Shattered Applause

The Eva Le Gallienne Story

Robert A. Schanke

Foreword by
May Sarton

Barricade Books Inc.
New York

Published by
Barricade Books Inc.
150 Fifth Avenue
New York, NY 10011

by arrangement with
Southern Illinois University Press

Copyright © 1992 by the Board of Trustees,
Southern Illinois University
All rights reserved.
Printed in the United States of America
Edited by Jill Butler
Designed by Natalia Nadraga

First Printing

Library of Congress Cataloging-in-Publication Data

Schanke, Robert A., 1940–
     Shattered applause: the Eva Le Galliene story / by Robert A. Schanke.
     p. cm.
Includes index.
ISBN 1-56980-023-5: $18.00
     1. Le Gallienne, Eva, 1899–   . 2. Actors—United States—Biography. 3.
Lesbians—United States—Biography. I. Title.
PN2287.L2896S3 1995
792'.028'092—dc20
[B]   94-13104
                                          CIP

To Jack

Contents

Illustrations

Foreword

May Sarton

At the highest level in all the arts genius communicates a vision of life. Of course we recognize a Virginia Woolf world, a Wallace Stevens world, a Stravinsky world—a few lines, a stanza, or some musical phrases would have in each case a recognizable signature; but when we come to the performing arts the aperçu becomes subtler and harder to pin down. Eva Le Gallienne was one of the very few actors I have seen who did communicate a vision of life.

After more than sixty years I can still recapture and meditate upon two moments I saw when I was still in high school. The first was the way in which Eva Le Gallienne as Sister Joanna of the Cross in *The Cradle Song* said goodbye to the young girl she and the other sisters had brought up in the convent. Sister Joanna is speaking of human love. She describes it as "a drop of honey spread upon our bread each day which we must receive gladly, but with trembling, for it will surely pass away." As these words were interpreted by Miss Le Gallienne the audience witnessed an act of the spirit. We were not being told about something; we were given the grace to experience it. It was happening before our eyes and also in some miraculous way within each of us.

The role of Hilda Wangel in *The Master Builder* gives us a character at the opposite pole from Sister Joanna of the Cross. Hilda does not renounce, she attacks. In act 2 Hilda sees Master Builder Solness treat a young rival without generosity out of fear. After the young man has left the room, Hilda says, "That was a very ugly thing to do." The very long pause Eva Le Gallienne took before uttering those words is not written into the text. It is a good example of her genius at work. For in that long silence, we saw, as if we were inside Hilda, her fury and her pain grow and change, so that when she finally spoke it was not so much an attack as a deep grieving. In that minute she had grown and she would make him grow, so we understood, for we had been somehow taken into a human soul.

Purity, depth, the complex movement of the soul—was this what acting could be? I felt that I had been changed in some unexplored region of the psyche, and would never be the same again. At sixteen I wanted to get inside the mystery, to be not a witness but a participant, and a year later I had managed to persuade my father to let me go to New York and to enroll as an apprentice in the Civic Repertory Theatre. Although I was in the end to become a writer, not a theatre person, my three years there, plus a winter in Paris when the "Civic" was closed, taught me more, I believe, than the college education I missed as a result. I mention this only because what I have to say of an analytic nature is based on watching Miss Le Gallienne at work in hundreds of rehearsals and performances.

Eva Le Gallienne was at her greatest when she could serve a great playwright. When I think of her genius I come back always to her roles in Chekhov, Ibsen, Shakespeare, Molnar, Giraudoux, Schiller. The range here is quite fantastic, from sophisticated comedy to high tragedy, from roles of the greatest inwardness to roles where wit and poetry of language are paramount, from roles that require complete realism to roles that require the "grand manner."

To encompass so much, intelligence of a high order must be at work. I do not believe that Eva Le Gallienne ever would have played a role with which she could not identify with her heart and soul. But in the preparation, intelligence is the prime requirement for a time. Some actors rely almost entirely on intuition, on what will happen at rehearsal. Eva Le Gallienne always began by steeping herself in the period and in the playwright. Slowly and patiently she built up a world.

Preparing to play Queen Elizabeth, Le Gallienne began months before the first rehearsal. Her blue-walled library in Weston, Connecticut, was cluttered with books—biographies, histories, poems, journals of the period—as well as reproductions of all existing portraits of the great queen. During those months Eva Le Gallienne was becoming an Elizabethan first, then thinking and feeling her way into the woman who dominated the century. I can imagine no actor who would approach a role with a more acute sense of the writer's intention, nor with greater respect for the text, for the weight of each phrase, for "tone," for what is also between the lines.

And so we come to the mysterious powers of an actress of genius, and to an acting style forged out of the control and deployment of unique characteristics. Because the actor must use his own person as an instrument, what is poured into a given role springs in some sense from all he has thought and felt, read and known up to that moment and is expressed by a total human machine. When we deal with genius growth is implicit. It was moving to see how Eva Le Gallienne's performance of certain key roles grew over the years, as she herself had more and more within her to bring to them—Hedda Gabler, Masha, for example. So in the end what constitutes genius in the actor is at least partly the communication of his perception of life. And it is the quality and depth of her perception that sets Eva Le Gallienne in a high place.

It would be a mistake to overlook Miss Le Gallienne's whimsical, witty, or clownish humor. From the moment of her entrance when she literally "flew down" as the White Queen in *Alice in Wonderland*, she was greeted by a solid wall of laughter. The White Queen is a true clown, making us laugh even as we are stabbed by something about her that reminds us of ourselves at our most imaginative and grotesque.

Yet in all this something eludes me, the genius itself, unique, never to be seen again. What is it? Here we come close to mystery, the mystery of personality itself. The tragic and enraging fact is that for many years Eva Le Gallienne was not used by our theatre. We allowed this gift to be wasted, and we "wasted" ourselves for lack of it. There may have been actors who could project passion as well or better than Eva Le Gallienne. None I have ever seen could project the soul itself, the "inwardness" of a human being, as she did. And when we come to this, it is perhaps always close to tragedy.

This genius was at her most glorious when playing the least glorious of roles—when she came closest to the naked human soul in each of us, for it is there that we meet something lonely, passionate, even despairing that we recognize as the human truth—the longing to be more than we are, and to understand ourselves. It is there that we weep the cleansing tears of revelation and of acceptance.

Preface

"A national treasure," "another Duse," "a reminder of what greatness in the theatre can be"—this is typical of the praise showered on Eva Le Gallienne as she approached her eightieth birthday. In 1977 President Gerald Ford cited her "excellence of achievement." A decade later President Reagan awarded her the National Medal of the Arts, the highest honor any artist can receive from the United States government.[1]

At the age of twenty-seven, this daunting and determined maverick dared to challenge the male-dominated Broadway system of long runs, high prices, and typecasting and established America's first and only classical repertory theatre (1926–35). In later years she founded the American Repertory Theatre (1946), either acted in or directed the world's great plays—Shakespeare, Ibsen, Chekhov, Sheridan, Molière, Schiller, Euripides—and earned a Tony, an Emmy, and an Oscar nomination.

A few years ago a professor from Tufts University was preparing to introduce me for a paper I was presenting and asked for comments he could make. I told him that I was working on a biography of Eva Le Gallienne. Though one of Le Gallienne's several honorary degrees was from Tufts, and though the professor was a theatre historian, he looked puzzled and asked, "Who is she?"—not an uncommon response, since today she is virtually unknown to most Americans.

This grand dame of the theatre was first presented to me back in my undergraduate days at Midland College in Nebraska. Professor Sara Hawkinson, inspired many years earlier by Le Gallienne's touching performance in *Liliom*, impressed upon her theatre students that Le Gallienne was one of America's greatest actresses.

My personal crusade to promote her name began a number of years later when I wrote a term paper about her, under the excellent guidance of Tice L. Miller at the University of Nebraska. My assignment ultimately took me to libraries and archives around the country. I spent an entire summer examining the papers Le Gallienne had donated to the Beinecke Library at Yale University. What a glorious wealth of information—programs, letters, clippings, pressbooks, photographs, and promptscripts. By 1975 that fifty-page paper somehow led to my Ph.D. dissertation, "Eva Le Gallienne: First Lady of Repertory."

But my fascination did not culminate with such an academic tribute. I loftily prepared to advance her standing in the annals of American theatre history. I originally set out to publish her biography, which, as I reflect, was little more than an extension of my doctoral work, heavy with accolades and bows. I sent proposals to publishers and met with a number of editors. At every turn I was asked how Le Gallienne's personal life orchestrated her creative work. It seems that they expected a biography to tell her whole story. Since nothing in all my research explained sufficiently the various reversals in her life and career, I soon realized that, as a biography, my dissertation was vastly inadequate.

Since I was not prepared to continue the research at the time, I set the project aside for several years. At first I was absorbed by another book I was authoring, *Ibsen in America: A Century of Change*. But soon after its completion, I resumed my interest by conferring with several of Le Gallienne's closest friends and executors, such people as Eloise Armen and Anne Kaufman Schneider.

They also recognized that an account of Le Gallienne would be incomplete without an understanding of her private struggle and that a person's intimate life, especially that of an artist, is clearly part of the creative process. The two cannot be divorced. We more clearly understand the works of other artists—Van Gogh, Strindberg, Dickinson, and Hemingway, for example—when we know about their personal challenges, so we will come to appreciate Le Gallienne more when we realize hers.

While this is Le Gallienne's first biography, she herself wrote two autobiographies, *At 33* (1934) and *With a Quiet Heart* (1953). Both are litanies of her achievements and salute her renouncing Broadway stardom for a life among the classics. Certainly they were well intentioned, but both are literary shrines to a woman that Eva always wanted to be, not to the woman she was. She did an admirable job of camouflaging herself behind portraits that rob her achievements of their sinew and texture.

This is the story of a woman who has been called "the Nureyev of the twenties." Her budding reputation took a dramatic shift around

1918 when she initiated an affair with the exotic and notorious Alla Nazimova. In the next thirty years she would charm many women. For most of her life, she chose to live in shadows. Like many women of her generation who loved other women, she viewed herself as a man trapped in a female body. Her sexuality became her nemesis and defined her great need for privacy, coloring her selection of scripts, casting, management practices, style of acting, and ultimately her critical reception.

Louise Brooks, an icon of movie history and a contemporary of Le Gallienne's, once wrote the following:

> In writing the history of a life, I believe absolutely that the reader cannot understand the character and deeds of the subject unless he is given a basic understanding of that person's sexual loves and hates and conflicts. It is the only way the reader can make sense out of innumerable apparently senseless actions. To paraphrase Proust: how often do we change the whole course of our lives in pursuit of a love that we will have forgotten within a few months.

Even Le Gallienne's own father, who was equally unconventional, once explained to an interviewer that a "biography is only interesting if true. All should be told," he argued. "If a man is really great, he is great enough to carry off his follies."[2]

But there is another important reason for my needing to tell her complete story. It is impossible to fully appreciate the achievements of such artists as Michelangelo, Tchaikovsky, Walt Whitman, or Tennessee Williams without knowledge of their sexual orientation. Yet as I discovered more about my own sexuality, I became increasingly aware of how gay history is invariably concealed or denied. Biographers are allowed, even encouraged, to analyze emotional and sexual issues, as long as they are traditional. Unorthodox themes are laundered, and struggles with homosexual identity are still generally suppressed. The *New York Times* obituary for Aaron Copland, for instance, reduced his private life to a three-word summary: "a lifelong bachelor." The article detailed his education in Europe, analyzed his music, and explored his sympathy with communism in the thirties, but it totally censored his homosexuality and his lifelong relationships with men. Missing was any suggestion of the special love he shared with another man for forty-four years.

When actress Glenn Close narrated a comprehensive television documentary called "The Divine Garbo," newspaper ads ballyhooed with Garbo's line "I've always wanted to live two lives, one for the movies and one for myself."[3] A sweeping account of her life was the promise, but the script fell flat. With the Broadway set from the award-winning *The Grand Hotel* as a backdrop, they spared no cost. The film highlighted Garbo's sensuality, her rare beauty, and her torrid affairs with various men, yet it conveniently ignored her bisexuality and her frequent romances with women.

In his film documentary about the golden years of Hollywood, Gene Kelly featured Rudolph Valentino as the consummate lover—once again, nary a hint that the screen's dashing cavalier was anything but one of the guys. Actually, both his marriages were to lesbians and were stage-managed for the public by the doyenne of Hollywood's lesbian community, Alla Nazimova. Such repressive whitewashes of history are not only shams but shameful. The time when our gay heroes are invisible must end.

My formal introduction to Le Gallienne was set for July 17, 1974. Although this date was canceled abruptly, she asked in a telegram that I phone her to arrange another time. I soon learned that even though she was guarded with her comments, Le Gallienne was always generous and supportive with her personal interviews, telephone conversations, correspondence, and backstage visits. On July 26 I arrived at her doorstep, nervous not just because I was meeting this legend but because she had warned me that she could spare only about twenty minutes. How could I ever cover a sixty-year career in twenty minutes?

She opened her front door, stood there in her blue jeans and denim shirt, and said, "You're not German, are you? You are . . . Norwegian with some Danish blood. Come in." She was right on the mark, and from that moment on, all barriers disappeared. She ushered me to her Blue Room and pointed to a chair where I could relax. Leaning back in her chaise opposite me, underneath a poster of Sarah Bernhardt, and cuddling her little dog to her side, she chuckled when I asked if I could record our discussion. After all, she reminded me, the Nixon/Watergate scandals were still headlines. Twenty minutes blossomed into four hours!

Four days later I returned, accompanied by my wife, Ruth, and our six-year-old daughter, Julie. Le Gallienne handed Ruth and Julie a children's book to look at while she and I visited. Before we left, she escorted us on a short stroll through her woods, pointing to where she put out salt lick for the deer and to the bench where she had always studied her scripts. She described how she had naturalized daffodils throughout the woods. As we were about to climb into our car, she reminded us that her mother's name was also Julie. Then she bent down, kissed my daughter on the cheek, and handed her an auto-graphed copy of a book she had written, *Flossie and Bossie*. At seventy-five years old she seemed so fragile and so very sincere. Through the next ten years, she never stopped asking about Ruth and Julie.

When I finished my degree the following summer, I could not wait to hand her a copy of the dissertation. She was rehearsing *The Dream Watcher* at the White Barn Theatre in Connecticut at the time and asked me to stay for a dress rehearsal. As we chatted under an umbrella on the sunny patio of the theatre, she appeared so tired and old, and I wondered if she would be able to perform.

The rehearsal was magic. As soon as the curtains opened, she had miraculously shed twenty years. Her adrenaline was flowing, and her mind was razor sharp. I was charmed by her performance and wept as the curtains closed. No more than five minutes elapsed before she came out to get my response.

"How was I?" she asked.

"Beautiful. I've never seen a performance so moving."

She reached up and grabbed my shoulders. "Please, tell me the truth! Nobody tells me the truth!" she begged.

As I repeated my words, her eyes filled with tears and she began to weep. A few minutes later, playwright Barbara Wersba thanked me for my praise. It seems that Le Gallienne was beginning to doubt her own ability to act; after all, it had been five years. I did not go backstage on opening night, since she was mobbed by so many fans. She asked me later if I would write and share my responses to the performance. I did.

The next time I saw her was backstage at the Kennedy Center a few months later, when she was making her phenomenal comeback in *The Royal Family*. She told me how impressed she was with my dissertation, the research, the accuracy. I remember being so enthralled I felt my knees buckling. When I told her how I enjoyed her performance, she shrugged, "Oh, dear me, I haven't been in such a silly play since *The Swan*." That, incidentally, was in 1923. No one could convince me, however, that she was not overjoyed with all the publicity she was again receiving. I saw her backstage on at least two other occasions during *The Royal Family*, and she always asked, "Is it fresh?" On one visit, she even met with a dozen of my students who had accompanied me.

Up until the mid-1980s I talked and corresponded with her on many occasions. I doubt if many people have had more access to her than I have enjoyed. When I lived in England from 1980 to 1982, I researched her early years growing up in London and Paris and spent a weekend in the little country village of Chiddingfold. I even persuaded the current owners to show me through the manor house where she lived as a child. I traveled to Paris and walked the streets and gardens where she played. Knowing of my research and dissertation, Greenwood Press commissioned me to prepare a two-hundred-page, annotated bibliography on her life and career, which they subsequently published in 1989.

I spent the last few years interviewing Le Gallienne's friends and colleagues—producers, actors and actresses, directors, press agents, designers, playwrights, and students. Each time I thought I had completed my last interview, someone would suggest another name or two; by the end the list of contributors surpassed a hundred. Some had known her for over sixty years and others only briefly. Some have risen to the top of their profession; others are retired or still aspiring. Because of their candor and sincerity, I discovered the complexity of Le Gallienne's personality. She was truly a Jekyll and Hyde, kind one moment, vicious the next. Having become so intimately aware of her weaknesses and foibles, I occasionally questioned whether I wanted to complete the book. When I began this project, Le Gallienne was flawless. When I finished, she was immensely talented, but human. Her lifelong friend May Sarton provided my answer: "There is no criteria for genius. All of us, especially geniuses, are a bundle of opposites."[4]

For more than fifty years, Eva Le Gallienne pursued an unshakable goal with invincible drive—to establish a repertory theatre in this country, classical in scope and affordable. Her singlemindedness brought her the attention of friends and foes, praise as well as challenge. Her story, complete with both feats and follies, might serve as a barometer of the changing values, tastes, and attitudes of American society.

I could not have come this far without my partner, Jack Barnhart. He accompanied me on several research trips and helped prepare the outline. He read, reread, and scrutinized every phrase and word of the manuscript. His background in theatre, his gregarious and optimistic nature, and his zest for life have enriched not only my world but also the text of this book. Like Eva Le Gallienne and most gay people, I have sometimes felt ashamed of who I am. But my partner has provided boundless love and encouragement and has helped me grow in pride and self-confidence. I dedicate this book to him.

Acknowledgments

Many people assisted me in writing this book, especially Eloise Armen and Anne Kaufman Schneider. They granted several interviews, opened many doors, and provided moral support.

I am grateful to the following individuals for interviews, correspondence, and ideas: Margaret Adams, Jane Alexander, Marnie Andrews, Eloise Armen, Jim Aull, Joseph Baldwin, Paul Ballantyne, Jack C. Barnhart, Richard J. Beckley, Rod Bladel, Virginia P. Boyd, Jeanne Brady, Ellen Burstyn, Emily Camp, Helen Crich Chinoy, Paul Reuben Cooper, Staats Cotsworth, Margaret Cruikshank, Vincent Curcio, Dalton Dearborn, Michael Dewell, Gwyda DonHowe, Andrew Edmonson, Peter Falk, Tedd Fetter, LeAnn Fields, Tim Fish, Hal Floyd, Burry Fredrik, Farley Granger, Herbert D. Greggs, Uta Hagen, T. Edward Hambleton, Lorraine Hansberry, Harriet Harris, Julie Harris, Rosemary Harris, R. C. Hart, Nancy Hartley, Signe Hasso, Al Hirschfeld, Shirley Herz, Margaret Hilton, Norris Houghton, Trina Hyman, Anne Jackson, Glenda Jackson, Doris Johanson, Jessalyn Jones, Sabra Jones, Gordon A. Juel, Michael Kahn, Jonathan Ned Katz, Caroline Lagerfelt, Barbara Lee, Eva Le Gallienne, David Leopold, Bobby Lewis, Ted Lockwood, Lucille Lortel, Bernard Marquez, Robin Martin, Kate McDowell, James McKenzie, Burgess Meredith, Mary Merrill, Tice L. Miller, George Morfogen, William Morgan, Tharon Musser, Connie Nelson, Fred and Sandy Nelson, Richard O'Donoghue, Ronald C. Olson, J. Richard Phillips, Levi D. Phillips, Eileen Porch, Ellis Rabb, April Raynell, Rosemarie Rogers, May Sarton, Terence Scammell, Julie A. Schanke, Ruth Schanke, Anne Kaufman Schneider, Tonio Selwart, Carole Shelley, Sloane Shelton, Gina Shield, Jim Sirmans, Katherine Squire, Barry Stavis, Haila Stoddard, Tim Summers, Megan Terry, Paul Vincent, Eli Wallach, Richard Waring, Warren Watson, Berenice Weiler, Barbara Wersba, Anne Whelpley, Ann Wilhite, Clifford Williams, Mary Louise Wilson, Andy Wolvin, Mark Wolff, and Irene Worth.

Staff members at the following libraries were also of invaluable help: Joseph Regenstein Library of the University of Chicago, Chicago Historical Society, Wisconsin Historical Society, Beinecke Library of Yale University, Butler Library of Columbia University, Theatre Collection of the Museum of the City of New York, Billy Rose Theatre Collection of the New York Public Library for the Performing Arts, Free Library of Philadelphia, Cleveland Public Library, Detroit Public Library, Amherst College Library, Princeton University Library, Library of Congress, National Archives, Wesleyan University Library, Westport Public Library, Lilly Library of Indiana University, Mugar Library of Boston University, University of North Carolina Library, Seattle Public Library, Gleeson Library of the University of San Francisco, Stanford University Library, Humanities Research Center of the University of Texas, the Margo Feiden Gallery, the Kinsey Institute, the British Museum, and both the Haslemere Educational Museum and Godalming Library in Surrey, England.

I am particularly grateful to Michael Dewell and the National Repertory Theatre for providing numerous photos.

I would also like to thank my editors at Southern Illinois University Press—Jill Butler and Teresa White.

Shattered Applause

1

Water Baby

Each summer thousands of Americans visiting England make a special pilgrimage to the home of Charles Dickens, one of London's colorful tourist attractions. Armed with maps and cameras, they board the Piccadilly Line Underground and exit at Russell Square, via a creaky and cramped elevator that shakes and shimmies as it chugs to the surface. Once the elevator doors open and the visitors get their bearings, they walk east to Doughty Street, passing the playgrounds of Coram's Fields on the way. Doughty Street is a quiet, wide thorough-fare, lined with rows of brick, Georgian, terrace houses built in the late eighteenth century. Originally, both ends of the short street had gates attended by porters wearing gold-laced hats and the Doughty coat of arms on the buttons of their mulberry uniforms.

It was while Dickens lived at 48 Doughty Street that the great Victorian author's fame was established. It is a handsome, three-story home, with a formal dining room, a morning room that over-looks a little courtyard garden at the rear, and a dignified Regency staircase that leads to bedrooms, a study, and a drawing room. During the two brief years he lived there, 1837–39, Dickens penned some of his most distinguished literary works. His evenings were often spent entertaining. Artist Leigh Hunt, illustrator George Cruikshank, or popular romantic novelist W. Harrison Ainsworth were frequent guests.

As tourists approach the home of this famous novelist and social reformer, they take no notice of another historic address so very close by. Today, at 42 Doughty Street, can be found the offices of the Society of Graphical and Allied Trades and the London Home Counties Area Organizers. But sixty years after Dickens left Doughty Street for a larger home, this address was shelter to another important person, a woman who eventually migrated to America and, like the Victorian writer, became a great artist and reformer—Eva Le Gallienne. She was born at 7:00 A.M., January 11, 1899, two months after her mother had taken up residence in the shadow of the birthplace of *Pickwick Papers*, *Nicholas Nickleby*, and *Oliver Twist*.

It was a significant time in English history. Mid-nineteenth century had marked the climax of British power, prestige, and prosperity. By 1880 Britain's colonial possessions covered about 7.7 million square miles, with 268 million inhabitants. Clearly, Brittannia ruled the seas and assumed the "white man's burden" to extend dominion over a vast commonwealth. But now it was the end of the century, the *fin de siècle*, the end of an era that began with Queen Victoria's coronation in 1837. During the funeral for Alfred Lord Tennyson in 1892, all of London had stood hushed and bareheaded outside Westminster Abbey. Many, including Eva Le Gallienne's father, had viewed his death as a fore-shadowing of the Queen's death and, subsequently, of the passing of the old Victorian order.

Indeed, the last quarter of the century saw Britain's supremacy questioned within several international arenas. People were well aware that they were living amidst changes and struggles. Weary of centuries of exploitation by the English ruling classes, the Irish renewed their drive for independence. But in 1886, when Gladstone introduced the first Home Rule Bill to provide a separate parliament for Ireland, it split his Liberal party, aroused bitter debate among the voters, and eventually lost him the election. A second attempt to pass the bill was thrown out by the House of Lords in 1893. Passions became so heated that the country soon teetered on the edge of civil war. The struggle to overpower the Dutch and rule supreme in South Africa created even more tension. Only a few months after Eva was born, Parliament declared war on the two Boer Republics of South Africa. Expected to last only a few months, it wore on for over two and a half years and caused great internal dissension in England.

But there were changes at home as well. The quadrupling of England's population during the nineteenth century resulted in large-scale unemployment and poverty. Slum conditions were so severe in some areas, in fact, that even as late as 1900 every other child was dead by the age of one. By the 1890s most large cities were considered giant polluted bedlams. Women spent the major part of each day cleaning house, due to the increased amount of dirt in the air. The trams, railroads, petrol-engined buses, underground trains, and horse carts produced deafening clatter in the streets. More than seven hundred horse-drawn buses passed London's Bank of England every hour, creating half-hour traffic jams and leaving endless layers of horse droppings estimated at six inches deep. Smells of burning coal, stale food, and mounds of uncovered trash added to the stench. Pessimism was so prevalent that between 1886 and 1888 more than 51,000 Englishmen migrated to other continents.

English social life was also changing. Smart entertaining no longer took place in private homes but in hotels and large, glittering restaurants backed with spacious kitchens and vast wine cellars. Women could even go unattended. People did most of their shopping at newly developed department stores, such as Harrods and Whiteley's. For amusement, they frequented the newly built pubs, labeled "the modern plague of London" by the National Temperance Society, or attended music hall productions of such lavish extravaganzas as *The Belle of New York* and *Florodora*. More serious theatregoers attended Gilbert and Sullivan or performances of Henry Irving and Ellen Terry. Every evening thousands of Londoners flocked along the Thames River Embankment to view the new fad of yacht racing. Men met their friends at their private clubs, and ladies held "at homes," during which they received their friends, drank tea, and ate scones, cakes, and cucumber sandwiches. "The world was beginning to realize that work and duty were not everything," Richard Le Gallienne explained many years later, "and that life was meant at least as much for play." [1]

The arts were characterized by "the new." H. D. Traill wrote of "The New Fiction," William Sharp of "The New Paganism," and Oscar Wilde of "The New Remorse." When Grant Allen referred to "The New Hedonism," he opened his essay with these words: "Not to be new is, in these days, to be nothing." The use of the word spread until it embraced ideas of the whole period—New Humor, New Drama, New Realism, New Journalism. A popular, penny-weekly periodical sprang up with the name *The New Age*. The goal of disillusioned and dissatisfied artists was to revolt against the old, idealized, and highly moralized Victorian standards. It meant breaking down old frontiers and establishing new outlooks.

This was the milieu that greeted Eva Le Gallienne's parents when they set up residence on Doughty Street. It was no surprise to them, however, since they had both moved to London years earlier. Le Gallienne's father, Richard Thomas Le Gallienne (1866–1947), was born the first of ten children in Liverpool and lived in the lower middle-class area of Everton with its long, dull streets of identical brick boxes of houses, grimy shop windows, and murky alleyways. His father, the son of a sea captain, had moved from the Isle of Guernsey to Liverpool, where he worked as a secretary for the Birkenhead Brewery Company.

There was constant conflict between Richard and his father, John Gallienne, a sober, self-righteous Puritan who considered literature and poetry senseless trivia. An inflexible autocrat, when he wanted to speak at the table, he rapped his glass with his spoon, and all conversation ceased. Richard's mother, by contrast, was much more tolerant, had a poetic sensibility, and often interceded for her children. Tension in the Gallienne home caused a severe asthmatic condition that plagued Richard till his death.

One of the family's conflicts concerned Richard's romantic adventures. When he was a mere twelve years old, Richard had an intimate fling with a miller's daughter. By the age of nineteen, he had managed affairs with easily half a dozen young women. Sex was never mentioned in the Gallienne household, ironically, for the children were instructed to show no interest in dating until the age of twenty-one. To enforce his policy, Richard's father censored his mail and used a stout stick on him when he learned of his disobedience.

Although his father planned a career in accounting for his first-born, Richard held more artistic aspirations. When he was only sixteen, he and close friend Jimmy Welch formed a literary society called "The Squires and Dames of Books and Pens," which met each Friday in a member's home to hear literary papers, read plays, and plan pilgrimages to birthplaces of famous writers. They would often sneak off to the theatre and creep back home late at night.

Inspired by an 1883 lecture by Oscar Wilde, Richard began to see himself as another William Wordsworth, or perhaps a latter-day Charles Lamb. Reading the latest books became such an obsession for him that he was frequently in heavy debt to the local bookstores. During this time he adopted the prefix *Le* for his surname, wore his hair nearly to his shoulders, and sported a long flowing Inverness cape lined with scarlet silk. As his biographers suggest, it was "the flaming banner of his own particular guerilla war upon the dull and colourless."[2] With relentless optimism, he refused to consider the possibility of failure. Therefore, he would become a writer.

Soon after the arrival of his first book, *My Ladies Sonnets*, in 1887, Richard moved to London, where he hoped to enter into the major literary circles. He discovered that the restless atmosphere of the era was reflected by the men of letters. The 1890s was the "mauve decade," "le mal du siècle," or as the Germans put it, a time of "weltschmerz." Writers like Richard were determined "to escape from the deadening thraldom of materialism and outworn conventions, and to live life significantly—keenly and beautifully, personally and, if need be, daringly."[3] Influenced by Baudelaire and Verlaine, they sought not a realistic and functional art but an intensity of feeling, with strong emphasis on symbolism, music, and color. The founder of the English aesthetic movement, Walter Pater, declared, "Not the fruit of experience, but experience itself, is the end." He believed that people must live intensely and with no regard for morality.

Soon after Richard arrived in London, he befriended the movement's chief spokesman and his idol, Oscar Wilde. In his sensational personal life, Wilde put Pater's theory into practice, bringing himself considerable disgrace as well as great popularity. His comedies, which appear to modern audiences as delightful farces, were intended as satires on Victorian manners. His hero in *The Picture of Dorian Gray* is in search of intense sensations. In his quest for pleasure, Gray bans every belief and every feeling that limits pleasure. After the book appeared in 1890, Wilde's name became synonymous with all that was immoral. His extravagance created a flock of Ivory Tower, velveteen-clad aesthetes, whose ecstasies were expressed in thrills over sunflowers, peacock feathers, and objects of art. Richard delighted in belonging to this circle.

The exact nature of his friendship with Wilde is not conclusive. Certainly, Richard's youth, quiet and feminine voice, flowing hair, and handsome features appealed to Wilde, who often compared the younger poet to the angel Gabriel in Rossetti's *Annunciation*. In 1888 Wilde presented his disciple with a copy of *Poems* inscribed "To Richard Le Gallienne, poet and lover, from Oscar Wilde." Richard responded with a poem in which he wrote, "With Oscar Wilde, a summer-day / Passed like a yearning kiss away," and he included the inscription "This copy of verse I have made for my friend Oscar Wilde, as a love-token, and in secret memory of a summer day in June '88." In April 1889 Wilde wrote Richard another letter, hoping they could soon "meet and make music." In a letter dated December 1, 1890, Wilde went on: "I want so much to see you: when can that be? Friendship and love like ours need not meetings, but they are delightful. I hope the laurels are not too thick across your brow for me to kiss your eyelids."[4]

By the time the two men had met, Wilde was already a skilled connoisseur of likely-looking young men. His charm and mastery of language, as well as his rich, syrupy voice with its Irish intonations, could almost always bring a smile. As one of his biographers put it, he had become "consumed with his passion for moving swiftly from one to another of the boys he met. . . . Wilde was hypnotized not by any individual but by his conception of pleasure, of supermanship. . . .

Wilde was a highly sexed and promiscuous man."[5] Although most of Wilde's friends in London were homosexual, there is no clear evidence of a physical relationship between him and Richard. If anything intimate did occur, it was probably short-lived, for Wilde usually dropped his young disciples after the first flush of enthusiasm. No evidence suggests that Richard ever participated in any other male liason.

In any case, Richard lost little time penetrating London's world of letters. At first, he became literary secretary to actor Wilson Barrett. After his successful biography of George Meredith appeared in 1890, he began writing a regular column on men and works of literature for the London *Star* and entered into the routine of newspaper life. He was elected into the exclusive Hogarth Club and began associating with all the major writers and editors of the period. He sipped inexpensive claret at the posh Café Royal, which was decorated in Second Empire style, with Bohemian glass chandeliers, red plush upholstery, and nude figures painted between the masses of gilding on the ceiling. Another of his favorite drinks was absinthe, a highly aromatic, yellowish-green, hallucinatory liquor that was later banned in many countries. Unkempt, haggard-looking, and often wearing brigandish hats, he could be found drinking hot gin and water at The Crown on Charing Cross Road, a homosexual pub renown for its male prostitutes.

In 1891, in an attempt to revive the spirit of the literary tavern, Richard, William Butler Yeats, and Arthur Symons founded the Rhymers' Club. The monthly meetings at the Chesire Cheese Restaurant on Fleet Street began in the downstairs bar, moved to one of the gloomy, ill-lit dining rooms for dinner, then adjourned to an upstairs smoking room, where the poets would read their works while drinking from tankards of ale and huge bowls of steaming punch. The hushed readings were profoundly solemn and rarely broken with smiles or laughter. The members were not of the establishment: Francis Thompson was an opium addict who slept among the tramps and beggars of London, John Davidson was incapable of adapting to London society and eventually committed suicide, Lionel Johnson was addicted to absinthe and became an alcoholic, and Ernest Dowson was ill and emaciated and died at the age of thirty-three. Though not a member, Oscar Wilde was a frequent guest.

One of the most shocking products of the club appeared in shop windows on April 16, 1894. The *Yellow Book*, a quarterly periodical that lasted three years, was devoted to art and literature and became the symbol of 1890s decadence. The flaming cover of yellow sported a pen and ink drawing by Aubrey Beardsley, already a cause célèbre for the scandalous, seminude illustrations he created for Oscar Wilde's English language edition of *Salome*. The *Yellow Book's* innovative and abstract cover design was related to poster art in its daring use of black on yellow. Its economy of line was influenced by Japanese prints. For the spine and lower cover, Beardsley drew a frieze of women's heads. His most notable drawing in the first volume was a portrait of Mrs. Patrick Campbell, then playing the lead role in Pinero's *Second Mrs. Tanqueray*. Among the literary contributors in the first issue were Henry James, Max Beerbohm, George Moore, Edmund Gosse, William Watson, and Richard Le Gallienne.

Immediately, the "respectable" press set up a howl, describing the new publication as a combination of English rowdyism and French lewdness. One outraged editor demanded an Act of Parliament to make such periodicals illegal. The criticism naturally boosted sales; the first printing of 5,000 was sold out in just five days and was twice reprinted. Le Gallienne contributed to all but four of the thirteen volumes before it ceased publication in 1897.

During the three years of the *Yellow Book*, Richard continued his interest in the theatre. He became a good friend of actress Lillie Langtry. In 1892 Oscar Wilde sent him a special invitation to the premiere of *Lady Windermere's Fan*. He attended many productions that featured his boyhood friend and roommate Jimmy Welch, who was recognized as one of London's most brilliant young actors for performances in such plays as *Oliver Twist*, *Enemy of the People*, *Arms and the Man*, and J. T. Grein's Independent Theatre presentations of *Widowers' Houses* and *Alan's Wife*. Inspired by Grein's production of *Ghosts* in 1891, Richard traveled to Norway with his publisher John Lane, in anticipation of meeting Ibsen. Knowing the playwright usually lunched at the Grand Cafe in Kristiania, they waited there expectantly:

> Punctually on the stroke of one, there entering the doorway was the dour and bristling presence known to all the world. . . . The great ruff of white whisker, ferociously standing out all round his sallow, bilious face, as if dangerously charged with electricity, the immaculate silk hat, the white tie, the frock-coated martinet's figure, dressed from top to toe in old-fashioned black broadcloth, at once funereal and professorial. . . . He might have been a Scotch elder entering the kirk. . . . As one man, the whole cafe was on its feet in an attitude of salute. . . . All remained standing till he had taken his seat, as in the presence of a king.[6]

Ibsen represented to Richard the ultimate in modern playwrights. He was startling, ruthless, and gallant. Like Oscar Wilde, he refused to compromise.

About eight months before he traveled to Norway, Richard married his first wife, Mildred Lee, a woman he had known for some time in Liverpool. When Richard was unable, because of his asthmatic condition, to accompany his employer Wilson Barrett on his theatre tour to America, he returned to Liverpool and asked Mildred for her hand. For two years they lived in the London suburb of Hanwell, a quiet, leafy village, complete with a charming old church and a traditional inn. They named their semidetached, Queen Anne-style home "Meadowsweet," because it overlooked a park of splendid old trees. His letters relate accounts of country walks, long and lazy afternoons along the Thames River, meals of sheepshead and shepherd's pie, visits by Arthur Bennett and the musician Frederick Delius, and his little garden with its miniature flower beds. But according to Bennett, all was not bliss. He visited the Le Galliennes in the summer of 1892 and suspected some difficulties when he discovered Richard's study cupboard filled with empty wine bottles and only four books, damp, dusty, and sticky with spilt wine, and lying forlorn and neglected amidst the grubby bottles. In September 1892, Richard appealed to his father for financial assistance, claiming, "our exchequer has sunk pretty well below zero."[7] Although he had been receiving money from his writing, his current expenses had become a grave burden.

In October 1893, explaining to friends that the Hanwell cottage was too small for entertaining, the Le Galliennes moved to the less expensive Mulberry Cottage in Brentford. Another London suburb, Brentford was an unattractive, industrial, country town, with a long and narrow High Street cramped with old-fashioned shop fronts. On the north side of the street, however, was a prosperous, residential quarter of middle-class villas. Their new home included a long, rambling flower garden, with a great and venerable mulberry tree in the center. From the house, there stretched, as far as one could see, a gently undulating ocean of parkland, dotted with ancient trees and grazing cattle.

Two months after the move, their daughter Hesper was born. Though this should have been a happy occasion, it was not. Mildred was ill for the next five months and died on May 21, 1894, of typhoid fever. After her death, Richard became even more of a drunkard, vagrant, and womanizer. Part of his grief may have been a sense of guilt, since even during their few short years of marriage, Richard was known to wander. In his bereavement, he wrote:

Yes! we had once a heaven we called a home
  Its empty rooms still haunt me like thine eyes,
  When the last sunset softly faded there;
Each day I tread each empty haunted room,
  And now and then a little baby cries,
Or laughs a lovely laughter worse to bear.[8]

Richard's sorrow was so great that he carried with him for the next twenty-seven years an urn with Mildred's ashes. "It was her ghost he was condemned to pursue for ever down the years," explains biographer Whittington-Egan. "This is the key to the whole of the rest of Richard's life. Over and over again the same wistful note recurs in his writings and letters. He looks back, back, back, incessantly, to youth, to spring, to the Mildred of the golden years." "I don't think our little Mildred will ever die," he wrote to his parents on September 25, 1894. "She lives more and more in me each day."[9]

After a brief drinking holiday in Paris, Richard set out on the lecture circuit. His name was quite familiar now, since he had published four more books and had continued writing for London newspapers. In November he addressed the Liverpool Teachers' Club on "The Revolt of the Daughters." Prolonged applause followed his declaration that "man's absurd tyranny in the past had compelled woman to be one of two things—doll or devil." The inflammatory speech gained extensive coverage in the press, and his name was recognized all over England. He repeated it later in Glasgow and in Birmingham. The following month, on December 9, 1894, he lectured to the members of the Playgoers' Club in London on "The World, The Flesh, and The Puritans," attacking "technical Christians" and hypocrisy. Illogical laws meant to contain passions by damning them up, he argued, actually make passions break out in dreadful ways. If brandy helped a man do his duty, then it was his duty to drink it. Finally, in support of the "New Hedonism," he scorned the sacred institution of marriage.[10]

In the audience on the evening of December 9, 1894, was Julie Norregaard, the woman who would become Richard's second wife and Eva's mother. There is little information about Julie's background. She was born in Flensborg, Denmark, but before her first birthday, her parents fled with her to Copenhagen in order to escape the German invasion of Schleswig-Holstein. Her family was very interested in the arts. One distant relative, in fact, was actor Michael Wiehe, a leading man with the Danish Royal Theatre, who was praised for his romantic lyricism. His performances had led Ibsen to hold him up as the finest actor he had ever seen. On one memorable occasion, Julie and her family saw a performance of Ibsen's *Doll's House* starring the actress who created the role of Nora, Fru Dybvad.

Little is known about Julie's formal education. By the 1890s she had come to London to sell samples of traditional Danish peasant embroidery at a little shop at the Danish Art School in Bayswater. Since most of her customers were great ladies, she began making extra money by selling short society pieces to the Danish and Swedish newspapers. Eventually she became a regular correspondent for Denmark's well-known newspaper *Politiken*, and she wrote occasionally for the *Star*, using "Eva" as her pen name. A profile she wrote of Georg Brandes appeared in volume 8 of the *Yellow Book*, and at the time she met Richard, she was about to edit an anthology of Scandinavian writing.

The story goes that when Richard finished his lecture at the Playgoers' Club, Julie "turned to her companion and firmly announced, 'That is the man I shall marry!'" An educated, engaging woman, she was striking, with close-curling blonde hair, blue eyes, and the carriage of a princess. She was always interested in exciting adventures and liked the "glamour in the theatre — the latest successes, the spectacular hits."[11] Undoubtedly she had read Richard's poetry. Undaunted by the scathing reactions he was receiving from the Victorian middle class, she was overwhelmed by his raven locks, his pale face, his bright blue eyes, and his air of independence.

But their relationship was slow in forming. During the first half of 1895, Richard had other plans. In March he and John Lane sailed from Liverpool to New York City for a lengthy lecture tour. But plans were abruptly canceled. All New York was buzzing with the Oscar Wilde sodomy scandal that had just surfaced. Although homosexuality was considered a crime, the problem was not that Wilde was homosexual but that he had been less than discreet. Indeed, the Victorian code of behavior allowed sinners and transgressors to cavort in private, but in public, people were to be proper ladies and gentlemen. Breaking this code was considered an ill-bred mistake that could lead to certain denunciation. When the affair of Wilde and Lord Alfred Douglas became public, even the most liberal-minded Americans were prejudiced against long-haired poets preaching gospels of decadence and revolt. If Richard had ever considered a homosexual tryst, the imprisonment of his friend and mentor must have eliminated all such fantasies.

In less than a month, Richard was back in London, where he resumed an affair that he had begun with Mrs. Chevalita Dunne

Clairmonte, who used the pen name George Egerton. When Clairmonte became pregnant by her husband, however, Richard turned his attention to Julie. By mid-May he was once again in love and wrote passionate letters to his "lapland witch." May 17: "Dear nightingale that has nested in my heart. How you are singing there, so wildly and sweetly—in heart, in blood, in brain!" May 20: "You have given me the keys of the garden, where grow those magic flowers." May 26: "I love, love you, *love you* . . . and I will be that man you pray me to be." May 30: "Soft lights, vermouth, and your own white limbs, Fie! Tomorrow night I shall be with thee in Paradise!"[12] The romantic couple spent considerable time together that summer and sent letters and telegrams, sometimes in English, sometimes in French.

During their courtship, Richard was working on his next book, *The Quest of the Golden Girl*. It is a long, romantic novel, in which the narrator searches for his fantasy love. Commentators have suggested that the narrator was actually Richard thinking back about one of his first encounters. "How lovely she used to look with the morning sun turning her hair to golden mist, and dancing in the blue deeps of her eyes," he dreamed. "And once when by chance she had forgotten to fasten her gown, I caught glimpses of a bosom that was like two happy handfuls of wonderful white cherries."[13] Though the novel solidified his popularity, it did not bring him great wealth. He later said that "the publishers got all the gold and poor Richard got the girls." One of the girls he managed to get—the one who became his own "golden girl"—was Julie Norregaard. They were married on February 12, 1897.

Alas, the marriage seemed destined for failure. From the very beginning they established a pattern of living separately. Although they spent occasional days together in the country, Richard mostly remained in London, where he felt he could concentrate more on his writing. Is it a wonder that his wife felt lonely and soon became suspicious of what he was doing with his leisure time?

Indeed, Julie had ample reason for suspicion. The very month Richard had applied for their marriage license, he initiated a two-year affair with Ethel Reed, an American artist who had contributed to the *Yellow Book*. But even more infuriating to Julie, her husband had taken for a mistress her Danish friend and companion Agnes Slott-Möller. Richard denied the importance of these triflings, but his new bride still felt threatened. Perhaps in retaliation for her husband's dalliance, Julie embarked on her own amorous adventure with Danish photographer Frederick Riise.

Still another threat to the marriage was Richard's obsessive grieving for his first wife. During his courtship with Julie, he wrote in a letter to her, "every day is the day that Mildred died, and day and night without ceasing my soul is kneeling at her altar." Only five days after his marriage, in a letter to his parents, he praises "the many little ways in which she [Julie] shows her tenderness for dear Mildred's memory."[14]

Their problems began to multiply. Neither Richard nor Julie liked their home at Kingswood Chase in Haslemere, which was simply a dormitory settlement inhabited by working-class Londoners. The strain began to show. Heated quarrels became frequent. He began to drink dangerously heavy doses of whiskey and absinthe and was treated by a doctor for his alcoholism. They were so destitute by the end of the year that they dismissed their servants, closed up the house, and hid from their creditors—Julie fleeing to Copenhagen with Hesper, Richard to a small London flat on Chancery Lane.

Subsidized by John Lane, who was sponsoring Richard in a lecture tour, the couple sailed early the next year for New York, where they stayed at the exclusive Waldorf-Astoria Hotel. They wined and dined with New York society. Hailed as the leader of the English decadents, he created quite a sensation with reporters when he confessed in front of his new wife, "I have not worn anything but black for some time. I lost my wife about three years ago and I am in mourning for her and shall continue to mourn her all my life."[15]

On March 30, they attended the American premiere of *Hedda Gabler*, starring their friend Elizabeth Robins, the American actress who had premiered many of Ibsen's plays in London. Julie was clad in decadent green. Richard reportedly "posed most artistically," as he walked down the theatre aisle with his raven locks fluttering in the stir. Dozens of curious young men with similar haircuts flocked around the notorious couple. When the *New York Telegraph* described the event the next day, the Le Galliennes were singled out as typifying the intellectual audience. To Richard's delight they were called "members of the elect."[16]

While on the lecture tour, Richard began an affair with Louise Theresa Wooster, a witty, Vassar-educated woman from Connecticut. They had met after one of his lectures in Bridgeport, and according to Miss Wooster's niece, he "proceeded as if no wife had been present."[17] Once Julie became aware of this latest escapade, she departed hastily for Copenhagen, leaving her husband to spend much of the summer in and around the Wooster home. He escorted "Tess" to concerts, picnics, and lectures. They were known to spend many evenings drinking absinthe. In a correspondence to Julie, he even confessed, "Tess and I are head over heels in love with each other."[18] By July, however, Richard reluctantly sailed for Denmark. He had learned that his wife was to have a child.

The couple's reunion was brief. About a week after he arrived to live with Julie in a rented house outside of Copenhagen, Richard moved to a hotel. Insisting that his asthma was once again flaring up, he left abruptly for London in October and stayed at his small flat on Chancery Lane. When Julie finally joined him in November, rather than sharing the flat with Richard, she took her lodging at 42 Doughty Street. On a chilly morning in January, long before the sun reached above the horizon, Richard received word that he would soon be a father.

The Le Galliennes had expected a boy and had planned on naming him Michon; instead it was a plump, round-faced baby girl they christened Eva. Richard was so gladdened by her birth that he dedicated his next book of poetry to her:

> When Eva talks and knows all that I say
> Oh won't that be a most exciting day!
> When Eva talks,
> When Eva walks—
> Oh won't that be a most exciting day!
>
> I am afraid we'll sit up long past seven—
> I have so much to ask her about heaven.
> When Eva talks
> When Eva walks—
> I am afraid we'll sit up long past seven!
>
> Eva, we are so glad you came,
> For life is such a lonely game
> With only one to play it, dear—
> As Hesper found for six long years;
> But now the games you have, you two!
> We are so glad you came—are you?[19]

Richard and Julie had become lonely people. Their marriage of two years was heavily mired in debt, drinking, and dalliances. Richard could be loving, charming, and considerate, but he could also be mercurial, cruel, arrogant, and venomous. Julie wanted to love him, but his holding on to memories of Mildred seemed an affront to their own "lesser" love. When Eva was born, therefore, it was not a tranquil, traditional home setting that greeted her.

After a few months back at their oppressive Kingswood Chase home, the family moved to the quaint, country village of Chiddingfold in Surrey. One spring day, Richard was cycling down a country lane thick with trees, when he came upon a gabled house with a Georgian facade, covered with neatly barbered ivy. "The Old Manor" (as it came to be called) had yellow tea roses clinging to its red bricks and a well-groomed lawn studded with gnarled, old trees and a sundial. The mossy-walled garden, filled with a tapestry of color from the primroses, hyacinths, and violets, convinced Richard that he was in a fairyland, a dreamer's paradise. He could see that the front room of the house looked out on the village green with its peaceful pond. It was in every way a home fit for a poet, and he knew immediately that this must be his family's new residence. It would allow him and Julie another chance to make their marriage work, and it would provide a perfect setting for entertaining—for weekend fetes, autumn pheasant hunts, bridge parties, picnics, and horse racing. Surely they could afford the rent of one hundred pounds per year.

Even as they were preparing the house for occupancy, hope for a smooth marriage was wishful. Soon after Eva was born, her parents resumed their theatregoing, and in June they traveled to Stratford-upon-Avon to see Sarah Bernhardt star as Hamlet. Finding her portrayal "interesting, personal, intellectual, and in parts electric," the Le Galliennes waited for the star outside the stage door after the performance. Richard later said that as she opened the door, "the wonder was enchanting. She had bloomed in the doorway, half orchid, half Queen. . . . We gazed . . . at the strange beauty, the imperious distinction, the siren charm, of Sarah Bernhardt."[20]

According to Julie, the episode did not end quite so innocently. There were officials waiting with the mayor to escort Madame Sarah to the train. She "bloomed in the doorway," smiled at these men, then suddenly spied Richard in the crowd. "When Sarah caught sight of him," Julie later described, "her smile became genuinely dazzling. The 'siren' stretched out her hand and went toward him: 'Mon poete, votre bras!' she said in that magical voice as she handed him one of her carnations. Not content with taking him to the station in the mayor's carriage, she insisted on his accompanying her to London."[21] Julie never disclosed how long her husband stayed away. "La Grande Sarah" reportedly kept a photograph of the young and dashing poet on her bedroom mantle for many months to come.

By August, however, they moved into Chiddingfold with its population of fifteen hundred inhabitants. Both Richard and Julie became intrigued with the village's rich and colorful history. Nearby were ruins of Roman buildings and Celtic funeral barrows dating back to A.D. 400. A thriving glass industry that supplied glass for both Westminster Abbey and York Minster existed from 1225 to 1617 and made Chiddingfold the chief glass-making center in England. For many years a local iron factory exported products to Spain and supplied some of the balustrades for the current St. Paul's Cathedral.

By 1300 the little village gained such renown that Edward I granted the inhabitants a royal charter to hold an annual fair and a weekly market on the green. In 1552 Edward VI and his four thousand followers stopped at the Crown Inn, the local pub. As recently as 1814 the prince regent (George IV), the emperor of Russia, and the king of Prussia passed through the village. To celebrate the jubilees of both George III and Queen Victoria, the victory of Waterloo, and the coronation of Edward VII, villagers decorated with flags, rang the church bells, and sponsored a feast on the green for the entire parish.

There were many tales of smugglers finding the village a good route to the north—tales of boldness, ferocity, and brutality. It was a depot for contraband, a place of late-night rides with illegal spirits, tea, and tobacco. The smugglers rode from the nearby coast and exchanged horses in Chiddingfold. After the payment of a keg of spirits, few questions were asked. The countryside was dotted with caves and underground vaults where the smugglers hid their treasures. Press gangs were known to penetrate this far inland, to carry off by force able-bodied men to serve on board ships in wartime.

The Old Manor, the Le Galliennes' new home in Chiddingfold, was first noted in the poll tax of 1380 and was originally described as comprising ten to twelve acres of land known as "Swanland." By the time the Le Galliennes moved there, it was considered a freehold estate that included five bedrooms with powdering closets, a large dining room, a breakfast parlor, a paved kitchen with a roasting spit and an apparatus for brewing beer, and a cellar with whitewashed wine bins. Also on the property were a dairy, a large brewing house, a piggery, a two-stall stable, and a coach house. The two acres of land included an orchard of two hundred fruit trees, a garden, and a small meadow.

At first, they found happiness in Chiddingfold. Julie entertained; Richard wrote. Looking after Eva and Hesper was their "Nanny," Susan Stenning. Nanny tended to their needs, packed picnics on lazy days, and played games with them in the garden. She occasionally took the girls on long walks through the village. They strolled to the lower end of the green to see the village cross and the stocks, sometimes stopping to watch the smithy at work in his shop. For a special treat, she walked them to the ancient church, entering through the newly built lych-gate and walking along the paths that separated the arched brick graves. Undoubtedly, Nanny recited to her young charges some of the local superstitions: "If a bumble bee flies into a room it is a sign a stranger will call"; "When the blackthorn is in flower there is to be a spell of bad weather"; "If children take a green broom into the house, they won't grow."

Soon after Nanny came to their home, she presented Eva with the child's first doll, which Eva named Bessie. Originally it had a delicate, white, china face and a pink-and-white calico body. The story goes, however, that when Eva first received it, she threw it immediately from her perambulator, and it broke into a thousand pieces. Nanny quickly repaired the doll with a new calico face and with features drawn with india ink. For the ten years that Nanny cared for Eva, she often mended Bessie, creating a brand new face with each surgery. Bessie was the only doll Eva ever loved, and she treasured it her entire life.

By the end of September, the idyllic serenity in Chiddingfold had ended. Eva's parents were once again battling over Richard's roving eye. He had not ended his liason with Ethel Reed as he had promised, so Julie was threatening to leave him. Apparently he sought an ideal relationship. "Is it not possible," he pleaded in a letter on September 24, 1899, "that there may be a joy which we can all three equally share, and that the dream of our three-fold union in the spirit . . . may come true." He argued that Julie, Ethel, and Hesper were "the only human beings necessary" to his life. The solution, as he saw it, would be for him "to renounce the senses," so that he could "see and worship you two great and beautiful women."[22] Julie's rejection of his proposal brought their marriage even closer to the brink.

Eva's first Christmas at The Old Manor was hardly a merry one. In a letter to his wife on December 26, Richard wrote, "I understand that forgiveness for last night must seem impossible and is probably unwise. . . . I am, by sad inheritance, a drunkard." Still he hoped that Julie would not hate him for hitting her "in a frenzy of epileptic possession."[23] Once again he was staggering from heavy debt. So eager to escape the stigma of his working-class upbringing, he had overextended himself in leasing The Old Manor. Even though friends had assured him they would help pay his overdrafts, and he could count on some money from Julie's earnings and from his father, he discovered he could not afford the staff of servants, the remodeling of the house, and the small flat he kept in London as a private retreat.

On Christmas day Richard had tried to escape his depression and sense of failure through whiskey and absinthe. Indeed, he became so drunk that he lashed out at his wife. His raging drunkenness was so severe that Nanny locked Hesper and Eva in the bathroom and guarded the door when she saw him waving a carving knife. Eva was less than a year old when she and her older sister cowered and cried in the corner of that tiny room. She may have been too young to understand fully what was happening, but she was not too young to be terrified of her father. It was an ugly, traumatic moment that the sisters would vividly recall in later years.

The turn of the century did not improve the marriage. In February Richard published his novel *The Worshipper of the Image*. The story concerns a poet who lives in a lovely country house with his wife and children. He acquires a plaster mold of a suicide victim that bears an uncanny resemblance to his wife. The poet falls in love with the image and proceeds to neglect his wife, who eventually commits suicide. A rather morbid fantasy, the book detailed the author's continued mourning for his first wife. Julie was livid with the publication.

A few weeks later, Richard left Chiddingfold. With his Chiddingfold home behind him, the first thing he did was visit with his old friend Jimmy Welch, who had married Richard's sister Sissie a few years earlier. Jimmy and Sissy expressed great concern about the Le Gallienne marriage and pleaded with Richard to end his affair with Ethel Reed. Shortly after this visit, while on a two-month trip to Paris and Italy, he took their advice and announced that Ethel Reed was "no longer a reality in my life." "Try and forget those last hard foolish words," he implored of Julie. "They were only a part of the madness—from which I am going to recover after all." Apparently his apology was too late. A few weeks later, Julie answered rather bluntly, "I am happy. I have an ideal home, the children, my work and you . . . there far away, which means peace."[24] When he returned to England in May, he spent most of his time in London rather than joining his family in Chiddingfold.

The family was reunited again in August of that year, when they traveled to Normandy for a brief holiday. When that ended in September, they could not return to The Old Manor, since they had rented it out for a number of months. They took rooms instead at 34 Bedford Place, in the heart of the Bloomsbury section of London. It was only a few yards away from the British Museum and the spacious gardens of Russell, Bedford, Woburn, and Gordon Squares. Apparently the reunion was not very successful. In October, Julie and Eva moved to another flat at 10 Kensington Crescent, Hesper went to live with Richard's mother, and Richard sailed for New York, not to return to England for eighteen months.

Eva was less than two years old, and already she had lived at six different addresses. She seldom saw her father, and when she did he was often drunk, depressed, or both. Now she was being separated from both her sister and Nanny. Instead of stability and security, her life was filled with confusion, disruption, and loneliness.

Once Richard arrived in the United States, he not only renewed his affair with Miss Wooster but began another. Veda was a ravishing and sensuous South American beauty who worked as a governess in the employ of Minneapolis millionaire James Carleton Young. She soon quit her job and joined Richard at his New York apartment, where they lived off and on for the next three years. In 1903 Veda bore him a son, but the infant died the following year. Strangely, during the early days of their affair, Richard was still wooing Julie. In answer to a letter in which Julie referred to the dead old days of their marriage, he replied, "Does it seem all so far away—and if that future does come, there is only one woman in the world I want to share it with."[25]

A dark day for Richard came when he learned of Oscar Wilde's death on November 30, 1900. He dreamed that he saw a bedraggled and wretched Wilde toiling up a hill one sunny afternoon. When Wilde approached Richard's door, he asked for help, but Richard turned him away. "I often wish I had made some sign to him in those days," Richard later explained, "but, God knows, my own hill needed climbing."[26] Was he embarrassed by Wilde's extravagant behavior, was he fearful of personal scandal, or was he perhaps denying his own homosexual tendencies? Regardless, Richard was left with the guilt that he had rejected his former mentor.

For most of 1901, Julie and Eva were back at The Old Manor, joined by Hesper and Nanny. Although this initially strengthened her sense of family, a new complication was soon to enter Eva's life; her mother began to notice another man. Dr. Folmer Hansen, a young Danish diplomat, became a frequent visitor to The Old Manor and seemed to worship Julie. A few years later, Julie even made tentative plans to settle with him in South Africa. Eva liked him quite a bit, yet she was uncertain of his place in her life and was fearful that he would leave her as her father had so many times earlier.

Richard spent the first part of the year writing for William Randolph Hearst's *New York Journal*, earning the handsome sum of sixty dollars per week. He occasionally managed to send money back to his family. But when his literary contributions came to an abrupt end in April, he turned once again to heavy drinking. In letters to Julie, he bemoaned their separation and yearned to return to The Old Manor at

Chiddingfold. "I am staying away all this time not merely for practical reasons," he explained in a letter, "but because I don't want to see you again until I can say I have conquered." By the end of the year, at Christmas, he wrote, "Dear dear home—shall I ever see it again! . . . let us make one more hard try to hold on to the old house this year—shan't we? I cannot tell you how dear it is to me, and how it haunts my imagination."27

Toward the end of the year, Richard began working on his pastoral, *An Old Country House*. In the chapter "Our Tree-Top Library," he reminisces how his young daughter Eva wandered from the children's corner of the garden one day to show him a fallen bird's nest. After some gymnastic scrambling to return the nest, he found himself seated on a branch some twenty feet above his daughter—"wondering eyes, looking up at me like daisies from the grass." He was so inspired by the moment, he built a reading room in the tree so he could study "alone in a palace of leaves."28

Another chapter, "The Joy of Gardens," intensifies his love for country living and gardening. "To live in town, in a row of houses where all the necessities of life are delivered daily by parasitical, piratical tradesmen, is to live by proxy. It is a life where all the real work of living is done for you," he argued, "and therefore not life." He describes the joy of growing flowers and vegetables, rearing chickens, and milking cows. Part of the joy of the garden was taking tea in a shady corner of the lawn and watching his children play. "Nothing in the world needs so much love," he confesses, "but nothing gives you so much pure love in return."29 He may indeed have spent little time with Eva during her formative years, but somehow his love of gardening and nature made a lasting impression on a spirited little girl who delighted in building flower chains and playing ring-around-a-rosy.

Whether these two chapters were based on fact or were pure fiction is impossible to determine. But the concluding chapter of the book, "Perdita's Christmas," was certainly a far cry from the only Christmas Richard ever spent with his family. Here he recounts celebrating an old-fashioned holiday: the house decorated with holly and mistletoe, guests dressed in Elizabethan costumes, and a feast featuring mulled wine, boar's head, roast goose, mince pie, and the traditional English plum pudding. Candles in the front windows shone out across the village green to help welcome the arrival of Aunt Sissie, who always brought boxes of chocolates, and Uncle Jimmy, who played animal games with the children. The evening ended with the appearance of Father Christmas, caroling, and a festive dance. The perfect celebration was a sad contrast to the Christmas when Eva was locked in a bathroom to protect her from a raging father with a knife.

When the handsomely bound book appeared in December 1902, Julie was appalled by her husband's blatant untruths. The stories said little about their real country life and even less about their marriage. To her, they were sweet, wishful fantasies and nothing more. Since she was lonely and tired of being isolated in the country, she found the idealism an impossible frustration that mocked her ordinary world.

Richard was also feeling discontent. Unable to afford living in New York without a higher salary and lonely for his family, Richard returned to England in May 1902 and joined Julie and Eva. Because they could no longer meet all the expenses of country living, the family rented The Old Manor to their actor friend William Faversham and his wife and took their lodgings at 5 Bedford Gardens in the Campden Hill section of London. An agreeable, residential quarter, the area contained, in addition to Kensington Palace and Gardens, several large mansions with extensive grounds, giving the neighborhood the appearance of a rural district removed from the metropolis of London.

Again the family reunion was short-lived. In July Richard took an alcohol cure at a doctor's home in Wimbledon. Ashamed of his weakness, he told friends that he was suffering from a nervous collapse and asthma and that he was taking a cycling holiday through the countryside. Julie and Eva left Bedford Gardens and moved into the Southdown Hotel in Eastbourne. They were joined by Richard in August. By September they were living at 16 Clifton Hill in the London suburb of St. John's Wood.

This originally salubrious suburb was established early in the nineteenth century as a luxury for the privileged classes. The conservative Victorians whispered that the three-story detached homes, each with its own walled garden, were places where rich men installed their mistresses. Names of earlier residents—George Eliot, Thomas Huxley, and Charles Bradlaugh—lent the area the vague scent of impropriety.

By the time the Le Galliennes moved in, however, St. John's Wood was a middle-class neighborhood with swift and direct train service to central London. Their home was a modest villa, with a kitchen, a bathroom, four bedrooms, and a drawing room with two fireplaces. On the ground floor was the nursery, with doors out to the garden. Nearby was the famous Lord's Cricket Ground. Toward the rear of the garden was a little log house where Richard wrote during the few weeks he lived there. Little Eva often looked in at the window with an "affected, innocent look, a definite purpose of seduction in her baby heart." Though she knew she was not supposed to interrupt her father, she would want to play truant together, hunt butterflies and wild flowers. Unable to resist her "little broad indomitable face," he would stop his work and carry her up to the gorse-lit moorland nearby.[30]

One day, when he saw an adder while walking through the woods, he decided to lure Eva away from her dolls so she could see it. He hid behind a hedge of flowering laurel, plucked a red rose from a nearby bush, and threw it on her lap. "If there is one thing I love about her," he wrote later, "it is the calm way she takes surprises." She looked silently at the rose, then with her strong, quiet eyes gazed around to see where it had come from. Once she caught sight of her father, they went running off to one of their secret hiding places, a hollow of fern surrounded by birches.

"Daddy," Eva asked, "why are some roses red and some white?"

"I will tell you, Eva," he replied, "when you can tell me why sister's hair is black and yours is golden."

The answer made a profound impression on Eva, and she pondered it "in the unfathomable deeps of her baby brain." She began questioning everything that grew or sang or moved in the woods. "Eva is of a different temper," her father noted a couple of years later. "She is an exact scientist, and insists on knowing the name and the how and the why of every leaf and flower and insect that crosses our path." She even wanted to know what the birds were saying.[31]

A major highlight of the year was Eva's attending her first play, *The Water Babies* by Charles Kingsley. In spite of their grave financial situation, Richard and Julie scraped together the money for tickets so that Eva could experience this popular theatrical event. The fairy tale is about Tom, a chimney sweep who is employed by the bully Mr. Grimes. Tom runs away, falls into a river, turns into a water baby, and becomes friends with colorful sea creatures. Awed as only a three-year-old can be by such a fantasy, Eva stomped up and down the room when they returned home, repeating, "I will be a water baby. I must be a water baby." Her mother replied, "To be a water baby one must be able to read and write, and you can neither read nor write."[32] Julie consented with amusement to take her daughter to the theatre manager once she had learned.

Soon, Eva's sense of family was disrupted again. Her father left for New York in early October. The reasons were many. He had come to realize that publishers in England were no longer impressed by his work and that the style of the nineties was "not only dead, but buried." He missed New York and his relationship with Veda. But also, he needed once again to escape from his creditors. Even though he and Julie had cut their expenses by renting out The Old Manor, they were still plagued by debts amounting to over two thousand pounds. They were even threatened with the seizure of their Chiddingfold furniture. Both Richard's father and Jimmy Welch had lent them money, but they agreed to waive their claims until the other creditors were paid.

Probably a final blow to the Le Gallienne marriage was a telegram Julie received quite by accident. It was an amorous and flamboyant telegram that Veda intended Richard to receive before he left for New York. When she read it, Julie was wild to learn that Richard's earlier visit to the United States had not been as dull as he had complained, and she thundered at him for his Bohemian, vagabond-artist airs. Richard subsequently apologized for the telegram but not for his affair with Veda, insisting that his sinning was quite sincere.[33] At about the same time, Julie learned that his repertoire also included authoress Zona Gale.

The next year, 1903, was one of great transition. In July Richard discovered that Julie's relationship with Dr. Hansen was thriving and warned her in a letter, "Think very long before you put it away from you."[34] He suspected that their own marriage was doomed and that Julie should be careful not to lose a man who seemed to dote on her. Still hoping against hope, however, he returned to England in August to pursue some sort of reconciliation.

What a pathetic reunion it must have been. He drank heavily and again became abusive. "It was the old filth and poison of my mind coming again to the surface for no reason," he pleaded in a letter. "It was the madness in me, and not me, talking. Will you try to forget it? . . . Julie, who shall deliver me from the body of this death!"[35] Though utterly sorry and miserable, he could not dissuade Julie this time. The only sane solution to the mockery of their partnership was now clear to her. She returned his ring and went home to Copenhagen. Richard returned to New York, and the girls went to stay with Nanny in Farncombe. Although he continued to write her long, diarylike letters, there was no hope of saving the marriage.

The time spent in Farncombe must have been a delight for the girls after the months of tension in their household. The little Elizabethan cottage where they stayed was made of oak and covered with ivy. There were creaky staircases, uneven floors, low-hanging corners, and narrow passages. In the rear was a traditional English garden, filled with apple trees and bordered by hedges of hop. Nanny's sister Juden pampered them with rice pudding, roast joints, and all the traditional English dishes—porridge, steak and kidney pie, trifle, bubble and squeak, lamb stew, and treacle. In the front room on Christmas day, they had a tree topped with a Danish angel of wax, with tinsel wings and a star in her hair.

Soon after Christmas, though, life was jolted once more for Eva. Dining one day in New York with Theresa Wooster, his Bridgeport beauty, Eva's father was informed, much to his supposed surprise, that his wife was suing him for divorce. Miss Wooster remarked, "He was thunderstruck! This was the first he had heard of it! And I was sorry to bring him the news, for he was like a maniac." He insisted there was no foundation to the rumor and produced a letter from his wife that read, "We are growing into the perfect married understanding, free from all hypocrisy. I love you to tell me all you do, to be frank with me as I am with you."[36] Regardless of Richard's protestations, the Le Galliennes permanently separated by the end of the year—as he saw it, because of his "will to romance."

Eva did not see her father again until 1917. But in spite of those years of separation, he left a lasting mark on his young daughter. Eva's mother was her daily authority figure, the parent who disciplined, the one who tried to curb her aspirations in earlier years and even cautioned her that she might be tiring people with her endless talk of the stage. Richard, on the other hand, was the absent parent who was idolized. Eva cherished the man who refused to run with the herd, and she clung to the thought that more than a little of her was very much like this famous and infamous man. "Although we had seen so little of each other," she wrote many years later, "I felt deeply bound to him."[37]

While the divorce proceedings were beginning, Eva, who was still at Farncombe, learned of another impending move—she and Nanny were to join her mother in Paris. Once again she would be separated from Hesper, who had been made a legal ward of her uncle, Jimmy Welch, and would attend school in Littlehampton. Now barely four years old, Eva had lived in more homes than many of her playmates would know in a lifetime. But this move was especially difficult for her. She had no idea how long they would be in Paris, no idea when she would see her sister again, no idea if her father would ever join them, no idea if she would ever return to The Old Manor, and no idea if she would ever be able to fulfill her dream of becoming a water baby.

2

Mad about Her

Eva and her mother were not the only foreigners flocking to France. Soon after the Universal Exhibition of 1900, Paris suddenly became the premiere school of Europe, the acknowledged center of intellectual, cultural, and artistic activity. Cézanne, Picasso, and Miro came from Spain, Chagall, Nijinsky, and Diaghileff from Russia, Gertrude Stein from America, and Modigliani from Italy. In 1903 King Edward VII of England paid his first state visit to France and helped form a new Anglo-French alliance. Greeting these guests was a new bridge crossing the Seine, the impressive Pont Alexandre III, as well as two great buildings of the Exhibition, the Grand and the Petit Palais des Beaux Arts.

These years before 1914, when Eva lived in Paris, are often called "La Belle Epoque." They were glorious, brilliant, exciting years. Sarah Bernhardt was performing in *Camille* and *L'Aiglon*. Toulouse-Lautrec was immortalizing the music hall world with his posters and canvases. The Moulin Rouge and Folies Bergere were attracting local, as well as curious, foreign, crowds. Little cafés in Montmartre, like Lapin Agile, attracted writers — Anatole France, Verlaine, Mallarme, and Gide — and there, such artists as Manet, Seurat, Degas, and Renoir argued their latest theories on impressionism and symbolism. The popular Maxim's restaurant on the Rue Royale offered discreet rooms for guests to dine in private with their courtesans.

There were other highlights. The first Metro line opened in 1900. Marie and Pierre Curie were awarded the Nobel Prize and made their world-shaking discovery of radium. Louis Lumiere produced color film and furthered the popularity of moving pictures, and Louis Bleriot flew the English channel, inspiring many Frenchmen to become pioneer pilots. The bicycle, now within the purchasing power of the masses, led to the the annual Tour de France, and Louis Renault founded the great automobile factory.

It was only natural that Julie Le Gallienne would move to Paris. She wanted to start over, away from the memories of her husband, but she also wanted to live in a bustling, artistic atmosphere. Paris was the perfect answer. Their first home was an apartment on the fifth floor at 60 Rue de Vaugirard. Low-ceilinged but spacious, it consisted of six rooms, with a large area on the courtyard doubling as the kitchen and dining room.

The street was in the heart of the Fauborg St. Germain area of the Left Bank. Such expatriate, artistic women as Natalie Barney, Edith Wharton, Gertrude Stein, Isadora Duncan, and Colette settled here. Later labeled "the Left Bank of Lesbos," by 1900 the neighborhood had an international reputation as a haven for lesbians. Because the Napoleonic Code did not address homosexuality, such life styles were not banned by law and were a dominant element of the culture. As one salon hostess commented, "All the noteworthy women are doing it."[1] In the fashionably risqué salons, women of the demimonde mixed with royalty. While homosexual men appeared in rouge and wigs, the women sported tuxedos with monocles tucked in their pockets.

As Eva witnessed this liberal behavior in her early years on the Left Bank, she also learned that the general community viewed lesbians as men trapped in female bodies. When a woman was discovered as being lesbian, she was usually advised to seek a cure for her pathological drives. The private salons seemed to allow safety from embarrassing public exposure.

The best part about their new lodging on the Rue de Vaugirard was its proximity to the Luxembourg Gardens. Nearly every day, Nanny walked her charge through the park, which was always filled with children floating their toy boats around the artificial lake and rolling hoops with bells. Nurses, wearing long capes and starched white caps, pushed perambulators down the long, flower-bordered walks and sat on benches under the majestic chestnut trees. If Eva was good during the day, Nanny bought her flavored soda water or licorice from one of the candy booths. They often walked through the gardens into the Petit Luxembourg and down the boulevard Saint-Michel, where they stopped at a pastry shop for a cake or praline ice. On special occasions they hired a horse-drawn coach to return them to their apartment.

Eva's mother managed to eke out a very frugal living. She translated and continued writing newspaper articles for *Politiken*. Fortunately, Nanny agreed to work for over a year without pay. But regardless of the strenuous life Julie was facing, she never regretted leaving her husband. Richard was "always very charming, when he *was* charming," she explained to author and friend Arnold Bennett, and clearly "he had never bored her." Nevertheless, she insisted she had tolerated "enough of the artistic temperament."[2] Her understatement gave no indication of her real anger and disgust.

Julie occasionally pleaded with her husband for financial help, but he had little to send. In fact, his manuscripts these days were regularly rejected by publishers. Even when he was forced to sell most of his personal library and took in nearly five thousand dollars at an auction in New York, he had virtually nothing left after he paid his creditors. In 1905 he earned less than fifteen hundred dollars; the following two years were even more severe. In 1907, when he was most desperate for money, he sold the last of his library, including a treasured letter from Robert Louis Stevenson. He suffered not only from his customary asthma and alcoholism but from bouts of cold and hunger and was on the verge of a complete nervous breakdown. At one point, he wrote to Julie that he was embarrassed that his sister and husband were paying all of Hesper's expenses. "As to Eva, I should, of course, only be too happy to do whatever I could—though seeing that she will practically cease to be my child, and that I shall have no share or say in her, such a demand certainly strikes me as unfair."[3]

Even though Julie had limited funds, in late autumn of 1905 they moved to a larger apartment at 5 Rue de Regard. It was a delightful occasion for Eva. Not only would they have more space, but more importantly, they would be joined by Eva's half sister, Hep. With her mother occupied with making a living for them, Eva had been spending most of her time with Nanny and longed for a youthful playmate. Aunt Sissie, whose marriage with Uncle Jimmy was disintegrating, joined the family circle.

Opposite the new apartment was an old convent-school that Hep and Eva attended. A few years earlier it had been one of the well-established and flourishing Catholic private schools, but when the anticlerical government broke off relations with the Vatican and began expelling monks and nuns by the thousands, the dedicated teachers at the school dropped out of their religious order. Their action made them eligible for state funds and thereby able to preserve the school.

One of Eva's vivid experiences at the school occurred during a St. Catherine fete. The children, in a game much like that of the Mexican pinata, each had their turn striking a wooden mallet against an earthenware pot suspended from the ceiling. The girl who broke the pot received the prize inside. The Le Gallienne sisters created quite a row when they discovered the prize was a poor, terrified rabbit and cried deeply when they saw that it was bruised and frightened and could barely breathe. Their upbringing, they were learning, had been quite different from these city girls, for they had been taught to treat all animals with love and dignity.

Birds were Eva's favorite animals. Her Danish grandmother, Bet, came to Paris on a visit and surprised her with a cage bursting with a dozen tropical birds. Their colors and songs brought considerable joy into the impoverished home. Still, Eva's favorite bird was a common baby sparrow she found in the courtyard of their apartment, carried to her bedroom, and nursed with sugar and water for weeks.

During their Easter holiday, the entire family visited Arnold Bennett at his lovely home at Fontainebleau and was treated to a drive in his new motorcar. Nanny was apprehensive, for she considered these newfangled inventions nasty and smelly. She much preferred a peaceful walk on a country lane. Eva remembered that the automobile "was shaped like a governess cart (this comforted Nanny a little!); Mr. Bennett sat next to the chauffeur on a very high seat like a carriage-box. We clambered into our seats through a little door at the back of the car, and sat there perched very high, in considerable trepidation."[4] After a number of explosive misfires, they gathered speed until they were zooming at fifteen miles per hour. When they finished the ride, Bennett presented the girls with a rare treat—a bagful of chocolate-cream eggs. What a delightful day! The brief holiday was a welcome interlude from the hard times they were facing in Paris. With no advance notice, *Politiken* abruptly discontinued Julie's "Eva" articles, cutting off most of her income. Since coal was scarce and expensive, the family lived mostly in one room during the bitterly cold winter. Nanny became so critically ill with bronchitis that Julie strained her slender purse and bought the medicine that returned her to health. When Sissie and Hep returned to London in November 1906, Eva, her mother, and Nanny moved to a smaller apartment at 1 Rue de Fleurus—a street lined with art studios and secondhand bookshops—just a few doors from the home of Gertrude Stein. Once again Eva was separated from her sister. It seemed as if she would never experience stability and a place to call home.

Julie decided that the solution to their financial problems would be to open a millinery shop, but first she needed thirty francs to pay for a six-month apprenticeship program. She reluctantly appealed to her father-in-law, John Gallienne, for help. Embittered by his cold refusal, she wrote to Sissie later that winter that the pious, narrow, self-glad tone of his reply deeply infuriated her:

It made me set my teeth hard and I realized that only in the strength of my own nature lies salvation for Eva and me in the future. . . . I cannot help thinking how many crimes are committed in the name of Christ even nowadays, and if one compares two very opposite theories as that of your father's and Grant Allen's, how finer and far truer Christian in spirit is then the pagan. . . . At all events I have given up all hope of help from that quarter. I won't be sentimental, too much is at stake and I must go ahead. Well, sweet Sissie, I have had a hell of a time, I am in the midst of it all yet, but a quiet strength has grown out of it and I believe firmly I shall come out top—yet. You know I have always had an absurd faith in my own star, that I should go down in the whirlpool I simply refuse to believe, so with a tiny bit of luck I still believe things will come right.[5]

To raise the necessary funds herself, Julie began selling her personal treasures—a sideboard, an Empire table, a dress and matching lace coat. Friends supplied the rest.

Since she already knew most of the fashionable people in the American and English colony of Paris, her shop, which she called "Mme. Fédora," quickly became a thundering success. Such people as H. G. Wells and Arnold Bennett sent all their friends. The shop was actually in their apartment on the Rue de Fleurus. In the daytime the drawing room was converted into a bustling salon; in the evening all the hats, along with ribbons, feathers, and flowers, were stashed in boxes.

Little Eva was usually unaware of the struggle, and Mams, as Eva now called her mother, tried her best to hide it. Finances rarely kept them from the adventures around town. They often went on Sunday excursions to the Bois de Boulogne, the Louvre, the Musée de Cluny, or the Tuileries. Whenever they visited Versailles, they lunched at a little restaurant at the foot of the *tapis vert*. But their favorite excursion was to Ville d'Avray. Here they dined beside the pond immortalized in Du Maurier's *Peter Ibbetson*, then they walked back to Neuilly through the woods and returned to Paris by way of a little river steamer on the Seine.

To help celebrate Christmas, Eva's mother sacrificed and bought tickets for them to attend a dramatization of *The Sleeping Beauty*, starring none other than Sarah Bernhardt. Eva could not believe that she was actually going to see "La Grande Sarah," the greatest actress of the day. Shortly after the play began, the scene changed to a large hall in a castle; an old woman was sitting in front of her spinning wheel. Years later, Eva remembered the event vividly:

Suddenly, from off-stage came the sound of a voice — high, clear, vibrant, electric, unforgettable — and through the archway upstage left appeared the Prince. . . . I sat in a kind of daze, completely under the spell of this extraordinary creature, who to me was Prince Charming personified. . . . I remember thinking, in a confused kind of way, that this Prince was more radiantly *alive* than anyone I'd ever seen; as though he lived more intensely, more joyously, more richly than other people.[6]

At the time, Mams wondered if her little, seven-year-old daughter would believe in a Prince Charming played by a sixty-three-year-old woman. A worry in vain. Eva was completely entranced, as she fantasized once again about her dream to become a water baby.

A few days later, Eva read about another theatrical performance. The notorious writer and actress Sidonie Gabrielle Colette had performed in a revue at the Moulin Rouge and was almost arrested for enacting a lesbian love scene. Further performances of the play were banned, Colette's husband was discharged from his position on a Paris newspaper, and Colette was forced to stop living openly with her female lover. Surely for Eva, the risk of public pronouncements and the danger of scandal did not go unnoticed.

On her eighth birthday, Eva was given a toy theatre. With Hep, who was visiting with them in Paris, she made costumes from her mother's wardrobe and acted out plays and pageants. "Once after we had seen 'Kismet' I appropriated mother's tiger skin rug and triumphantly turned myself into an Eastern slave," she later wrote. "On another occasion with the aid of a red striped bathing suit for tights I played an ardent Romeo. We reproduced every play we saw."[7]

That summer they all went back to England for a long holiday, but their reunion was interrupted by the sudden death of Aunt Sissie. Eva and Hep were sent to stay with Nanny's married sister, who lived on the edge of Epping Forest. Although their time was colored by their sorrow, the two girls managed to have many adventures playing in the woods and seeing all the wild animals. Eva's imagination seemed to soar. She wanted to know what characters in books and plays really looked like; she wanted to actually visualize them. Once Hep came into Eva's room and found her pulling the most awful faces in front of the mirror. "I asked," explained Hep, "'Why, Baby, what in the world are you doing?' Eva replied, 'Pretending people,' and went right on pulling faces."[8] The girls were rather lonely children and did not enjoy dressing up and going to parties. They had a better time by themselves, spending many leisure hours playacting. At the end of the summer, Eva was heartbroken to learn that Hep was being sent to live with Nanny in Farncombe. Eva and her mother would leave for Paris alone.

Soon after their return, Eva began attending a school that her mother had chosen very carefully, the Collège Sévigné, located at 8 Rue de Condé in the old Hotel de Condé. Fortunately, she was a child interested in reading and study, for the school was heavily academic, a kind of college prep school, priming girls for the Sorbonne. The school's intellectual atmosphere encouraged her obsession with books. Her mother, who treated her always as an adult, allowed her to read anything she wanted. She began with *Robinson Crusoe* and continued with *The Count of Monte Cristo*, *The Three Musketeers*, novels by Dickens and Thackeray, and even *Grimm's Fairy Tales*. She continued her education there for over five years.

Eva attended classes in the morning only, listening to lectures and taking detailed notes. In the afternoons, she frequently played in the Luxembourg Gardens. She especially enjoyed helping Madame Coudret and her daughter conduct donkey and goat-cart rides for children. Besides being fun, the work also provided a few leisurely coins. When her mother discovered she was doing such menial work, she not only stopped it but took away Eva's allowance for six months.

If Mams disapproved of this innocence, it is fortunate she never learned of Eva's next scheme. She was still determined to make some spending money, and since the Luxembourg Gardens were now off-limits, she turned to the Bois de Boulogne. She stationed herself at one of the busy crosswalks, placed her large straw hat at her feet, and proceeded to perform, singing Danish and German folk songs as well as English music hall favorites. As the crowd gathered, she passed the hat around. This new venture was even more rewarding, for on a good day she collected as much as five francs.

Christmases were usually spent in Copenhagen with her mother's family. It was a wonderful time for Eva to learn and practice her Danish. But it was also a time when she could experience the real warmth of a family. Naturally, there were all the festive foods of the holiday—julekake, lutefisk, rice pudding, red pudding, and cream porridge. When the tree was finally presented with its real lighted candles on Christmas Eve, there was a hushed silence. Then presents were distributed. What a thrill for Eva when she was once given a miniature wooden sleigh pulled by a team of hand-carved reindeer.

These holiday visits were a time to renew friendships with relatives, such as her cousin Mogens and her Uncle Kai. Grandmother Bet always took time to read from the old sagas or to tell the story of the family's flight from the Germans during the invasion of Schleswig-Holstein. One of Eva's favorite stories was about her mother's meeting with Hans Christian Andersen. When Mams was five years old, Andersen had visited her school room. After seating himself at the podium, he had looked around the room and motioned for her to come to him. Grandmother Bet described how "he had helped her climb onto his friendly, bony knee and had kept her there—now and then offering her a sip from the glass of barley water that stood on the table beside his chair—while for an enchanted hour he had told his fairy tales."[9] From hearing the story so often, Eva felt that she actually knew the man.

In the evenings they sometimes went to the opera or to the Royal Theatre, where Eva noticed the words "Ej Blot til Lyst" (Not Only for Amusement) carved over the proscenium arch. One Christmas she was given a toy replica of the Royal Theatre. She proceeded to fit it with special scenery for the various plays she had seen and made footlights, borders, and spots with candles. Bits of colored glass served as color media for the lighting scheme. She was particularly proud to show her relatives her rain effect. To simulate torrents of water rushing down on the stage, she made a floor out of plastic, and above the stage she rigged a piece of gas pipe with holes in it. As she poured water into the pipe, it would run out of the holes and onto the stage below. There was a trap door in the stage with a bucket underneath. When she was cast in *Not So Long Ago* in 1920, she refitted this toy theatre and dramatized the play, taking all the parts, as a voice hovering above the theatre. Her characters were dolls dressed in the fashions of 1870.

In the summers, Eva and her mother always returned to England, often staying for two or three weeks with the Favershams at The Old Manor in Chiddingfold. In 1911 Eva spent the entire summer there. Whenever Hep visited, they kept busy with their creative projects, acting out scenes from *As You Like It* and *Romeo and Juliet*, presenting vocal concerts of popular songs, and publishing a little magazine called *The Arrow*, the only readers being close family friends and Mrs. Le Gallienne.

One of the girls' pastimes involved Dame Bicknell, a colorful, eighty-three-year-old woman in the village, who was rumored to be a witch. One story Eva and Hep heard many times was that Dame Bicknell caused the illness of a local girl. When the girl's father consulted a witch-hunter, he was advised to beat the witch the next time she came near his house. After he followed the advice, he was taken to court and fined. To cure the illness of a little boy, Dame

Bicknell boasted she would catch a white mouse with no blemish, cook it alive over a slow fire, and make the boy eat it as she chanted. Intrigued as young and imaginative children might be, Eva and her playmates were terrified of the old lady as she walked along the village paths. They spent many afternoons creating little plays with Dame Bicknell as the central, wicked character.

By chance the Favershams were also visited that summer by the successful London actress, Constance Collier. When Eva first came upon her, she was sitting on a low stool beside the big fireplace in the great room of The Old Manor. She was dark, with a vivid, glowing face, and she wore an exciting red dress with no jewelry, only a spray of flowers pinned to her bodice. Eva was a mere twelve years old, but for some curious reason, she felt an unusual attraction for this glamorous lady. Sixty years later, she told her close friend Anne Kaufman Schneider that she sensed even at this age that whatever she was feeling was the first glimmer of her own sexuality. [10]

How thrilling for her, then, that this enchanting actress agreed to give Eva her first lessons in acting. Driven by an unconscious infatuation, Eva was determined to please. This was truly a dream come true. Maybe she could even become an actress. They worked together on the roles of Juliet in *Romeo and Juliet* and Ariel in *The Tempest*. Under her mentor's guidance, Eva discovered the values in the poetic speeches, working to bring out the music without losing sight of the meaning. Collier explained to her the dilemma of either intoning the verse and therefore losing all the feeling of reality or being too natural and disregarding the poetry. "Such a brilliant teacher," Eva thought, and she dreamed of one day performing on the same stage with this beautiful woman.

Collier quickly saw the spark of greatness in her young student. When she played games with the other children, Eva was always the organizer. Even the boys obeyed her. Collier noticed that these games were different. "They did not play as ordinary children play. There was meaning in their amusement. It had a beginning and an end." She was quickly drawn to Eva's eyes and remarked, "There was a tremendous look of earnestness and determination. . . . Those eyes of hers, that are so wide and penetrating! They are the most characteristic thing about her; brilliant and star-like, they seem to shine out of the Nordic sky."

In her autobiography, Collier recalls an incident that occurred that summer. Eva, who was a Girl Guide, decided to camp out one evening. A particularly hard rain knocked her tent down, pinning her underneath the muddy canvas. The next morning, when most girls might have come crying home, Eva returned for equipment to strengthen her tent. When Collier asked her if she had cried for help, she responded, "No, of course not. I built it up again." "Typically Eva's attitude toward life," she thought.[11]

Eva's first offer to act professionally came during that summer. Faversham and Collier were rehearsing several new productions for the coming Broadway season, including *Romeo and Juliet* and *Julius Caesar*. Impressed with Eva's potential and desire, Collier asked Mams to allow her daughter to play the part of Lucius in *Julius Caesar*. What an opportunity! This was the culmination of what Eva had been hoping for the past nine years. But permission was refused. Eva's mother insisted that her daughter needed more education before she embarked on a stage career. The refusal came as a blow. Eva could not help but question her mother's decision. Was it truly about her education, or was Julie anguished over her husband's "artistic temperament" and hoping to stifle it in her young daughter?

Adding tension to the summer were the divorce proceedings that Julie and Richard had initiated eight years earlier. It was not an easy matter with the two of them living on different continents. Their original plan had been for Julie to bring a case of desertion against Richard after he had taken up residence in Rhode Island for one year. When that proved futile, they forged a case of adultery. In response to Julie's financial demands, Richard drew up a will that granted half of his copyrights to Eva and the other half to Hesper. The divorce on grounds of adultery and desertion was finally granted on July 3, 1911. Although Eva was aware of some of her parents' problems and had not seen her father for eight years, the finality of the decree was very upsetting. Richard had rarely written to Eva through the years and had seldom sent her any financial help. Since Mams had now refused her permission to travel to America with Constance Collier's theatre production, Eva wondered if she would ever see her father again.

At the end of the summer, Julie returned to Paris, leaving Eva in England at a boarding school in Bognor, a dreary, ugly, seaside town, with aspirations of becoming a resort like Brighton or Bath. The town was so depressing, in fact, that Englishmen coined a popular expletive—"bugger Bognor." All the girls at the school wore the usual uniform of a long skirt with a high-collared shirt. In contrast to the progressive and challenging Collège Sévigné, Eva found this school intensely dull. The rigid codes of behavior and the routine instructional methods were too much for her. She had been a "latchkey child" from the age of eight, and now she was treated like an infant. Unaccustomed to such a stifling atmosphere, she frequently sneaked out of her little room at night, climbed over the wall, and ran along the sandy beach to freedom. How she yearned for the beauty of Paris and the glamour of the theatres.

However the school did provide Eva's first opportunity to act and direct before an audience. The dramatic production at the end of the first term was about Queen Elizabeth, and Eva was cast as Lord Burleigh. Recognizing that the rehearsals were not moving as they should, Eva asked to be appointed as director. This was an exciting challenge, though she could not convey it to her fellow students. Most of them had never set foot in a theatre. They refused to learn their lines and could not understand Eva's enthusiasm and intensity.

During the Christmas holidays of 1911, Eva joined her mother in Paris and began a succession of visits to the theatre to see "La Grande Sarah" in productions including *La Dame aux Camélias* and *La Reine Elizabeth* in 1912; *Jeanne Doré* in 1913; *Phèdre* in 1914; a series of one-act plays and scenes from *L'Aiglon*, *Jeanne d'Arc*, *Cléopatre*, and *La Reine Hécube* in 1916; and *La Reine Hécube* again in 1917. These performances were critically important to this hopeful actress. Besides being inspirational, they laid some of the groundwork for her later techniques in acting.

In 1912 Eva saw Bernhardt's portrayal of Marguerite Gauthier in *La Dame aux Camélias* and was greatly impressed by the feeling and clarity she projected. The story of a beautiful and sensitive prostitute with a fatal disease, the melodrama allows the actress to play profoundly upon the emotions. Bernhardt did just that. Eva found that her acting was "full of fire and often charged with genuine feeling. . . . I myself had cried so much that the front of my dress was soaked."[12] The effect was due in part to the way Bernhardt developed her character. Many actresses, even great ones, would begin playing Marguerite's death scene almost from the first act of the play, but Eva saw that Sarah "did not fall into this trap; she gave herself plenty of scope for variety and progression. She was wise enough to know that a woman in Marguerite's position—that of a highly successful demimondaine—could not afford to appear sickly, neurotic or melancholy. If she did her vogue would be short-lived."

Bernhardt analyzed the role and decided to allow her character to develop during the full course of the performance. In act 1, her Marguerite was no ordinary tart but an aristocrat. A sharp contrast occurred when she moved to the country. Eva observed "the tenderness, the lyricism with which Sarah played this scene. She seemed to be living a poem of sheer happiness. The brittle gaiety of the first act had given way to a deep inner serenity, and the shattering of this serenity by Armand's father was almost unbearably poignant." In the last act, Bernhardt stressed Marguerite's gallantry, yet remnants of her former brightness shone through. Although she was only thirteen, Eva was moved by a consciously studied style of acting that was still "full of fire."

Because her mother did not force her to return to school at Bognor, Eva saw Bernhardt later that season in Emile Moriau's *La Reine Elizabeth*, a play about the Elizabeth-Essex story. It was enormously impressive—almost heroic. This time Eva witnessed that great acting could, and indeed should, be based on careful research, but with an eye for theatricality. Eva knew from her study of English history that the Elizabeth of history lay on a pile of cushions for several days as she was dying. Sarah's portrayal staged the scene with this in mind. Several steps led to the throne, and at the foot of these steps was a mound of pillows. Eva saw how Sarah's Elizabeth mounted the steps with great difficulty, "stood in front of the throne for several moments as though determined to die as Queen, then swayed and plunged down onto the pile of cushions." It was another electric moment that made Eva even more resolved to become an actress.

Perhaps Eva's best observation of Sarah's ability to combine technical skill with emotional power came with the performance of Sardou's *Cléopatre* in 1916. Eva noticed that Bernhardt seemed aware of all the details:

> The virtuosity, for instance, with which through the power of her imagination, she convinced us of the reality of the asp hidden under the rose petals; the effort of will one saw her make as she gazed at the basket, seeing death there, hands poised above it—hesitant. Then the sudden pounce of the fingers and the struggle beneath the petals to catch and hold the wriggling muscular creature, and the swift movement with which she placed it at her breast. And the moment—very restrained, under-stressed—when she felt its "sharp teeth" in her flesh. It was impossible to believe there was nothing there—no snake, no sharp teeth, no death. It had all seemed so real—so fantastically real. For Sarah's acting—contrary to her legend—could be very naturalistic, though always in a studied way.[13]

Eva learned that it was possible to have both polished technique and genuine feeling.

Clearly, she was more than inspired by Bernhardt's acting. But an event that occurred a few months later was even more stimulating—

Eva actually met Sarah Bernhardt. On December 16, 1913, Mrs. Le Gallienne took her daughter to the opening night presentation of Tristan Bernard's *Jeanne Doré* in which Bernhardt played the mother of a boy who has been condemned to death. After the performance, they went backstage for a prearranged meeting with the actress. Amidst the usual confusion, Bernhardt finally appeared before an awestruck teenager. Eva was startled by the amount of makeup: "The strange grey-green eyes were heavily framed in blue. . . . Her face was quite pale but her mouth was a gash of bright scarlet. When she smiled at me I noticed that small flecks of the scarlet paint had stuck to her teeth."[14] The young girl was amazed at how the actress was treated like royalty, by both her retinue of servants and the crowd of admirers. This, she thought, was how a star should be treated, and she began dreaming of the day that she would have such crowds gathering around after one of her performances.

Fortunately, this was not their last meeting. A few months later, William Faversham's wife asked Eva to deliver a message to Sarah. With the intention of making the delivery afterward, Eva attended an afternoon presentation in which Sarah was cast as Racine's Phèdre. Through the entire performance, all she could think of was the coming meeting. As the curtain descended, she rushed down the seven flights of stairs to the backstage area. After a short wait, during which she watched a number of fans dismissed, her turn was announced. As she entered the mirrored room, she saw Sarah sitting at a huge dressing table, still wearing her jeweled costume and diadem. She looked like a real queen. The aging actress turned to the girl before her and suddenly laughed, "Mais, mon Dieu, c'est un bebe!" As the laughter in the room mounted, Sarah realized Eva's embarrassment and stopped it "with an imperious gesture."[15] After a short conversation wherein Eva delivered the message, she accepted some flowers from Sarah and departed. At first she was frightened by the crowd and disappointed in her idol, but she later came to appreciate how sensitive and responsive Sarah had been to her situation.

When Bernhardt's *Memoirs* were published later that year, Eva was determined to own a copy of her own. Since she had no money, she borrowed the book from a family friend and copied in longhand every word of the eight hundred pages. Sometime later, Edmond Rostand, author of *L'Aiglon*, was visiting the Le Gallienne home and saw the girl's work. When he later informed Bernhardt about it, she sent for Eva to bring the book to her and inscribed on the flyleaf: "Dear and adorable child, I am touched at the great pains you have taken to copy this long book. I wish you great happiness throughout your life and I embrace you tenderly. Signed Sarah Bernhardt." Eva had seen her perform, had visited her backstage, and now she had an actual written message from her. It was her first autograph from a major celebrity.[16]

By the fall of 1916, Bernhardt had become Eva's god. After she saw Sarah perform in *Camille*, she was given the flowers the actress wore in the performances, along with a note saying, "a souvenir of Sarah Bernhardt." Eva confessed to a reporter, "I put the flowers in a locket which I wear always. It is my talisman!" When Eva was appearing in *Mr. Lazarus* in New York, she announced, "I watch her gestures, her hands, the expression of her whole body. I listen to her French—her voice is music and her enunciation is like a bell. I am mad about her!"[17]

Truly, Sarah was the epitome of everything Eva worshiped. Eva explained to friends and to herself that her infatuation was simply the height of admiration. Perhaps it was admiration, but it was not that simple. There was a strange magnetism that she would not fully understand for several more years. Eva would soon begin to struggle with a part of her world that would burden her at every turn. It was the same struggle that Sarah had faced a generation earlier, though she had refused to accept it as a burden. Sarah Bernhardt was among other prominent women of Paris at the turn of the century who openly loved their own gender. They freely lived beyond the restrictions of bourgeois society but were protected against censure by their own class and social standing. Though Eva would soon share that standing, she never allowed herself the luxury of this protection. Instead, she worked tirelessly to hide her Sapphic spirit from most people. It would prove to be her nemesis.

The last time Eva talked to Bernhardt was in 1917, during Bernhardt's tour to the United States in *La Reine Hécube*. After the lights went up on Sarah seated in a huge throne-chair placed center stage, and after the applause died down, Eva realized:

> She was utterly exhausted—so exhausted that she scarcely knew what she was saying, and much of the time the lines she spoke made very little sense. It all sounded well. Her voice still had that extraordinary magic. She made all the famous gestures, and they were still beautifully effective. The many years of discipline sustained the old tired body, but the mind—the spirit—simply wasn't there.[18]

It was a sad experience for Eva. She did not want her god to grow old. She did not want her to lose the magic.

The performance over, Eva went backstage. She approached the star's dressing room and found the door open. The room was large, plain, and cold. In contrast to the earlier meetings, Sarah was alone. She was absorbed in counting out sums of money and arranging them in piles on the shelf beside her. It seemed to be the payroll for her company. Eva felt embarrassed, as though she should not be watching. This was a mundane chore and one beneath the dignity of her idol. As she turned to leave, Sarah looked up, and suddenly it was like a light had been turned on. The dreary dressing room was transformed by her entrancing smile, her graciousness, and her charm. Eva went over and knelt beside Sarah's chair. She looked up at the extraordinary face; the makeup was heavier than ever, and so carelessly applied. "La Grande Sarah" was tired, so tired. She looked a thousand years old yet somehow ageless.

In 1914, only a year after she first met Bernhardt, Eva's own career was officially launched—with her professional debut in theatre. Constance Collier, who had been keeping in touch with the family through the years, asked Mrs. Le Gallienne's permission to have Eva appear as a page in matinee performances of Maeterlinck's *Monna Vanna*. Although the play previously had been banned from public performances because of its sexual overtones, J. T. Grein had managed to gain the rights for production at his Independent Theatre. The theatre was a real trailblazer. In fact, only eight days earlier Grein had presented—to scathing reviews—the first licensed production of Ibsen's notorious *Ghosts*. Although the London *Times* made no mention of Eva's brief debut, it was a memorable event complete with royalty. In attendance at the premiere were Queen Alexandra and the dowager empress of Romania.

As the play approached the end of its engagement, Eva made plans to study theatre in Munich. But fearful of the impending war, a close family friend, Ralph H. Philipson, suggested that Eva remain in London and enroll in Herbert Beerbohm Tree's Academy for actors on Gower Street. Mr. Philipson had taken great interest in the Le Galliennes, often asking them to stay in his apartment at 74 Portland Place for long periods of time. Prior to her first opening night in *Monna Vanna*, he had given Eva a very expensive makeup kit, which she treasured for years. Now he offered to help pay for her lessons at Tree's Academy, then under the direction of Ralph Kenneth Barnes.

During her two terms at the school, Eva was enrolled in a number of classes, including dancing, fencing, voice production, elocution, and Delsarte. Her ability to speak polished French won her the role of

Pierrot in De Banville's *Le Baiser*. She also had her first introduction to the coveted role of Juliet. A number of girls had been asked to prepare the farewell scene. The student presenting the best audition was to play the role at a public performance. After all the other girls had finished, Eva's moment finally came. When it was over, she remembered absolutely nothing of what she had done. Believing she had failed, she ran to a corner of the room and hid her face. Then, very quietly, her teacher said, "I think all of us will agree that Miss Le Gallienne should play the scene at the performance. It was beautiful, my dear."[19] Perhaps her audition was inspired, but her performance was a disappointment. She was stiff and unmoved. All attempts to repeat her earlier portrayal simply failed. The experience was devastating. But she came to realize that an actress cannot rely solely on inspiration of the moment or on repeating past performances; she must develop a system to arouse the emotions on demand. This became Eva's goal.

Toward the end of the second term, she was cast in the role of a cockney in one of the academy's plays. Having spent considerable time working in the war kitchens in Covent Garden during the previous months, Eva had developed a fine talent for speaking in the dialect. Impressed with her performance at the school, actor-producer E. Lyall Swete offered her the role of a cockney maid in his West End production of *The Laughter of Fools*. This would be a difficult decision, for she could not remain at the academy if she accepted the role. But a couple of strong considerations prompted her answer. She and her mother were desperately in need of money, and the thought of acting professionally raced her imagination. Besides, this might provide a chance for her to be noticed by someone who could really boost her career. She accepted Swete's offer. As fate would have it, the minor role was a plum — the kind novices dream about. No sooner did Eva make her first entrance and say "yes'm," than she received roaring laughter from the audience. Each entrance brought the same reaction. At one point when she tumbled and broke all the crockery, the audience went wild. On her final exit, she received her first exit applause. After taking two curtain calls with the company, she was led onstage to take her first solo bow. The London *Times* wrote that the hearty laughter "in the case of Miss Eva Le Gallienne, who played the comic maidservant with a fresh and piquant humour, was thoroughly deserved."[20] Her first review! Well, at least her first notice, albeit a single line. But it was positive. She read it a hundred times a day.

Suddenly Eva was besieged by interviewers and offered a number of roles. During the summer she gave one performance of *Peter Ibbetson* with Constance Collier. In attendance at this royal benefit for the war effort were Queen Alexandra, Princess Royal and Princess Maud, Princess Victoria, and the Grand Duchess George of Russia. Elsie Janis, a well-known American performer who was visiting in London at the time, recalled that Le Gallienne was heralded as "among the foremost actresses of London."[21] She had performed in only three professional productions, two of them attended by royalty—not bad for a water baby!

By late July Eva had to make a more frightening decision. David Belasco was considering a Broadway production of *The Laughter of Fools*, and Eva knew that she would be asked to repeat her role. She was encouraged that her name might be familiar to Americans because of her father's popularity: "My name has been a great help in the past, for managers were much more likely to choose the daughter of Richard Le Gallienne than Jane Smith because of the interest they thought she might excite."[22] But on the side of caution, she knew she could tour through England, repeating her popular role in *The Laughter of Fools*, or accept another play within the comforts of London. Still, England was embarking on the Great War with Germany, which might force a decline in London theatre activity. Should she stay or leave? Should she take her success at home or try her luck in America? Encouraged by her acclaim and new confidence, advised by family and friends, and determined to conquer a whole new audience, sixteen-year-old Eva Le Gallienne and her mother packed their bags, boarded a ship, and headed for New York.

3

Tout Sera Bien (All Shall Be Well)

When Eva and her mother arrived in New York in August of 1915, they saw little evidence of the war panic they had left behind in Europe. Only three months earlier, a German torpedo had sunk the *Lusitania* off the coast of Ireland, killing 1100 people, but Americans seemed oblivious.

Instead, hope and optimism were in the air. Business was thriving. It was a time of rebellion against Victorian prudery and mediocrity, a time of promise and expectancy. Freud and Jung were gaining prominence. Art of all types was breaking away from tradition and creating new forms. Progressive magazines appeared: *New Republic*, *The Nation*, *Vanity Fair*. Such literary periodicals as *Little Review* and *Poetry* launched unknown writers: James Joyce, Robert Frost, Ezra Pound, Gertrude Stein. *The Green Hat*, a novel by Michael Arlen, which was later dramatized in New York, completely symbolized the spirit of the times. Heroine Iris March was totally reckless but always gallant. At the end of the novel, she drove her Hispano Suiza off a mountain top. Bold and dangerous were in a sense the passwords of the period. A person could do almost anything, as long as it was done with panache.

On Broadway, the parade of 133 plays produced the year before Eva's arrival was nearly double the number at the turn of the century. Top attractions luring people to the box office were such forgettable hits as *Twin Beds*, *Sinners*, and *On Trial*. The lavish Ziegfeld Follies boasted gorgeous showgirls, magnificent costumes, elaborate production numbers, and the talents of Ina Claire, Ed Wynn, and W. C. Fields. Five new theatres had recently been built to accommodate the wealth of productions in search of a stage. Eight companies toured across America with the Cinderella story *Peg O' My Heart*, which was filled with warmth and sentiment. Peg charmed her audiences with her innocent line: "Sure, there's nothing half so sweet in life as love's young dream."

Providing an element of class to this roster of frivolous offerings was a revival of *Othello* presented by Eva's family friends William

Faversham and Constance Collier. Other revivals included Maude Adams in *Peter Pan* and Grace George in a series of plays by George Bernard Shaw.

Just as significant, however, was the founding of little theatre groups committed to producing artistic but noncommercial plays. Indeed, the very year Eva arrived, three were begun in New York—the Neighborhood Playhouse, the Washington Square Players, and the Provincetown Players. Influenced by the recent New York visits of Max Reinhardt and Harley Granville-Barker, they inspired new playwrights as well as a younger generation of designers and actors. As the American answer to the art theatres of Europe, they concentrated on new, American plays. "They wanted whatever the established theater would have none of," explained critic Joseph Wood Krutch, "and in the beginning that included a great deal—the esoteric, the radical, the intellectual, and the merely shocking."[1]

Regardless of the hurly-burly in the theatre circles, the first few weeks for Eva and her mother did not live up to their dreams of the New World. Initially, they stayed with William Faversham at his summer house at Mattituck on Long Island. Their hopes were soon shattered, however, when Eva learned that Belasco had rejected his plan to produce *The Laughter of Fools*. Her easy entry to Broadway and stardom began to fade.

Her mother's attitude added to her troubles. For some unknown reason, once Eva started her career as a professional actress, Mams never again sought employment. The full burden of their finances, therefore, fell on the shoulders of this lonely and homesick teenager. In early September they moved to Manhattan and began searching desperately for affordable housing. Nothing materialized. In the end, Faversham helped them secure a small apartment at 206 East Seventeenth Street and furnished it with an odd assortment of stage furniture from his storehouse. Eva then began to make the rounds of managers and agents. She touted her few London credits, but no one was very impressed. More than once she overheard "too British for Broadway." She began to doubt her decisions. Should she have stayed in London? Would work ever come? Would she ever be able to support her mother properly? Should they book the next boat home?

Finally, in late September, as their finances were running dangerously low, Eva received a call for work. She had been chosen for the cast of *Mrs. Boltay's Daughters*. What excitement! Her first professional assignment on Broadway. She accepted without knowing anything about the play. Not until the first rehearsal did she learn that she was cast as a Negro maid. She had never seen a Negro maid, let alone heard one talk. How might a girl "too British for Broadway" pass herself off as a domestic, and a Negro to boot? She sought help from a fellow cast member. On opening night, Eva appeared in a kinky wig and blackface that circled her bright blue eyes, and she used a voice that was a queer mix of Irish and cockney. Ironically, Richard Le Gallienne attended one of the few performances: "My God! Is *that* my daughter!" This was the first time he had seen Eva in more than ten years.[2] The play closed after seventeen performances and left her once again among the ranks of the unemployed.

During the next few weeks, Eva repeated her rounds of the Broadway managers, stopping at the public library on Fifth Avenue between appointments. She began to read the plays of Henrik Ibsen. A few years before, her mother had given her a copy of *Brand*. But now she read some of Ibsen's later works—*Hedda Gabler* and *The Master Builder*. Both topped the list of plays she intended to do before she was thirty-five. The others included *Peter Pan*, *La Dame aux Camélias*, *Romeo and Juliet*, and *L'Aiglon*. An ambitious list, especially for an actress whose Broadway credits consisted of a dismal run of *Mrs. Boltay's Daughters*.

Somehow Eva learned that Austin Strong was planning to produce his new play, *Bunny*, and that in it was a cockney role like the one she had portrayed in London. The next day she waited her turn to read. Amazed at the poor attempts the others made at the cockney accent, Eva was convinced she had won the part. She was dumbfounded afterwards when she heard a voice say, "Her cockney isn't very good, is it?" Even though the author preferred Eva, the director thought she lacked experience. Another rejection. To her astonishment, she received a telephone call from Strong a few days later. They had reconsidered. She was to begin work the next morning.

After a short rehearsal period, the play premiered on Christmas Eve in Elmira, New York, then proceeded to Rochester and Syracuse. When it finally opened on Broadway, the audience applauded Eva with enthusiasm. According to the *New York Times*, Eva arrived "on the stage with a flourish, acting an affectionate slavey with high spirits and no little skill."[3]

With critics now calling her the "most promising of youthful ingenues," she soon landed the supporting role of Patricia Molloy in the new play, *Mr. Lazarus*. The playwrights had fashioned a whimsical comedy about a presumed dead man who returns to his family. When he discovers that his daughter is mistreated by her stepfather, he announces his identity. In playing the role of the daughter, Eva received top, featured billing. The late spring opening in Washington, DC, was so successful that the producers booked the play for a summer run in Chicago, where she was touted as another Maude Adams. Her picture was even printed on the cover of the entertainment section of the *Chicago Sunday Tribune*.

Before opening in New York, *Mr. Lazarus* was to play in Atlantic City. The authors came to check it out for one last time, since they had not seen the production for several weeks. Eva's performance had changed—her overconfidence had led to overplaying. They complained that she had lost the necessary charm and sincerity of the character. Regardless of criticism from the authors, Eva refused to alter her performance, especially since she was paraded by the New York critics as the "new leading lady."[4]

Certainly fueling her new arrogance was the knowledge that David Belasco wanted her for a leading role in a Sacha Guitry play he was producing. Eva was fully aware that Belasco had made stars of Mrs. Leslie Carter, Blanche Bates, and David Warfield. She felt, however, that he wanted to take complete possession of her career, that he would insist on absolute loyalty. After discussing the offer with him, she turned it down. To refuse a Belasco offer was unthinkable, but Eva simply could not make herself submit to his demands. Besides, she was confident that fame was easily in sight.

Her next acting assignment proved her wrong. Impressed by Eva's performance in *Mr. Lazarus*, Oliver Morosco offered her the lead and a six-week guarantee in a new play called *Mile-a-Minute Kendall*, clearly her most important role thus far. Five years earlier Morosco had made a star of Laurette Taylor. Under the guidance of director Robert Milton, Eva and her costar tried to portray sincerity and tenderness. But when Morosco attended the final dress rehearsal, he objected and spent several hours redirecting, putting the focus on speed and energy.

Eva was unable to change the mood on such short notice and objected to Morosco's tampering. The result was confusion and bad reviews. By the end of the tryouts, Eva was fired. At this point in her career, it came as a serious setback. Morosco let the Broadway establishment know that Eva was uncooperative, smug, and pretentious, confirming earlier rumors that this young upstart from England was barely directable. During the next four years, Eva received no offers for major roles in New York and was relegated to playing in bit parts or on the road. She was forced to prove herself all over again.

An added frustration in her life was a recent decision by her half sister, Hep. In past years, they had always been extremely close, romping together in Paris and London, playing tricks on their Nanny, and comparing notes about their notorious parents. But now came a sharp turn in their relationship. Despite opposition from grand-parents, aunts and uncles, and even Mams, when Eva's father begged Hep to come to America and live with him, Hep agreed.

Eva was hurt and jealous. She felt not only rejected but betrayed. She had always longed for an intimate bond with her father, but instead she had found emptiness. Through the years she had received amazingly little from him — a calendar, a book about natural history, a dollar bill on her fourth birthday, a dedication of a book. Seldom had he sent money to help pay her expenses. When she and Mams were struggling to make ends meet in their first few weeks in New York, he offered nothing. Never had he asked Eva to live with him. And now she had the constant image in her mind of her father doting on her half sister only a few hours away in Connecticut. Even after she learned that all was not well with Hep, that she was suffering from Richard's alcoholism and abuse and was living on the edge of a volcano, Eva's resentment did not thaw. To get over the hurt, she plunged ahead with her career.

Since Morosco had blackballed her in New York, she had to go elsewhere. She began by accepting her old role in *Mr. Lazarus* and touring with William H. Crane through California and the mining towns of Arizona. It was an exhausting tour — one week in San Francisco, another in Los Angeles, and then several weeks of one-night stands. When the tour ended, Eva quickly accepted a position with San Francisco's Alcazar Stock Theatre rather than return to the rejection and disappointment of New York. She appeared in *The Cinderella Man*, *Rio Grande*, and *Pierre of the Plains*, playing twelve grueling performances a week.

Complicating Eva's life was her leading man, Richard Bennett. Though Bennett was considerably her senior, he was attracted to Eva and frequently sought her companionship. She was seventeen; he was forty-three. Perhaps she looked on his attention as something of a father substitute. She genuinely enjoyed his company, sat mesmerized as he told her anecdotes about his many years in the theatre, and warmed to his mentoring. Although she had never felt sexual longings for a man, she had yearned for intimacy. This frightening episode taught her to be cautious. She mistook his interest in her for sincere companionship, not as sexual maneuvering. She confessed years later that as the season was about to end, Bennett had made his intentions more clear.[5] How could she be so gullible? Eva returned promptly to New York as soon as she could.

For the next year and a half Eva performed with Ethel Barrymore on Broadway and on tour, playing Barrymore's daughter in both *The Off Chance* and *Belinda*. Although they were small parts, Eva again attracted attention with her charm and radiant beauty. As important to Eva as the reviews, however, was observing Ethel Barrymore at work. After her daytime rehearsals for *The Off Chance*, she was awed as she watched the older star perform at night in *The Lady of the Camelias*. She had been moved by Bernhardt's portrayal a few years earlier, but that was through the eyes of a child seated in an audience. Here was another theatre legend, but this time Eva had the supreme fortune to work with her and actually share her stage.

The year of her Broadway engagement in the Barrymore repertory boosted her career, but it was more important perhaps for other reasons. She developed a lifelong friendship with another young actress, Mary Duggett, affectionately known as Mimsey. During those months they were inseparable. They dined together and walked to rehearsals together. She was Eva's confidante. One evening, while discussing J. D. Beresford's new novel, *House-Mates*, and his treatment of lesbianism, they both confessed to having sexual yearnings for other women. As they shared each other's innermost secrets, Eva began to fantasize about having her first intimate encounter, and her imagination soared. She knew exactly who it would be.

When Eva had first arrived in New York, she had tried to attend as much theatre as she could possibly afford. One event she had refused to miss was a vaudeville performance of *The War Brides* starring the renowned actress Alla Nazimova. The exotic Russian had created a sensation a decade earlier, when she had presented a season of Ibsen on Broadway, and had overnight become one of America's leading ladies. A crush of articles had appeared in all the periodicals, and by 1910 the Shuberts had even remodeled one of their theatres and had named it Nazimova's 39th Street Theatre.

In the three years since Eva had first observed her, Nazimova's popularity had soared even higher. She had made a successful movie version of *The War Brides* and had signed a contract with Metro films awarding her the phenomenal salary of $13,000 per week. The press was abuzz with her purchase of a huge estate on Sunset Boulevard, which she dubbed the "Garden of Alla." Indeed, she had become one of the first superstars of Hollywood. Rumors traveled around the theatre circles that Nazimova was not only exotic but a lesbian who had an interest in teaching attractive, younger women.

As soon as Nazimova announced another season of Ibsen for the spring of 1918, Eva dashed to the box office for tickets. She could not miss this sensational star performing her favorite play—*Hedda Gabler*. Although the critics complained of her sinuous, serpentine portrayal, Eva was compelled by her seductive beauty and lurid acting.

When Eva went backstage after the performance, there was a noticeable spark between the two. They talked incessantly about their fascination with Ibsen. "I rebel against the eternal love theme in drama," chided Alla. "Always woman represents love. . . . With women it is always the same sort of thing—always the man and the woman and the result. In contrast, Ibsen forces the actress to think, think, think," she argued.[6] On the heels of Eva's encounter with Richard Bennett, the point was well taken.

But the two women had more in common besides Ibsen—European backgrounds, interest in music, and ambition. Although she was twenty-years older, Nazimova's dark and penetrating eyes, raven black hair, slender and supple body, fiery personality, and soft Russian accent dazzled Eva. They spent many evenings together exploring Ibsen, new directions in art, and the flourishing homosexual underground in New York City.

It was not without danger for women to love other women in 1918. Although such courageous feminists as Emma Goldman and Edith Ellis toured the country lecturing on behalf of the Sapphic spirit, they were often ridiculed and jeered. Goldman even spent two years in prison for promoting her radical beliefs. Most psychologists argued that same-sex love was dysfunctional and that women afflicted with love for other women were abnormal. In some parts of the country, in fact, living a lesbian life was grounds for being committed to an insane asylum. These condemned women were thought to be suffering from androphobia (fear of males) and were labeled "twisted," "inverts," and "degenerates."

This homophobia sharply challenged Eva's attitudes toward her own feelings. As she grappled with this confusion within herself, she recalled the plight of Oscar Wilde—the tragedy, the public scandal, the humiliation. She remembered reading that in England homosexual propositioning was punishable by flogging. Searching for some answers, she turned to the new literature that dared to discuss the subject—Mary MacLane's autobiography, short stories in *Century* and *Ladies' Home Journal*, and Clemence Dane's *The Regiment of Women*. In most cases the women she read about were feminists with powerful egos whose same-sex love produced self-loathing and even suicide. Nothing she read was at all comforting, yet she knew she could not change. She knew that she would probably experience periods of ridicule and disgust, but she also knew that she could not reverse this strange attraction. Besides, her desire to succeed as an actress would not allow her to submerge her ego for a husband and family.

Soon after her contract with Ethel Barrymore ended, Eva decided it was time to assert her independence. Until now she had always lived with her mother and appreciated all her encouragement: "She never impressed her ideas or tastes upon me. . . . She opened doors for me—and left me alone to explore what lay behind them. She treated me always as a mental equal, discussed my ideas, allowed me to have my own opinions, even if she didn't always agree with them." "I simply ran away," Eva explained. "I always supported my mother [financially], but I couldn't live with her anymore, as much as I admired her."[7] Soon after Eva moved out, Mams returned to live in London.

Although mother and daughter respected each other, they were definitely not compatible. Both women were strong-willed and had clashed over the future of Eva's career. Mams's dream to see her daughter's name illuminating Broadway billboards collided with Eva's intellectual and artistic aspirations. They battled over clothes and deportment—Mams insisting on femininity and glamour, Eva on masculinity and utilitarianism. Although she thought of herself as liberal-minded, Mams had an aversion to lesbianism and her daughter's sexual adventures. What really tormented her was the fear that her ex-husband's nature would reappear in Eva. Mams had often accused Eva of being just like her father, and now it ironically seemed as though her charges were true. They both had artistic temperaments, endless charm, exceptionally strong personalities, and an eye for women.

During a brief reunion with her father at his small apartment on Waverly Place, Richard asked Eva pointedly why she had moved out. "Oh, you should know," she retorted, "nobody can live with Mams." And at that point the two of them fell into hysterical laughter until they cried. It was pointless to mention, no doubt, that she also needed her freedom to pursue a relationship with Alla Nazimova.[8]

Eva's first apartment was actually a small back room at the Algonquin Hotel. Such frequent residents as Dorothy Parker, Heywood Broun, Alexander Woollcott, and Noel Coward would gather each evening at a large round table in the Rose Room. As their private waiter served them drinks and food, these wits lashed out at the inadequacies of the establishment and the ills of society. As word spread about this group's liveliness and outrageous repartee, the room grew to overflowing. Actress Blyth Daly once remarked that she, Tallulah Bankhead, Estelle Wynwood, and Eva were such popular lesbians at the Round

Table that they were dubbed "the four horsemen of the Algonquin."[9] Though Eva was truly ashamed of her lesbianism, she refused to deny it. After all, was this not a time to live gallantly and dangerously?

A definite turning point in Eva's career finally came in 1920. The Shubert office indicated they wanted her to play the lead in Arthur Richman's *Not So Long Ago*. A romantic Cinderella story set in the early 1870s, the play centers on Elsie Dover, a poor seamstress girl who pretends that a rich man loves her. Eva knew she wanted the part as soon as she read the script. Not only was it the lead, but it was also the best role ever offered her.

The New York opening night was exactly what Eva had hoped. Time and time again, she and her costar Sidney Blackmer were called before a thunderous audience. Kenneth Macgowan of the *New York Globe* described Eva's performance as one of extraordinary charm and humor and remarked, "it is hard to say anything nice enough in praise of her beauty and skill." For the first time in her career, the critics praised her technical proficiency. Her voice, face, and gestures seemed in complete control and portrayed her character perfectly. Following the second performance, the Shuberts offered her a three-year contract with a salary of $250 a week! After nearly five years in America, she was finally recognized as a leading lady.[10]

Soon after the production closed, Eva accepted an invitation for a prolonged visit to Nazimova's Garden of Alla in Hollywood. A reigning movie queen, Nazimova was busy working on her film *Camille*, with Rudolph Valentino as her leading man. Eva enjoyed the days, wandering quietly among the four acres of cedars, palms, tropical flowers, and roses. During the lazy afternoons, she sunned beside the mammoth pool.

In spite of the relaxing atmosphere, however, Eva felt quite alienated from her hostess. At the evening house parties attended by such lesbian protégées as Jeanne Acker, June Mathis, and Natacha Rambova, Eva witnessed Nazimova's narcissistic posturing and affectations. Instead of being treated as a special friend by Nazimova, she felt like just another plaything in a menagerie of misfits.

When Eva was invited to view the daily rushes of Nazimova's *Camille*, she was repulsed by the exoticism and perverseness of the interpretation—Camille dressed in a lizardlike dress and hinting lesbianism, Armand portrayed as sexually starved. All she could think about was how freakish this production was in comparison to those by Bernhardt and Barrymore. As soon as she could, Eva contacted a friend and begged her to send a telegram insisting that Eva was needed back in New York immediately. Not many months later their three-year relationship ground to a halt. The exotic siren went on to film a critically acclaimed version of Ibsen's *Doll's House*, but her bold, all-gay screening of *Salome* destroyed her reputation and forced her into bankruptcy.[11]

If Eva's portrayal of Elsie Dover in *Not So Long Ago* had made her a star, her next role established her career. Joseph Schildkraut had seen her performance and now insisted on having her as his costar in the Theatre Guild's production of Molnar's *Liliom*. The producers had other actresses in mind, but Schildkraut insisted, "I wanted to play with no one else. . . . She was so beautiful, and I was impressed by her great sensitivity and the honesty of her acting."[12] Four years earlier, Eva had been offered the same role in an adaptation called *The Daisy*. She had wanted to do it then, but the project was canceled.

A major obstacle now, however, was the contract Eva had just signed with the Shuberts. Knowing they had nothing definite in mind for her, she went to Mr. Lee and begged, "Let me do Julie in *Liliom*. After all, (and I knew this would please him), it isn't going to run, you know. It's one of these artistic plays, and it'll only run for six weeks or so."[13]

Once she received Lee's permission, Eva immediately began rehearsals. Everything did not go as smoothly as she had hoped. When she had rehearsed Elsie Dover, the Shuberts had allowed her almost complete freedom to direct herself, and now she wanted the same arrangement. Miffed by comments from director Frank Reicher after the first rehearsal, she informed Theresa Helburn of the Theatre Guild that she refused to work under him. She would quit the show rather than be bullied. Though Reicher boasted impressive directing credits in both Europe and America, Eva thought she had better ideas. Helburn reluctantly agreed to Eva's mandate that he leave her alone for at least two weeks.

Friction also began to surface between Eva and her costar. In contrast with her total seriousness, Schildkraut was playful and even devilish. Theresa Helburn recalls that "one night Peppy [Schildkraut] infuriated Eva. With great control she went through the moving love scene. Then, when the curtain fell she slapped Peppy's face with a ringing sound that echoed backstage." Many years later, while she was directing a revival of *Liliom*, Eva admitted what happened. As she was kneeling and praying over Schildkraut's dead body toward the end of the play, he would sneak his hand up and "pinch my tits."[14]

Eva's total reverence for technique and her art seemed to egg Schildkraut on. Knowing full well that she would fly into a rage, he frequently pinched her during the play's long run. Although the two actors later became intimate friends and he even proposed marriage, at this time their personalities more than clashed. Members of the company gossiped about Eva's egocentric, reserved behavior and said that she seemed very limited in her ability to relate to others.

Prior to opening night, the Theatre Guild began to fear they had made a mistake in selecting *Liliom*. It had failed miserably when first produced in Budapest in 1909. Its lyricism and episodic structure were considered alien to the usual Broadway menu. The final dress rehearsal went so poorly that Helburn warned, "The play is lousy, nobody out front, none of the invited guests likes it—let's terminate our contract and not open tomorrow night. Just let's forget about this play, it's not for America."[15]

But when the play bowed in New York on April 20, 1921, the critics were unanimous. Alexander Woollcott of the *New York Times* called it "the most important and the most eventful [production] in America." As coproducer of the Theatre Guild, Lawrence Langner had been skeptical along with Helburn, but he later admitted that it became one of their outstanding successes. Nearly everyone agreed that Eva's acting was near perfection: "She was not 'poetic'—she was poetry"; "There is a breath of the spiritual in it."[16] With intelligent restraint and control, Eva projected a wistful melancholy that became poetic.

To achieve this spiritual tone, she concentrated first on all the external details of the character, especially Julie's costume. The blouse designed for her was made of gingham, pale blue with a small plaid of white. With short sleeves that were cut a deliberately awkward length, just above the elbow, it was "broken down" with mended rips and gray stains. Her skirt of mid-calf length was a nubby, dark gray cotton, gathered at the waist with a heavy band. Eva felt this much of the costume was good; it visualized the character and her peasant background. To find just the right pair of shoes to go with it, she went to a little second-hand shop on Hester Street in the New York slums, where she selected an old pair of men's shoes. As she told a reporter from the *Boston Herald*, "My friends urged me to have them fumigated—they certainly aren't very prepossessing."[17] Attractiveness, however, was not her goal.

Eva found it necessary to wear a costume that would help enrich her character, not simply to achieve a sense of naturalism, but to stimulate her own imagination. Unlike many of her contemporaries who were content with presenting their own personalities on stage, she sought ways to transform herself into her character. As Konstantin Stanislavsky was to recommend to actors three years later in his revolutionary *An Actor Prepares*, she looked for conscious means to arouse the subconscious. By concentrating on little details and on Julie's inner thought pattern, she allowed herself to be transported out of the surface reality and into the realm of the spiritual.

Needless to say, the production ran longer than the projected six weeks, and Eva was determined to remain in the spotlight. She remembered some advice she had received a few years earlier from David Belasco: "If you want anything out of a manager get hysterical. Cry and scream and just become wild. Then they'll give you anything because they can't stand it." When she returned to the Shuberts for an extension, she staged the kind of scene that would have made Belasco proud:

> I screamed and shrieked and wept and jumped up on the window seat. I said I was going to throw myself out the window. I carried on like a lunatic. It did the trick. Mr. Lee began ringing bells under the desk; various people appeared. He said, "OK, OK, OK. You stay with them then. But they've got to pay you what I'm paying you. Otherwise, I won't let you stay."[18]

Thanks to the Shuberts, she not only stayed with *Liliom* but received a raise in pay from $75 to $250 a week.

Eva became so popular during the long run that reporters began hounding her for stories on everything, from her acting style to what she ate for breakfast. They knew she idolized Sarah Bernhardt and often asked if she was trying to imitate Bernhardt's style. Eva denied any comparison, pointing out that it would be fatal to copy another actress. "People who merely imitate others remind me of flying fish," she quipped. "Their flying doesn't amount to much, compared with that of the birds they imitate. Therefore, I'd rather be a success as a fish than a failure as a fish trying to be a bird."[19]

In preparing a role, Eva found it essential to work in privacy, so she could think intensely with no interruptions, "trying to make the character a vivid reality—an actual personal experience." Instead of learning lines, she tried to set the thoughts of the character in her mind, knowing that the words would come spontaneously. She knew there were complaints that she studied too much. "I think a girl's got to have brains, with a capital B to succeed as an actress," she argued. And yet she believed that the most important step in creating a character was something "sublimely unconscious. . . . We are not practically aware of what we are doing. We are mediums."[20]

Besides showing interest in her approach to acting, the media began to exploit her appearance. They had suddenly noticed her petite figure, light brown hair, clear blue eyes, and melancholy expression. "Rare would be a synonym for her," raved one critic, "so would luminous."[21] Her picture was suddenly everywhere, promoting every-thing from theatre to cosmetics to fashions. In the August 1921 issue of *Theatre Magazine*, Eva is seen modeling golf and riding clothes for Abercrombie and Fitch. Some well-intentioned advertising man even points out how well she wears sports clothes, especially those that are of a "mannish style."

In one interview a reporter asked Eva to share her beauty recipe. It is "of the spirit; beauty is from within," was her reply. Perhaps thinking about the turmoil she was experiencing with her sexuality, she added that to achieve spiritual beauty "you have to suffer criticisms, snobs, jeers, deprivations, and often see far less worthy persons apparently getting far ahead of you."[22]

One of New York's most eligible bachelors decided to pursue her. The dashing young conductor and composer Dirk Fock was certainly of the cultured class. The son of the Governor General of the Dutch East Indies, Fock had studied in Amsterdam and Berlin. Prior to his New York debut at Carnegie Hall in 1920, he had held prestigious positions with the Göteborg Symphony in Sweden and with Amster-dam's Concertgebouw. Ever since his arrival in America, gossip colum-nists had followed his adventures.

Fock escorted Eva to concerts and parties. They dined in fashion-able restaurants. But when he made it clear that his interests were more than platonic, Eva tried to be equally clear. To escape his advances, she sailed secretly for Europe, only to discover that he had learned of her plan and had booked passage on the same ship. During the entire voyage, he tried to impress her with his musical compositions and his artistic brilliance. He sang selections from his operas and from his latest composition, *Songs From the Chinese*. He thought he could surely change her mind, but Eva remained cool to all his attention and repeated her position: "I do not like men!"[23] Spurned by Eva, Fock accepted a position at Vienna's famed Konzertverein.

Actually, Eva was interested in another woman. A few years earlier, she had begged her friend Betty Pierson to introduce her to Mercedes de Acosta, a woman who was notorious for wearing pants and slicking back her jet black hair with brilliantine. Eva was aware that this woman had also been involved in a brief affair with Alla Nazimova. They began their arranged lunch at the Ritz Hotel by comparing notes on the great actress Eleonora Duse, and they ended by returning to Mercedes's apartment. Eva was quick to learn how to charm a woman.

She saw much in Mercedes that she liked. Mercedes was almost reptilian in appearance, with her pale white face, black hair, and thin red lips. She had a thirst for knowledge and reading. She knew many people in the arts—Augustin Daly, Ada Rehan, Sarah Bernhardt, Ethel Barrymore. She had met Toscanini and Caruso. As a child, she had traveled extensively in Europe and had lived an aristocratic, cultured life in a large house near the home of Teddy Roosevelt. She seemed to have endless energy and a free spirit. In fact, she "never cared a fig what anyone thought. As long as I feel 'right' within myself," she told Eva, "society's opinion never influences me for a second."[24] Mercedes definitely made a statement with her mannish pants, pointed shoes trimmed with big buckles, tricorn hat, and cape. When Eva later learned, however, that the eccentric young woman was soon to be married, her attentions cooled.

Eventually, Mercedes pursued the affair herself, going to Eva's dressing room one night after a performance. A whirlwind of socializing followed. Whenever possible they attended Bob Chanler's legendary parties on East Nineteenth Street. Part of the social, artistic, and Bohemian fabric of New York, Chanler held parties that mixed intellectuals, artists, races, colors, titles, vagabonds, homosexuals, rich, and poor. Some evenings Eva and Mercedes would rush up to Harlem to explore the speakeasies and sit in rooms filled with smoke and the smell of bad gin. One of their favorite pastimes was visiting Stark Young, then editor of *New Republic* and a theatre critic for the *New York Times*. The evenings with Young and his lover at their home on Broad Street always passed quickly as they discussed books, plays, music, and art.

Eva and Mercedes often dined at the Russian Eagle, a restaurant on Fifty-seventh Street where all the help were Russian refugees. On one occasion they escorted the internationally famous ballerina Tamara Karsavina to the restaurant. It was a memorable evening, because they were joined by Konstantin Stanislavsky and members of his Moscow Art Theatre. Regardless of Prohibition, the head waiter provided a flow of vodka and Scotch.

Even with all the activity in her life and the attention she was receiving from *Liliom*, coping with another long run made Eva restless. For a diversion, she agreed to play Selysette in Arthur Row's matinee production of Maeterlinck's *Aglavaine and Selysette*, with Mercedes designing her costumes. The result was dreadful. Alexander Woollcott reported of the bored audience that the "lack of demonstration was maintained out of respect for the players." The production was so poor that "the civility of the spectators was really extraordinary." Tallulah Bankhead summed it up as she nudged Woollcott in the lobby and remarked, "There is less in this than meets the eye."[25]

Not long after the *Aglavaine and Selysette* presentation, *Liliom* closed on Broadway and set out on tour with plans to spend the entire summer of 1922 in Chicago. After a few weeks, Eva's schedule began to take its toll. She staggered to the theatre, then staggered back to her hotel room. She began fainting after the fifth scene, and when she recovered, she couldn't walk. She was suffering from a complete nervous collapse, and the tour was postponed. The press reported that the strain of playing Julie's repressed emotions nightly for over a year had proved too much for her.

Following a week of rest in New York, she and Mercedes sailed for "Old Nurse Europe," where Eva hoped to relax and recover more fully. Since Eva had been invited to Hungary by *Liliom*'s playwright Ferenc Molnar, they headed for Budapest but stopped along the way in Paris, Genoa, Venice, Munich, and Vienna. When they finally arrived at their destination, they were met by Molnar, a brass band, and banners with "Welcome Julie" printed in Hungarian. Eva was handed bunches of flowers and embraced by hundreds of people, and photographers snapped pictures of her with the playwright. Masses of uninvited fans swarmed to their suite at the Dunapalata Hotel. During their stay in Budapest, they were toasted and praised at nearly all turns. The excitement of meeting the playwright and seeing Budapest made Eva eager to play Julie again. Following a brief stopover in London to visit her mother, Eva returned to New York and began rehearsals to revive the tour.

With her contract with the Shuberts set to expire at the end of the season, Eva faced the decision of renewing it. In one of her conversations with Mr. Lee, he urged her to capitalize on her new popularity. He advised that "to be successful I had to develop a type, create my own exaggerated mannerisms so the public would know what to expect." He believed the audience wanted instant identification. Eva disagreed and told him, "I want to be an actor. I want to live a hundred different lives."[26] Afraid that if she signed she would always be given sad, melancholy parts like Julie, Eva left the Shubert management.

While waiting for another good offer to come along, Eva appeared in a showcase production of Mercedes de Acosta's *Sandro Botticelli*.

The acting was compared to a scene by Mme. Tussaud. Mercedes had developed a short drama about the beautiful Simonetta Vespucci, who offers to become a nude model for Botticelli in order to encourage a romantic relationship. Eva was sharply criticized for her portrayal of Simonetta, for she conveyed none of the passion necessary to make the character believable.

Eva and Mercedes had decided to sail again for Europe once the production closed. As they were preparing to leave, producer Gilbert Miller offered Eva the leading role of Princess Alexandra in Molnar's *Swan*. Although the management had been negotiating with Billie Burke for the part, Molnar had insisted on Eva.

The Swan is a romantic comedy that involves a love triangle—a princess, a prince, and a commoner. Because she desires to become a queen, the princess rejects her love for the commoner. Eva accepted eagerly, thinking the role would be a good contrast to Julie. However, she insisted that she be listed with the rest of the cast as one of the featured players rather than be given star billing. She did not want the pressure of being labeled a star.

Since the rehearsals were not to begin until fall, Eva and Mercedes proceeded with their plans for Europe. Just before sailing, they learned that Eleonora Duse was rehearsing in Paris for a comeback tour. The morning Eva and Mercedes arrived in Paris, they started off at once for the Tuileries Gardens and stood opposite the Hotel Regina where Duse was staying. As they looked up at her window they felt they had witnessed a miracle—sitting there on a balcony, wrapped in a blanket, was Duse herself. Mercedes whispered, "We should kneel."[27] Eva immediately cabled her old friend Ralph H. Philipson that he must purchase tickets for them when Duse opened in London.

Because France had no legal sanctions against lesbianism, the days Eva and Mercedes spent in the country were a joy. Part of the time, they looked like a pair of gypsies, as they embarked on a walking trip through Brittany. With only a small bundle of clothes for baggage, they walked along the countryside until they came to a town called L'Arquest, where they stayed with a fisherman and his wife.

Back in Paris they partook of afternoon tea at the famous Rumpelmayer's *patisserie* and analyzed Andre Gide's new novel *Corydon*, which called for someone to lead the attack against homophobia. In the evenings, they attended the famous Le Monocle and Magic City, both music hall promenades that specialized in transvestite dances.

One Friday evening, they even attended a soiree hosted by the infamous lesbian Natalie Barney. In the rear garden of her home at 20 rue Jacob, Eva and Mercedes were served tea with cakes and cucumber sandwiches as they listened to poetry and observed the other sexual rebels being entertained by their hostess. They were intrigued by Barney, who was known for her inconstancy and for collecting new women to add to her collection of souvenirs. Eva concluded that she was like Barney in that she, too, stalked and pursued women when she was interested. It was an exciting environment, where she did not have to hide her sexual preference or view herself as an unnatural outcast.

When Eva and Mercedes finally arrived in England, they learned they had tickets for Duse's first performance in London. Eva had always suspected that Bernhardt was the world's greatest actress, but seeing Duse in *Cosi Sia* changed her mind:

> I saw the stage take on an added dimension; I felt the vast audience grow still and sit as though mesmerized in the presence of a frail, worn woman who, with no apparent effort, through the sheer beauty of the truth within her, through the sheer power of her spirit, reached out to each one of us and held us all enthralled. I saw "the impossible" come true.

Exalted by the performance, Eva purchased flowers on her way home that evening and sent them to Duse. Years before, she had seen a photograph the great actress had signed with the words "strength and faith." The words came back to Eva now, and on her enclosure card she wrote, "You have given me strength and faith to live."[28]

The day after the performance, Eva and Mercedes returned to Paris, where Eva was to have costume fittings for *The Swan*. A few days later, she heard that Duse had also arrived in Paris and was staying once again at the Hotel Regina. Eager to meet her, Eva and Mercedes went to the hotel and sent word to her room. A few minutes later, Duse's companion, Désirée, handed them a note that read, "Thank you for your good words; thank you for the flowers. Regret today impossible—perhaps tomorrow. E. Duse."[29] Désirée added that Duse was leaving for Switzerland soon, but since she was planning a tour to the United States in the fall, they might see her then.

Eva soon returned to New York and began work on *The Swan*. Although the out-of-town tryouts in Detroit and Montreal seemed to predict another success, she was still quite nervous about the New York opening. A few days before the scheduled date, Duse arrived in town for her announced tour. Hoping for encouragement, Eva tried to see Duse on the afternoon of her opening, but again Désirée said it was impossible. Later in the day, however, Désirée came to Eva's apartment with a message: "Dear, beautiful child, Dear Artist who is suffering for her Art! I would so like to console you—tell you to be SURE of yourself. I scold myself for not coming to find you—and I dare not leave this room! Forgive—and be happy. 'You are in the light.' Eleonora Duse." Désirée then asked Eva to return with her to see Duse. During their brief meeting, Eva noticed how different Duse was from Bernhardt. She did not act like an actress; she had no retinue of followers. When they talked, Duse listened intently to every word. There was nothing patronizing about her. She made Eva feel that she really mattered. As Eva began to leave, Duse said, "Strength and Faith! You will play well tonight—I know it!"[30]

Duse was right. The audience rose in standing ovations at the ends of acts 2 and 3. As with *Liliom*, the critics were unanimous in their praise, agreeing that Eva had never been better. John Corbin of the *New York Times* described her Princess Alexandra as "admirable alike for its artistic restraint, its renunciation of all easy and obvious effects, and for the potency of its inward fires." Corbin emphasized that Eva had played the truthfulness of each individual moment in the play and had captured the varying moods. A critic for the *New York Telegram* praised her ability to convey regal dignity. He pointed out that her pensiveness, coupled with her personal attractiveness and vocal beauty, led to an "exquisite . . . delightful performance."[31] With this credit, Eva had proven that she could play more than melancholy waifs.

In the weeks that followed, Eva saw Duse perform many times and began to study her style closely. With Bernhardt one was always aware of technique, but with Duse everything seemed so effortless, so easy. She seemed to actually have no technique at all; it was perfectly concealed. Duse did not need makeup, wigs, physical motion, or even facial expressions to convey her thoughts. Eva believed that "she conveyed them because she really thought them—she did not merely pretend to think them. She did not pretend to listen—she really listened." She noticed this particularly in the first act of *Ghosts*, when Mrs. Alving tells Pastor Mandors the truth about her marriage:

During Manders' pompous outburst, when he berates Mrs. Alving and accuses her of being a bad wife and a bad mother, Duse sat quietly watching him, and listening; one felt the irony and the contempt behind her stillness. Then, after a silence, she began to speak. At first the words came with a certain reluctance, as though she disdained to justify herself, yet was forced by the very absurdity of his attack to let him know the truth at last. Then, as she began to relive in her mind the pain and humiliation of her years with Alving, the tempo became rapid, broken, with moments of silence while thought took shape in words sometimes difficult to find. It was impossible to believe that these words had been printed on a page and had been learned by heart. Mrs. Alving was really talking, expressing these thoughts for the first time.[32]

Eva saw the production three times and was amazed that nothing ever varied. It had all been worked out very carefully. But more important, the meticulous planning had all been concealed. She saw a woman thinking, not an actress working.

Eva realized that Duse's power to listen and to think enabled her to use bold silences. There was a moment at the end of the first act of *Ghosts* that especially impressed her. It came after Mrs. Alving tells the pastor, "I shall forget that such a person as Alving ever lived in this house—there'll be no one here but my son and me." Then came the crash of the overturned chair and the laughter from Oswald and Regina. Eva observed that when Duse heard them, she "did nothing; she stood absolutely still; the blood drained from her face; her eyes grew enormous; life seemed to flow out from the tips of her fingers; she seemed cold—numb. Then very quietly—in a whisper—she spoke: 'Ghosts—those two in the conservatory—Ghosts—They've come to life again.'"[33] To Eva, it was a triumph of economy and thinking, and she was inspired by watching Duse's technique.

Before Duse left New York for the remainder of her tour, Eva talked with her often. On one occasion, Duse said she had been sitting quietly for several hours "in prayer." She was performing that night and explained that she was "trying to forget myself—to free myself from self. . . . That way, perhaps I won't be so afraid." When Eva replied that she was so often afraid, Duse exclaimed, "Ah! That abominable fear! One must conquer it. One must forget self. . . . Forget self. . . . It's the only way!" Duse sought to eliminate self totally in order to make herself a better servant of the script. It was a significant conversation for Eva: "I began to realize from that moment that in playing, as in any other art, one should abolish the personal and try to place one's instrument at the service of a higher, disembodied force."[34]

"Strength and Faith"—those words of Duse's were helping Eva embrace a personal concern. Even though she was now a recognized star, she foresaw shortcomings in her future career. Earlier in the year, critics of *Sandro Botticelli* had mentioned her inability to play feminine passion. Now Arthur Hornblow of *Theatre Magazine* noticed the same weakness about her performance in *The Swan*. He praised her performance overall but noted that "when it comes to showing feminine tenderness . . . the actress is on less sure ground. . . . Miss Le Gallienne seldom rings true in scenes where she is called upon to reciprocate masculine ardor. The soft, feminine note is missing—a matter of temperament, probably."[35]

Advice from her agent added to Eva's dilemma. Sam Lyons had signed her on after he had seen a performance of *The Swan*. He thought Eva was the absolute epitome of what was glorious and wonderful, so he could not understand why she was not a bigger commercial star. She was admired and respected, but he felt something was keeping her from becoming a superstar like Bernhardt. When he learned of her lesbianism, he confronted her immediately. "You know, you gotta get a fella," he bellowed. "I don't care what you do with him, but you gotta get one. Who knows, you might like it."[36]

At first, Eva flatly rejected the idea. She had vowed that she would never again lean to the desires of a man. She had been betrayed too often and could not trust them. Besides, she knew her strong preference for women. But her career was another matter. Maybe she did need a convenient marriage to serve as a cover. After all, both Katharine Cornell and Lynn Fontanne had recently chosen that option. With a husband at her side, she could confound the critics and keep the public in the dark.

The man she ultimately selected was her costar, the dashing young actor from England, Basil Rathbone. Although she told a good friend that she was "bored after ten days," at one point during their courtship, Eva thought she was pregnant. When she told Rathbone, he promptly ended their affair. Even though the pregnancy was false, she once again felt rejected by a man.[37]

This experience coincided with another shock for Eva—the death of Duse. During her tour engagement in Pittsburgh, Duse developed pneumonia and died. When her body arrived in New York, Eva and Mercedes kept vigil in the little chapel, prayed beside the coffin for many hours, and watched as the black ship carrying her body glided out of the pier for Italy. Eva's goddess had died, and suddenly she felt ashamed. She had disappointed Duse. By accepting a male lover, she had not been true to herself. She had been thinking of her reputation, not her art. Many years would pass before she would again consider a relationship with a man.

The long run of *The Swan* finally came to an end in June 1924. Rather than spend the summer in Europe as usual, Eva decided to join Jasper Deeter's Rose Valley Theatre in Moylan, Pennsylvania. Away from the scrutiny of New York critics, she wanted to attempt a new kind of role, a role where a woman has a strong influence over a man. Although by her own admission her performance of Hilda in Ibsen's *The Master Builder* was not very good, it gave her the experience of playing a strong-willed, masculine woman and served as a foundation for her later productions of the play.

Following a short Broadway run in September, *The Swan* toured for the entire 1924–25 season. Ten weeks were spent in Chicago, where the play was hailed as refreshingly brilliant and wholesome. Unable to escape to other projects as she could in New York, Eva grew weary. After four months on the road, she wrote to a friend:

> We open in Boston February 16th and play there probably until the end of March, when with God's help we close. I am so mortally tired of *The Swan* — and though ever grateful for what it has done for me, still I shall be happy when it is ended. I am frantic to get on to something newer and finer.[38]

Although the character of Princess Alexandra was in some respects a contrast to Julie in *Liliom*, a tone of delicacy and melancholy prevailed in both. Eva was ready to try something more daring.

Mercedes had written a new play for Eva about Joan of Arc. Two years earlier the Theatre Guild had offered Eva the same role in Shaw's *Saint Joan*, but she had turned it down, saying, "It should have been called Saint Shaw."[39] This offer was a more exciting one. The women had engaged Norman Bel-Geddes to direct and design the show; and Fermin Gemier, director of the Odéon Theatre in Paris, had arranged for the production to premiere in Paris under the auspices of the Ministry of Beaux-Arts.

What appealed most to Eva, however, was Mercedes's treatment of Joan. The playwright was not concerned with history or any philosophical statement. This Joan was a character that was human and sincere, a simple woman whose great spiritual forces and powers ultimately deserted her. Joan was determined, independent, and a martyr who refused to compromise her beliefs. There seemed to be an affinity between the way Eva saw the role and the way she saw herself. Maybe this production could change her image with the critics.

As she left for Paris in late March 1925, Eva was filled with anticipation. She wrote to her good friend Irina Skariatina, a former Russian countess, "It is all so terribly exciting — such a thrilling adventure! And whether we fail or succeed, nothing can prevent it from being that. . . . I am terrified at the thought of playing in Paris—and all the terrific work of the thing takes my breath away—though the work itself, no matter how strenuous, never frightens me."[40]

That there was terrific work ahead was an understatement. Since the Odéon Theatre, which they had been promised rent-free, was too small for Bel-Geddes's sets, they had to go elsewhere, reluctantly settling on the Theatre de La Porte Saint Martin, which cost them $7,000 for thirty days. Eva and Bel-Geddes had raised a total of $12,000 before leaving New York, thinking that would be sufficient. Suddenly, more than half their funds were depleted. With their agreement to use the Porte Saint Martin, they were also forced to use that theatre's permanent company of actors. When it came to extras, Bel-Geddes insisted on hiring a minimum of 150, a third of whom were Russian immigrants who spoke neither French nor English. For the first rehearsal, they were offered free use of the big Trocadero Hall, only to discover the next day that they had to pay several thousand francs for alleged damages.

By the first of May, Eva's anticipation had turned to exhaustion, which she tried to explain to Helen Lohmann, a woman she had met at Duse's funeral in New York the preceding spring:

> The difficulties have been *immense* and at times seemingly impassable— but they have so far been overcome, by a kind of strength and courage which has seemed *dictated* to me. . . . The people are all devils and have but one thought in their heads: How can they get the most for themselves? without giving *you anything*.

Only a year before, Eva had been inspired by Duse's strength and by her phrase, "Tout sera bien," (All shall be well). In her letter to Helen Lohmann, she now explained:

> "Tout sera bien." I have thought so *constantly* of Her and of how she would have enjoyed the Battle. And I have prayed in my innermost self every moment of the day to Her, for strength and some kind of guidance. Sometimes it has almost been as though I were obeying definite orders to *go on*, not to give in, not to turn tail as many advised me to do. God knows what I am doing it all for—except that I feel it should be beautiful and *must* be done—for something stronger than myself *wills* it. No one may like it—it may utterly fail, and yet I should still know that it had been *right*.[41]

Believing that the great Duse was behind her, giving her orders to go on, Eva continued with the project. When they finally opened on

June 12, 1925, Paris was filled with anticipation. The press had capitalized on the novelty of an American author and actress presenting, in French, a play about one of the French heroes. As Alexander Woollcott observed, it was like a French actor electing to appear in New York in some new play about Abraham Lincoln. In attendance at the sold-out premiere performance were the American ambassador to France, a representative of the French president, and artists Constance Collier and Ivor Novello.

The excitement was short-lived. Bel-Geddes had conceived the production as a spectacle, emphasizing on lighting, sound, and movement of the actors. He designed a single, architectural setting with multilevel platforms. By means of banners, costumes, and properties, he transformed the stage into the Dauphin's throneroom, Rheims Cathedral, the battle of Compeigne, and a Rouen market place. The French critics were impressed with the color and pageantry, but they were in unanimous agreement that Bel-Geddes had exaggerated his role as designer. Lucien Dubech, critic for *l'Action Francaise*, insisted, "The stage setting should only be the servant. It only has interest and value if it is subordinated. Otherwise, it is like a slave which usurps a throne." A critic for *Le Matin* concluded, "Poetry, literature, history, and philosophy are treated like poor relations. . . . It is a 'great show' for the eyes, and nothing at all for the brain and spirit."[42]

Eva's portrayal of Jehanne suffered from all the dazzle. Alexander Woollcott noticed that sometimes ten minutes would pass before a word of dialogue could be spoken. One French critic was so overwhelmed by the visual display that his only comment on her acting was that she spoke "French without the slightest accent." A critic for *Le Temps* made no mention of her performance! Perhaps her best notices came from a reviewer for *Le Journal*. Although he provided no explanation for his observation, he mentioned that Eva was "perfect, especially in her attitudes."[43]

Nearly fifty years later, Eva complained about Bel-Geddes work with the actors: "He wasn't a 'director' at all in my opinion. . . . Certainly in *Jehanne d'Arc* he didn't direct the actors at all. He did move the crowds of supers around in masses to enhance the visual effect— but that's about all. . . . The production would have been a thousand times better if he had left the direction to someone else." Eva's desire to convey a human, simple, and sincere woman was overshadowed by Bel-Geddes "great show for the eyes."[44]

When Eva and Mercedes boarded the *Majestic* for their return voyage to New York at the end of the summer, their relationship was near an end. They were exhausted, disillusioned, and embarrassed over their resounding failure. The original plan for *Jehanne d'Arc*—to present it on Broadway after Paris—needed reevaluation. Since the original cost estimate of $12,000 had mushroomed to $40,000, neither of them felt they could go another step. Fellow passenger Noel Coward complained that during the entire trip the two women "alternated between intellectual gloom and feverish gaiety—and wore black, indiscriminately, for both moods."[45]

Also on board the *Majestic* was the object of Eva's next involvement, Gladys E. Calthrop. Serving as scene designer for Noel Coward's plays, Gladys was accompanying him to New York to prepare for his Broadway debut of *The Vortex*. Even though Mercedes objected, Eva spent considerable time with Gladys and argued that it was impossible for her to be faithful to just one woman. She had learned that she could not be monogamous, that, indeed, she was "prone to feelings about women that she could not entirely control."[46] Like her father, Eva needed a relationship where both parties could pursue other people with no rage and no jealousy. By the time the ship docked in New York, Eva had replaced Mercedes with Gladys as the significant woman in her life, and Mercedes soon began her colorful affair with film goddess Greta Garbo.

Passionate to work again, Eva quickly joined the newly reorganized Actors' Theatre, formerly the Equity Players, Inc. Among the leaders of the organization were many of her old associates and friends: Clare Eames, Ethel Barrymore, and Dudley Digges, who had played the Sparrow in *Liliom*. When they asked her to take the leading role of Marie in their upcoming production of Arthur Schnitzler's *Call of Life*, she readily accepted. A sullen drama, it reveals the torment of a young woman who poisons her crippled yet oppressive father and runs away to her lover.

The reviews were a disappointment. A critic for the *New York Times* found her characterization unbelievable, claiming she appeared so sad and defeated that there seemed to be no reason for a man to love her. Percy Hammond of the *New York Herald-Tribune* was more caustic. He complained that her acting was "obviously make-believe" and labeled her performance "a bit cadaverous." Most critics agreed that once again she had failed to portray a woman with passions and feelings.[47]

Unimportant by themselves, these reviews represented something bigger. The male-dominated Broadway establishment undoubtedly considered her a threat to their masculine superiority. By this time, everyone knew that this young actress was no clinging vine who could be ordered around like a giggling chorus girl. Her challenge to the authority of authors, directors, and producers alike was rapidly preceding her. Inspired by Duse's mysticism, she truly believed that through her acting she was a channel for something other than herself. Though humbled by this revelation, she was also tremendously arrogant.

As her reputation grew and as knowledge of her affairs became more widespread, many major critics routinely dismissed her acting as cold and intellectual. To the layman, it appeared as if they were simply describing her restrained, quiet, controlled style. At first, even Eva was amused by the description and regularly telephoned actress friend Clare Eames on her opening nights and laughed, "Well, how was I? Cold and intellectual?"[48]

As the tag persisted, however, Eva began to fight against waves of depression. She longed for recognition and artistic praise. It was becoming clear that the words "cold and intellectual" were code words identifying Eva as a dykish snob whom the press wanted to expose. Questions whirled in her mind: Were the critics using her sexuality against her? Were they repulsed by her lesbianism? Does the fact that she loves women mean that she cannot show love for a man on stage? Was she getting blackballed by the Broadway establishment?

As Eva wrestled with these questions, the words of Duse echoed faintly in her ears: "Strength and Faith," "Tout Sera Bien." The once inspiring phrases were getting weaker. Eva knew that she must find a way to break down the wall of resentment if she was to continue her career. Maybe she needed to stop bowing to the patriarchal Broadway system, she thought, and instead strike out on her own. If she was refused entry into their club, why not start her own.

4

Abbess of Fourteenth Street

Eva was beginning to feel strangled by a lack of professional appreciation. She realized that she was moving outside the mainstream of what was expected of actresses of her generation. Nevertheless, she felt she deserved better and refused to be brushed aside. She had fought to keep her private life from the public and resented those who insisted on viewing her work through her sexuality. At the same time, she knew she could not disregard their sneers.

As soon as *The Call of Life* closed, Eva suggested that the Actors' Theatre produce *The Master Builder*, with herself as Hilda Wangel, the assertive, masculine, radical heroine of the play. She was convinced that a successful performance would soften the rumors and strengthen her career. When the board of directors rejected her proposal, arguing that the play lacked box-office appeal, Eva decided to become her own manager and to produce and direct the play for special matinees at the Maxine Elliott Theatre. Her romantic attachment, Gladys E. Calthrop, agreed to design.

Contrary to all predictions, the play was a stellar success. The announced run of four matinees was extended to twelve and then switched to a regular evening engagement at the Princess Theatre. The notices were perhaps the best Eva had yet received. Alexander Woollcott, who marveled at her determination to present the play, reported that her last moments were "aflame with a finely communicated exaltation." More descriptive was the *New York Times*, which called her performance "a luminous portrait":

[She] strips it of every embellishment. Through all three acts her costume is not merely plain but ugly. . . . Her acting likewise is severe; she does not soften it with a gentle flow of gestures. . . . On the contrary, the different elements are kept distinct; and she flies from one to the next with an evanescent precision. Her voice is a fine instrument. . . . Nothing is more remarkable than the rhythm she applies to the prose of the

66

dialogue; and the punctuation, emphasis and inflection she supplies through the suppleness of tone quality.[1]

Eva's conviction had served her well. For a number of years she had wanted to play Hilda on Broadway. In fact, in one of her conversations with Eleonora Duse, she had been strongly encouraged to do it. Suddenly she was being hailed among the foremost of dramatic actresses.

When the play opened on November 10, 1925, it marked the start of Eva's career as director-producer. Knowing her reputation was at stake, she approached the production with a ruthless zeal, flung herself into it "with all the confidence and assurance of youth and never stopped to question or analyze."[2]

One of Ibsen's late plays, *The Master Builder* focuses on Master Builder Solness, a middle-aged architect who has given up his dream to build churches for God, in order to build homes for the wealthy. The young and romantic Hilda Wangel, who comes to visit, inspires him to reach for his dream once more. In her role as Hilda, Eva could forget the repressed and melancholy women she had played in the past, the "supine, bloodless parts," as she called them, and let herself go. Instead of the ankle-length skirt that most Hildas wore, Le Gallienne's costume was (for that time) much more scandalous: brown corduroy breeches, very high mountain boots, open-necked shirt, a knapsack with straps, a wooden hiking stick, and a pair of jewelled earrings. Accenting her costume was a silk waistband, whose violet color had been a symbol of lesbian love from the time of Sappho. To Eva, her costume was "expressive of Hilda's 'esprit de contradiction'—her defiance of the 'customary,' of the rules of convention."[3] She even smoked cigarettes and snapped her fingers impatiently at the Master Builder.

Complaining of producers who present Ibsen's characters mournful and lugubrious and who literally drape the stage in crepe, Eva seemed intent on playing a variety of moods. Her Hilda was sensitive and always thinking, always listening, which provided Eva the opportunity to let her character change and develop during the play. In act 2, when Hilda sees her idol Solness raging at his assistant, Eva tried to pull the audience into her character's inner thought process. She sat looking at the floor for a long time in silence, shaken and subdued. She turned and looked angrily at Solness. As he met her eyes, he turned, then faced her again. Holding the pause for what seemed an eternity, she turned away and with effort said very simply, "That was a very ugly thing to do."[4] Through the power of her concentration, economy of motion, and prolonged pauses, she added a whole sequence of feeling and thought to the line.

With the success of *The Master Builder*, she started thinking seriously of breaking with the commercial Broadway theatre and establishing her own company. That way she would not be forced to bow to the supremacy of other managers, producers, and agents. Broadway, she chided, was like "an Indian Totem Pole, never growing in stature but gaining merely in the number of new grimaces carved on its surface."5 She yearned for a theatre without stars, without long runs, without high prices, and without typecasting. And she yearned for recognition as an important artist.

At the suggestion of Egon Brecher, who was playing Solness, she chose to inaugurate her new venture by producing Ibsen's *John Gabriel Borkman*, alternating it with *The Master Builder*. An austere drama, *John Gabriel Borkman* presents a man who sought financial success. In order to achieve his goal, he renounced his love for Ella Rentheim and married her coldhearted sister. The play occurs many years later and reveals the two women's bitter struggle to dominate Borkman and his son. Eva realized she was much too young to play the eighty-year-old Rentheim, but as she admitted later, "I thought I could do anything. You know how one is when one is young."6

At the final dress rehearsal, everything looked like failure. Unable to begin until after the evening performance of *The Master Builder*, the rehearsal wore on for nearly eight hours. The sets were not finished, the snow machine did not work properly, and light cues were not set. By opening night the mechanics were still not resolved. While Eva was emoting during the last act snowstorm, a metal coat hanger fell from the grid and struck her on the head.

In spite of the problems, Eva achieved another success. Richard Watts, Jr., of the *New York Herald-Tribune*, called it "one of the events of the season." Praising the ensemble quality in the production, Brooks Atkinson remarked that Eva gave fresh proof of her versatility. She was "the apotheosis of daring youth" in *The Master Builder*, yet pulled off a melancholy octogenarian in *John Gabriel Borkman*. Her intelligent acting always suggested the changing moods and resulted in a sharply etched characterization.7

Eva's work with Ibsen had triumphed. Now it was time to test another theory. She had always resented the high ticket prices of Broadway theatres and wondered what would happen if she reduced them. As an experiment, she gave two special 10:30 A.M. performances of her Ibsen repertory for $1.50 top, one-third of the standard fare.

Both performances were entirely sold out! She was convinced that if she established a theatre, she could attract large audiences by keeping her ticket prices low.

In a speech at Yale University in December 1925, Eva stated her goal for the American theatre:

> One of America's greatest needs is to build up the theatre. . . . The theatre is yet far away from its loftiest possibilities. To restore or to attain these the actor must take his vow to God as does the priest. . . . Of the stage and its condition today we might use the words of Christ of the ancient temple: "This was a house of prayer and ye have made it a den of thieves."[8]

Eva Le Gallienne wanted a theatre where she could devote her life to producing fine drama, developing her talent, and reaching the people. For the next ten years, she tried to achieve her "house of prayer."

During this year of her Ibsen experiment, the Broadway theatre reached an all-time peak of activity. A record number of 255 new productions had been presented during the year. Yet no theatre group was committed to Eva's ideals—to provide the best in theatre at the lowest possible rate and to present plays in repertory. The Actors' Theatre, Walter Hampden's Theatre, and the Theatre Guild espoused the same intent but fell short. They charged regular prices for tickets and arranged for long runs with their hits.

Determined to realize her goal, Eva contacted theatre benefactor Otto H. Kahn for help, knowing that he was an old friend of her father's. At Kahn's suggestion, she embarked in the spring of 1926 on a tour with her two Ibsen productions, traveling to major Eastern cities and as far west as Chicago. Kahn believed her proposal would benefit from the tour's publicity.

Every aspect of the tour was encouraging. The critics described the productions as "spirited," "thrilling," "taut and tense." Theatregoers began to line up at the box offices for SRO tickets. Through speeches before local organizations, Eva promoted her scheme for a new theatre. If productions of great masterpieces were available at all times, she argued, the theatre would not be limited to producing best-sellers. "Repertory," she proclaimed, "keeps the plays alive just as though they were in your library." She was not interested in a theatre whose aim was to make money, and she boldly attacked efforts to put the control of art in the hands of corporations and syndicates. She pleaded that "the theatre should be free to the people just as the Public Library is free, just as the museum is free. It should belong to them, should be free just as churches are. It must be so. . . . I want the theatre to be made accessible to the people."[9]

This rebel from Broadway drew the attention of the press in nearly every city she visited. For a star actress to renounce Broadway and what seemed like a flourishing career was astounding, especially when she was merely twenty-six years old. As interest in her project grew, she began to receive commitments for financial help, and in May she wrote to Kahn, "These last few days have been a concentrated effort as you foresaw—and they have been enormously successful. We are within $10,000 of the amount needed." With a religious zeal, she had badgered many wealthy people. "I am giving nine-tenths of my earning capacity to this idea, and I have nothing," she reasoned. "I only have my earning capacity, and I'm willing to give up nine-tenths of it. You are a millionaire. Now you've got to give me $50,000."[10]

Never during the three-month tour did Eva consider abandoning her goal. Even when financial backing seemed unsure, she continued her preparations and proclaimed, "My faith in the plan is so firm that I am convinced the *need* of it will enable me to carry it through."[11] By the end of the summer, more than 8,000 subscribers had promised her a total of $68,000 for her first season. Leading the list with a pledge of $18,000 was Otto Kahn.

Eva mapped out her plan in detail. Her original idea to call the company The People's Repertory Theatre had to be scrapped when she learned another group had claimed that name. Ultimately, she settled on Civic Repertory Theatre and initiated plans to open in the fall with a permanent company of actors. Although their salaries would be lower than the Broadway scale, she would guarantee twenty weeks of employment. During the first season, she would direct her Ibsen duo, Chekhov's *Three Sisters*, and Benavente's *Saturday Night*. Every four or five weeks, she would open a new production. Since her ideal of making all performances free was financially impossible, she insisted on a top price of a dollar fifty, with cheaper seats sold at fifty cents.

In forming her acting company, Eva selected actors who shared her ideals. She was not interested in stars, but in actors with experience, training, and the versatility to perform a number of roles in repertory. For her nucleus she hired the seven-member Ibsen company, which included Egon Brecher, Beatrice Terry, J. Sayre Crawley, Beatrice de Neergaard, Harold Moulton, Sydney Machat, and Ruth Wilton. Most of the other actors who joined the troupe—Alma Kruger, Paul Leyssac, Leona Roberts, Walter Beck, and Donald Cameron—had the same type of professional background. They had at least a brief amount of formal training and had performed the classics in stock theatres and on tour.

With her acting company set, Eva put together her professional staff: Gladys E. Calthrop, designer and vice president; Mary Duggett Benson (Mimsey), secretary and general manager; Mrs. William Laimbier, treasurer; Mrs. Joseph Drum, press representative; Rae Rabinowitz, subscriptions; and Mary Ward, business manager. The composition of the management was perhaps one of Eva's first errors. Although she felt more comfortable working with women, having no men in the ranks set her up for obvious criticism. From its inception, the Civic Repertory Theatre was viewed as a feminist theatre, and because of Eva's touted relationships with Gladys Calthrop and Mary Duggett, there were rumors that it was a den of lesbianism. In fact, critic George Jean Nathan referred to it derisively as "the Le Gallienne sorority."[12]

Eva's next step was to locate a theatre large enough to handle all the scenery needed for repertory. She learned there was an old theatre available on Fourteenth Street, just west of Sixth Avenue, that had a huge stage and a seating capacity of eleven hundred. Constructed in 1866, the theatre had been used in recent years as a burlesque house. Paint was peeling from the front facade. Inside, the aisles were lined with well-worn linoleum, the floor of the auditorium sagged and buckled, and many of the seats were broken. It was far from glamorous. Yet Eva was struck with its sense of dignity and believed it would fit her plans.

While the building was being refurbished, Eva invited her company to rehearse in Weston, Connecticut. She stayed at the country home of Mimsey, while the rest of the company resided at Cobb's Mill Inn. Especially in rehearsing *The Three Sisters*, she wanted to avoid the distraction of the big city and to build a group feeling. "We sat around in the beautiful fields and woods near Weston trying to identify ourselves with the various characters," she explained. "We called each other by their names and frequently started work by discussing in character things not actually in the text." Though this may have given the company a tremendous sense of ease and reality, Noel Coward rebuked such lofty techniques. Rehearsals were postponed, he quipped, after some actors sat in beds of poison ivy and were sent to the hospital for treatment.[13]

Eva knew her directing of this intimate drama must approach the characters as real people with human dimensions, so she instructed her actors to handle the lines not as speeches but as actual conversation.

During the usual ad lib moments, she urged them to talk on relevant topics. To make the dramatic action clear, she labored over the blocking and stage compositions. Nothing could be left to chance.

While Eva's troupe was busy rehearsing in the serenity of Connect-icut, New York was buzzing about a play soon to open — *The Captive*. It eventually became one of the most notorious and most highly pub-licized dramas in American theatre history, and it introduced lesbian-ism to Broadway. The story deals with a wealthy young woman who tries to hide her sexuality from her family by marrying. She eventually confesses to her husband that she is a sick person who needs help: "There are times . . . when I don't know what I'm doing. It's like — a prison to which I must return captive, despite myself." Her lover, who is likewise married, is never seen on stage but sends frequent bouquets of violets. The distraught husband refers to lesbians as "shadows," mysterious and menacing creatures that must be shunned at all cost.[14]

When first produced in Paris, *The Captive* was hailed as a master-piece and compared to Greek tragedy. Productions were soon dupli-cated in Berlin, Vienna, and Brussels. The New York reaction was quite the opposite, however, and revealed the country's antagonistic homo-phobia. Brooks Atkinson of the *New York Times* despised the "revolting theme," the "loathsome possibility" of a "twisted relationship with another woman." To him it was nothing more than a "warped infatua-tion." Other review comments were equally evocative: "a cancerous growth," "gangrenous horrors of sex perversion," "a decadent wo-man." In an editorial, the influential William Randolph Hearst ranted that the play was "vicious and obscene." Even the usually liberal George Jean Nathan joined the chorus. He called the play "the most subjective, corruptive, and potentially evil-fraught play ever shown in the American theater" and fumed that it was "a documentary in favor of sex degeneracy."[15]

Many critics noted that the gilt-edged, first-night audience in-cluded such stars as Billie Burke, Ruth Gordon, Norma Talmadge, Anita Loos, and, of course, Eva Le Gallienne.[16] When the production was finally closed four months later, after a sensational police raid, stars Helen Mencken and Basil Rathbone were arrested. Prompted by this production, a bill to amend the penal law in relation to immoral plays soon became a New York State law. In essence, it outlawed the presentation of homosexuality in the state's theatres, and it remained on the books for forty years, until 1967. Although Eva refused to miss *The Captive*'s pivotal premiere, the public outrage convinced her to keep her lesbianism more private.

When the Civic Repertory Theatre finally opened its doors on October 25, 1926, Eva was frightened. She had chosen Benavente's *Saturday Night* because of the large cast, thinking it would be a good choice to show off her company for the first time. But the reviews were a disaster. The script was attacked for its mixture of moods, superfluous characters, and allegorical pretentiousness. Eva "was terrible," wrote Noel Coward, "the production awful, and the play lousy!"[17] Eva later admitted that it was "a ghastly hopeless failure." With such an obvious disaster on her hands, she knew that the future of her grand experiment was riding on the next evening's offering of Chekhov.

Fortunately, that performance, the premiere of New York's first English production of *The Three Sisters*, was a major success. Even though Eva played the female lead, she was praised for a performance absent of stardom. The close harmony in the acting resulted in an unusual spirit of ensemble. The high-quality production prompted Alexander Woollcott to warn that Eva meant business with her idea of a classical repertory theatre. "As a General she leads her generation in the theatre," he wrote. "All our players sigh ostentatiously for the great plays. Miss Le Gallienne merely acts them."[18]

By the end of January 1927, Eva had added two comedies to her roster—*La Locandiera* and *Twelfth Night*. Even though five of her first six productions were artistic and critical successes, she could see by the box-office reports that they were not all popular. To her dismay, the Civic was attracting audiences of only sixty percent capacity. To cover the expenses of repertory, she knew she needed a top attraction.

When Eva opened the Sierras' *Cradle Song*, the future of her theatre was assured. For the first time, the Civic Repertory Theatre had a decided hit. Set in a Spanish convent, the play is about a group of nuns who rear a girl from infancy until she is eighteen. Eva's portrayal of Sister Joanna of the Cross captured the sentiment and tenderness of the script. Woollcott applauded: "Not this season in the theatre anywhere in this town have I been part of an audience so obviously and so genuinely moved."[19] Virtually all the fifty-six performances in the spring of 1927 were sold out. When Burns Mantle asked the New York critics to select the ten best dramas on Broadway that season, nearly half of those responding named *The Cradle Song*.

But the play's triumph brought new problems. Broadway managers urged Eva to move the production uptown. She would make a fortune, she was told, and the money could be used to strengthen the Civic. She knew, however, that the ticket prices would be about three times as much. As she explained, "There was the matter of integrity. If it had gone up to Broadway . . . we would have gone back on our promises. Our policy would have been disrupted."[20] It also would have meant bowing again to the male-dominated Broadway establishment.

Even though the move would have guaranteed her future, Eva proclaimed, "If you have a clear idea, the only chance of failure lies in compromise. Don't compromise. . . . People who have no direct line in their heads are the ones who fail. If you have a conviction, don't take anybody's advice."[21] Though her decision may have pleased her faithful theatre patrons, it certainly alienated the Broadway management even further. This young woman, a lesbian at that, was refusing to play according to their rules.

Ironically, Eva's last play of the season, Susan Glaspell's *Inheritors*, dealt specifically with the subject of compromise. The story tells of a woman who is persecuted and reprimanded by government officials because she harbors a conscientious objector. Like Eva, she is constantly pressured to compromise her ideals. But rather than play the lead role herself, Eva cast Josephine Hutchinson as the fearless and idealistic young radical. The critics were pleased that Eva was finally presenting an American play, yet they concurred that this script was solemn, tiresome, and dated.

The performances were probably weakened by a tragedy at the Civic. A few months earlier, Sydney Machat, an actor who had been with Eva since the days of the Ibsen tour, had suffered a complete collapse and had been diagnosed as temporarily insane. A brilliant young man and a promising actor, he apparently had snapped under the pressure of acting. *The Inheritors* was to be his comeback, but a few days before the play opened, he committed suicide. Although Eva recast the part, the company was shaken and gave an uneven performance.

The casting of Josephine Hutchinson was probably ill-timed. Though she had striking red hair, she did not possess a commanding appearance. The twenty-two-year-old ingenue was slender, gentle, and fragile, with a delicate, cameolike face. She had made her stage debut about seven years earlier and for three years had been a member of the Ram's Head Players in Washington, DC. Soon after Eva caught her Broadway performance in *The Unchastened Woman*, she had been invited to join the Civic. Although she had been featured in other productions during the season, this was her first starring role. Unfortunately, the young actress was not the appropriate choice for such a taxing assignment.

Perhaps swaying Eva's opinion in her casting was the fact that she and "Josie" had become more than friends. The intimacy she had shared with Gladys Calthrop had disintegrated into simply a working relationship, and Eva was looking for more fulfillment. As her charm worked its magic on Josie, she was convinced that she was establishing the most meaningful and enduring relationship of her life. She was certain she would overcome the resentment of Josie's mother, who incidentally was also an actress with the Civic. Although Josie had married director Robert Bell three years earlier, she quickly succumbed to the spell of the experienced, older actress.

In early May, Eva closed her first New York season after twenty-eight weeks. It had been a rewarding year. Six of her eight productions had been critical successes, and she could boast that her company played to audiences averaging seventy-eight percent of capacity. She had yet to prove, however, that such a theatre as hers could be financially solvent. Even though she had grossed over $245,000, the net loss for the season, exclusive of donations raised, stood at $101,000.[22]

In recognition of her achievement, *The Nation* magazine selected Eva for its Roll of Honor for 1927, placing her name alongside those of Charles Lindbergh, Eugene O'Neill, Ernest Hemingway, Will Rogers, and Max Reinhardt. From Tufts University she received the first of her many honorary degrees. The Society of Arts and Sciences awarded her a gold medal for making the most important contribution of an individual to the drama during 1926.

Stories proclaiming her success appeared in newspapers throughout the country. Most significant, perhaps, was the backing she received from the National Woman's Party, the most militant and uncompromising of the many women's associations in the country. Along with Gloria Swanson, Pearl Mesta, Mrs. Randolph Hearst, and Edna St. Vincent Millay, Eva had been an active member and had served as chairman of the Actress Council of the organization. Through the party's nomination, she won the annual $5,000 prize from *Pictorial Review* magazine, for founding the Civic.

Praising her determination and self-sacrifice became vogue. Journalists were quick to print the altruistic motto on her programs—"The theatre should be an instrument for giving, not a machinery for getting"—and to note that there was no billing page listing herself as star and director. In one year, reporters were hailing her with such titles as "The General," "The Colonel," "St. Eva," and "The Abbess of Fourteenth Street."

The frequency of such ribbing annoyed Eva. "I think sometimes people imagine that we are rather a bunch of high-brows down there who think we are making sacrifices for the sake of art," she complained. "That is all nonsense. I have not made one bit of sacrifice. I have had no courage. I have just believed a thing and tried to do it, and in trying to do it I have been happy. I have been selfish."[23] Her humble denial provided even more fodder for the media and ammunition for the critics.

Confident of the future, Eva signed a ten-year lease for the building and, following a short trip to Europe, began plans for the new season. To answer critics who thought she should refrain from taking all the leading roles, she announced plans to devote more time to directing. But she explained, "I have played leading parts for economic reasons."[24] Of all the members of her company, Eva was the only one who had a well-known professional reputation. She believed that the immediate success of her theatre depended on her name.

Eva's opening production of the second season, Herman Heijerman's *Good Hope*, started the year on a roll. Based on actual accounts of a damaged fishing schooner lost at sea, the play illustrates the agony of those who are left at home. What appealed to Eva most was not that it dealt with the social problem of abusive shipping laws but that it portrayed the lives of human beings. Critics compared the production's realism to that of the famed Moscow Art Theatre of Stanislavsky. John Mason Brown ranked it as good as *The Cradle Song*, and Brooks Atkinson called it "exhilarating, cathartic. . . . theatre in its finest manifestation."[25]

In sharp contrast, the next production was considered vulgar and indecent. In an attempt to add some variety to her repertory, Eva scheduled what she thought was going to be a daring experiment, Gustav Wied's theatrical satire, $2 \times 2 = 5$. In a mood of fantastic artificiality, the plot concerns a radical novelist who is married to a rigid, moralistic, and highly proper society woman. After he is imprisoned for writing scandalous literature, he compromises his ideals and becomes an editor of a conservative newspaper.

Egon Brecher, director of the production, requested designer Boris Aronson to come up with a futuristic set with illogical juxtapositon of visual elements. The first act living room, for example, revealed a mixture of Victorian and ultramodern Danish furniture. Character movement was equally unique. An actor might demonstrate his pomposity by prancing like a pony, or his indifference by cartwheeling across the stage. Most critics felt that the aim of the play, which was to deal with the question of compromise, was clouded by all the absurdity. The Civic's subscription members were so disturbed by the peculiar style that when Eva called a meeting to discuss the complaints, more than 600 disgruntled people showed up. They did not like her daring experiment and demanded the play be removed. After sixteen performances, she reluctantly agreed.

Suddenly Eva seemed plagued with bad productions. Hoping to alleviate charges that she was neglecting American authors, she turned to a new play called *The First Stone*. Eva directed and played Sarah Peri, a young Cape Cod woman married to a truck driver. Her husband discovers that while he has been traveling, his wife has been engaged in a romantic affair with another man. But Eva once again seemed unable to convey the physical passion required of her character. When she should have been a hearty, man-hungry, earthly woman, she was prim, pinched, cool, and self-possessed. So much so that it prompted Alexander Woollcott to conclude that Eva's performance was "a fresh reminder that she can do everything in the theatre except act."[26]

The most cruel comments came from George Jean Nathan. Never her fan, he had become her enemy since the days of the controversy over the lesbian themes in *The Captive*. He now accused her of incompetent, amateurish work and called her a reincarnated Joan of Arc with "unmistakable overtones of Jesus."[27] Perhaps his objection to homosexuality colored his attitude. He could tolerate lesbian actresses who married, for he saw them trying to blend into the fabric of American society. It made them appear as if they were sorry for their affliction and wanted to lead acceptable lives. But Eva was different. All he perceived was arrogance. He had no way of knowing that she was deeply hurt by the attacks and was hiding her shame.

Not until late March did Eva finally have another financial success, *Hedda Gabler*. This began her long association with the play. By 1964 she had starred in the role six times in New York, played in two coast-to-coast tours, cut the first full-length American recording of it, and directed a national tour. Although her approach to the play changed throughout the years, she had a clear concept of what she wanted, even with this first production in 1928.

Intent on bringing the play closer to modern audiences, Eva avoided setting it in the 1890s. Her mother, along with Civic actor Paul Leyssac, prepared a revised translation. Instead of the common Victorian set with all the fussiness, her new Civic designer, Aline Bernstein, used taupe draperies for the walls, accenting them with touches of blue in the curtains and furniture. Hedda herself was a stylish woman of the 1920s. She smoked cigarettes, wore her hair in a boyish bob, and lounged in a fashionable yellow moiré gown, trimmed with silk braid.

Only two years earlier, Emily Stevens had gained recognition for her portrayal of a Hedda who was something between a visible demon and a slinking cobra. Eva objected, describing Stevens as "all nervous and jumpy as if she was taking dope all the time. She was totally wrong."[28] To Eva, Hedda was more tragic than evil. Her obsession for power sprang from an uncontrollable pathological condition, not from conscious plotting.

Instead of nervous and demonic, Eva wanted Hedda to convey a cold unruffled repose. The physical image she found most appropriate for Hedda was that of a cat. When Thea first mentioned Lovborg, Hedda watched her carefully from "behind her eyes — like a cat." As she became amazed at Thea's courage, she sat on an arm of the sofa, put her hand on Thea's shoulder, and gave "the impression of a cat's paw, claws barely concealed."[29]

Eva planned frequent pauses that allowed the audience to grasp Hedda's inner thoughts. When Thea says to Hedda, "I only know that I must live here where Eilert Lovborg is — if I am to live at all," a long pause followed before Hedda replied. She was amazed at Thea's courage, as well as resentful of it. She herself was far too conventional to ever dare what Thea did. Certainly Eva's most dramatic pause came at the end of act 3 after Lovborg leaves. Holding the stage for two and a half minutes, Eva crossed silently to a table below the sofa and lit a cigarette, circled up to the desk that held the manuscript, crossed back to the sofa and sat, returned to the desk, then went back to the sofa once more, before finally going to the desk to get the manuscript. During that time the thought of the child kept knocking on her brain. She was drawn to the manuscript as though mesmerized. Once she had it in her hands, she tore it into a thousand pieces and, with a fanatic, almost brooding joy, burned it. Her ability to concentrate and to hold such a long pause prompted young actress May Sarton to say, "I remember we used to keep away from Eva on the nights she was playing Hedda Gabler!"[30]

Financially, the production was a great success. All fifteen performances in the season were sold out. Of her five new productions of the second season, it was the only one to show a profit. Artistically, however, its success was not so clear. Eva's attempt to portray a modern Hedda did not work. As Glenda Jackson pointed out a half-century later, "A part of Hedda's problem is that she can't get out; she has no outside world." There are no telephones or television. "She moves in a very solid, proper, polite, bourgeois world. You need to see her corseted and her sense of isolation in Norway." The vast majority of the critics agreed with John Anderson, who reported that the inspiration for Eva's portrayal came "out of the icebox. . . . At no point did her picture . . . take on the intensity of repressed emotion, or the excitement of reckless temper."[31]

From the time Eva had opened the Civic, her acting had come under attack. In mounting frequency that culminated in their reactions to her Hedda, the critics accused her of being rigid, cold, and intellectual. Even though they could see she had carefully preplanned the development of her characters, they failed to see her bring subtextual thoughts and feelings to her portrayals. They accused her of indicative, superficial acting that revealed an inability to express the inner life of a character. Even company member Tonio Selwart noticed that her "love scenes were a little bit sticky. They were not free. They were half gestures, artificial."[32]

In spite of the financial success of *Hedda Gabler*, the Civic's second season had been less successful as a whole than that of the first—box-office receipts were down nearly $3,000. In hopes of broadening her subsidy, Eva instituted a campaign at the beginning of the season to enlist members into the Civic Repertory Club. Dues of $1.00 per year provided a reduction in ticket prices, invitations to special meetings, a subscription to the Civic magazine, and the opportunity to win a $1,000 prize in a contest for the best review of a Civic production. With the active support of literally hundreds of people, including artists such as Laurette Taylor and Richard Boleslavsky, she had registered 39,000 members by the end of the year and, combined with other donations, raised a total of $60,000. The massive effort was of little help, however, for she had spent $34,000 to finance the campaign.

During the Civic's second season, Eva expanded her operation by opening a free school for actors called The Apprentice Group. Each spring she auditioned some 300 applicants and selected twenty to thirty students. Those who were accepted attended all rehearsals of the Civic Repertory and played as "supers" in the productions. They were charged no fee, and though they were guaranteed no salary, they were not allowed to have outside employment. The four best apprentices each year were paid to remain for a second season, through a scholarship fund provided by Mrs. Edward Bok of Philadelphia.

Under the guidance of Anne Moore, Walter Beck, and Giorgio Santelli, the students attended daily classes in fencing, speech, makeup, and movement. They became a close-knit group, often running to Child's Restaurant for coffee and even rehearsing scenes in the theatre after the evening performances. At the end of the season, they performed their scenes before invited guests, and Eva would provide a critique. She was known to be severe but honest. "This is my opinion," she would begin. "Take it or leave it." She would advise some of the young women to try something else. Apprentice Richard Waring remembers the warning she gave one student: "You have a lot of talent," she admonished, "but one thing I cannot understand is that you come late to rehearsals, and your work is sloppy. It's as if God has given you this talent and you are spitting in his face." The student was Burgess Meredith.[33]

What drew the students to the school in the first place was the reputation of Eva, who was regarded as a "Young Goddess, an inspiration." Regardless of her criticism, Burgess Meredith proclaimed that when he first joined the school, the high royalty of the American theater consisted of five people—Katharine Cornell, Helen Hayes, Alfred Lunt, Lynn Fontanne, and Eva. "To have a role in one of their plays was more than a privilege," he remarked. "It was a kind of knighthood." Although Lee Strasberg established a different approach to acting when he founded the Actors' Studio in the 1940s, he recognized that the only place to learn acting in the 1920s was "at the feet of Eva Le Gallienne."[34]

Among the apprentices who started their careers under Eva's tutelage were John Garfield, Arnold Moss, Howard da Silva, Bobby Lewis, May Sarton, and J. Edward Bromberg. The young and yet unknown Bette Davis auditioned for the Apprentice Group, but Eva felt she had too many mannerisms for stage acting. By the Civic's sixth season, five among the twenty-eight actors in the permanent company had come up through the apprenticeship program.

As the opening of the third season approached, theatre circles were stunned when they learned that two major stars were signed to join the company. Eva needed box-office draws for her struggling enterprise and performers to assume some of the leading roles. Her first surprise addition was none other than Alla Nazimova. She had seldom talked with her former mentor and paramour since they had separated so abruptly seven years earlier. But now the two women needed each other. Nazimova had lost her fortune and fame after a series of disastrous films and was desperate for work; Eva needed a star. The reunion seemed a natural solution for both.

Eva's other new addition was Mary Morris, a well-known actress who had only four years earlier overwhelmed Broadway with her passionate portrayal of Abbe in Eugene O'Neill's *Desire Under the Elms*. "We would like to invite you into the company," Eva explained to the full-bosomed Morris, "because the critics are complaining we are too flat-chested down here at the Civic."[35] Though she did sign a contract,

Morris played only in the season opener, before leaving to join the Group Theatre.

Still another problem facing Eva was the Civic's ongoing reputation as serious and intellectual. This attitude had become so widespread that Noel Coward parodied it in his 1928 review, *This Year of Grace*. In one scene, a tragic young woman made up to look suspiciously like Eva rocked back and forth as she sat before a table and moaned, "Oh, the pain of it!" Because of their highmindedness, Coward dubbed it the Civic Raspberry Company.[36] Though Eva had included comedies in her repertory—*La Locandiera* and *Twelfth Night*— they had not proven very successful. She hoped her opener for the third season would remedy the situation, but her amateurish and tiresome production of Molière's *The Would-Be Gentleman* convinced nobody that the Civic was adept at comedy.

Eva's next venture, *The Cherry Orchard*, saw Alla playing Mme. Ranevsky and Eva directing. An inspiring touch came toward the end of act 4, when Varya, played by Eva, hopes for a proposal from Lopahin. Following a few lines of awkward groping for words, Lopahin crossed away to the large French windows, as Varya knelt on both knees before a low trunk, pretending to look for something. After Lopahin informed her that he was "off to Harkov—by this next train" and that Epihodov was staying behind, Eva as Varya kept her hands in the trunk as if searching, but her eyes revealed the truth. She looked over the top of the trunk, calmly but sadly. She knew there would be no marriage proposal. At the same time, Lopahin crossed quietly behind her, held his hands out as if wanting to touch her, and looked as if he desperately wanted to speak. Lacking courage, he crossed back to the window in silence.[37] The repressed tone Eva gave to the role seemed to suit her personality.

Because of Alla's sensational star status, many critics were amazed at Eva's ability to blend the company into an ensemble. They compared the result to the Moscow Art Theatre and proclaimed the production one of the Civic's best. Due to the great demand for tickets, Eva played *The Cherry Orchard* for sixty-four performances during the season— more than any previous Civic offering. Inviting Alla to join the company had proven to be inspired.

About six weeks after *The Cherry Orchard* opened, Eva launched a new production for the Christmas season, one of decidedly different mood—Sir James Barrie's *Peter Pan*. Eva hoped once again to dispel the idea that her company could present only classical, highbrow productions. Audiences and critics were delighted. Different from the

Maude Adams 1905 portrayal in which Peter was romantic and sentimental, Eva's Peter was agile, muscular, and mercurial. Instead of an icy Hedda or a practical Varya, she became a boyish, elfin Peter Pan. For her costume she insisted on tight blue leotards that would show her legs, blue suede sandals, and a blue jerkin trimmed with green leaves. On her head she wore a small pointed hat; the color was a daring violet.

Determined to fly, Eva hired the same people that had supervised Maude Adams. With an intricate system of wires, counterweights, and pulleys, complete with a ten-pound harness, she began rehearsing her flies a month before opening. Once perfected, she added a swoop out to the second balcony of the theatre for her curtain call. Audiences went wild with their cheers and hoots. Sometimes the children in the audience ran frenziedly down the aisles to help conquer the pirates. When Peter finally felled Captain Hook to the ground, the performance had to pause for the choruses of thundering cheers. Once, swinging back from the dangerous "audience fly," Eva almost missed the stage and nearly broke her legs on the edge of the orchestra pit. It may have been hazardous, but according to Eva, "It was great fun!"[38]

Believing that *Peter Pan* was an excellent means to interest children in the theatre, Eva announced plans to keep it in her repertory and to make it the Civic's "gala play, the play which will come to life year after year, and especially at those holiday periods—Thanksgiving, Christmas, and Easter—when everyone, old and young, is a child again."[39] True to her word, she revived the production each November as long as she managed the Fourteenth Street Theatre. With frequent Saturday matinees and one free, annual Christmas matinee for orphans and underprivileged children, she played the title role for a total of 129 sold-out performances.

As the Civic's third season came to an end, the future looked better than ever. They had been playing to 91 percent capacity. Box-office receipts totaled nearly 30 percent more than in their first year. With this record of achievement, Eva was able to persuade Yiddish actor Jacob Ben-Ami to join the company, promising him that he would play opposite Alla in *The Sea Gull*. In the middle of the summer, however, after Ben-Ami had committed himself, Alla resigned. Neither she nor Eva would explain, but a representative for the Civic said Alla had been "too temperamental" and had objected to billing in which Eva's name as producer preceded the alphabetical listing of the performers. She may have been angry, too, when she learned that her weekly salary for the next season was to be only $250, which was $50 less than Ben-Ami's.

In any case, Eva proceeded with plans to begin her fourth season with *The Sea Gull*, casting Merle Maddern as Irina and Ben-Ami as Trigorin. The critics were enthusiastic, applauding the orchestrated, ensemble acting as well as the truthful and sincere characterizations. Eva's portrayal of Masha was rated by many as her greatest achievement in years. She was convincing as the sensitive, desperate woman who loved in silence. Once again she was praised not for revealing passionate feelings but for suggesting repressed emotions. The performance ended with a five-minute standing ovation.

The unexpected highlight of the year, however, was Eva's revival of *Romeo and Juliet*. At the first rehearsal, she told her cast that the play "had been written by a young man just a few days before. It's a young, vital, gay, passionate and romantic play . . . and isn't the Bible."[40] She wanted to impress on them that they were presenting a real situation, not a historical classic.

The unit set she designed along with Aline Bernstein provided for a variety of locales yet retained possibilities for swiftness and excitement. The performance began with a roll of drums, then the curtain opened to a terrific fight taking place among the servants, who came right down onto the apron. Entrances were made from the aisles as well as the orchestra pit. She cut the opening chorus, since she wanted to establish immediately that this was a fighting play: "Swords clash, blood is shed. It ought to be like lightning."[41]

At first Eva hesitated playing the title role herself, feeling she was too old for the part and weary from slurs by the critics about her depth of emotions. Once Josie refused the role, however, she felt compelled. This time she was determined to make the characters real. "From the first kisses which Juliet experiences at the ball, where she glimpses Romeo for the first time," she explained, "her maturity is taking rapid effect. Her second meeting with her lover . . . is invested with a strange glamour of something which inevitably must happen."[42] Even though most of Eva's sexual experiences had been with other women, she set her mind on doing all in her power to squash the critics. She vowed to portray a woman with real passion, a woman who was not static and sentimental and repressed, but who changed and grew stronger and more resolved as the story progressed. She would prove beyond a doubt that she could create sensuality on the stage.

Once again Eva used her trademark silences and inner monologues to capture the audience's attention. After Juliet experiences intimacy with Romeo, for instance, and then hears her mother say she must soon marry Paris, Eva insisted that Juliet is filled with the blood and energy of youth: "Her body and soul is still permeated with Romeo. The thought of another man even touching her is horribly distasteful to her." Eva held a long pause, therefore, before saying, "Now by Saint Peter's Church and Peter too / He shall not make me there a joyful bride."[43] Eva wanted to infuse the poetry with the richness of human thought.

May Sarton remembers Eva discovering richness in even simple lines of dialogue. At one point, Juliet says to Romeo, "My lord, my love, my friend." Most actresses utter these words on a simple rush of feeling, making no differentiation between them. Eva however, "took them slowly, seemed to be discovering them as they were uttered so that for us in the audience the reality of a true marriage was suddenly made clear in all its beauty."[44] Over and over again, the audience could perceive the thoughts of a living, thinking Juliet.

The success of Eva's portrayal overwhelmed the press. Gilbert Gabriel observed, "This is a Juliet well acquainted with the facts of life and the persuasions of love." Joseph Wood Krutch said, "The blood that runs in Tybalt's veins runs in Juliet's too. . . . Obviously she is no model maiden." And Percy Hammond added that Eva showed "a burning enthusiasm for what appeared to be her soul's mate." Virtually everyone agreed with Brooks Atkinson's observation that this was "the finest and most elastic performance of her career." Eva acted with "a new fulness of emotion." One witness to her stunning performance was Richard Waring, who played Romeo: "She was warm, vibrant, and sensitive. So young, so soft, so beautiful." Following their night together in her bedchamber, Juliet embraces Romeo. "It was so real," Waring recalls, "so passionate."[45] So passionate, indeed. Waring fell in love with Eva and actually proposed marriage.

Of the twenty-seven productions presented at the Civic from 1926 through 1930, *Romeo and Juliet* was one of the most popular. It emerged as a play born of action, and it surged onward not as a teenage love story or as a vehicle for the stars but as a tragic misadventure of an ancient feud.

Perhaps one reason for Eva's personal triumph was that Juliet's goal to defend and fight for her Romeo corresponded with the actress's own personal journey at the time. While Eva was rehearsing and presenting the production, she was desperately seeking to justify her own love for Josephine Hutchinson. Both Josie's mother and her husband, Robert Bell—grandson of Alexander Graham Bell—were pressuring Eva to abandon the relationship. Eva refused. The blood that ran in Tybalt's veins ran also in Eva's.

Though she appeared strong, Eva continued to suffer from the guilt of her lesbianism. The public furor over Radclyffe Hall's notorious novel *The Well of Loneliness* reminded her of her own predicament. In the haunting novel, a lesbian named Stephen is driven from her family's aristocratic society into the fashionable lesbian culture of 1920s Paris. Considered an indecent invert, Stephen is eventually forced to sacrifice the woman of her life to a man who can offer respectability. She learns that females are expected to remain passive and weak. An aggressive woman, particularly a lesbian, posed a threat to men.

At first banned in both England and America on grounds that the very theme of lesbianism was indecent, the story pleads for pity and understanding. It closes with Stephen praying, "God, we believe; we have told You we believe. . . . We have not denied You, then rise up and defend us. Acknowledge us, oh God, before the whole world. Give us also the right to our existence."[46] Eva, like Stephen, felt shameful and apologetic. More important, she feared that one day she might lose Josie's love.

Eva's fear was compounded because her lesbianism had become such public knowledge. Adoring women at the Civic copied her dress and walk and wore slouch hats that matched Eva's. When May Sarton wanted to join Eva's Apprentice Group in 1929, her parents were warned against letting their seventeen-year-old daughter enter into that "den of evil." Her father even went backstage one night and, while Eva sat in her Peter Pan costume, asked bluntly, "Are you in love with women, and if so, will you leave my daughter alone?" At parties that Sarton attended during those years, she frequently heard people refer to Eva as "that terrible lesbian woman." When actor Tonio Selwart arrived in America from his native Germany in 1931, friends immediately told him that she was a lesbian. "She was discreet and delicate," he recalls, "but everybody knew it."[47]

As Eva's notoriety grew, she became the brunt of countless rumors and many cruel jokes. One relayed the story of an avid fan who rushed to her dressing room one night with a bouquet of flowers. With great panache he flung himself at her feet: "I must have you for my wife." Eva supposedly replied, "Oh, really! When shall I meet her?" Another exchange described Eva a number of years earlier, when she was questioning her sexuality. She barged into Joseph Schildkraut's dressing room one night while they were performing in *Liliom*. "Pepi," she begged, "you have to marry me." "Oh, Eva," he laughed, "I can't. You're a dyke!" Another version of this encounter had Schildkraut proposing to Eva and her confessing that she was a lesbian. Gossips buzzed about the erotic gatherings she hosted in her hotel room when she was on tour. The parties reportedly included a parade of young women in various stages of undress.

Eva's popularity as a prominent New York lesbian became the subject of ugly satire by all the media. In a magazine cartoon depicting two people in a romantic embrace, the characters were drawn to look suspiciously like Eva and Josie. Josie sits demurely with her head tipped, eyes gazing full front. She wears a plain gingham dress, and her hair falls loosely down her shoulders. Eva, seen with sweater and slacks and close-cropped hair, has one hand stretched around her lover's back, while the other clasps Josie's hands to her bosom. She is looking seductively into Josie's eyes. In the background is a flowering vine, perhaps intended to suggest violets. At first glance the picture appears to be a typical male-female pose. With tongue in cheek, the caption reads rather pointedly, "You are wrong in thinking that the young man in the sweater is Eva Le Gallienne."[48]

As she became an icon of lesbianism, Eva developed an even greater need for privacy. Her one escape was the country. Back in 1926, when Eva had stayed with Mimsey in Connecticut during rehearsals for the Civic opening, she had decided to buy a wild, rustic, four-acre piece of land near Weston. Though it was shaded with large elms, maples, and dogwoods, from a high vantage point she could see as far away as Long Island Sound, some seven miles in the distance.

Something about the gently rolling hills and the wooded terrain had reminded Eva of The Old Manor in Chiddingfold and of the times she had enjoyed with her father, Mams, Hep, and Nanny. She had lived in so many places since the days of her childhood, most of the time in apartments in large cities. Now she yearned for a permanent, country retreat, a quiet place where she could be alone and out of the public eye, where she could occasionally forget her work and the biting scrutiny of the press. With this purchase, she helped to popularize the surrounding area as a getaway for theatre personalities.

Eva had christened her new estate Toscairn, a name derived from her regular companion, a tiny cairn terrier called Tosca. The only remaining house on the property, a pre-Revolutionary War wooden frame, was located at the point of the triangular-shaped lot that bordered South Hillside Road. It was easy, and almost an adventure, to get snowbound for days on this isolated lot, since the road was dirt and nearly abandoned by the town. The house itself was quite primitive— no electricity, no running water, and an outhouse in the back. The wood-burning stove provided the only brace against the brutal winters.

Aided financially by Alice De Lamar, a wealthy lesbian friend who lived nearby, Eva, Josie, and Mimsey had set out immediately to revive the run-down estate. A new dormer on the second floor became a studio, where Eva built theatre models and miniature sets. The woodshed attached to the rear of the house became the kitchen.

Their first Spring at Toscairn saw the birth of their garden. Besides a long hedge of peonies, they planted a typical, English-cottage garden complete with dozens of Queen Elizabeth hybrid roses and masses of lilies. From seed, they grew miniature dahlias, phlox, Michaelmas daisies, carnations, and chrysanthemums. The flowers brought Eva great comfort and filled many a joyous afternoon. Partly because the flowers changed before her eyes, lived and died in a few days, she felt in touch with the process of life and with reality. Perhaps her need to create this garden revealed her basic English sensibility. In any case, she would often stand "in silent awe before the exquisite perfection of some tiny blossom, some spray of foliage. The myriad miracles of nature" filled her "with amazement and humility."[49]

The animals, too, brought her much delight. She erected a large kennel for her nine cairn terriers, but roaming free was a virtual menagerie, many with names—Rosy the cow, Little Eyolf the goat, Dinah the cat, and Camille the donkey. Completing her zoo were two love birds, a flock of chickens, two sheep, a horse, and a canary. For the many skunks and raccoons in the area, she built a wooden trough, which she filled every night with scraps of marshmallows, chicken, bread, and doughnuts. Salt lick was set out for the deer. She spent endless hours with the animals, training them, feeding them, and nursing them. Her patience was greater with them than with people, because the animals were more acquiescing, loving, and accepting.

Yearning for this country retreat, Eva and Josie returned to it in May 1930, after the Civic closed for the fourth season. For nearly two months they divorced themselves from all concerns of the theatre. When she wanted to read, Eva walked through the wooded paths to a secluded bench hidden among the trees. She found peace in the solitude of the garden and the fields and felt almost childlike as she cared for the animals. In the decades to follow, Eva looked back to this precious time and saw a relentless thirty-one-year-old woman who was experiencing, in her young theatre, the most productive period of her career. As youth would have it, there was no thought of disruption. Even in spite of the stock market crash and the chaos that was everywhere, the future appeared bright and promising. Eva could not imagine that the serenity, the joy, and the dream were about to die.

5

My Life in Two

On July 8, 1930, Eva's struggle for privacy abruptly ended as she became front-page headlines across the country. The cause—Josie's explosive divorce from her husband of six years. Attempts to hush the divorce by going through the courts in the distant town of Reno, Nevada, only peaked the gossip-hungry media. Claiming "sex in the office" between Eva and Josie, they reported that her husband, Robert Bell, filed for the divorce and named Eva as corespondent. He was even quoted as complaining that he never had a chance to have lunch with Josie, since she was with Eva "morning, noon, and night. If my wife had not joined Miss Le Gallienne," he charged, "this would not have happened." Further, they wrote that Bell's lawyer sought absolute secrecy and that he accordingly filed the divorce papers under a code name and had them sealed from public scrutiny. The divorce was reportedly granted to the indignant ex-husband within minutes of his application, on the grounds of mental cruelty.[1]

Avoiding direct accusations of lesbianism, the press did all they could to expose Eva and Josie's intimate relationship. Headlines in the *New York Daily News* read "Le Gallienne Shadow Actress Is Divorced," "shadow" being the common euphemism at the time for women who loved other women. "The girl had become Miss Le Gallienne's protege," the article read, "and she and the older actress were inseparable." A columnist for the *New York Daily Mirror* commented that "some people will regard this as a new angle in the old love triangle. But the affinity of one girl for another is older than the pyramids."[2]

The divorce did indeed take place in Reno, but this was practically the only shred of accuracy among the various accounts. Josie, not her husband, filed for the divorce. In her official complaint, Josie states that though she "conducted herself in accordance with her marital duties," her husband treated her with extreme cruelty. For particulars, she cites his morose and sullen behavior, his refusal to be agreeable to her friends, and his ignoring her on holidays. "As time went on," she claims, "plaintiff and defendant developed tastes that were more and more divergent from each other." They had become unsuited for each other and for some time had "not lived together as wife and husband." At 3:40 P.M. on July 7, 1930, District Judge Frank S. Dunn ruled in Josie's favor and, in open court, proclaimed that the marriage was dissolved absolutely and forever. He further clarified that neither plaintiff nor defendant had "any right, claim, or interest of any kind . . . against the person or estate of the other."[3] Eva is never mentioned or referred to in any of the legal accounts.

Regardless of the documents, the public preferred the press accounts. Sixty years later, theatre professionals still persist in referring to Eva as the actress who was the first lesbian corespondent in a divorce. Whenever Eva could, she tried valiantly to correct the rumors, but no one wanted to believe her. Her protesting was simply viewed as screening the truth. After all, people knew of her sexuality and concluded that Josie and her husband had probably arrived at an agreement out of court. If he refrained from charging lesbianism and allowed Josie to file for the divorce, she would not ask for a financial settlement.

The last half of the summer of 1930 was devastating. Eva could see that any attempt to keep her private life to herself was hopeless. For a woman who was so emotionally guarded, the scandal came as a humiliating disgrace. What people recognized as her abnormal perversion was now more publicized than her theatre, and the social degradation she felt only strengthened her resolve for privacy. A bolder person might have admitted the truth and ended the rumors, but Eva's shyness and fear of exposure prevented that. The courage she had exhibited in challenging Broadway and founding her own theatre unfortunately did not transfer to her personal life.

Terribly tormented by this episode, by early August Eva was admitted for exhaustion into New York's Doctors' Hospital, where she remained for two weeks. Because her doctors urged her to rest in the country until September, she was ultimately forced to announce a delay in opening her season at the Civic.

Though this traumatic experience strengthened the bond between Eva and Josie, Eva naturally felt uneasy about the future of her career. Just four years earlier, a book had appeared discrediting the work of Amy Lowell. The author had argued that Lowell's lesbianism prevented her from being a good poet and that nonlesbian readers would find nothing in her verses. Two years later, Emily Dickinson's niece published her aunt's love letters, and Eva learned that the author, in a pointless attempt to protect her aunt's reputation, had edited out all hints of Dickinson's lesbianism.[4] Eva naturally wondered if the validity of her own theatre work might now be questioned even more than before the scandal.

She certainly had reason to fear, because the attitudes and values of the American public seemed to be changing. With the onset of the Great Depression and difficult economic times, a growing conservatism prevailed. In the film industry, for example, the studio bosses saw the need to establish the Motion Picture Production Code in order to quiet the critics. This self-censorship, an answer to the public outcry over immorality on the screen, prohibited such indecencies as low cleavages, the depiction of lingerie, and even the hint of passion. Above all, morality and the sanctity of the home were not to be endangered. Anything smacking of sexual diversity was clearly forbidden.

When Eva finally began her fifth season at the Civic Repertory Theatre, she tried to proceed as if nothing had happened the previous summer. To begin with, she initiated a new producing organization composed of graduates of her Apprentice Group. Eleven actors were selected, including Howard da Silva, Burgess Meredith, Arnold Moss, and May Sarton. The plan was to present six plays during the season at six-week intervals. Calling it The First Studio, Eva hoped to encourage new and untried authors. Under the direction of Civic actor Robert Ross, the young actors used all the equipment and facilities of the Civic. In order to allow for more experimentation, Eva decided on private performances free from critics.

When the first new major production of the year was finally introduced in late October, it revealed the turmoil Eva was suffering. Jean Giraudoux's *Siegfried* had been tremendously popular in Paris two years earlier, but New Yorkers were unimpressed with this American premiere. In this story of a French soldier who developed amnesia during the war, Eva played the crucial role of the soldier's French fiancée. Since the play dealt with a person's struggle for identity, it could have been a personal catharsis for Eva, who was certainly experiencing the same sort of crisis. But once again the critics found Eva's portrayal lacking. The part demanded a passionate performance, but she seemed sluggish, heavy-footed, restrained, and ill-prepared. Never did she suggest a heartsick maiden longing for her lost lover.

Perhaps the greatest outcry from the critics during Eva's tenure on Fourteenth Street came with her next production, Susan Glaspell's *Alison's House*. It was a daring choice, since the story revolved around Emily Dickinson, widely known by this time as a lesbian. The curtain goes up some twenty years after the death of the poet and reveals her spirit brooding over her old house and family. The conflict that emerges concerns the discovery of some unknown poems that tell the story of the poet's thwarted love. Her embarrassed elderly brother wants to burn them, but the younger, more enlightened members of the family fight to save them for posterity. The issue of privacy was one Eva certainly recognized.

Eva's directing promptbook for the production reveals fascinating business for the characters. In order to suggest intimacy and warmth, she introduced lots of touching and embracing. Eva cast herself as Elsa, the niece who had been banished from the family because she refused to renounce her love for a married man. In one scene, she takes the hands of her young cousin Ann and kisses her twice, looking after her as she exits. At another point she crosses the room and rests her hands tenderly on Ann's shoulder for a prolonged moment.[5]

The critics were outraged. They complained in print of sentimentality, perfunctory acting, stereotyped prose, and absence of conflict. Their wrath was obviously rooted in their knowledge of Eva's recent scandal. Coming only five months after the divorce, the play and the character were too much for the critics to tolerate. Whatever Eva's intention with this production, it appeared to backfire.

To everyone's shock, toward the end of the season the play was awarded the Pulitzer Prize for drama. Predictably, the New York critics were furious and accused the panel of judges of narrow vision. In overlooking Maxwell Anderson's *Elizabeth the Queen*, Kaufman and Hart's *Once in a Lifetime*, and Lynn Riggs's *Green Grow the Lilacs*, they rewarded Eva for her theatre enterprise rather than for quality of production. As critic Richard Lockridge argued, the judges seemed "determined to give art a boost, forgetting that there is a difference between a boost and a crown."[6]

If *Alison's House* was controversial, Eva's last production of the year was an undeniable triumph. On January 26, 1931, Eva joined the ranks of nearly 4,000 other actresses through history and presented her interpretation of Marguerite Gauthier in *Camille*. Instead of the emotionalism of so many of her predecessors, however, she was determined to make the character as real as one of Ibsen's or Chekhov's: "It's got to be played true. If you play it true, it's devastating."[7]

Setting the play's action in the 1870s, she was especially concerned that her costumes suggest the development of Marguerite's character. For act 1, designer Aline Bernstein created a lovely, deep beige, satin gown. The matching skirt of lighter beige rayon, along with its draped overskirt, was trimmed with braid and tassels. Over the dress, Eva wore a deep cream, lace shawl. The costume focused on the shimmering glamour of Marguerite, a fashionable demimondaine. Her dress in act 2 was strikingly different, since now she was living at her country house. She wore a fluffy white, organdy dress, whose skirt was made of a series of organdy ruffles trimmed with white Valenciennes lace. Pinned at her waist was a small nosegay of blue cornflowers. It was fragile, very romantic, and showed that Marguerite had become a changed woman.

Artifacts housed in the theatre collection of the New York City Library reveal even more of Eva's attention to reality and truth. Two stage letters that she wrote as the character of Marguerite have been preserved. In act 2 Marguerite writes to Varville, the man she has reluctantly agreed to marry. Eva would neither fake the letter nor scribble, but rather wrote as the character. In fairly legible handwriting, Eva wrote, "My dear Varville, I'm coming to you tonight at last! Be very glad—faithfully *yours*. Marguerite." In act 4 Marguerite learns that her good friend Nichette is getting married. Again Eva wrote an actual letter, saying "My Nichette—I'm dying but so happy for you—Come here when—Marguerite."[8] The penmanship of the second letter was more forcibly strong, and her signature was barely legible, suggesting a woman near death.

Camille became the greatest box-office success the Civic had ever known. Tickets were sold out for all performances. Box seats were filled to overflowing, and standees at the back of the theatre were clumped together as thickly as straphangers in a subway. Critics raved about the improvement in Eva's acting. Only a few years earlier, it had seemed that she was able to play only quiet, reserved characters, but now she showed a much greater range. Perhaps one reason for this remarkable victory was that Eva had hired actress Constance Collier to direct and could therefore devote all her energy to her acting. Perhaps another reason was that Eva could identify closely with Marguerite, an attractive beauty who had fallen out of favor. Both women were social outcasts who hoped for sympathy and understanding.

In spite of her stunning triumph, Eva abruptly announced, the day after *Camille* opened, that she would close the Civic for one year at the end of the season. The last five years had been rewarding, she said, but they had left her exhausted. She needed time not only to rest but to reassess her work. "The Civic Repertory Theatre does not satisfy me," she admitted, "for to be satisfied is to die."[9] She planned to spend the year visiting major theatres in Europe in order to get ideas on how to proceed with her own company. To quiet skeptics who believed this marked the end of her theatre, that Eva would not reopen the Civic in 1932, the editor of the *New York Sun* encouraged her to "be as good as her word; she must take her vacation and come back. Whatever the form of the Civic Repertory's future," he stressed, "it is important that it have a future."[10]

The encouragement was refreshing. Eva was weary of being put on the defensive and of steeling herself against the press. "I'm doing the best I can," she said, "and, I hope, getting better all the time." There were two things that she believed were necessary to make a good actress. "She must develop her personality, must be a woman," she said, "and she must become a good technician." Eva had no doubts about her technical ability, but she knew that she needed time for herself, time away from the theatre. After the harrowing events of the previous year, she feared that unless she took that time she might easily become negative and bitter. "Bitterness is smallness. It isn't warmth," she said, "and you can't be a good actor and be bitter."[11]

From the early days of the Civic, Eva had refused the comfort and diversion she might have found with a more normal social life. She rarely frequented the crowded New York night spots and seldom accepted invitations to large parties. Besides, her schedule of daily rehearsals and nightly performances simply did not allow for that kind of light socializing. The theatre was her life—morning, noon, and night. Her rigid routine was interrupted only by endless fund-raisers, where Eva found herself regularly surrounded by wealthy patrons and champagne. As the Depression dragged on, the fund-raisers started to dwindle. Regardless, Eva began to enjoy the relaxation that champagne could provide.

When the curtain came down on nights when there was no fund-raiser, Eva and Josie would head upstairs to their apartment and prepare a nightcap, usually white wine or Scotch and soda. No doubt the scandal further accelerated their drinking, and without realizing it, Eva was more and more turning to alcohol for comfort. She found that the pressures of the Civic seemed to be more bearable within her and Josie's own private retreat, where they could enjoy the solace of each other, and perhaps a second glass. Although the public was unaware of her growing problem, the theatre company could tell, for Eva occasionally suffered from hangovers during morning rehearsals.

The problem was particularly shocking because Eva's father had been such a renowned drunkard. But recent publications of the National Association for Children of Alcoholics show that 50 to 60 percent of children raised in an alcoholic family become alcoholic themselves, and that adult children of alcoholics, such as Eva, are extremely susceptible to emotional, physical, and spiritual problems. These adults tend to be overly serious, overly self-reliant, unable to trust, and unable to cooperate. They need to be in control and in charge. "These responsible adults," write researchers Herbert L. Gravitz and Julie D. Bowden, "also find that the sense of responsibility and control weighs very heavily upon them. Sometimes they shed this burden of responsibility by taking a drink."[12]

Though written in 1985, these words seem to describe Eva a half-century earlier. She had a compulsion to keep tight reins on her expressions and feelings, and she needed to direct, lead, and supervise others. In most of her relationships, she was unwilling to reveal her innermost self, a problem psychologists now term intimacy-phobic. Indeed, she had a tendency to flee intimacy, since it meant the sharing of feelings, of thoughts, and of herself. When she became intimate with someone, her feelings were aroused, and thus her ability to control was weakened. The phobia certainly affected her acting, for she was often unable to reveal intimacy and feminine passion. But since the phobia was now affecting more of her private life, Eva knew she needed a break from her work.

Almost one year exactly after the divorce shocked people around the country, Eva's name was once again in the headlines. As she and Josie worked in their rose garden on the afternoon of June 12, Eva learned from her maid that the hot-water heater in the caretaker's house that she had recently built would not light. She promised to check it once she finished with her roses. About thirty minutes later, she entered the house and started down the basement steps, striking a match on the side wall. The explosion was deafening, and the whole cellar became a flaming inferno. Apparently a valve had been left open, and for the past half hour, the odorless, propane gas had poured into the cellar. Instinctively, Eva threw her hands in front of her face, ran upstairs, and doused the flames by rolling on the grass.[13]

With massive burns covering her entire body—legs, arms, face, and hands—Eva was literally burned within an inch of her life. In fact, some newspapers actually reported that she had burned to death. Immediately her name was put on the critical list, where it remained for over a week. None of her doctors were confident she would live. Fortunately, since she had worn heavy clothes, had lighted the match at a distance from the heater, and had covered her face with her hands, her life was spared. But her hands suffered terribly. Before she blacked out, she saw that they were hanging in long bloody strips. When she regained consciousness in the emergency ward of the hospital, she felt excruciating pain, as though her hands had been "separated from the rest of her body; they were remote . . . as though they had assumed an entity of their own."[14] The first time the bandages were removed, Eva saw two masses of swollen flesh, utterly shapeless. There was no trace of fingers or bone structure of any kind. She was terrified that she would never again have the use of her hands.

For two weeks Eva bore the pain without the help of drugs of any kind. Doctors told her the more pain she could stand, the better her chances of recovery. Every other day, her doctor treated the lumps of burned meat, picking away the dead flesh. Gradually, with great skill and patient care, he was able to whittle down to the healthy cells that would build her hands again. As time passed, Eva received injections of morphine that provided release from the pain. "It was as though my hands were unscrewed from my arms and went off somewhere, taking their hell with them," she recalled, "and I was left in peace."[15] To hasten the healing process, a new treatment was used. Instead of painful skin grafts, the burned areas were exposed to warm light, causing new skin to grow rapidly.

For a long time the doctors forbade Eva to look in a mirror and actually allowed no mirrors in the room. She looked so hideous, in fact, that Mimsey stationed herself outside the door to warn visitors not to be horrified when they saw her. She looked like a monster. All her hair was charred, jet-black stubble; she had no eyebrows; and her face was red, severely swollen, and covered with dark brown scabs. The one sign of her beauty that remained in tact were her bright blue, Lake Tahoe eyes. Fortunately, the only permanent damage to her face was a slight sagging of her right eyelid.

During the long weeks of recovery, rumors flew. Was she permanently disfigured? Could she walk? Did she still plan to reopen the Civic in 1932? The most vicious rumor described the tragedy as a brawl between two women that ended with a kerosene lantern thrown in Eva's face. When Eva left the hospital, she and Josie, rather than returning to the scene of the accident, visited Eva's benefactor Mrs. Bok in Camden, Maine. Then they drove with Eva's nurse to Provincetown, where they stayed with playwright Susan Glaspell.

Once Eva's strength returned, she and Josie decided to resume plans for a trip to Europe. They dreaded returning to their home and the site of the accident, and Eva did not want to be seen by her public. In fact, for several months she hid her hands with gloves and refused to be photographed. Although they had intended to visit Moscow and Copenhagen, they limited themselves to warmer climates because of Eva's sensitive hands.

Most of their time they spent in Paris, where they stayed at Alice De Lamar's deluxe apartment on the Rue Git-le-Coeur. Trying desperately to strengthen her damaged hands, Eva endured many painful hours playing an accordion. For relaxation, her favorite haunt became the Cirque d'Hiver, one of the city's permanent circuses. The Fratellinis, famous European clowns, appeared there all winter. To Eva, their timing, discipline, and ability to get a laugh made them artists on the level of Bernhardt or Duse. She frequented the circus rehearsals so often that she eventually received an actual offer to appear in an equestrian act.

One autumn day in September, Eva visited her father, who had moved to Paris only a few months earlier. Ironically, the apartment he now shared with his wife, Irma, and his stepdaughter, Gwen, was at 60 Rue de Vaugirard, the same address where Eva and her mother had first lived when they moved to Paris twenty-seven years before.

It was an awkward afternoon tea. Eva did not care for Gwen. She resented the attention her stepsister received from her father and objected to her taking his surname. Since he had not officially adopted her, and since she had none of his blood, she had no right to use his name, and Eva thought she was a cheat. But even more, Eva disliked Gwen's apish behavior. She copied Eva's hair, her clothes, and even her speech pattern. To make matters worse, Eva learned that Gwen had approached lesbian entrepreneur Natalie Barney for a loan, using Eva's name as a reference, and that she had been involved in a police raid in a lesbian bar.

Other guests for tea were Eva's half sister, Hep, and her husband, Robert Hutchinson. It was the first time the two women had been together with their father for over twenty years. Although they had patched up their differences years earlier, the sisters seldom saw each other, since Hep had moved back to England when she married in 1920. Their reunion was a tearful one, since Hep had not seen Eva since the scandal and fire.

Following a few more months in France, Eva and Josie returned to New York so Eva could undergo surgery on her right hand. The main tendon in her little finger had been almost totally destroyed and had to be freed from the scar tissue then cut and spliced together again in order to make it long enough to serve as a finger. This was only the first of dozens of operations Eva suffered through in the next few years.

As this initial bout with surgery healed, Eva wrote most of her first autobiography, *At 33*. It is not surprising that this book says very little about key issues in her life. Not only is there no hint of her sexual orientation, but there is no indication of any kind of intimacy, male or female. She mentions her female attachments—Mimsey, Nazimova, Mercedes, Gladys, and Josie—but only in terms of their professional relationships. She does not discuss the divorce scandal or her growing problem with alcohol. The tragic fire had just occurred, but that, too, is almost absent from the text.

Writing the book could have been therapy for her, a confessional wherein she could have examined her soul. Relating personal challenges and weaknesses could have gained her sympathy from the press and public. But just as she adamantly opposed visiting psychiatrists, so she refused to bare personal secrets in her writing. Apparently she decided that opening up not only would have meant admitting shortcomings and diversions but would have made her more vulnerable to criticism. Eva had always thought of herself as being strong. She could solve her personal problems by herself and did not need assistance. Admitting weakness and need for help was unattractive. Although the book enjoyed critical acclaim and even reached the best-seller list, it was a sham as an autobiography.

Meanwhile, it appeared as if Eva's future was promising. In the last two years, she had received superior notices for her portrayals of both Juliet and Marguerite. As recently as 1930, *The Nation* magazine had placed her for the second time on their Roll of Honor. That same year, she had received two honorary degrees, and eight of the best-known New York critics who chose America's leading actors had ranked her number three, coming after Alfred Lunt and Lynn Fontanne. In a preference poll in Philadelphia, voters had selected Eva as the actress they most wanted to tour with a play, beating out both Helen Hayes and Katharine Cornell.[16] Eva's personal life looked equally optimistic. Josie had damaged her relationship with her mother and had renounced her husband—both because she loved Eva. Even during Eva's bouts with drinking, there was no question that Josie would do anything to maintain her loyalty and love. Their five-year relationship appeared not only in tact but permanent.

Yet Eva was more plagued with doubt and fear than ever before. It was as if the fire had burned away her shell, the outer layer of skin that protected her, and she had become overly sensitive to all outside stimuli. Because of the scandal, she had lost her privacy and now felt naked in front of the public. Because of the fire, she had lost her radiant beauty and now questioned her attractiveness. During her "tussles with the bottle," as she later called her binges, she would tell people to look at her and examine the two very different sides of her face. "This side is the demon," she would say, pointing to her left cheek, "and this side is the good one."[17] More and more she could see the truth in her mother's accusations; she was indeed her father's daughter. As her doubts and fears grew, her former bold and arrogant nature was tempered with growing guilt and shame. The demonic side was taking over. Her already low self-esteem plummeted to new depths.

Eva ends her first autobiography with these words: "All over the country people seemed to be sending me kind thoughts; I'm sure they helped me through an ordeal that had somehow cut my life in two."[18] Although she is specifically referring to the fire, the scandal had been the other half of her personal hell. The events of the last two years had changed her life forever. Her personal life and public career would never be the same.

6

The Greater Depression

As the summer of 1932 approached, Eva was ready to tackle the re-opening of the Civic. During her sabbatical year, she had kept a nucleus of her staff and acting company on a small retainer's fee and assumed they were prepared to resume their work. She discovered otherwise. Her strongest performers—Jacob Ben-Ami, Egon Brecher, and Alma Kruger—had chosen not to return. Their absence not only damaged the company morale but meant Eva needed to find solid replacements.

She began by contacting her former *Liliom* costar, Joseph Schild-kraut. For the past few years, Schildkraut had been acting in films for Cecil B. deMille. When offered the opportunity to join the Civic, he accepted, primarily because of his great friendship and admiration for Eva, but also because his own career was floundering in Hollywood. To complete her replacements, Eva elevated former apprentices Howard da Silva, Burgess Meredith, and Richard Waring into lead performers in the acting company.

Over the months, a new insecurity had been mounting. Eva now worried about her appearance, especially her hands. Dreading that audiences would stare at her crippled fingers, she developed an elabo-rate makeup for them, which she used for the next fifty years. Using tempera paint, she shadowed and highlighted her fingers to give them a realistic appearance. She studied the angles in which they looked best and developed special techniques to achieve these positions. She had never believed in consciously planning movements and gestures, but that was before the fire.

As the opening of the season drew near, Eva reaffirmed her ideals and once again attacked Broadway: "The theatre has fallen into the hands of real estate men and syndicates and those who have no love or interest in the stage or its life, but who have considered it principally as a means to make money."[1]

Although she still appeared arrogant and confident, she was actually very frightened about the future. The economic picture had altered considerably since the time she had founded the Civic in 1926. During her first five years, donations had averaged a little over $100,000 per year, making it possible for her to have a deficit of only $5000 at the start of her sabbatical a year earlier. But during the season that the theatre was dark, gifts dropped dramatically. Because of the maintenance expenses of that year, she was left to begin her new season with a deficit three times that amount.[2]

Desperate for both a popular and an artistically strong comeback, Eva opened the Civic's sixth season on October 26 with a revival of one of her former triumphs, *Liliom*. The overall production was rated as one of the Civic's finest. A critic for *Theatre Arts Monthly* maintained that Eva's portrayal of Julie had "gained in depth and poignancy. Her voice is full and clear, her movement quiet and eloquent. Her Julie possesses a heartbreaking tenderness."[3]

One emotion Eva had definitely achieved was the ability to convey a sincerity in her acting, especially in the scene after the death of Liliom, when Julie sits quietly in her misery, reciting the Beatitudes. Actor Paul Ballantyne remembers that Eva "was always overwhelming in this scene; she would start to read from the Bible, and very soon one realized she wasn't reading at all—she had long known, and had lived every word by heart."[4]

Immediately following the opening of *Liliom*, she revived *Camille*, with Schildkraut as Armand Duval. Since Lillian Gish was to open a few nights later at the Morosco Theatre in Robert Edmond Jones's production of the same play, Eva thought she could capitalize on all the advance publicity and advertised hers as the first performance in New York that year.

The two interpretations were quite different. Eva continued her attempt to make Marguerite Gauthier a believable woman who could exist in 1932. As she explained, "The problem which existed socially then [when the play was written in 1852] exists fundamentally now. The play is based on love and gallantry and bravery, and you know there's nothing more true than these." Gish, however, viewed the character as a person of "great delicacy and charm, . . . a Ming porcelain."[5]

The critics rushed to compare. One reviewer thought Gish "was a cough all dressed up in the costumes of 1875," whereas Eva was a live person. A critic for *The Stage* complained that Gish made Marguerite "a rare girl, too tender and yielding to survive in the jazz atmosphere of today." He preferred Eva's portrayal for having more "blood and sinew" in it.[6] The Gish version lasted fifteen performances; Eva's continued to draw lines at the box office throughout the season. Eva's overwhelming success with *Camille* ever since her first revival in 1931 undoubtedly inspired Hollywood moguls when they filmed Garbo's version only three years later.

In mid-November, Eva directed the premiere production of *Dear Jane*, a new play by Eleanor Holmes Hinkley, based on the life of Jane Austen. To lighten her load, old friend Constance Collier helped with the directing. Josie was cast in the title role. In a prologue set in London's Chesire Cheese Restaurant, Samuel Johnson declares that women are superficial and could never become creative artists. The remainder of the play reveals Jane Austen's determination to be a novelist, as she forsakes three suitors who wish to marry her. Most criticism of the production centered upon the writing; it lacked a conflict. Eva had been attracted by Austen's dilemma, but she had again misjudged the value of a script.

Eva's most remarkable production of the season came shortly before Christmas, when she premiered *Alice in Wonderland*. The project had actually begun while Eva was recuperating in Paris. She and Civic actress Florida Friebus worked to adapt Lewis Carroll's texts of *Alice in Wonderland* and *Through the Looking Glass* into an acting version. Irene Sharaff and May Sarton spent endless hours dreaming with her about design options. Their goals were unanimous: to appeal to adults as well as to children, to adhere closely to the Carroll text, and to costume the characters exactly as they were dressed in the popular Sir John Tenniel drawings.

In the end, Sharaff gave the costumes a one-dimensional quality. Most of the colors, except for characters in the dream, were kept in black and white. The lines were sharpened and drawn in vertical parallels to blend with the background and scenery. The idea was to make the characters appear to be cardboard figures pasted upon a flat surface. Sharaff chose white buckram and sailcoth for fabric because they would retain their stiffness and shape, and she padded some of the costumes so heavily that they weighed almost fifty pounds each. Remo Bufano designed seven-feet-tall Walrus and Carpenter puppets and one-foot-high oyster puppets that danced in boots.

Eva insisted on keeping Alice always on stage, hoping to suggest that all the places and characters of Alice's dream came to her. As the various Wonderland people appeared, Eva introduced descriptive, fantastic musical tags. The Queen of Hearts had a saxophone, and the White Rabbit, a flute. Each character had his own particular instrument as a kind of signature.

Because it was a complex production costing $23,000 and including more than 120 cast members, they had all the staging worked out on paper in advance. Using a diorama, rolling platforms, and a scrim, Sharaff achieved a continuous action with no scene breaks. Josie starred as Alice. Assuming the role of the White Chess Queen, Eva used her previous experience as Peter Pan and actually flew on and off the stage. When she got angry, the White Queen rose into the air.

Critics hailed the production as a new triumph. A sharp departure from the seriousness of Ibsen and Chekhov, the emotionalism of Molnar and Dumas, and the lyricism of Shakespeare, the production was praised for its lightness, enchantment, and fantasy. Of her directing, John Mason Brown recorded that Eva was "in her most dauntless mood, tackling a task of superhuman difficulty, and succeeding where most of her uptown competitors, with much more time at their disposal, would fail."[7] Columbia Pictures contracted with Eva to bring the production to the screen, but the project was shelved after Paramount released their own adaptation.

Less than six weeks after Eva's premiere of *Alice in Wonderland*, the Civic experienced a financial crisis. On January 19, 1933, Eva announced the temporary closing of her theatre. On January 30 she took her production of *Alice in Wonderland* to Broadway as a short-term, emergency measure. She realized she was near defeat and knew her only hope was to cash in on her current success with *Alice*. Eva was learning what countless theatre moguls before and after her had discovered. Good notices do not necessarily pay the rent.

Eva had tried other solutions. Since her poorest business was always on Monday nights and Wednesday matinees, she had appealed to Actors' Equity for permission to replace them with two performances on Sunday. Equity refused. She then sent her patrons a form letter describing the Civic's achievement and begging for help: "We are doing what few theatres in New York are doing, playing to capacity houses. We are now in the eighteenth week of the most successful season we have ever had." No doubt the public was impressed, but the money only trickled in. By the end of the 1932–33 season, Eva had received only $43,000 in donations. Her options were dwindling. Without moving to Broadway she could not meet her weekly payroll for a staff of 115 people.[8]

A major factor in her economic problems was losing Otto Kahn's financial support. He had helped sponsor her first Ibsen tour of *The Master Builder* and *John Gabriel Borkman* in 1926, had donated substantial amounts to the Civic every year, and had guaranteed the annual

$20,000 rent for the theatre. His assistance had not been a mere business transaction. Before he had met Eva, Kahn had known her father Richard. They had corresponded and had even dined in each other's homes. In a letter written in 1930, Richard Le Gallienne thanked Kahn for the interest he had shown in his daughter's career. In deep admiration, Kahn replied, "As for your daughter Eva, she is one of the artistic treasures of New York, apart from being a rare and delightful person. I owe her much more than she owes me."[9]

By 1933, however, the economic depression and ill health plagued Eva's major benefactor. Kahn testified before the Senate Banking and Currency Committee that he had been unable to pay federal taxes in 1930, 1931, and 1932. He had resigned from the Board of the Metropolitan Opera and from the vice-presidency of the New York Philharmonic Symphony Society. In 1933 he took several trips to Europe, seeking cures for his debilitating health. He was in no position now to help Eva and her fading dream.[10]

Eva's move to Broadway unfortunately did not rescue her finances. The Civic's share of the box-office receipts amounted to less than the money taken in on Fourteenth Street. The uptown, Broadway theatre-goers were slow to buy tickets. As Richard Lockridge of the *New York Sun* observed:

> We have talked over much, perhaps, of "art" in relation to the Civic. We have given the impression that it is all very high-minded and worthy, but not on the whole much fun. . . . And it has also been pointed out, rather too often, that the Civic just now needs public support. A visit to "Alice" has been held up too much in the light of a duty, and not enough in the light of a lark.[11]

The critics' references to Eva's noble sacrifice, her dauntless determination, and her dedication to the classics, coupled with her own bullish attitude about Broadway, did not settle well with many theatregoers.

In hopes of increasing business and maintaining some semblance of repertory, Eva persuaded Alla Nazimova to revive their production of *The Cherry Orchard*. In spite of the glowing reviews, she still finished the season with a debt of almost $22,000.[12] It was clear she could not afford to return to her theatre on Fourteenth Street in the fall, yet she was hell-bent on keeping her company together. Eva sublet her theatre and scheduled a national tour of *Romeo and Juliet* and *Alice in Wonderland* for the 1933–34 season. By December of 1933, she had played in New Haven, Boston, Providence, Springfield, Hartford, Newark,

Baltimore, Washington, DC, Philadelphia, Pittsburgh, Cincinnati, Columbus, Louisville, Indianapolis, and Chicago.

Surprises were always a treat for Eva. But when the curtain went up, she always had a short sense of humor. The tour was fairly routine, productions running according to schedule and to script—the way Eva insisted. Washington, however, was different.

On the opening night of *Romeo and Juliet*, the routine took a turn. Eva always prided herself with strict discipline backstage—there was no time for carelessness. She had asked her Romeo, Richard Waring, to use a special little dagger for the final tomb scene. Because it had a tendency to slip out of his costume, he had instructed the stage manager to place it on his funeral bier each night. Since nothing had ever gone amiss during rehearsals, Eva expected this performance to be no different. On this particular evening, however, the stage manager forgot. When Eva reached for the dagger, there was none to be found. She paused momentarily and reached—above, below, and around. Still nothing. Waring was supposed to be dead, so he was of little help. Besides, his eyes were closed, and he did not know what was going on, only that there was an extraordinarily long, deadly long, pause.

Eva knew she must somehow find a way to kill herself, and quickly. She climbed slowly off the bier and stumbled over to Paris's body on the floor. She ran her hands frantically over his body, but discovered that in this scene he did not carry a dagger. By this time Eva was wild. How would she ever end the play? Desperate, she finally grabbed Paris's sword, crawled back on the bier, recited her dying line, "O happy dagger, This is thy sheath! There rust, and let me die," and dropped down on the sword with a thud. By the time the curtain dropped, she was in a rage. So much for routine performances! Still, not a single reviewer noticed the altered ending.

Although both *Romeo and Juliet* and *Alice in Wonderland* were well received, they were a mistake to tour. With casts and crews totaling seventy people and numerous sets for both shows, just the running expenses for each week reached nearly $10,000. Each move the company made within a week added another $1,000. Since Eva received only 70 percent of the ticket sales, she needed to gross at least $14,500 a week to break even. By December 30, 1933, her net loss amounted to almost $19,000. She was drawing enough to cover her weekly running expenses, but not enough to pay for her original production costs.[13]

In spite of her setbacks, Eva continued to hold on to her vision. In the midst of her struggle, she wrote to May Sarton that she felt fortunate that she had "won her spurs in the regular (and often horrible) mill of the commercial theatre before starting to fight the Wind Mills of idealism." And fight she did. "I do believe in miracles," she confided. "You should know that I will never let Tinker Bell die without a battle. I also know the rocks in the road."[14]

Eva received a nod of immense encouragement during the tour. Following a performance in Washington, DC, Mrs. Franklin D. Roosevelt invited her to the White House to discuss the status of the American theatre and the problem of unemployed actors. At the First Lady's request, Eva proceeded to map out in detail her plan for a national theatre. Essentially, she wanted theatres like her Civic at a number of locations in the country, all with free acting schools and all subsidized by the government. "The government would furnish the financial support. And why shouldn't it? It provides funds for purely material schemes. Spiritual or artistic pursuits are essentials, too." When asked if such a theatre might not become a means of disseminating political propaganda, Eva replied, "I think that could be avoided. A State theatre would be rather like a State museum. Not much politics there."[15]

Soon after the meeting, Eva sent a copy of her proposal to President Roosevelt and received an invitation to leave her tour for a few days so she could meet with him and Harry Hopkins, head of the Federal Emergency Relief Administration. During the conversation, the president urged her to apply for the directorship of the National Theatre Division of the Works Progress Administration, soon to become the Federal Theatre. However Eva's concern was for quality theatre rather than creating jobs. The president "wanted to save hungry actors from starving. . . . I wanted to make the theater a way of life only for those with talent and determination enough to qualify."[16] Eva was so intent on her own ideas that she lacked the foresight to see other possibilities for saving her theatre.

In a move Eva would come to regret bitterly, she refused the president's offer. Under Hallie Flanagan's supervision, the Federal Theatre soon attracted such artists as Elmer Rice, Eddie Dowling, John Houseman, and Orson Welles. During its four years of existence, over eight hundred plays were produced in regional theatres from coast to coast, with titles ranging from *Macbeth* to *Ghosts* to *Emperor Jones*. Forty-five plays toured. Several times, the Federal Theatre had successful plays running simultaneously on Broadway and throughout the country. At one point, 10,000 people were on the payroll of the Federal Theatre. With her brash decision, Eva missed an opportunity to make her Civic the flagship of a national federation of theatres.

Eva's rationale at the time is cloudy. She may have hoped that if she played her cards right she could secure government backing for the Civic without the burden of supervising the entire national circuit. After all, Hopkins had promised her that he would investigate finding funds specifically for her theatre. A few weeks later, when she returned to Washington at Hopkins's request, a substantial subsidy looked hopeful. In conferences with Hopkins and Madame Perkins, the secretary of labor, Eva agreed on $90,000 annually. Accepting their word that everything was settled and that she could count on the money, Eva rejoined the tour.

On December 18, 1933, Eva sent Hopkins a telegram from Chicago, informing him she would return to Washington if he needed to confer with her. Nine days later, she wired another telegram stating, "Vitally important to talk to you at once. Where can I reach you tonight or in the morning? Sorry to bother you but desperately worried." Although Eva has written in her autobiography that Hopkins never responded, a carbon copy of a telegram in his official papers shows that he asked her to telephone him the next day. The exact content of that telephone conversation is unknown, but on January 2, 1934, Eva received a telegram from Hopkins stating very clearly, "No hope for direct subsidy from government. Terribly sorry."[17] Her hopes at securing federal aid were dashed.

Eva found the remaining months of the tour terribly frustrating, and for the first time in her career, her nightly bouts of heavy drinking began to show. In one of her letters to May Sarton, Eva noted that the most important goal of hard work should be happiness. Work is rewarding "if one can find joy in it now and then."[18] But at this point in her life, joy was fading.

For the first time, Eva began to show another side to her audiences. In Philadelphia she failed to keep a speaking engagement, declaring there was a "complete misunderstanding." When she finally did appear along with Ethel Barrymore, the two actresses berated their audience. Eva insisted she had never broken an engagement in twenty years. "I would think by this time you would have a little faith," she scolded. Only days later in Pittsburgh, she presented a lecture before the Drama League and complained of the loudspeakers echoing her voice. When a photographer took her picture, she reportedly threw up her hands and shouted, "Young man, you don't know what that means to me. I nearly lost my hands in an explosion. I'm really quite sick."[19]

When the company reached Detroit in late January 1934, Eva was forced to try another survival ploy. She decided to keep only a small nucleus of her company together to tour an Ibsen repertory—*The Master Builder*, *A Doll's House*, and *Hedda Gabler*. She earnestly believed that if they could stick together for another year, some miracle might come along.

The Ibsen trio of plays appeared at first to be the answer. They were certainly less expensive. During the next three months Eva toured from Minneapolis to California, returning to the East through Texas, Kansas, and Nebraska. All but two stops showed a very healthy operating profit. But even though these plays had surprised her critics by actually paying for themselves, they could not erase the earlier large deficits resulting from *Romeo and Juliet* and *Alice*. She ended the season with a total net loss of $17,000.[20]

Soon after Eva had changed her tour repertory to the Ibsen plays, the company arrived in Minneapolis, Minnesota. Following an evening performance of *A Doll's House*, Eva went to the Municipal Auditorium, where she had agreed to auction off birthday cakes in honor of President Roosevelt. As she started the bidding, she said, "I am not going to raffle off these cakes as cakes alone. They represent the struggle of a man to overcome a tremendous physical handicap. They are your opportunity to help others do the same." Apparently miffed with the poor response to her plea, she marched to a microphone, which she had previously refused to use, and decried:

> I came to Minneapolis proud of my Viking ancestry, and I'm still proud of it. You can't be Vikings. You aren't even good Americans. You make me ashamed of the country I have chosen as mine. You are lousy Americans and unpatriotic dollards. . . . Who said Minneapolis is the Scandinavian capital of America? You haven't a drop of Viking blood in your veins.[21]

Although later insisting that she called them "terrible," not "lousy," Americans, her inflammatory denunciation made headlines across the country.

At Eva's performance of *Hedda Gabler* in Oakland, California, only a thin partition separated the stage from 7,500 cheering high school youths at a basketball game. According to a United Press release, Eva became so furious with the noise that "she went to the footlights and told her audience what she thought about it. 'We are sorry,' she said, 'that we could not do better.' There was an icy restraint in her voice."[22] Some newspapers reported that she emphasized her remarks by brandishing Hedda's guns.

Certainly compounding Eva's turmoil during the Ibsen tour was the unexpected disruption in her personal life. The relationship between

Eva and Josie had always been unique. Josie was content in playing the role of the faithful, obedient, loving spouse. She needed to nurse someone and wanted to be the perfect helpmate. Eva, however, was not so noble. She insisted on her independence and would not agree to monogamy. From the very onset of their relationship, Eva had pursued other women. More than once, she brought her latest interest home and asked Josie to take a long walk so they could be alone. Because Josie desperately wanted the relationship to last, she resisted confrontation and allowed Eva most of the freedom she wanted. She was the perfect enabler, making it possible for Eva to continue with her cruel and selfish behavior.

By 1934, however, even the dutiful Josie had reached her limit. As financial problems plagued Eva, Josie found herself faced with a self-centered partner who had become an alcoholic. Josie might have survived Eva's brief dalliances, but what led to her ultimate departure was the hurtful introduction of another relationship. Sometime the previous year, Eva had met Marion Evensen; the exact time and location are unknown. Marion, more commonly known as "Gun," was an actress who had moved to New York from the Midwest. A very tall and handsome woman eight years Eva's senior, she looked typically Scandinavian. Only an adequate performer at best, she was awestruck with the famous, even notorious, Eva Le Gallienne.

Because of Eva's passionate infatuation with Gun, Josie decided by early spring of 1934 to end this impossible liason. As she explained to May Sarton, she could tolerate almost anything from Eva except her wanderings. She simply could not accept anyone, especially her own mate, having "more than one person at a time."[23] Josie's first and only relationship with a woman had proved to be a disaster. Josie agreed to finish the scheduled tour in which she was playing Thea Elvstead in *Hedda Gabler* and Nora in *A Doll's House*, but she adamantly refused Eva's offer to perform the Ibsen repertory on Broadway in the fall. Josie had successfully passed a screen test during their California engagement, had signed a long-term contract with Warner Brothers in mid-April, and knew she must remain in Hollywood if she wanted to make a clean break from Eva. It was announced that Josie's film debut would have her starring opposite Dick Powell in Mervin LeRoy's *Gentlemen Are Born*. When the film was finally released later in the year it brought her little satisfaction. Reviewers echoed their criticism of Eva's attempts at playing love scenes. They did not believe Josie in her romantic scenes and complained that she did not know how to kiss.

For a brief time after the tour ended, all three women—Eva, Josie, and Gun—lived in Eva's Connecticut home. The atmosphere was frigid. Once Josie announced her decision to leave, Eva wanted nothing to do with her. As May Sarton observed, "When Eva finished with a person, she finished!"[24] Eva and Gun stayed upstairs while Josie packed her bags.

But when Josie finally left in early May, Eva fell into an unusually deep depression and began to behave oddly. Almost daily she drove to New York and was seen getting drunk in the bars. One late night, as she was driving back to Connecticut after a night on the town, she slammed into a large boulder at the entrance to her home. She was so distressed and lonely at one point that she even turned to religion. She dressed like a nun, carried a beautifully bound missal, and attended mass daily.[25] Finally, on May 12, the very day that Josie arrived in Hollywood, Eva once again sailed for "Old Nurse Europe."

Eva never fully recovered from the split with Josie, who was to be her most consummate love throughout her years. Although she swore she would never be unfaithful again and vowed to remain with Gun forever, theirs was not a great romance. When Josie married a man one year later, Eva's sense of rejection was overwhelming.

In the midst of this upheaval, Eva wrote some advice to May Sarton, who was experiencing some discrimination over her own lesbianism.

> The best one can do is be a decent person and realize that lack of understanding always promotes a kind of cruel criticism and censorship. People hate what they don't understand and try to destroy it. Only try to keep yourself clean and don't allow that destructive force to spoil something that to you is simple, natural, and beautiful.[26]

If only Eva could have heeded her own advice. The forces within her had spoiled her beautiful union with Josie.

When Eva returned to New York from Europe, rather than search for a new script that might suit her talents or even a classic that might suit her gender, she began preparations for a production of Rostand's *L'Aiglon*. Ever since she had seen Bernhardt's portrayal in 1916, Eva had wanted to play the role. She did not seem to realize that the dated play was not right for the times, nor could she predict that the practice of actresses playing men's roles was no longer in fashion. It was ingrained in her that she needed to play certain parts before she was thirty-five, and this was one of them. She would proceed, regardless of what it meant to her reputation. She would dare to play a man.

Written especially for Sarah Bernhardt, the romantic drama was popularized in America in 1900 by Maude Adams. It focuses on the psychological dilemma of Napoleon's son, the duke of Reichstadt. Referred to as "The Eaglet," he longs to regain his father's lost empire but is physically too weak and dies of tuberculosis. Eva would direct and also play the duke. Supporting her were many of her loyal Civic actors—Richard Waring, Donald Cameron, Leona Roberts, Walter Beck, Paul Leyssac, and Sayre Crawley—as well as Ethel Barrymore and Eva's new partner, Marion Evensen.

Newspapers in such remote places as Portland, Oregon; Jackson, Mississippi; and Knoxville, Tennessee, announced that Eva's twenty-year dream was finally being fulfilled. The project became so widely publicized that rumors were started that she planned to make a film version of the production.

Eva wanted to avoid the complaints other actresses had received when playing the role of the duke. Sir Max Beerbohm had criticized Bernhardt because she looked, walked, and talked like a woman. William Winter had complained that Maude Adams was effeminate. Eva argued that it was "a mistake to play the part as a languid weakling from the beginning. The duke had an intense, burning energy, inherited from his father. . . . He was a fine horseman, fond of putting his regiment through maneuvers."[27] She chose to play the duke with as much strength and masculinity as she could muster.

Although some of the New York critics felt Eva still played too intellectually, nearly all agreed the performance was one of her best. It was a three-dimensional portrayal, with subtle shades of tenderness as well as fierceness. Brooks Atkinson complimented her clarity of outline and rated the production on a par with the Civic's *Alice in Wonderland*. The production proved so successful that the original four-week run was extended another month.

About two weeks after *L'Aiglon* opened, Eva and Gun attended a performance of a play that ripped through Broadway like a thunderbolt. The play was Lillian Hellman's masterwork *The Children's Hour* wherein a closeted lesbian kills herself after confessing her love for her best friend. The theme clearly expressed that lesbians were viewed as outcasts. Although the play enjoyed a long run in New York, it was banned in Boston because of its portrayal of "perverts." Fearing public outrage, Samuel Goldwyn changed the story into a heterosexual love triangle for his 1936 film version and forbade any reference to the original title. The total impact was lost.

In 1979 the original producer, Herman Shumlin, remarked that he now found the suicide unconvincing and unrealistic, but that in 1934 it had seemed very natural: "I remember how stunned everyone was in the 1920s when Le Gallienne's affair with Josephine Hutchinson hit the headlines. People thought it was simply frightful, and I wondered how they would have the courage to go on with their careers or simply to go on."[28] When Eva saw the last scenes of *The Children's Hour*, she was outraged. Even with all of her personal struggles, suicide had never been in her thoughts. She was furious that Hellman had offered it as a solution, and she stormed out of the theatre during the curtain calls.

After *L'Aiglon* closed in late December, Eva took the play on a three-month tour subsidized by the Shuberts but under the banner of the Civic Repertory Theatre. Wherever she played, the production was praised. When the tour ended in late March, she had played a total of 200 performances in twenty-seven cities. At one point, she was suffering from ghastly pain due to a nine-pound tumor on her leg, but she never missed a performance.

If only the box-office draws could sustain the failures, but Eva's Civic was no different than most other ambitious art projects. Survival was always a battle. Later that year, Eva was planning to launch another adaptation of Ibsen, but this left a span over the summer without work and, worse, without income. Vaudeville was in full swing by now, and the need for bookings was profound. A new experience—what could be better?

"Four-a-days" was the popular format, so Eva found herself doing programs preceding the four showings of the featured film. During one particular week at New York City's Capitol Theatre, the management had booked a Scotch comedian, a seal act, and Eva. Later she starred in Alfred Sutro's one-act play *The Open Door*. After closing in New York, she and Donald Cameron played the balcony scene from *Romeo and Juliet* at a movie theatre in Washington, DC. Although it was exhausting and light on prestige, it helped pay some bills.

At the beginning of the 1935 fall theatre season, Eva began her Ibsen tour by featuring her own translation of *Rosmersholm*. It was a final attempt to hold it all together. She directed and assumed the female lead of Rebecca West, an emancipated woman who attempts to make a man the instrument of her will.

After a monthlong tour to Baltimore, Boston, and Buffalo, Eva opened the play in New York for a limited two-week engagement as a prelude to a national tour. A complex drama, its elusiveness and subject matter appealed to Eva, but in this assessment, she stood alone. Nowhere was the production well received. The typical comment was expressed by a critic for the *Boston Herald*, who wrote, "The play is filled with talk, eloquent, fervent talk, but talk that deals with issues no longer clear or especially important."[29]

The New York critics were baffled to say the least. Especially with rumors of financial collapse, they could not understand why Eva chose to spend her energy on such a stodgy and dated play. Richard Lockridge of the *New York Sun* put it most succinctly:

> Even if Miss Le Gallienne's traveling museum of the stage has brought us one of its better exhibits . . . it might be well for Miss Le Gallienne to strike the old flag, and let the library bury its dead amid the moan of the professors. . . . Instead of producing rather dull plays by Ibsen because they are by Ibsen, it would be heartening if she would join the theatre of 1935.[30]

In the decade during which Eva had resurrected the plays of Ibsen, audience's tastes had greatly changed. They no longer could see that his issues were relevant. More and more, they wanted American plays dealing with American problems.

The familiar cycle, the same shared by other dreamers in the theatre, was now complete. A need was discovered, an artist emerged to meet the challenge, and for a moment or two there was magic. The tragedy is that these theatrical eras are so unpredictable and short-lived. It was all too clear that Eva's moment was also about to pass, and after ten years of struggle, it was time to finally admit defeat. After a short engagement in Philadelphia, the Civic Repertory Theatre disbanded for good, and the players were left to go their separate ways.

Even though Eva's dreams had dimmed, she had proven her major theories. The thirty-seven plays presented by the Civic were plays Eva believed should be as available as books on a library shelf. Besides five of Ibsen's dramas, she produced two of Shakespeare's, two of Rostand's, and one of Molière's. Her championing of Chekhov prompted Modern Library to announce that her Civic Repertory Theatre "undoubtedly has done more to familiarize America with the work of the great Russian dramatist than any other group."[31]

Although most of the Civic's productions were modern classics, Eva did not restrict her selections to plays that had proven themselves on Broadway. Her production of Chekhov's *The Three Sisters* was the New York premiere. *The First Stone*, *Alison's House*, and *Dear Jane* were new works by American playwrights. *The Good Hope* and *The Cradle Song* had been presented on Broadway previously but not successfully. She introduced New York to plays by Goldoni, Giraudoux, Bernard, Wied, Anet, and Mohr. She recognized that some of these plays would not become popular attractions but argued their selection on her theory of repertory—"the strong plays must help the weak ones."[32] Even a theatre specializing in the modern classics, she believed, should find room to produce unproven scripts.

Though Eva might be faulted for not presenting more American plays, she did try. During her second season, she bought the rights for *Harlem*, a play about a mixed marriage, and planned to star Paul Muni. She was forced to abandon the project at the last minute, however, when Muni went off to Hollywood. In 1929 she was offered Elmer Rice's *Street Scene*. She subsequently refused it after lengthy discussions, because she felt it needed a larger number of experienced actors than she had in her company.

For ten seasons Eva had maintained her goal of repertory. In the year before her sabbatical, she presented eighteen productions, five of which she had opened in her first season. *The Cradle Song* was offered for seven seasons; *The Master Builder*, six; *John Gabriel Borkman* and *Hedda Gabler*, five; and *The Three Sisters*, *The Cherry Orchard*, and *Peter Pan*, four.

By keeping her ticket prices low, she developed a loyal audience composed of students, secretaries, shopkeepers, and clerks. The location of the theatre on Fourteenth Street attracted many foreign-born Americans living in Lower Manhattan. They were not wealthy, well-groomed playgoers, but because of their enthusiasm, they created an excitement that leaped from row to row like an electric spark. According to one critic, the atmosphere in the audience was always of "people who have come to the theatre not for something to do after dinner, but because they love the theatre. One really ought to go there about once a month just to recapture the feeling of theatregoing."[33] During the years when the Civic was permanently situated in a theatre, the average attendance had risen from 78 percent of capacity to nearly 94 percent.

In spite of her failure with *Rosmersholm*, Eva's acting had vastly improved since 1926. She had played thirty-one roles. As she predicted when she began the Civic, work in repertory broadened her compass as an actress. Each time she repeated a role, she brought to her characterization new depths and richer subtexts. By 1935 she had developed an approach to acting that would remain with her for the rest of her career. Intent on making her characterizations appear realistic, she carefully plotted their logical development in the play. Constant attention was given to maintaining her technical skills of vocal control and bodily movement. But when rehearsing and performing, her acting was dependent on her concentration. She tried to think and listen as the character, often including pauses to draw the audience into her thought process. Frequently, her approach to acting was considered cold and intellectual, because she sometimes projected her characters' surface intentions without the subtle richness of a subtext. But as her acting developed at the Civic, such criticism came less frequently.

Directing thirty-three plays had also developed Eva's talent as a distinguished director. At the first rehearsal, Eva always read the play to the company, making no attempt to act it out but rather to set the tone. This was followed by several full-company readings, until the meanings were clear and the actors had clear ideas about their characters. Only then did they begin to explore on the stage. From the very earliest rehearsal she insisted on a complete conception of the play: "Doubt is fatal. . . . Everything must be definite in one's own mind. One must not say to one's actors: 'Do you think so and so?' There must be unity about the conception. It must be one person's idea. Actors know when a director is befogged."[34]

She had clear concepts not only of the characters but of all the technical elements, from the lighting to the smallest prop. She was so involved in all areas of production that her head carpenter once said the crew "wanted to resent her at first, until they discovered that she not only knew their jobs as well as they did, but oftentimes, much better."[35]

Eva's most vital function as a director was building an ensemble, one in which each actor was important for his unique contributions, and in which all worked as a harmonious unit. Rather than direct as a dictator imposing her ideas, she looked at rehearsals as a collaborative effort, saying, "I leave my players alone. I want their minds to be free to work intelligently. We have so few real actors and actresses because the directors want to do it all."[36] She assured the actors, however, that she would keep a tight rein on the overall rhythm and would make sure that their contributions fit her concept.

Eva's success was due to her ability to build a sense of trust and loyalty. Many company members were friends she had known for years and had performed with in earlier productions. Several were actually related: Beatrice de Neergaard was a second cousin to Eva; Leona Roberts was Josie's mother and the wife of Walter Beck; Sayre Crawley joined the company with the understanding that his wife, Mary Ward, would also be taken on; and Donald Cameron and Eva became so close that they were practically considered brother and sister. By the end of the fourth season, fourteen of the twenty-five members of her permanent company had been with her three years or more. The years of playing together clearly had an effect. As Brooks Atkinson remarked, the Civic had become a first-rate company. Such an esprit de corps developed that Howard da Silva remarked, "With us there may have been a little of the feeling that we were art and that everything else was junk."[37]

The stories of two actors illustrate Eva's concept of loyalty. J. Edward Bromberg started with the Civic's Apprentice Group and rose in the ranks until he was playing leading roles. He was beginning to build quite a following and was often credited for improving the quality of Civic performances. But when he announced in the fall of 1930 that he wished to join the Group Theatre at the end of the season, Eva released him immediately. If he was not going to be loyal to her ideals, then she did not want him around.

Eva hired Tonio Selwart when he migrated to this country from Germany in 1932. A handsome man, he was often called the new Rudolph Valentino. With his vast amount of acting experience in Europe, Eva knew he would be an asset to the company, and she began making plans to have him play leading roles opposite her. She knew he would be a perfect Romeo or Liliom. Some directors eager for immediate results would have rushed him into those major roles, but Eva would not offend her family of actors. She demanded loyalty, and she exhibited it as well. Tonio would just have to wait.

As a director, she worked very quietly, almost inconspicuously. Actor Paul Ballantyne remembers that she very seldom, if ever, spoke to an actor from the auditorium during rehearsal. "I never heard her lose her temper or berate anyone. She would climb up the steps, cross the orchestra pit, take the actor by the arm, and walk slowly upstage, talking to him or her."[38] Eva used this technique because she knew it was easier to discuss something—even a pointed attack on characterization—alone. It was less embarrassing, less threatening, and more helpful than discussing it in front of the others.

Undoubtedly Eva's determined personality created the unity in the company. Though a very quiet, reserved person, she had boundless energy and could put in a thirty-six-hour day every day. She assumed many of the leading roles and directed all but three of the plays. She assumed minor roles in six productions, and in another six, she did not appear at all. Her company knew she had given up an established Broadway career, had little use for stardom, and was willing to work tirelessly for her ideals.

Like all theatre companies, the Civic productions evolved their share of lore. Very few practical jokes were played, however, for Eva was deadly serious backstage. She demanded adherence to rules and strict discipline. During one performance of *Peter Pan*, however, she exited the stage with howls of laughter. Some spirited person had dressed up her cairn terrier Tosca to look like one of the Indians. The actors loved to tell the story of Egon Brecher's mistaking which play was slated for performance one evening and entering the scene wearing the wrong costume. And they often talked of the time the company played a whole act without one of the principals. Merle Maddern had forgotten a specially booked matinee and was ultimately discovered resting in her hotel room. The performers' desperate but brilliant improvisation managed to fool the audience, as well as several of the apprentices watching from the back of the house.

In spite of her many achievements, Eva's stubborn refusal to compromise certainly contributed to her downfall. Because she insisted on performing in repertory, American playwrights were slow in offering her their plays, believing they could make more money with a long run on Broadway. And finding actors interested in performing in repertory was difficult. Theatre historian Alfred L. Bernheim articulated the commonly held opinion of theatres like the Civic: "It matters not a jot how artistically perfect a stock company may be. It is still a stock company, and that means of a low order, in the minds of the public. . . . The stock or repertory company is déclassé. Actors who can make Broadway do not play in stock."[39] Even though Eva could guarantee actors more weeks of work than they could find elsewhere, she could not offer the prestige that most performers sought on Broadway.

When she did manage to engage top performers like Nazimova, Ben-Ami, and Schildkraut, they did not remain long. Although Nazimova agreed to revive her role in *The Cherry Orchard* in 1931 and in 1933, she was a permanent member of the Civic company for only one season. Ben-Ami remained for two seasons, and he did not return to the Civic after Eva's sabbatical. After one year of repertory, Schildkraut returned to Hollywood. Top talent among the apprentices Eva discovered and groomed—such actors as Arnold Moss, John Garfield, and Bobby Lewis—left the Civic when tempted by more lucrative offers.

Too much of the Civic's success depended on Eva alone. She established the philosophy, set the budgets, hand-picked the actors and staff, arranged the rehearsal and performance schedules, directed and starred in most of the productions, supervised all the designs, and organized the fund-raising. As May Sarton quipped, "She did everything except play in the orchestra."[40] When in a reminiscent mood many years later, Eva admitted that she had been wrong in not allowing others to share her responsibilities.

Although there were occasional disagreements about some of Eva's decisions, who was to utter a word? The company fawned over her. She was so worshiped that many of the younger actresses began imitating her style of dress, her walk, and even her acting techniques. If someone had challenged, Eva would not have listened. She needed to remain in control and refused alternative views and outside assistance. Her vision was set in stone. When one of her latest hits could have sold every ticket with an extended run, she refused to alter her plans and insisted on maintaining her repertory schedule. Indeed, some of her own performances may have been improved if she had submitted to the will of guest directors.

Her most insurmountable problem, however, was financial—the inability to continue the Civic without outside subsidy. Even during the 1928–29 season, when she played to 91 percent of capacity, she had lost $100,000. As of August 31, 1935, the Civic Repertory Theatre had a net capital deficit of $94,000.[41] In a time when America was still bailing out of the Depression, the debt was monumental. Eva had built a large and faithful audience, but her insistence on low ticket prices was her unraveling.

At the young age of thirty-six, Eva seemed out of touch with the temper of the times. Serious audiences were interested more in contemporary social commentary than in her menu of European classics. Among the current attractions in New York were Group Theatre productions of Clifford Odets's *Waiting for Lefty* and *Awake and Sing*, Maxwell Anderson's *Winterset*, and Sidney Kingsley's *Dead End*. The leftist sentiments in these plays appealed to theatregoers caught in the severe economic crunch.

When she was forced to sublet her theatre on Fourteenth Street in 1933, it should have served as an ominous signal to Eva that the new tenant was The Theatre Union, a company dedicated to these new ideas. But Eva was unable to perceive that she was out of touch. Instead, she put the blame on her audiences: "People more and more are losing the power of either listening or thinking in the theatre."[42]

For ten years Eva maintained her "house of prayer." During that decade she weathered significant losses—her privacy, her beauty, and her lover. Now she was faced with another loss, her theatre. Although her accomplishments had been impressive during those years, she could not go on. But she was not yet ready to admit her weaknesses and her mistakes. Rather than view her seasons as would a football coach, with a numerical win-loss record, she fought to justify her work and to excuse her limitations: "What does so-called success or failure matter if only you have succeeded in doing the thing you set out to do. The DOING is all that really counts."[43]

Obviously, Eva had done a great deal. Her monumental efforts were the result of an artist with passion for her work, but the doing is not all that counts. At least as important is the quality of the doing, not just of the productions themselves but of the management decisions. She must have felt that her greatest accomplishment would have been to continue the Civic indefinitely or at least to have been respected for her efforts. By 1935 neither was possible. She had failed.

Shortly before Christmas, Eva and Gun packed their many trunks and drove the one-hour journey from New York City to their Connecticut retreat. Snow was falling gently. As the car passed the houses and farms along the way, Eva could see that everyone was busy preparing for the happy holidays. The joy she saw around her added to her own misery. During the long silence, Eva wondered what the New Year would bring for her. It all looked so very bleak.

As a two-year-old.
Author's Collection.

Eva, her Nanny's two sisters, her Nanny, and Hep, her half sister, enjoying afternoon tea at Nanny's home in Farncombe. Author's Collection.

As an eight-year-old playing the role of a shrimp-gatherer in a school play. Author's Collection.

At the age of fifteen with her half sister, Hep, on the
right. Author's Collection.

By the age of nineteen Eva was supporting Ethel Barrymore in *The Off Chance*, 1918, and beginning a relationship with Alla Nazimova. Author's Collection.

Alla Nazimova was starring as Hedda Gabler when she
first met Eva (1918). Courtesy The Billy Rose Theatre
Collection, The New York Public Library for the Performing Arts, Astor, Lenox and Tilden Foundations.

Eva with Evelyn Chard in *Liliom*, 1921.
Author's Collection.

My Fashion

Correspondence

By PAULINE MORGAN

"As Eva Le Gallienne wears sports clothes so effectively, she has consented to pose in two of our smartest models. The golf outfit is an imported tweed in green, blue and brown plaid, with knickers cut on mannish military lines that button at each side—there is likewise a button cuff below the knee. A knee length coat is worn with this—a full belted model with huge pockets and an inverted pleat at the back.

"For riding, the covert suit adds a waistcoat made exclusively by us, of tan and brown homespun. It has a silk back, is made surplice fashion and fastens at the back with a button. Both outfits are designed and made by us, and cannot be found elsewhere."

Abercrombie & Fitch Co.

She modeled "mannish" fashions for Abercrombie
and Fitch in *Theatre Magazine*, August 1921.
Author's Collection.

As a doll, Eva Le Gallienne
shows that some quality of
restraint which marks her
Julie in "Liliom"

A new toy rage was to create dolls delin-
eating characters in Broadway plays,
1923. One of the first dolls made was ordered by Eva, who presented it as a gift
to Alla Nazimova. Author's Collection.

Eva Le Gallienne, in *The Swan*. The Princess exposes her ears but not her heart, and pities men more than she loves them.

As early as 1923 subtle hints about her alternative life style began to appear, as in the caption provided for the above caricature. Author's Collection.

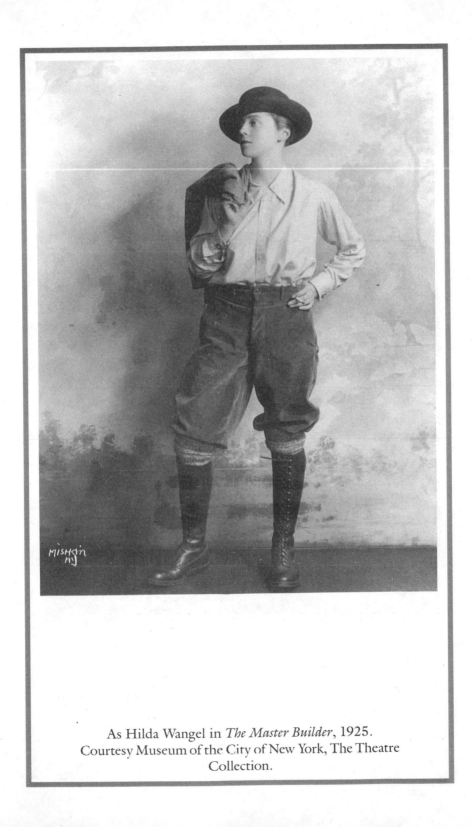

As Hilda Wangel in *The Master Builder*, 1925.
Courtesy Museum of the City of New York, The Theatre
Collection.

She opened the Civic Repertory Theatre on Fourteenth
Street on October 25, 1926. Author's Collection.

EVA LE GALLIENNE
in "Three Sisters."

Caricature by MATIAS SANTOYO

Her production of *The Three Sisters* in 1926 was the
English-language premiere. Author's Collection.

A bobbed Hedda Gabler, 1928. Courtesy The Billy
Rose Theatre Collection, The New York Public
Library for the Performing Arts, Astor, Lenox and
Tilden Foundations.

Eva, Sayre Crawley, and Alla Nazimova in *The Cherry Orchard*, 1928. Author's Collection.

The Theatre
Perishing!
Says St. John Er...

Don't You
Believe
Answers the Edi...

Eva Le Gallienne in the title role of "Peter Pa...

Eva makes the cover of *Theatre Magazine*, March
1929. Author's Collection.

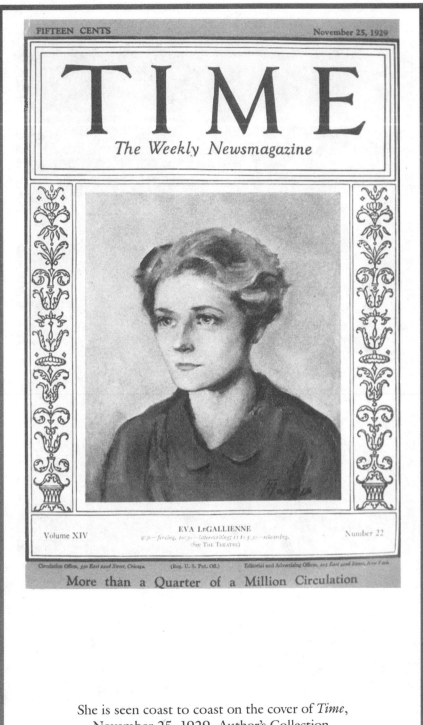

FIFTEEN CENTS

November 25, 1929

TIME

The Weekly Newsmagazine

Volume XIV

EVA LeGALLIENNE
9:30—fencing, 10:30—letter-writing; 11 to 5:30—rehearsing.
(See The Theatre)

Number 22

Circulation Office, 350 East 22nd Street, Chicago.   (Reg. U. S. Pat. Off.)   Editorial and Advertising Offices, 205 East 42nd Street, New York.

More than a Quarter of a Million Circulation

She is seen coast to coast on the cover of *Time*,
November 25, 1929. Author's Collection.

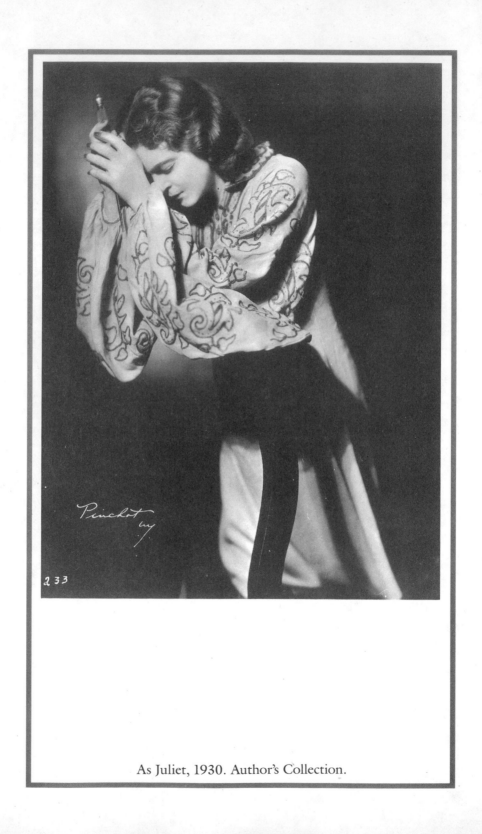

As Juliet, 1930. Author's Collection.

CLEAN DRAMA

Then there is the play which straightens
out everything in the last act by getting
the heroine into gingham and winding up
her romance in front of a canvas meadow.
You are wrong in thinking that the young
man in the sweater is Eva Le Gallienne

This cartoon and caption
appeared in a magazine in
the early 1930s and is included
in the "Lesbian Scrapbook"
at the Kinsey Institute.
Courtesy the Kinsey Institute
Collections.

As Marguerite Gauthier in *Camille*, 1931. Courtesy
The Billy Rose Theatre Collection, The New York
Public Library for the Performing Arts, Astor,
Lenox and Tilden Foundations.

As the White Queen in *Alice in Wonderland*, 1932.
Author's Collection.

Josephine Hutchinson in the title role in *Alice in Wonderland*, 1932. Author's Collection.

Richard Waring and Eva in *Camille*, 1935. Courtesy
The Billy Rose Theatre Collection, The New York
Public Library for the Performing Arts, Astor, Lenox
and Tilden Foundations.

May Sarton, c. 1937. Author's Collection.

Lois Hall and Eva in *The Cherry Orchard*, 1944. Author's Collection.

As Elizabeth I in *Mary Stuart*, 1957.
Author's Collection.

Eva and Farley Granger in *Ring Round the Moon*,
1963. Author's Collection.

Dolores Sutton, Farley Granger, Eva, Signe Hasso, and two unidentified women at a reading for *Liliom*, 1964. Author's Collection.

Margaret Webster, Sylvia Sidney, Leora Dana, and Eva rehearsing *The Madwoman of Chaillot*, 1965. Heavy street makeup was typical for Eva after her tragic fire. Author's Collection.

Eva and Sloane Shelton in *The Trojan Women*, 1965.
Author's Collection.

In her front garden at Toscairn, her home in
Connecticut. Author's Collection.

In her workshop at Toscairn. Author's Collection.

As Queen Marguerite in *Exit the King*, 1968.
Author's Collection.

A Hirschfeld caricature during the run of *The Royal Family*, 1976. © Al Hirschfeld. Drawing reproduced by special arrangement with Hirschfeld's exclusive representative, The Margo Feiden Galleries Ltd. New York.

Ellis Rabb, Rosetta Le Noire, Joseph Maher, Mary Louise Wilson, Sam Levene, Eva, Rosemary Harris, and Mary Layne in *The Royal Family*, 1976. Courtesy Cliff Moore.

Eva and Nana, 1976. Author's Collection.

Eva and Tim Wilson in the Seattle Repertory Theatre
production of *The Dream Watcher*, 1977.
Author's Collection.

Ellen Burstyn and Eva,
1979. Author's
Collection.

Kim Hunter and Eva at the Alley Theatre in the world
premiere of *To Grandmother's House We Go*, 1980.
Author's Collection.

Eva auditioning pigs for *Alice in Wonderland* with
Anne Kaufman Schneider standing in the *upper left*,
1982. Courtesy Wide World Photos.

Eva's last commercial photograph, 1982.
Author's Collection.

7

Beyond Joy

The Connecticut terrain was wild and rustic. Eva wanted nothing more than to withdraw from the public eye and to forget the agonies of recent years. The first six months of 1936 were spent in the solitude of her home. During heavy snowstorms, the half-mile, ruddy old lane leading to the house from the main road was usually closed to traffic. The isolation was perfect medicine.

Eva set about making improvements on her farm. Since she needed space to accommodate all of her theatre memorabilia, she decided to remodel her nearby caretaker's home and move in there. Her prized addition was her new study, the Blue Room, named for its blue Italian walls. Bookshelves were everywhere in the room, with one shelf devoted to the works of her father. On another shelf, the two-volume biography of Sarah Bernhardt that Eva had copied in longhand some thirty years earlier sat like a shrine. Eva gained strength surrounded by her memories of better times — Hedda's armchair, a sofa from *Camille*, the spinet from *Dear Jane*, a favorite old ottoman used in most of the Ibsen and Chekhov plays. Positioned strategically on her desk were Juliet's dagger, L'Aiglon's riding crop, and Masha's snuff box. Large windows behind her desk overlooked her magnificent rose garden.

On these wintery days of the new year, Eva took her breakfast in the Blue Room. Though Gun would usually prepare a large breakfast of fluffy scrambled eggs and bacon and even serve the food, she was seldom allowed to join Eva. Eva wanted her privacy. She would lie back on her chaise for hours, reading the prayers of St. Thomas Aquinas or those of religious mystics such as Anchoress Juliana of Norwich. On the wall behind her hung an original Mucha poster of her idol, Sarah Bernhardt. She would gaze through her large window at all the activity — in the mornings the birds at their feeders, in the evenings dozens of raccoons and skunks scrambling for food at their wooden trough. She had fun dreaming up names for all these creatures, some took on names from parts in plays and some from real people.

It was on one of these solitary mornings that Gun coined a new name for her partner. Eva had never liked her Christian name, but no nickname ever stuck. Gun finally came up with "LeG" as a pet name, "Miss LeG" for more formal occasions. This shortened version of her surname followed Eva throughout her life.

LeG's days in Connecticut were usually spent completely alone. Like her father before her, LeG had discovered that she felt more relaxed, comfortable, and creative in seclusion. She built a tiny, one-room cottage in a hidden, very peaceful meadow. It had a little kitchenette and combination library and sitting room. LeG called this private studio "Nuja," a name derived from the word "nugatory," which means of little value or worthless. But the remote hideaway was really of tremendous value. Throughout the long winter, LeG trudged through high snow drifts so she could spend endless hours by herself reading, meditating, dreaming—and weeping.

Gun knew that LeG was not to be interrupted when she escaped to Nuja. So many questions plagued LeG. Had she accomplished much in the last ten years? Was she truly the anachronism that her critics claimed? Had her time passed? How could she afford to continue supporting Gun? Could she find other means of making a living? How was she going to pay her bills?

One restless afternoon, LeG suddenly recalled a conversation she had with Duse in 1923. Though Duse was the supreme actress of her day, she became disenchanted and turned her back on the theatre for twelve years. "What is it really worth," she argued. She felt she would never be able to fulfill her dream of an ideal theatre, so she quit. She returned to the theatre after World War I out of sheer necessity—she needed money. Thirteen years earlier, LeG had only "dimly understood her meaning,"[1] but now it made sense. Should she also turn her back on the theatre?

A career woman who derived much of her identity and self-esteem from her work, LeG had a compelling need to achieve. She was against a wall, to be sure, but could she really give up? She recalled one of Duse's favorite expressions—"The dead help the living"—so she began to read all of their old correspondence. On one telegram were these words: "You will find a new strength in the new effort. . . . Very happy to find you again in full battle. . . . All shall be well." It was exactly the encouragement LeG needed: "I have sometimes felt that the memory of the things she said to me, some of them buried deep in my subconscious mind for many years, came to the surface, as I needed them, like messages from another world."[2]

Fortified to resume her work, LeG accepted a summer theatre role—her first in nearly twenty years. Assuming the part of the wise and witty heroine in Congreve's *Love for Love*, she performed with Van Heflin and Dennis King at Lawrence Langner's Westport Country Playhouse for a week. Pleased with the experience, she commented, "I felt audiences would be relieved to see me in something gay after a lot of gloomy parts."[3] It was a rewarding run. The local press gave her a good review, and ticket sales broke box-office records. Hundreds of disappointed patrons were turned away each night.

During work on the production, Langner and Theresa Helburn asked LeG to rejoin the Theatre Guild and play Mathilde Wesendonck, Richard Wagner's passionate mistress, in a new play called *Prelude to Exile*. The experience of submitting to another director and management was not a pleasant one. Nazimova warned her that director Philip Moeller never preplanned his rehearsals. To LeG's dismay, she soon discovered it for herself: "He had obviously worked nothing out in his own mind, and the movements and business were left to the improvisation of the moment. . . . He was very self-conscious and . . . more aware of himself than of the play or the actors in it."[4] The entire first week was spent in reading and discussion. Not until the third week did the cast rehearse on stage, and then they discovered that the floor plan was radically different than they had expected.

Following tryouts in Princeton and Philadelphia, the play opened in New York on November 31, 1936. No one cared much for it or LeG's performance. The critics thought the play contained weak dialogue and worse motivation. LeG's notices were predictable—playing a passionate mistress was not in her makeup. She was accused of worshiping Wagner with her mind rather than her body. Perhaps she should have known better than to have accepted this role, but her need for work clouded her reason.

LeG had predicted the critical response during rehearsals and had begged the producers to close before reaching New York. The thought of being attacked once again by the critics made her literally tremble. Her fear was compounded by a renewed desire to start another repertory theatre. As she explained to an admirer:

> Thank God the play I am in (which you can guess I am not very keen about!) closes next Saturday. I am then going to the country to do a lot of preparatory work on a new scheme I have in mind—for I have not given up! And I realize very clearly that the Broadway commercial theatre is not for me—it has no relation to the theatre I love.[5]

LeG's sad return to Broadway furthered her resolve to once again strike out on her own. To be sure, the Civic had collapsed around her. This company that had been viewed as the Great Hope, indeed the Saviour of American theatre, had, in the end, become an embarrassment. And yet for ten years, it had provided LeG with a venue for her art and her need to perform. She originally opened the Civic at least in part because she felt blackballed by the "old boy" network and feared her career was in jeopardy. Nothing had really changed. She still felt rejected and sincerely believed that she had no alternative.

After the five-week run of *Prelude to Exile*, she began to develop her new scheme in earnest. With financial backing promised from Mrs. Bok, LeG planned to gather a small company of actors. Rather than attempt the financial risk of beginning in New York, they would spend the fall and winter in Connecticut, rehearsing a repertory of plays to present prior to the regular summer season at the Westport Country Playhouse. As preparations for the new company continued, she again looked to summer theatre work for income.

In August, LeG followed the precedent set by Sarah Bernhardt and Charlotte Cushman and played another male role, the lead in *Hamlet*. When she had performed *L'Aiglon* successfully in Chicago in 1935, a critic had suggested, "And why not a Le Gallienne Hamlet? . . . I think this poet's daughter has the poet's mind for the part, the cerebral graces as well as the physical."[6] Since she had earlier considered playing the part, this was all the encouragement she needed.

To solve the discrepancy of a woman playing a man, LeG chose to play Hamlet as a youth. She hoped that playing the role as a boy would make the story more convincing:

> His melancholy, his thoughts of suicide, his hero-worship of his father, his mercurial changes of mood, and above all his jealous resentment at his mother's second marriage, are touching and understandable in a boy of nineteen, whereas in a man of thirty they indicate a weak and vacillating nature in no way admirable or attractive.[7]

LeG and other members of the company produced all the costume fabrics for the production on a hand loom she had purchased the previous summer. Executed by Helene Pons, LeG's costume broke tradition by not being totally black. Setting the play in the Viking eleventh century, LeG wore a black jersey leotard with padded shoulders, but her tunic was red, historically a dominant color in the Danish court. Cut with dolman sleeves and with the front fullness stitched together at the waist, the tunic helped to disguise the fact that the part was played by a woman. Appliquéd on the front was a stylized design of the three Danish crowns.

Reviewers came from both Boston and New York, even though LeG had decided to perform at the less prominent Cape Playhouse in Massachusetts rather than at Westport. Although a Boston critic described LeG's portrayal as "a rival to Bernhardt," the New York critics were not as laudatory. They compared her acting to a school teacher's recitation that lacked vigorous assault.[8] Once again, they complained there was not enough passion.

In spite of the unfavorable criticism, Lee Shubert urged her to play a limited engagement in New York, to be followed by a national tour. But through the years, LeG had been worn down. She dreaded the inescapable comparison with the John Gielgud and Leslie Howard Broadway productions of the previous year and declined the offer. She later wrote, "The thought of all the fuss and commotion and publicity, the quips of columnists, the storm of controversy that a 'female Hamlet' would in all likelihood provoke, filled me with dismay."[9] Why ask for trouble?

For a brief period LeG returned to her repertory plans. Using many of the *Hamlet* cast members, including Uta Hagen, who had played Ophelia, she began rehearsing several plays. She began to search for a highly experienced actor to play opposite her, but she failed to interest any leading man in the project. They would not gamble on her or on her new scheme. The reasons are obscure. Perhaps men felt uncomfortable teaming up with such a notorious lesbian. Perhaps her name had the stamp of failure. She soon disbanded the company.

Once again LeG went back to Paris. During the visit, she found her next vehicle, a new play about Marie Antoinette called *Madame Capet*. The author had taken for her theme a phrase from a letter written to the young Marie Antoinette: "You will have to suffer to find yourself." Antoinette is pictured in the play as a woman who is deprived of everything—her possessions, her title, her dignity, her family, and, at last, her life. LeG felt a kinship with the character. She purchased the production rights and sent a script to her New York agent.

When LeG learned several weeks later that Eddie Dowling had agreed to produce the play, she left on a brief sweep through Europe, visiting Ibsen's birthplace, then traveling to Bergen, Norway, where she examined the promptscripts Ibsen had made when he was stage manager for the local theatre. What meticulous directions he left. Every movement and piece of business was written out in detail. After visiting her mother in Copenhagen for a few days, LeG returned to America in time to begin work on *Madame Capet*.

After a three-week tryout in Philadelphia, the company arrived in New York to open on Broadway, October 25, 1938. When LeG entered her dressing room about one hour before the performance, she discovered the show's closing notice on her makeup table. What a shock: "This was the first and last time in all my theatre experience that a management had seen fit to announce the closing of a play before it has even opened!"[10] She begged Dowling to continue the run, but he closed it after a week. The reviews were devastating, and besides, Dowling had turned his attention to a new script he hoped to produce the next year, William Saroyan's *Time of Your Life*.

Without a Broadway run to cover her finances and her need for discipline, LeG had no choice but to return to "four-a-days." Vaudeville was barely tolerable during the mid-thirties, when LeG had preceded film showings and had considered it a lark. By the late thirties, vaudeville was getting even more seedy, but LeG felt she could get through a few weeks. Though it was a kiss of death and indicated a deteriorating career, she could not afford to worry about saving face. She was desperate for work.

Entertainer Frank Fay planned a two-month engagement in New York, to be followed by a short run in Boston. Engaging Elsie Janis as the headliner, Smith and Dale for the comics, and Maxine de Shone for a striptease, he hired LeG to play the *Romeo and Juliet* balcony scene as the "class act." Besides being an embarrassing comedown for a woman of LeG's background, it was also a financial disappointment. For nine weeks she received only $2,200, about a third of what Fay had promised her.[11] Business had been good, but Fay continually cited poor ticket sales when payday rolled around.

The entire month of August 1939, LeG toured summer theatres as the female lead in Noel Coward's *Private Lives*. Doing the strawhat circuit was a unique experience. It was blatantly a star package concept, with LeG as the box-office draw. After a two-week rehearsal in New York, the company drove to Westport for one rehearsal on Sunday. The next Sunday they traveled by car and bus to the next theatre on the list, carrying only their costumes and makeup. At each stop they had new scenery and props. Though highly touted for tourists in the local press, the typical summer production was mediocre at best. The quality mattered little to audiences, since the vacationing masses wanted light entertainment and a chance to see a star. But for LeG it meant a guaranteed salary and a percentage of the box-office receipts.

At the end of the summer, LeG prepared for a national tour that would keep her working for most of the 1939–40 season. Since the past two years had been rather dismal, she eagerly accepted the offer from Arthur M. Oberfelder and Fortune Gallo to tour *Hedda Gabler* and *The Master Builder* under the banner of the Legitimate Theatre Corporation.

Although LeG was playing her favorite roles again, she did not escape some glaring problems. The management had also booked tours of *Golden Boy* and *On Borrowed Time*. LeG's troupe had preceded the others during the first part of the season, and she was not aware of the quality of the other productions. Later, when she followed, she heard complaints of shoddy acting, incompetent direction, and shabby scenery. Unfortunately, the other companies were so inferior that their quality eventually affected her own ticket sales.

A more immediate problem was the sudden illness of LeG's leading man, Earle Larimore. She had chosen him because of his extensive experience playing major roles with the Theatre Guild. Three weeks before the tour ended, she learned he was in the last stages of pulmonary tuberculosis. Since he could not perform, she needed to find a quick replacement. Two performances of *Hedda Gabler* were played by her stage manager, before Civic actor Staats Cotsworth joined the company.

After spending most of the 1940–41 season on a dull and tedious lecture tour to universities and women's clubs, LeG was eager for a return to the excitement of live theatre and quickly accepted an offer from the Theatre Guild to direct popular-priced revivals the next season. Intending to introduce a new production every four weeks, the Guild announced the following schedule: *Ah! Wilderness, The Rivals, He Who Gets Slapped, R.U.R., John Gabriel Borkman, The Devil's Disciple, Desire Under the Elms,* and *Alice in Wonderland*. The announced roster of stars included such luminaries as Spencer Tracy, Raymond Massey, and Charles Laughton. Following a short tour, each production was to play a limited Broadway engagement.

Unlike her years at the Civic, when she single-handedly made all the decisions, LeG now faced working with a board of directors. From the beginning she had reservations about the board's casting of Mary Boland in the role of Mrs. Malaprop in *The Rivals*. During their engagement in Toronto, Lawrence Langner had provided a new song for the production. When Boland heard the satirical lyrics for the first time, she refused to perform unless the song was eliminated. Rather than play the lusty, broad farce that LeG wanted, Boland insisted on giving her character the delicacy of a Dresden china doll.

Although she grudgingly consented to perform, Boland caused more problems during the remainder of the tour. In St. Louis she refused to attend brush-up rehearsals. When she became ill prior to the New Year's Eve performance, LeG was forced to take over the role herself with less than two hours' notice. A few weeks later in Chicago, Boland suddenly cleaned out her dressing room, quit the company, and could not be found for two performances. She cited illness as the reason, but more than likely she was annoyed that costar Bobby Clark received better reviews.[12] LeG eventually replaced her with Margaret Anglin.

Haila Stoddard played Lydia Languish and has fond memories of the production. Because of LeG's vast scholarly and artistic background, she knew what she wanted. It gave her a unique sense of freedom, which she was able to give to the entire cast. She would urge them on: "I don't mind anything you try. I love being surprised at rehearsals." Encouraging freedom could have posed problems, since the cast reflected such contrasting styles—Bobby Clark the superb clown, Walter Hampden the classical tragedian, Mary Boland the flighty comedienne, and a young cast of neophytes. Yet LeG was able to blend all the disparate parts, the contrasting styles, into one whole, as if she were weaving a magical tapestry. They all respected and trusted LeG's judgment. It was such a wonderful, delightful experience—so wonderful, in fact, that the two-week engagement in Chicago was virtually sold out, and it was considered "one of the gayer moments of the [New York] season."[13]

Stoddard had the opportunity to play opposite LeG during several performances and to compare her performance of Mrs. Malaprop with that of Boland and Anglin. She could sense the difference the nights LeG played. She always felt there was a thin, beautiful scrim between LeG and the audience. Somehow, with many performers, an audience feels they know all about the person when they see them perform. But with LeG there was a slight veil, something remote about her. The company had great respect and admiration for her, but they realized that her long-cultivated air of privacy was also present in her work.[14]

The many months of rehearsals, performances, tours, battles with Boland, and last-minute stand-ins for her leading lady left LeG exhausted. She reportedly became very ill with pneumonia while waiting to begin the next production, so the series of revivals ended with *The Rivals*. After recuperating for two weeks in Arizona, she returned home.

Her reunion with Gun was a strain. During extended separations over the past two years, major problems had begun to surface in their relationship. The first few years they had been together, Gun had accompanied LeG on her tours and had taken small roles in productions. She had always worshiped LeG. She had cooked, kept house, and waited on her devotedly. Her entire existence revolved around serving LeG. Even in the early stages of their relationship, LeG had occasionally abandoned her partner for late evenings and new encounters, but now Gun was being left alone for long periods of time. Unable to drive a car, she was sometimes snowbound for weeks. She felt stranded in a countryside that may have been solitude for LeG, but for Gun it was downright desolate, especially when she could picture her lover cavorting with other women as she traveled from city to city. Gun's despair resulted in drinking. She became such an extreme alcoholic that when LeG would return home from a tour, she often found the cupboards bare, the house in total disarray, and Gun passed out on the floor.

It is impossible to answer certain questions. Did LeG's neglect cause Gun to drink more? Did LeG search for times to be away from home because she and Gun were incompatible? Did Gun's insecurity and fear of another woman create a barrier in their relationship? No matter what the answers, Gun's excessive devotion to LeG became mawkish.

In the beginning LeG wrestled with her initial vow to Gun that she would remain faithful and never leave her. In the end, however, she brought home a new companion. LeG did not ask Gun to move out, since she knew Gun had no means of supporting herself. She did, however, change their roles in the household. From this point on, Gun was little more than a cook and housekeeper. LeG was definitely fed up with having to keep Gun on, yet she was determined to uphold at least part of her vow; Gun would not be thrown out. Instead, as May Sarton observed, "she became LeG's cross to bear."[15]

LeG's new partner was Margaret Webster, better known as "Peggy." The two women had known each other since childhood in England. In fact, Peggy and her parents had even visited the Le Gallienne's Old Manor in Chiddingfold. Peggy had spent most of her career in England, appearing often with the Old Vic Company. In 1937, she came to New York to direct Maurice Evans in *Richard II*. During the four years that followed, she directed Evans in *Hamlet* and *Henry IV, Part I*; and for the 1939 World's Fair, she directed *As You Like It*, *The Taming of the Shrew*, *A Midsummer Night's Dream*, and *The Comedy of Errors*. Indeed, she had been dubbed by the critics as America's foremost Shakespearean director.

In so many ways, Peggy complimented LeG. She was jolly, witty, and very outgoing. Intellectually, she and LeG struck fire. They knew so many of the same people in the theatre world. They spoke the same language and could banter back and forth on ideas like players in a tennis match. They talked of Europe and England, of art, music, and history. At times they reenacted entire scenes from Shakespeare in the Blue Room and brainstormed hypothetical productions. They viewed themselves as cultured Europeans who were more enlightened than the crude, uneducated masses of Americans.

LeG's main criticism of Peggy was her smoking. Although LeG certainly smoked her share of Chesterfields as well, she despised Peggy's smoking as she walked down a street and talking with a cigarette stub dangling from her lips. It was gauche, and whenever Peggy persisted, LeG refused to acknowledge her presence.

Though Peggy kept her New York apartment on Twelfth Street, where LeG often joined her, she spent most weekends in Connecticut. The situation was almost impossible for Gun, the displaced lover. Not only was she forced to move downstairs to the first-floor guest room, but now she cooked and cleaned for Peggy as well. She struggled as she overheard them both attack American theatre and boorish audiences; she agonized over the romantic sounds from upstairs.

LeG seemed virtually unconcerned about Gun's feelings. Gun was a woman who had been her lover, who actually continued to love her and certainly doted on her. Yet LeG, who hid her inner feelings from the public eye, never concealed from Gun her obvious feelings for Peggy. Gun would actually bring them tea as they sat together hand in hand before the cozy fireplace. In the mornings, she would make the bed they slept in, as they ate the breakfast she had prepared. LeG had established these new roles. Gun was to be the housekeeper, and that was that.

About this time, LeG received an offer from Pepi Schildkraut to star with him in a new play entitled *Uncle Harry*. The story is about a kindly gentleman who plots against his possessive sisters, murdering one and placing the blame on the other. After his sister is convicted and sentenced to die, Harry attempts to confess. Although LeG's role of the convicted sister was a large one, the play's lack of literary quality concerned her. According to Pepi, "She consented to take the part . . . on one condition; as soon as *Uncle Harry* finished its run, I was to play Gaev opposite her in Chekhov's *The Cherry Orchard*."[16]

After several preview performances in New York, the play opened to rave notices. George Freedley of the *New York Morning Telegraph* announced it was the town's newest hit. "The fact that she [LeG] is a star has had the tendency of concealing the fact that she is one of the best character actresses on the American stage." The play was not a street massacre carried out by a gang of thugs but a cerebral drama where the characters plotted their deliberate course of action.[17] LeG's restrained style of acting was the strength behind her character. *Uncle Harry* ran 430 performances and became the longest running play of her career.

During the run, LeG's mother died of cancer. Mams had spent her last few months living with her daughter and Peggy in Connecticut. As might be expected, Gun cared for her night and day. Though LeG had never been particularly intimate with her mother, she still felt a deep sense of loss. "I can only say I am infinitely grateful that mother had no pain—no struggle—but it does feel awfully strange. I keep thinking she's in Europe and that I should be writing to her!"[18] She accepted that their values were quite different, and yet she could always count on Mams. LeG had always resisted sharing her personal life with out-siders, so Mams's death meant that she had one fewer person she could confide in, feel close to, and share ideas with.

Also, her mother's death reminded LeG of her own mortality. At the funeral service, one of LeG's friends hugged her and whispered, "Isn't it strange? Somehow we think our mothers will never die?" Odd, to be sure, but that was exactly LeG's thought. Even though she had witnessed the slow but steady deterioration of Mams's health, she was not prepared for her death. Suddenly she was no longer a child, a daughter, a woman of the younger generation. Her mother was dead, and she felt thrust into middle age.

During the long run of *Uncle Harry*, LeG and Peggy formulated plans for working together. To launch their partnership, they decided they would first produce *The Cherry Orchard*. They would use their own version, which they prepared with the aid of LeG's old friend, the Russian novelist Irina Skariatina. Mrs. Carly Wharton and Peggy would produce, LeG would direct and play Mme. Ranevsky, and Pepi would play Gaev.

LeG had always maintained that Chekhov's plays needed a special kind of acting. Actors accustomed to focusing on the star or to relying on theatrical tricks needed to discover a new method of working.

The quality of a Chekhov production depends so tremendously on what goes on beneath the lines, on the almost casual interplay between the various characters, on a truth and simplicity so thoroughly understood and digested that it becomes effective in a subtle unobtrusive way in no sense dependent on the usual theatrical externals. It is a sort of flavor that permeates the whole ensemble—a mood, an aura. . . . Instead of doing, one must simply be.[19]

In spite of her actors' previous experience or style of working, LeG insisted that they submit themselves to her methods.

When the production opened January 25, 1944, it marked the first Broadway presentation of the play since the Civic's 1933 revival. To LeG, it was a joy to be playing in a great play again. It ran for an unprecedented ninety-six performances. In September, the company embarked on a five-month tour to major cities in the East and Midwest, winding up with a one-week engagement at the New York City Center.

Before leaving on the tour, however, LeG acted as an adviser for Peggy and Cheryl Crawford's production of *The Tempest*. Since World War II had just ended, *The Tempest* seemed to be a particularly pertinent classic to revive, pleading as it does for peace and reconciliation. Two years earlier, LeG had become intrigued by the play and had devised a production scheme for it. Her plan called for Prospero's island to be mounted on a revolving stage that would rotate visibly. After the beginning scene of the shipwreck, the stage lights would never be dimmed or blacked out; each scene would flow quickly into the next. Because LeG was not a member of the Scenic Artists' Union, she could not be listed officially as the set designer. She did, however, receive title-page credit. Following one hundred performances on Broadway, the play was sent on a five-month tour.

The elaborate production was a nightmare to mount. One plan was to have Ariel fly when Prospero says, "Be free, and fare thou well." During the Boston tryout, LeG, who had flown as Peter Pan, tried to demonstrate the technique. Three times she flew up some thirty feet only to be dumped on the floor by clumsy stagehands. According to Peggy, they "were all scared stiff and looked on with white faces."[20] Eventually, the effect was scrapped, because the actress playing Ariel, Vera Zorina, did not want to risk the danger. There were additional tensions—the scenery got lost during a blizzard and did not arrive in time for one performance; the actor playing Caliban, Canada Lee, fell asleep onstage and was awakened by the stage manager prodding him with a stage brace; an electrician put the stage in total darkness for several minutes when he forgot to plug in Ariel's special lamp. LeG nearly went mad at the Broadway premiere: "I hadn't been to a New

York opening night in so many years I'd forgotten how *horrible* they can be—it makes you feel you never want to play again! I think it's so much worse when one's nervous for someone one loves, than when it's just for oneself."

The grind of touring *The Cherry Orchard* and the agonies of opening *The Tempest* left LeG exhausted. She wrote to May Sarton:

There *might* be fear of my not wanting to bother with the theatre anymore—in fact I'm pretty sure I should never act again were it not for the necessity of carving my living! Such an idealistic artist I am! You see the theatre as it exists in this country is becoming increasingly *impossible*. It is such torment to achieve anything even approximately good. All joy has been taken out of it—it is surrounded by a lot of barbed wire—prickly and uncomfortable with lots of petty, nasty, selfish, little rules and regulations. I *hate* it all.[21]

The remaining months of the winter and spring of 1945 found LeG relaxing in the divine peace and beauty of her home. She found it soothing to be snowbound with the sole companionship of simple creatures of the woods. In early April she penned another letter to May:

I can't tell you how heavenly the spring is here. . . . I wish you could walk down the lane here, with me—daffodils, poeticus and violets all over the place—and at the old house the hillside is covered with masses of naturalized daffodils—and the forsythia and bridal wreathes are beautiful beyond words. I don't know what I'd do without such things! I spend my days working in the garden now—and attempting frightful paintings—but at least they soothe me and keep me out of mischief—and I shall not attempt to inflict them on the world—so it's not an 'evil' occupation! . . . I am well and peaceful here—I wish I never had to leave.[22]

By autumn, however, LeG did leave—for another production on Broadway. She agreed to star with Victor Jory and Peggy's mother, Dame May Whitty, in an adaptation of Zola's *Therese Raquin*. She did not particularly like the play but looked forward to acting under Peggy's direction for the first time. Critics complained about both the play and the acting. Designed as a sensational melodrama, it was labeled monotonous, sedate, and superficial. They could see no development in LeG's character from the woman who cheats on her husband to the conscience-torn murderess. The production was a failure, but because of the numerous theatre parties booked in advance, it continued to run for three months. The play "ran just long enough to suit me," LeG confessed. "I don't think I could have born with her much longer. She was rather an exhausting wench."[23]

LeG had still not abandoned her dream of another repertory theatre. This time it would be with Peggy's help, for she would not make the mistake again of shouldering all the responsibility herself. Besides, the New York theatre scene looked different than it did ten years earlier when her Civic folded. There were signs of possible government subsidy and grants from corporations. Serious young playwrights such as Arthur Miller, Tennessee Williams, and William Inge were taking their first bows on Broadway. In 1944 Williams urged his friend Margo Jones to open a new theatre: "Right after the war there is bound to be a terrific resurgence in the arts. . . . Many, many boys will come out of this war with a desperate thirst for creation instead of destruction. There is your chance, Margo!—I believe that you are a woman of destiny!"[24] LeG undoubtedly agreed with Williams. Here was her chance; the timing seemed perfect.

Also encouraging her was the rapturous applause given the New York visit of Laurence Olivier as he led England's Old Vic in a repertory of four classics. If he could pull it off, why couldn't she? LeG was adamant! "If we can't swing it this time—I shall feel I've done my share of trying and call it a day—and concentrate on earning a decent amount of money somehow—and *retire*."[25]

Although Pepi was originally to be been involved, he left for Hollywood after the Chekhov tour, under a long-term contract with Republic Pictures. Cheryl Crawford now joined the planning. Her background made her a valuable addition. In the 1920s Crawford had served on the executive staff of the Theatre Guild, and in the 1930s she was one of the founders of the Group Theatre. More recently, she had successfully produced *Family Portrait*, *Porgy and Bess*, and *One Touch of Venus*. She also made an attractive partner because she blended in with LeG and Peggy's alternative life style.

By the beginning of the 1945–46 season, the three women had designed a format to permanently establish the American Repertory Theatre (ART). Their promotional efforts were endless. They spoke before fifty clubs and organizations during the year, traveling to Pennsylvania, New Jersey, Massachusetts, and Connecticut, and making pitches to such diverse groups as Kiwanis and Girl Scouts. They appeared on forty radio programs; fifteen were broadcast nationwide. In a promotional brochure, they attacked Broadway "Show Business" for its policy of "Best Sellers only" and demanded that the country needed a repertory theatre specializing in the classics.

In outlining their production scheme, they indicated plans to open with two plays in September 1946 and to add four more during the season. In the second year, they would tour coast to coast with the most successful productions and rehearse plays to supplement the repertory. They believed the theatre could become a self-supporting business enterprise within three years. An essential part of their plan was an educational program for the New York City public schools. To encourage student audiences, members of the company would conduct discussion sessions about the plays in high school classrooms.

By the time the ART opened in November 1946, the prospects looked good. They had sold almost $300,000 in stock, to more than 142 people. Joseph Verner Reed contributed $100,000; William Paley, $10,000; and Mrs. Samuel Goldwyn, $5,000. Among the other sponsors were Mrs. Efrem Zimbalist (formerly Mrs. Bok), Katharine Cornell, Carl Van Doren, Helen Hayes, Fredric March, Mary Martin, Peggy Wood, Robert Edmond Jones, and Jo Mielziner. By selling subscriptions at $6.00 each, they registered more than 5,000 patrons by opening night. The first week of ticket sales brought in $50,000 in mail orders.[26] Stories appeared in newspapers throughout the country, trumpeting the project. Who might have guessed from all the buildup and ballyhoo that the ART would last only two years?

Over the course of several weeks, LeG, Peggy, and Cheryl auditioned literally hundreds of eager actors. They wooed Marlon Brando by offering him such roles as Oswald in *Ghosts* or Hamlet. "You are all unusual women," he noted, "the likes of which one doesn't get the opportunity to know in a life's span."[27] He eventually rejected their offer—perhaps because of this same unique quality. One year later he would make theatre history with his legendary performance as Stanley Kowalski in *A Streetcar Named Desire*.

Among the younger, lesser-known recruits were Efrem Zimbalist, Jr., Eli Wallach, Anne Jackson, and Julie Harris. Wallach was just starting his career and had wanted desperately to be part of the company. He had read LeG's autobiography, *At 33*, and knew she was an innovator and pioneer, a star who "stuck to her guns with quality work and didn't take the glamour route." Looking back on those years with pride, Wallach remembers that the "attitude of the company was wonderful in the beginning; the spirit was great. Some of us only got paid $80 a week, but nobody cared about the money. We knew she was a stalwart, and we wanted to work for her."[28]

Thirty actors were finally selected for the permanent company. Although the top salary was only $500 a week, every actor was guaranteed two forty-week seasons. The total payroll amounted to $4,500 a week, only about a third of what the company could expect in a regular Broadway production.[29] But as the founders emphasized, even they were making financial sacrifices in order to establish the theatre. Both Katharine Hepburn and Mary Martin expressed great interest but declined because of the low salaries. In the end, besides LeG and Peggy, other prominent members of the acting company were Victor Jory, Richard Waring, Walter Hampden, and June Duprez.

Following tryouts in Boston and Philadelphia, the ART opened its first New York season on November 6, 1946—twenty years after the Civic—with Shakespeare's *Henry VIII*. One of Shakespeare's less popular plays, under Peggy's direction it was played for color and spectacle. The costume budget alone totaled $40,000, with each of Jory's *Henry VIII* costumes costing a minimum of $750.[30]

The following week, the company introduced the next plays of their repertory, Peggy's production of Sir James Barrie's comedy *What Every Woman Knows* and LeG's revival of Ibsen's *John Gabriel Borkman*. A month later they added Shaw's *Androcles and the Lion*.

By the end of the year, the company's future was predictable. During Philadelphia tryouts of *Henry VIII* and *What Every Woman Knows*, LeG and her partners had expected $23,000 in ticket sales but received only $19,000. Before opening in New York, Crawford had insisted on dropping the expensive repertory scheduling of a different play each night in favor of presenting each play for its own individual run. Forced to compromise, LeG and Peggy reluctantly agreed to rotate plays on a half-weekly basis to cut costs yet keep some semblance of repertory. Ticket prices were to remain as low as possible, yet when LeG arrived in New York, she discovered that Crawford had advertised a $7.50 top for the opening night and the customary Broadway prices for the rest of the season. In despair, LeG told Peggy, "That is the end of the American Rep. We might as well all go home!"[31]

Crawford's last-minute insistence on compromise was partially determined by union decisions. In early spring of 1946, LeG approached the New York Local Number 2 of the stagehands' union about their requirements. On May 20, 1946, union delegates finally agreed to meet with LeG but told her nothing. Three weeks later, she returned again. After two hours of arguing about union regulations, the delegates still refused to supply any information. As the meeting ended, one man turned to her and exclaimed, "If we want you to have your little theatre, you'll have it, and if we don't want you to, you won't — see?"[32]

Not until the plays were in rehearsal in October did LeG learn the union's demands. At the Civic the Stagehands' Union had permitted her to hire only a basic crew of ten men. Then, when she did a show like *Peter Pan*, she would bring in an extra crew for that performance only. For the ART the union demanded exactly the opposite. Since they needed twenty-eight stagehands for *Henry VIII*, they were forced to engage that same number for all productions, even when they only needed eight. Expenses soared!

The American Federation of Musicians, Local 802, dealt the theatre a further blow. Lehman Engel had composed music for *Henry VIII* that the union decided was part of the production and not merely entr'acte. The union insisted, therefore, that the weekly wage for the conductor and every musician performing for *Henry VIII* be raised 50 percent. LeG, Peggy, and Crawford agreed to the demands without a whimper. The union had previously consented to lowering the required number of musicians from sixteen to nine members, and the women feared that if they protested, the union would reverse their decision. "It is not from without that the theatre is in danger," LeG proclaimed, "it is from within. . . . I think it is a definite evil to make these unions so hide-bound, so drastic, and at times so ludicrous in their petty rules that they become the greatest impediment and obstacle in the path of sincere and honest stage activities."[33]

The attitude of the critics also helped to topple the ART. They refused to understand the objective to build a permanent company and treated each production as if it were done by a separate producing organization. The critics insisted on evaluating each actor's performance as a single unit, with no relation to his or her other roles in the repertory. Instead of evaluating the range of roles the actors attempted, they expected each actor to perform as if she or he had been typecast and had had a rehearsal schedule that focused on a single play.

To salvage the theatre, Crawford announced plans in late January to drop the repertory system temporarily in favor of regular runs, cutting operating expenses about $4,000 a week. LeG threatened to retire to her farm. "You see, I don't like show business. I love theater. That's how I feel after 30 years of service."[34]

Since chances for survival were slim, LeG turned to John D. Rockefeller, Jr., for help. He had recently donated land in New York City for the construction of the United Nations. LeG pressed for the inclusion of a United Nations Art Centre that would involve a resident theatre company. Arguing that such a theatre would draw nations together, she proposed two theatres equipped for repertory, a resident United Nations Repertory Theatre, and the invitation of foreign acting companies for guest appearances. Finally, she requested a donation that would allow the ART to tour its productions to South America. LeG hoped that if the company could remain intact, it could become the resident company at the United Nations. But Rockefeller's reply was negative. He granted that LeG's proposal had great merit, but he stated that he had no influence over how the land was used after it was donated. He also stressed that he always refrained from supporting theatrical ventures.

A concerted effort was begun to solicit funds for the ART. Headed by such notable artists as Helen Hayes, Jose Ferrer, and Raymond Massey, a committee was formed that managed to collect over $15,000 plus guarantees of free advertising and discounts on sound equipment. LeG and Webster agreed to work for no salary.

With these added funds, plans progressed to revive Sidney Howard's *Yellow Jack*. Many critics were puzzled with the selection. When the play was originally produced in 1934, it was not popular and closed with a financial loss after seventy-nine performances. The play is a documentary account of Dr. Walter Reed's long fight to find a cure for yellow fever. The elements of generosity and dedication seen in the characters of Dr. Reed and his scientific staff might have appealed to LeG and Peggy. And coming after the horrors of World War II, it celebrates the heroism of scientists and common soldiers.

The final production of their season was a revival of *Alice in Wonderland*. LeG had promised the role of Alice to Anne Jackson but instead cast Bambi Linn, who had just created a sensation with her dancing in *Oklahoma!* Everyone hoped her name would draw crowds to the box office. Because the company's financial picture was dismal, an arrangement was made with producer Rita Hassan to provide much of the financial backing. In return, she received a hefty 70 percent of the ticket sales. With the prospects for a second season very unlikely, all actors who were not in *Alice* signed releases from any claims on their two-year contracts with the ART.

As the ART's first season came to an end, the demise was in sight. One evening after a performance of *Alice*, the three women sat backstage gaunt, exhausted, and silent. As Crawford wrote, "There was nothing to say. Nothing to do. We had tried and failed."[35] Instead of a future of promise, all they could see was a dismal past. There were no hugs, no tears, just a heavy silence. To LeG it was even more shattering than to her partners, since this was her second company to fail. Expenses and salaries had been cut to the marrow. Often, as the curtain fell, LeG took center stage to beg audiences for contributions. No matter how much she rationalized intellectually that the failure was out of her control, she still felt embarrassed and guilty.

Many critics, including the usually faithful Brooks Atkinson, concurred with Robert Garland's conclusion that the management seemed more interested in "reviving plays in which the actors want to act, rather than plays the public wants to see."[36] This was a critical indictment of a company that was supposedly dedicated to serving the people.

LeG's nemesis, George Jean Nathan, was the most vehement. For many years he had been on a personal crusade to prove that LeG was "as poor an actress as lives." When she had presented *Madame Capet* eight years earlier, he had attacked her "efforts to soar like an eagle with only a pair of cuckoo wings at her command." Now he charged that the ART was "slipshod in its acting, often insufficient in its direction, stupid in the choice of most of its plays, ill-advised in much of its casting . . . and wholly devoid . . . of showmanship."[37] His nonstop diatribe damaged not only LeG's reputation but her confidence as well.

Contrary to all predictions, Broadway business began to decline after the war ended. Audiences were moving to the suburbs and spending their leisure time going to movies or watching a marvelous new invention called television. Those who did prefer live theatre did not wish to spend their money on European classics. When Anne Jackson recalls those early years of her career, she recognizes that "the American theatre was moving in a direction other than the classics. It was always, 'What's new?' Unfortunately, in the ART there was cobwebs and dust."[38]

But other problems challenged the ART. Insidious charges of communism were thrown at both Crawford and Peggy. Activities of both women prompted the criticism. Crawford had been one of the founders of the Group Theatre, a producing organization known for leftist leanings and attacks on traditional American values. She had directed Clifford Odets's *Til the Day I Die*, a one-acter with strong Marxist overtones. In 1935 she had accompanied Harold Clurman on a two-month pilgrimage to the Soviet Union, where they conferred with several prominent directors—Piscator, Meyerhold, and Stanislavsky. During the patriotic May Day celebrations, they took prominent positions near Lenin's tomb in Red Square. To the radical element in America, it appeared as if Crawford was a Communist sympathizer.

Peggy's profile was even more suspect. When she won election to the Council of Actors' Equity Association in 1941, actress Winifred Lenihan accused her in the New York press of communism. When Equity stood up for its members who were being physically assaulted, slurred, and threatened with violence for their political stands, the union was labeled a "Red" organization, and Peggy a "pinko." By the end of the year, she was reported to be affiliated with not less than nineteen Communist front organizations.

Reckless accusations, smear campaigns, and innuendoes were the order of the day. During the run of *Therese*, Peggy received a letter from a theatregoer threatening to "boycott any other play in which your name appears or in which you are connected." Early in 1947, actor Frank Fay rallied the lunatic fringe and, at a public meeting of Equity, accused Peggy of communism. Peggy and LeG began to receive abusive postcards: "Protest meeting being arranged by *Equity Membership*. Want to be investigated by F.B.I.?" Even though LeG had no interest in politics, she was "joined at the hip with Peggy," and the association affected her as well.[39]

Peggy wrote in her biography some years later that "no one touched the blacklist, witch-hunt pitch, without being lessened and to some degree defiled. . . . It was a miserable business from first to last; it did lasting damage to the United States and very few people emerged from it with any credit whatever." She felt her "career was undermined, if it was not ostensibly broken."[40] What direct effect this had on the fortunes of the ART is difficult to determine, but it must have played at least a supporting role in the financial drama at the box office.

Undoubtedly another factor, though perhaps more subtle, was America's opinion of women. At first it seemed as if the war had overturned old attitudes as women became a vital part of the labor force. By 1945 eight million women had entered the working world and composed 36 percent of the American labor force. Many of them performed "male jobs" and were granted equal pay for equal work. But after the war, a fourth of them were fired. Those that continued working found their salaries suddenly lowered, since they were now considered supplementary workers and not family providers. Very clearly, women were being told that their most important role was domestic. The ideal woman did not work but remained at home to create a nest for her husband and children or did volunteer things.

LeG and her two partners hardly fit the new mold. Instead, they were career women who challenged the establishment, and they were often derided for their aggressiveness. All the major theatre managers and producers, the people with power, were men. Somehow these three middle-aged women, with their new theatre devoted to the classics, posed a bit of a threat to them. To make matters worse, LeG was not even a native-born American.

For the women to be lesbians was downright repugnant to most people. Just three weeks after the ART opened, Jean-Paul Sartre's *No Exit* premiered on Broadway and fueled the prevailing stereotype of homosexuality. The story of three lost souls in Hell depicts a loathsome lesbian who has poisoned and destroyed the life of a married woman. A few months later, *The American Journal of Psychiatry* indicated that lesbians "are always lonely . . . frequently become psychiatric cases . . . [and] eventually develop a certain deviousness." Homosexuals were tagged "perverts" and became the frequent subject of witch-hunts. In fact, the national chairman of the Republican party went so far as to announce that homosexuals were "perhaps as dangerous as . . . Communists." These impressions surely colored the opinions of critics as well as theatregoers and very definitely contributed to the failure of the ART. As Anne Jackson reflected many years later, "Being a woman and a lesbian conspired to work against LeG. Why, even working with her put an onus on you."[41]

Unlike LeG's first year with the Civic, this season quite obviously did not end in a triumph. The company had received overtures to perform at the French National Theatre, the Dutch National Theatre, the Stratford-on-Avon Memorial Theatre in England, and the International Festival of Arts in Edinburgh. But ironically, the American Repertory Theatre had not been able to succeed in New York.

In the early summer of 1947, LeG and her partners met with their major investors and later reported they would dissolve the ART during the current tax year and accept their loss. It was agreed, however, to postpone any definite action until after the scheduled tour of *Alice in Wonderland* in the fall. The investors were gambling that the tour might save the theatre from collapse. But their hopes were shattered when the tour was abruptly abandoned after its first engagement in Boston. Even though critic Elliot Norton called the production "greatly imaginative" and said the actors played with "a touch of genius," the production's deficit after one week stood at more than $3,000.[42] In spite of good ticket sales, the high operating costs buried it.

Cheryl Crawford resigned from the company shortly thereafter. She believed it was now impossible to find a subsidy or to reduce operating expenses enough to hobble along. Although LeG and Peggy agreed with Crawford's assessment, they refused to give up. They did not know how, but they were resolved to continue the fight. For one more season, they struggled to continue.

As she sat down for breakfast one morning during the Boston engagement, LeG slowly opened the newspaper expecting to read yet another prediction about the future of the ART. Instead she saw headlines announcing her father's death at the age of eighty-one. For some peculiar reason, she remembered one of her last visits with him during her trip to Paris in 1931, a time when she saw the demon in him. "I felt as though I were in the presence of a stranger; his eyes were wild, almost evil, yet so tragic. . . . It made me understand the bitter struggle, the constant effort of will, the falling down, bruised and defeated in spirit, and the gallant climb upward again."[43]

The rejection she had suffered by her father had left scars. LeG began to sense her father's denial when she was barely two. Because little children normally see their parents as all-knowing and all-powerful, she had not questioned her father's attitude. Because he had left the household, something must have been wrong with it . . . and with her. The feeling of rejection did not go away; it was an emptiness that remained with her constantly, damaging her self-esteem and producing feelings of inferiority and inadequacy. It made her feel of little value as a person. She herself could not give love unconditionally with warmth and affection, because she regarded herself as incapable and unworthy, nor could she believe anyone could love her. Because of her feelings, she tried to conceal her real self from others. She thought that if anyone saw her as she saw herself, the result would be further rejection.

Ironically, LeG's hunger for affection continuously welled up and often became all-consuming. It was insatiable. As John Joseph Evoy has suggested in his psychological study, *The Rejected*, these women tend to develop into relentless affection-hunters.[44] It was certainly true for LeG. To satisfy her need for acceptance, she concentrated not only on romantic conquests but on her theatrical accomplishments. Sometimes she was so driven by her need to achieve that she felt she was "on a human treadmill, running with a frenzy."[45]

This overwhelming need to achieve kept her going, even when her world was crumbling around her. Late in November, LeG and Peggy accepted Louis J. Singer's proposal to present, in conjunction with the ART, a spring repertory of Ibsen's *Ghosts* and *Hedda Gabler*. At first they were reluctant because of Singer's reputation. Dubbed the "virgin from Wall Street," he was a wealthy, but stingy, New York City, investment banker with no understanding of theatre. He had even urged Tennessee Williams to give a happy ending to *The Glass Menagerie*; he wanted Laura to marry the Gentleman Caller.

LeG and Singer were bound to clash. After the tour ended, Singer insisted that LeG send him all her costumes, which he claimed he had purchased. She went into a rage. She had supplied her own negligee, all costumes, wigs, jewelry, shoes, furniture, and even some props. She had also declined a translator's royalty fee. When Singer filed a formal complaint with Actors' Equity, LeG admitted that he had paid for a new chiffon underdress for the negligee, so she ripped it in half and mailed him back his portion. If he wanted the rest, he could "send out a Union wardrobe mistress at union rates" to fetch it.[46]

Under Peggy's direction, *Ghosts* opened February 16, 1948, with LeG playing Mrs. Alving. The press was overwhelmingly negative; the play seemed tedious and dated. One week later, LeG opened her production of *Hedda Gabler*. Most critics concurred that her portrayal was too studied and mannered. Her nervous pacing, her gestures, and her awkward head movements destroyed the essential femininity of Mrs. Alving.[47]

The most destructive criticism came once again from George Jean Nathan. Of LeG's work in *Ghosts*, Nathan wrote that her acting was a mere recitation of the role. "The recitation is a clear and intelligent one, and hints that she has a profitable career open to her as a platform reader of the classics. . . . Of characterization there is nothing." Of LeG's Hedda:

> She is haplessly possessed of so frigid a personality . . . that her performances take on the air of an "Icetime of 1948." . . . She is so cold that a spectator is sometimes surprised that a frosty mist does not issue from her mouth when she opens it to speak her lines. . . . Even in roles themselves intrinsically cold, like Hedda, Miss Le Gallienne carries ice to Newfoundland.[48]

Nathan's venomous contempt for LeG's acting often rallied her friends. After the two Ibsen reviews, Lawrence Langner replied to LeG:

> I want to tell you how incensed I am at the article which George Jean Nathan just wrote about you. If it is any consolation, nobody gives a damn what he says. He is just a horrible old man and a blight on the theatre. All your friends love you and respect your courage and integrity. The hell with the lice that live on the blood of the theatre!

Peggy actually felt that a conspiracy was taking place. "Some of the critics," she wrote to Brooks Atkinson, "curdle your blood." They "write as if their principal aim were to attack Le Gallienne so viciously that she would finally be driven from the theatre."[49]

Whatever happened to the water baby, the young girl with dreams of a fulfilling life in the theatre? In the 1920s and even into the 1930s, LeG was one of New York's premiere leading ladies. She had starred in such hits as *Liliom, The Swan, The Master Builder, The Cradle Song, The Cherry Orchard, Peter Pan, Romeo and Juliet, Camille, Alice in Wonderland, The Good Hope*, and *L'Aiglon*. Most of these she had directed herself.

From 1934 through 1948, however, only two of her performances were truly critical successes—a revival of *Alice in Wonderland* and *Uncle Harry*. She was aware that her reputation was dying, but she still refused to recognize that another problem was her rejection of modern trends in American theatre. Her commitment to the classics was noble, but as Paul Ballantyne suggests, "The type of theater she loved and wanted to devote her life to went out of fashion."[50]

At forty-nine LeG was facing a personal crisis. She knew that the future would not search her out and that she would be denied jobs for so many reasons: she was overqualified; she was too old; she was too threatening; she was a woman. She had made so many sacrifices for her career, and the thought of more rejection began to haunt her. The changes in her body were also sobering. Her skin was losing its elasticity, and wrinkles were everywhere. Her hair was graying, and her joints were getting stiffer. The right eyelid that had been damaged during the fire was sagging more than ever. What a terribly frightening prospect to be aging with the added threat of being useless and unwanted.

One of LeG's most loyal friends had also observed a decline in LeG's professional stature. May Sarton saw her performance in the Ibsen plays and offered her the following thoughts:

> In some strange way it seems as if in these last few years of fearful struggle to make the frame in which you could grow and *be* what you are as an artist, you have outgrown the theatre as it is. You have not for some time loved the theatre, in the sense of finding your *deepest* joy within it. And when that happens it is time to stop and wait. There has been something forced in these last years due to the awful circumstances—I've felt each time I've seen you; for the sake of the theatre and what it might be, you have been forcing yourself beyond joy into some terrible place of effort.

Sarton suggested that LeG resist accepting another role until she found the right play, one "in which your inwardness can be made visible."[51]

Only days after the close of *Hedda Gabler*, application was filed for the dissolution of the ART Corporation, placing the financial loss at $340,000.[52] LeG's second attempt to establish a permanent repertory theatre had failed. Soon afterward LeG wrote to May Sarton, "I feel somehow that I should be *giving* in some way—but *how*? That's the difficulty—and the years go by—and I have done nothing—*nothing*—it's frightening—I who wanted to do so much—to *give* so much. I feel like old Firs in *The Cherry Orchard*. 'Life has gone by as though I'd never lived!'—Ah well—!"[53]

8

Buying Some Freedom

Once upon a time, in a far-off Connecticut farm, there lived two Bantam hens. Flossie, the scrawnier of the two, was downright ugly. Very shy and reserved, she often felt like crying for sheer loneliness. She often suffered from ill-natured gibes and malicious ridicule. Luckily, she did have a streak of gallantry in her, which she had inherited from her plucky father. Flossie dreamed of laying the perfect egg and felt pangs of jealousy as her neighbors admired the eggs of other hens. She was resolved to sacrifice everything for her chicks. She was such a loner that when she moved from the hen house no one even noticed she had gone.

Bossie, on the other hand, was considered a rare beauty and would often throw out her chest and arch her back. After all, she was First Lady of the Barnyard. She was clever and always kept everyone laughing. The other hens paid court to the vivacious and self-confident Bossie because of her sharp and stinging repartee. Rumor had it that she was being groomed for Hollywood! She gloated as her eggs were admired but resented the time they took away from her social life.

In a book published by Harper and Row in 1949, LeG dramatized a conflict between these two hens, a conflict that seemed to parallel her own life. One day both Flossie and Bossie are taken away to hatch chicks of their own. The amusing satire describes how each hen adjusts to motherhood and how their barnyard life is changed. At one point, an old friend of Flossie's scolds the other birds in a speech reminiscent of Ethel Barrymore's defense of LeG fifteen years earlier: "You don't even recognize a good hen when you see one! Flossie's worth more than the whole bunch of you, maybe some day you'll come to know it. Flock of sycophants! You give me a pain in my crop!" The old bird looked on with anger as the fickle hens continued to pay court to the latest favorite in the barnyard.[1]

Any reader who was at all aware of LeG's struggles to present the classics alongside the glamour and bright lights of the current Broadway fare had to recognize the analogy. Like Flossie, LeG had sacrificed everything for her dream, and also like Flossie, she was not missed when she was forcibly removed from the theatre scene. She had been ridiculed and jeered as younger and more alluring talents supplanted her. LeG was bitter, but since the book was marketed for a children's audience, her satire went unnoticed.

The American theatre was not the same as when LeG had been on top in the 1920s. Theatrical activity began a nosedive in 1928 and accelerated even more rapidly after the end of World War II. During the 1943–44 season in New York, ninety-seven productions were presented. By 1950 the number had dwindled to fifty-seven, and by 1960 to a low point of forty-eight productions. Because of the reduced activity, no new theatres were constructed in New York between 1938 and 1960.

A major cause for the decline was the emergence of television. Telecasting had begun as early as 1945. By 1948 there were 48 stations located in twenty-five different cities. In the decade that followed, the industry expanded so that it boasted 512 stations by 1958. To compete with this free entertainment that was finding its way into everyone's living room, theatre producers promoted well-known stars, lavish staging, and plays appealing to the widest possible population.

What especially excited theatre audiences was a new phenomenon, musical comedy. Before World War II, musicals had commonly stressed songs and dances at the expense of any clear story. But the incredible success of *Oklahoma!* in 1943 set the standard for the future, integrating plots and characters with music and dance. The popularity of this new format led to the overwhelming success in the next decade of *Carousel, South Pacific, My Fair Lady, The King and I, West Side Story,* and *The Sound of Music.* The dialogue, lyrics, and melodies encouraged people to "forget your troubles. Come on, get happy! Come on, chase all your cares away. Sing Hallelujah, come on, get happy."

The drama that continued to draw a following was of a different vintage. The postwar years were marked by interest in modern realistic theatre. Elia Kazan, Cheryl Crawford, and one of LeG's former apprentices, Bobby Lewis, founded the Actors' Studio in 1947 in order to train actors in "The Method." For the next ten years, the Studio was a dominant force in the theatre, and through the work of Lee Strasberg, it nurtured actresses such as Julie Harris, Jessica Tandy, Kim Hunter, Shirley Booth, and Geraldine Page, for masterpieces by Arthur Miller, Tennessee Williams, and William Inge.

LeG had no respect for this new style of acting that championed the Stanislavsky system. She had read the writings of the Russian master and agreed with his basic goal of searching for truth. But she vigorously opposed the Studio's emphasis on "emotional memory"— an exercise that instructs actors to examine their personal experiences in depth. LeG thought it fostered self-indulgence. Actors trained in the method "can't play anything but their own truth. They look into themselves only. Strasberg wants his actors to go to psychiatrists to learn more about themselves. But the actor is not supposed to be himself. He's supposed to be someone else." LeG believed actors must develop their imaginations and train their bodies to respond. Ironically, Strasberg eventually came to agree with LeG and even selected her some thirty years later as one of the "vivid examples of what American actors are capable of."[2] But at this time in American theatre, her opinions were ignored.

And yet LeG was able to spawn three intrepid female followers— Margo Jones, Nina Vance, and Zelda Fichandler. These women followed LeG's lead and waged a battle against the commercialism of Broadway. When Jones opened her Theatre 47 in Dallas in 1947, she inaugurated the regional theatre revolution. Both Vance's Alley Theatre in Houston and Fichandler's Arena Theatre in the nation's capital followed soon after. LeG may have failed to accomplish her goal in New York City, but these pioneering disciples carried her ideals into the nation's hinterlands.

Faced with what seemed to be insurmountable obstacles of musicals, modern realistic dramas, and method acting, LeG opted for a period of semiretirement that lasted six years. For most of her career, she had been proud that she could live up to her motto—"The theatre should be an instrument for giving, not a machinery for getting." But now circumstances had changed. Since the public no longer wanted what she had to offer and since she was not financially independent, she abandoned her lofty ideals in order to carve out a living. She renounced the New York theatre and began to look in other directions.

In October 1948, she began a six-month, nationwide lecture tour, where she combined brief talks about great plays with performances of selected scenes. During the spring of 1949, she agreed to tour summer theatres on the Eastern seaboard for ten weeks, starring as Miss Moffat in *The Corn Is Green*. Her decision certainly had no idealistic overtones. She confided to May Sarton that "it will be a good way I feel to 'buy myself' some further months of freedom. The garden here is glorious—the roses at their height—how I shall hate to 'tread the boards' again."[3]

A sentimental drama popularized in 1940 by Ethel Barrymore, the story concerns a Welsh schoolteacher who struggles to save her prize pupil from a life of drudgery in the coal mines. Although LeG liked the play and believed she could "do a good job on it without tearing myself completely to shreds,"[4] she accepted the role mainly because it was being packaged by her old admirer Richard Waring. He was to re-create his original Broadway role as Miss Moffat's student.

At first it appeared as if the production was going to bomb, even with the low demands of the summer circuit. LeG was testy during rehearsals and objected to the ideas of director Eddie McHugh, even though he had stage-managed the original on Broadway. She disagreed with some blocking choices and bits of business that he wanted. On opening night in Westport, she instructed Waring that she wanted to see both him and the director in her dressing room after the perfor-mance. Waring warned McHugh in advance that they must hold the line and not give in to her whims, particularly during the first week of the run.

Waring and McHugh expected an emotional outburst but came away completely disarmed. "You know, if old Doc Le Gallienne can't take direction," she said, "it's over. Believe me, you'll have no more trouble from me." She apparently had come to realize that she should respect their ideas.[5] In the end, the revival was so successful that LeG consented to repeat her performance for a limited, two-week engage-ment during the season of revivals that Maurice Evans was producing at the New York City Center.

Aside from the kudos and the welcome boost in her bank account, LeG found the experience to be therapeutic. Shortly before rehearsals had begun, she had resumed her "tussles with the bottle." "Thank God, this happens to me seldom now," she explained in a letter to May Sarton:

> But I had been upset and confused and unexpectedly troubled—and like a fool, I resorted to the wine bowl! I start rehearsals tomorrow for *The Corn Is Green*. I shall be glad to be at work in the strict discipline that the theatre must impose. I have a fondness for discipline. Do you remember that wonderful line in The Wisdom of Solomon in the Apocrypha?: 'The Care of Discipline is Love'—the whole passage is remarkable and beauti-ful—but that phrase in particular I find quite marvelous."[6]

Christmas of 1949 was a joy! For the first time in thirty years, LeG spent the holiday with her sister. Soon after Hep had married Robert Hutchinson in 1920, they had moved back to England. When the war broke out, they opened the Eagle Club in London, a club-canteen for the 20,000 American volunteers in the British services. They lived in the thick of the Nazi air raids during the Battle of Britain. Later they organized a club near Liverpool for GIs, and in the spring of 1943, they were put in charge of a large officers' club in Bournemouth. They continued this work until 1946 and were ultimately awarded the Medal of Freedom for their efforts.

In 1949, Hep and her husband returned to America and lived in the original old house on LeG's property before moving into their own home in West Redding, only ten miles from Weston. They celebrated Christmas with all the family traditions—decorating the tree, singing Danish Christmas carols, and feasting on all the delicacies coming from Gun's kitchen. It was certainly a contrast with that Christmas long ago but not forgotten, when the sisters had huddled together in a bathroom as their Nanny shielded them from their drunken father. With both parents deceased, LeG especially treasured these intimate times.

Another lecture tour filled most of the 1950–51 season. This time, however, LeG traveled with a company of four other actors, in order to offer more variety in the kinds of scenes that she presented. During one of the long breaks between bookings, she directed Chekhov's *The Three Sisters* for the Brattle Theatre, a Boston stock company, and starred in it along with Peggy.

The grind of the lecture circuit was almost too much. Week after week of one-night stands meant endless travel each day by plane, train, car, taxi, and even bus. It meant living with a suitcase, a different hotel room every night, strange restaurants, countless receptions, nonstop interviews, impossible train connections, and blizzards. Arriving just before the curtain minus lunch and dinner was fairly standard. Most important, however, the tour meant an end to LeG's restful days in the country.

By February she was bedridden. "I think I was quite close to a nervous breakdown—so *stupid*. It wasn't the work so much that tired me—I *love that*—but all the incredible machinations of the various booking agents nearly depleted me." Gun looked after her "like an angel. . . . I know what deep black holes one can fall into," she wrote to May Sarton, "but tout sera bien'!"[7] LeG did not clarify what she meant by the "deep black holes," but it is clear that her health had been threatened by more than just the demands of the tour. Her ten-year relationship with Peggy was about to end.

In the summer of 1950 a group of former FBI agents had published *Red Channels* and had listed some fifty pages of Communist organizations and a hundred and fifty pages of individual names. One of the names was Peggy's. The book quickly became the Bible for anti-Communists, and almost overnight Peggy felt the waves. There was to be a UNESCO conference in Paris, and Peggy had been unanimously chosen to represent Actors' Equity. When she applied for her passport, however, she was denied. Only by resorting to her British citizenship was she finally allowed to leave the country. Convinced that she would lose work in the theatre, Peggy chose to fight back.

During all this turmoil, LeG remained indifferent. When Peggy was called to Washington to testify before the House Un-American Activities Committee, LeG was aloof. She was busy working on lectures for her tour and preferred not to be bothered with Peggy's problems. She seemed to have no sociopolitical conscience. She was unaware of so much that was happening around her, especially if the subject did not concern her personally.

By contrast, Peggy was very political, even radical. She knew that ever since President Roosevelt had refused to save the Civic during the Depression, her partner had hated anything resembling liberal politics. In fact, Peggy had often joked that LeG was a conservative Tory at heart and would have voted for Napoleon if she could have. But this time Eva's blind eye and deaf ear was the last straw. As Peggy wrote in her autobiography, the Communist witch-hunt "had subtle side-effects, loosening some bonds and strengthening others. I got to know whom I'd like to be in a trench with and whom I'd just as soon not have on my side."[8] LeG and Peggy remained close friends and even worked together on future projects, but their romantic bonds were broken. For the third time, LeG had failed at love.

When Peggy finally moved out, LeG threw herself even more intensely into her work. For sixteen weeks she had her own New York radio show on which she read stories and scenes from plays. She also returned to her writing, praying it would keep her from another bout with the bottle. She had previously translated numerous Ibsen plays for production, and she now concentrated on refining her work for publication. She complained that the standard William Archer translations clung assiduously to the letter and therefore presented "a series of stumbling blocks to the reader's mind and of tongue-twisters to the actor. . . . The great Viking ship, with its clean, eliminated, uncompromising lines, has been muffled under Victorian drapery."[9] By 1961, twelve of her translations had been published by Modern Library.

In prefaces to her translations, LeG summarizes her thirty-year romance with Ibsen. In response to the many critics who label the plays "old-fashioned," she argues that their value is "the light they cast on the inner, secret lives of the characters presented in them." She praises them as "dramas of the mind, of the spirit." She allows that Ibsen's focus on the "inner content" of the characters is a challenge to the audience's intellect but insists that feature is precisely the reason for their greatness.[10]

She praises Ibsen also for his vivid gallery of female characters: Hilda Wangel, Hedda Gabler, Rebecca West, Ella Rentheim, and Mrs. Alving. They are complex and intricate characters. LeG maintains that Ibsen was the first playwright to present a woman who dominates "the stage as a full-fledged individual—interesting and complete in herself, quite apart from the men with whom she shared the action." Ibsen was not a feminist, she believed, crusading for the superiority of women, but a playwright concerned with human interaction. Even with *A Doll's House*, a play often viewed as Ibsen's statement on women's rights, LeG cautions that "the theme of the play that interests Ibsen most was not that of women's freedom—her so-called emancipation—but that of the different ethical codes by which men and women live."[11]

In 1952 LeG, Peggy, and Maurice Evans founded Theatre Masterworks, a company committed to recording a library of plays the commercial theatre would not touch. When the first record appeared, LeG stated the company's objective was to arouse in the "students of the drama . . . a desire to see these Theatre-Masterworks brought to full life on the stage."[12] Since the establishment of a repertory theatre now seemed impossible, she considered this the best alternative.

The new firm was not LeG's first venture into the recording of plays. In 1948 RCA Victor had recorded the ART's production of *Alice in Wonderland*. Two years later ANTA had asked a number of leading actors and actresses to record scenes from plays for its Album of Stars. Besides Helen Hayes in a scene from *Victoria Regina* and John Gielgud in *Richard II*, LeG was asked to record the first scene of act two from *Hedda Gabler*. LeG's other recordings had included *Romeo and Juliet* with Atlantic Records and her reading of Baudelaire's *Les Fleurs du Mal* with Caedmon.

Theatre Masterworks debuted with a recording of LeG's *Hedda Gabler*, the first full-length recording of the play in English. She made two additional recordings for the company. *An Evening with Will Shakespeare* included a program of readings that LeG had toured in 1953 with Basil Rathbone, Staats Cotsworth, Nina Foch, and Viveca Lindfors, attempting to raise money for Lawrence Langner's proposed Shakespeare Theatre in Westport. The other was a recording of LeG reading the poetry of great English and American writers.

Along with the translations and prefaces to Ibsen's plays, LeG published her second autobiography. Although it takes up where her earlier *At 33* left off, the work is again a victim of camouflage. The reader is given a rather homogenized and guarded portrait of a woman of accomplishment. There is no reference to her sexual orientation or to the importance of Josie, Gun, and Peggy in her life. May Sarton was one of her closest confidants, but her name is not even whispered. There is no hint of alcohol and no rumors of communism.

There is a noticeable difference between the two books, however. What had been a tone of defiance, energy, confidence, and joy in the first was replaced by melancholy and sorrow. By this time LeG had known anger and resentment, but she preferred admiration over pity. She ends the book with these words:

> I have loved every moment of my life and I thank God for it. I have been greatly blessed. I have been blessed with a good mind and a sound body, with talents and countless opportunities to make use of them. I have been greatly loved and have loved greatly in return. I have been blessed with enduring friendships and have received far more than my share of admiration and praise. There is no trace of bitterness in my heart toward any creature living or dead, and that is perhaps the greatest blessing of them all. I have enjoyed the past, I find the present good, and I look to the future with a quiet heart.[13]

In spite of what she wrote, there was indeed a trace of bitterness as well as anger. The painful reversals in both her personal and public life in the twenty years between the two books affected her style, even if they were not enumerated for the reader.

In the spring of 1953, LeG conducted a solo concert tour of California, reciting two stories by Oscar Wilde: *The Birthday of the Infanta* and *The Happy Prince*. She later remarked of the tour, "That was 57 pages of solid prose to learn. At least it proved to me the old girl still has concentration. If I can't find a play, it's a wonderful thing to have this."[14]

Much of her time was also spent translating *The Strong Are Lonely*, a French play by Fritz Hochwalder that was to be directed by Peggy. Set in eighteenth-century Paraguay, the story deals with a group of idealistic Jesuit priests who try to establish a Utopian society. Although it had previously enjoyed long runs in Vienna, Rome, Athens, Oslo, Helsinki, and Paris, the play's subject matter was considered foreign to American theatregoers. Some forty years later, the story was

the basis for a major, popular feature film, *The Mission*, but at this point
in time, the ideas seemed farfetched.

LeG's writing projects may have helped, but her finances were
again in chaos. She had no choice but to return to New York. Headlines
read "Le Gallienne Goes Contemporary." The role she accepted was in
the Shuberts' production of Diana Morgan's new play, *The Starcross
Story*. The play begins with the attempt of Lady Starcross to make a
film based on the death of her husband, a well-known explorer who
died during a heroic expedition. As the drama ends, he is revealed to
have been an unscrupulous egomaniac who knowingly set forth on a
deceptive quest.

After two weeks of tryouts in summer theatres, LeG anticipated a
New York success: "I know it sounds crazy, but I think I would go mad
if 'Starcross' went into a long run."[15] She need not have worried, for
the production closed after a single performance! It was little consola-
tion that LeG was credited with presenting a gracious and ghostly
dignity to the tight-lipped and faintly waspish Lady Starcross. She was
even applauded during several of her scenes.

The reasons for the abrupt closing were complex. Playwright
Diana Morgan was accused of plagiarism. Stanley Kauffmann, who
had written a novel entitled *The Hidden Hero* in 1949, maintained that
the playwright had lifted her story from his book. Although the
lawsuit was later dropped, the fear of a court trial led the Shubert
management to close the production. After this disappointing return
to Broadway, LeG went back to the country and the comfort of her
home. She wrote to May Sarton, "I escape to my little shack every day
for several hours—and am doing some writing. . . . It's good practice
and keeps me out of trouble."[16]

By late spring she found herself working on her first feature film,
serving as technical adviser to 20th Century-Fox's production of *Prince
of Players*, a film based on Eleanor Ruggles's biography of actor Edwin
Booth. Like most stage performers, LeG had little respect for this
industry of retakes, close-ups, and special effects. Film acting was to a
classical actress such as LeG what burlesque was to an opera diva. It
offered little prestige, but the money was good. LeG was actually
awarded the position through the back door. It had first been given to
Peggy, but when she became embroiled in the Red Scare, she convinced
LeG to take her place.

The management and director Philip Dunne cast Richard Burton
as the lead, hoping to exploit his recent success with the role of Hamlet
at the Old Vic in London. Although LeG played one short scene as

Gertrude to Burton's Hamlet, her contribution to the film was seldom even mentioned. She later said, "Everything I did as an adviser was 'wrong.' When I protested that things just didn't happen that way [in real life], the people in Hollywood had one great line for an answer: 'The public won't know the difference.'" According to Burton's biographers, the film became "the first notable box-office flop in Cinema-Scope."[17] When critics complained that it was boring, ill-conceived, poorly executed, and mistaken in historical accuracy, LeG had to swallow a smile.

After the film was completed, LeG returned to the stage, appearing on Broadway in another new script, John Cecil Holm's *Southwest Corner*. The author had fashioned a story around an eighty-three-year-old widowed schoolteacher who hires a housekeeper for companionship but instead finds herself trapped by a dominating stranger. The development of the scenes was not logical, and the characters were unmotivated. Under the direction of George Schaefer, LeG as the aged school marm sat quietly rocking in her chair during certain scenes, staring at the southwest corner of the house that held many family memories and drawing the audience into her inner thoughts. LeG gave a beautiful performance to a play not worthy of it, and after several weeks *The Southwest Corner* closed.

Purposely avoiding revivals of classics, LeG had turned to these modern scripts for her return to Broadway. Both vehicles she chose, however, were not great dramas. Even though her acting had been generally well received, the productions had failed to restore her reputation as an actress. More than two years passed before she had another opportunity.

During the summer of 1955, LeG began her long association with Lucille Lortel's White Barn Theatre in Westport, Connecticut. Founded in 1947, the summer theatre was intended to serve as a hub where writers and performers could showcase their talents. In the late 1940s, Sean O'Casey's *Red Roses for Me* received its American premiere. More recent seasons have seen the premieres of Eugene Ionesco's *Chairs*, Edward Albee's *Fam and Yam*, Murray Schisgal's *The Typists*, and Paul Zindel's *The Effect of Gamma Rays on Man-in-the-Moon Marigolds*.

Lortel offered LeG the opportunity to teach acting at the theatre, giving her a flat fee plus a percentage of the tuition. Since money was still tight during this period, LeG continued the classes for two additional years. She had always maintained that the best way to learn acting was by performing, so she taught by directing students in scenes from Ibsen, Chekhov, and Shakespeare. Among the young, aspiring artists were Peter Falk, Mariette Hartley, Paul Vincent, Tony Carbone, and George Morfogen.

The students were in awe of the celebrity—the legend—who was actually heading their class. George Morfogen's experience was typical. He had listened to her perform in his acting classes at the Yale School of Drama, when his teacher had used LeG's recording of *Hedda Gabler* to illustrate vocal music and the use of comedy in a tragedy. When he entered the room for his first interview and audition with LeG, the aura was striking. It was not like going into an ordinary room. He knew she was reading his innermost thoughts like no one before. He felt intimidated, but her genuine concentration on his work put him at ease.[18]

Before LeG arrived for the opening class, there was a nervous lull in the room where the neophytes waited for their master. "Then a small woman in lavender and violet swept up the aisle from the back of the house. Slow motion, fast motion, one of those moments never forgotten," Mariette Hartley remembered, "It was almost as if there were a light around her." Hartley admits that she "was in love with her, there is no question."[19] With her wispy, grayish-brown hair and translucent skin, she dressed always in cashmere sweaters of lavender or blue with gored tweed skirts and wedge-heeled shoes. To the family at the White Barn, LeG became something of a spirit mother.

LeG began by sitting at a little table with the class facing her in a semicircle. Intending to establish an air of formality, she called everybody by his last name; students called her "Miss LeG." She lectured on the three playwrights. "Ibsen is cerebral," she noted, "whereas Chekhov is emotional. Exploring Shakespeare is like seeing life under a magnifying glass. Exploring Chekhov is like peeking through a key hole." When she lectured, she implored, "Don't take notes; just listen."[20] The whole silhouette of the student rushing to "get it down" was too fussy and rigid. After parts were assigned, they worked on the scenes, with the goal of presenting a showcase of the best scenes at the end of the summer.

LeG taught largely through demonstrating, even to the point of giving line readings. One day she performed Hedda's first meeting with Thea. With no apparent preparation for the action, she kicked a footstool across the stage and trapped Thea in a corner of the set, a move certainly originating from one of LeG's actual performances. She then placed it at Thea's feet and sat on it. The action might seem extravagant for a polite hostess such as Hedda, but the students found it startling and totally in character.[21] It seemed to reveal Hedda's anger and bursts of passion.

Another day LeG demonstrated Lady Macbeth. She had been observing a young woman playing the scene where Lady Macbeth woos her husband. Apparently she could take no more. "Let me show you," she announced, as she climbed onto the stage and launched into it. It was very sexual. LeG grabbed her breasts and began a passionate embrace with Macbeth. The kiss dragged on and on and on and on. The students were glued to their seats. Finally they broke the kiss and came out of it. LeG turned, said, "Do you see what I mean now?" and proceeded with the next scene. Hours later, as they were all leaving the building for the day, LeG finally quipped, "It's been like Hollywood around here today, hasn't it." Everyone cheered.[22]

There were other lessons. When the students worked on Shakespeare, LeG assigned them to work through their scene in their head and not verbalize it. It was a tough exercise in concentration. She stressed tempo in dialogue, insisting that the movement of a line affected its meaning.

Not all lessons were academic. One evening, LeG attended a White Barn performance of *The Sign of Winter* starring Ruth Chatterton and Anne Meacham. As soon as she noticed that Meacham's bodice was gingerly plumped, she stormed out. "Why do actresses have to wear falsies?" she huffed. After she harangued over it with her students the next day, she marched up to one of the bustier young actresses and poked her in the bosom. "You're not wearing one of those, are you?"[23]

Not all the students flowered under her technique, but for the more advanced, it was truly liberating. They felt they were witness to absolutely impeccable readings and to an actress who was totally centered. Peter Falk claims that the students were "aware of being in the presence of someone out of the ordinary. She exuded intelligence and confidence. She knew what she was talking about. There was not much talking, no nonsense, no bullshit. I wish there were more like her. She is a vanishing species."[24]

LeG made a very active tool of her outside/in approach of demonstrating. By resorting to her own artistic integrity and to her diligent work as an actress, she intended these demonstrations to become little jewels of technique for the class to see. She then expected the students to do their homework and make the parts their own. Her coaching was always positive and loving but at the same time honest and tough. Sometimes she advised students to forget acting as a career; occasionally she offered a boost of encouragement.

Peter Falk thanked LeG thirty years after her classes: "I remember you with awe and I'll always be indebted to you."[25] For many years Falk had harbored a secret desire to be an actor, but he had been too embarrassed to admit it. He had dabbled in amateur productions, but his romantic fantasy of a career in theatre and his fear of failure had always stopped him. He had been holding down a mundane job as an efficiency expert in Hartford, Connecticut, but when he learned LeG was going to conduct acting classes, he knew he had to enroll. "I lied and went to the course. I was supposed to be a professional actor but went anyway. I wanted to be in proximity to other professionals."

Rather than take a two-week vacation during that summer, Falk convinced his employer to let him miss one day a week for the entire summer. Because of the drive, he was always arriving for class a few minutes late. One day, LeG's patience boiled over. "Mr. Falk," she barked as he entered the theatre, "why are you always late? An actor must learn discipline."

"I have to drive here each time from Hartford," he explained.

"From Hartford? What acting job can you possibly have in Hartford?" she challenged.

When he finally admitted in front of the class that he did not have an acting job and that he was not a professional actor, LeG stared him in the eye and said very pointedly, "You should be!"

Before that day ended, Falk drove back to Hartford and quit his job. "No one else but her could have done it. Only a few words from her mouth meant more to me than anything." In ending his letter of thanks he offers, "My very, very best and love from an old student to the lady who changed his life."[26]

Though there were some of the customary claims of favoritism and bad coaching, the students adored LeG. During their lunch breaks, they all ate yogurt together on the sunny patio. LeG had always remained unsocial with her peers. In fact, theatre owner Lucille Lortel seldom had lunch with her or socialized with her in any way, and she admitted that she was actually frightened of her. But every summer LeG really let down her guard and invited her students to her home. For the first time, she truly enjoyed entertaining. She hosted them all at a lavish reception at the start of classes. Quite frequently Gun would prepare a typical lobster clambake for smaller groups of students. Some students returned for two or three dinners. At one of the elaborate feasts prepared by Gun, LeG's feisty and hyperactive dog started chewing on the tablecloth. "You finally have a dog you deserve," Gun commented. LeG laughed uproariously at the comparison.[27]

But there was more than just entertaining. LeG seemed interested in sharing herself with these young thespians. Since they posed no threat and truly worshiped her, there was no need to feel intimidated by them. She accompanied students on leisurely strolls through her woods and showed them her theatre treasures. She told them stories about Duse and Bernhardt. Often she pointed to her complete set of Washington Irving. "He's magnificent," she sighed. She even agreed to give free, private lessons to some of the more promising students and awarded scholarships to those in need.

LeG loved her work at the White Barn. There artists had "a chance to experiment, untrammeled by the usual commercial pressures. Part of the fun of being allowed into such a laboratory lies in the sharing of the excitement and adventure of the search."[28]

Soon after her first summer of classes in 1955, LeG agreed to repeat her portrayal of Miss Moffat in *The Corn Is Green*, at the Fred Miller Theatre in Milwaukee, Wisconsin. As she boarded the plane for her flight to the Midwest, she had no way of knowing that she would soon meet a man thirty years her junior, who would eventually propose marriage.

Dalton Dearborn had amassed a number of credits in his twenty-seven years. He had studied at Erwin Piscator's Dramatic Workshop, where his classmates had included Rod Steiger, Walter Matthau, Ben Gazzara, Elaine Stritch, and Bea Arthur. While playing some fifteen plays a season for five years at a summer theatre in Pennsylvania, he had learned more than a few acting tricks.

In 1954, Dalton was invited to join the new regional theatre in Milwaukee, where they presented the typical Broadway staples— *Sabrina Fair*, *Kind Lady*, and *Three Men on a Horse*. Tall, slender, and delicately featured, Dalton was hired as the resident juvenile. After the first season, however, he was determined to never again play regional theatre. It was not acting. It was like working on an assembly line that never stops.[29] The audiences were uneducated, and friends back east had no idea that Milwaukee even existed. There was simply no prestige!

The only reason Dalton returned for a second season was the promise that he would play Morgan Evans to LeG's Miss Moffat. It would be a real play with a wonderful part and with the legendary Miss LeG. When she entered the theatre for the first rehearsal, he was stunned. She was teeny, so petite. He had envisioned the Statue of Liberty coming through the door, but here was this teeny, little lady dressed in purple and wearing a blue silk scarf.

Introductions over, Dalton watched LeG rehearse her first scene. He was awestruck. Her voice was as clear as a bell, her speech was absolutely impeccable, and her physical presence was electric. He felt he was in the presence of a god. He could hardly stand up; his knees began to shake; he could barely speak. He was frightened of having to act with her. As he was walking up the aisle for their lunch break, he felt LeG slide in under his arm and cozy up to him. She was so warm. She held his hand and said, "Don't worry. I'll coach you in the part."

For fourteen days of rehearsals and every night of the run, they worked alone in her dressing room. "You have to get the me, me, me out of the way," LeG implored, "in order to allow the character to come in. You will achieve a state of gratuitous grace by allowing the force to come in and take over. It will be a time of sublime ecstasy." She not only gave him acting lessons but told him many stories of her life in the theatre. Since Dalton had considered suicide the summer before, he perhaps needed a savior. He found one in LeG. At this point in her life, she seemed eager to reach out to groom and train young talent. She was a real-life Miss Moffat, nurturing her own Morgan Evans.

LeG and her new protégé possessed an incredible empathy for each other, so when they held hands or touched, it looked natural and unrehearsed. When Gun visited LeG and witnessed their performance, she was overwhelmed. "It's as if you've been playing together all your lives. He's like you when you were his age."

"Yes, isn't it amazing," LeG replied. Once again she slipped her arm into his and leaned on Dalton's shoulder. "He's wonderful to work with."

Some very poignant moments came at the very end of the play. LeG had fought with the management over the use of fans for air circulation. "The fans must be off during the performance. If they are not off, I'll be on the next plane to Westport!" A compromise was reached, and the fans were shut down during the final scene. The silence was chilling. People could hear the actors breathing, almost as though their souls were being carried out on their breath. The performance was an astounding success and drew standing ovations every evening. Within six weeks LeG repeated her performance for television's Hallmark Hall of Fame.

In the spring, LeG asked Dalton to meet her in New York. After he picked her up at her hotel, they strolled down Fifth Avenue like a proper couple, Dalton walking on the curb side and holding doors open. LeG was so very fragile, feminine, and seductive. She slipped her arm in his and hung on like she needed protection. They looked at the fashionable clothes and laughed at the immense diamonds in the windows of Tiffany's and Cartier's.

While dining at a French restaurant before they saw *Tiger at the Gates*, LeG said, "You have trouble with the boys, don't you? The chap in Milwaukee is in love with you, isn't he?" As Dalton sputtered in his soup, she continued, "That really doesn't matter. It's alright to be gay. It's in all of nature," and she proceeded to cite many instances of homosexuality in animals. She knew all too well, however, how critics could pounce on it and damage a career. Her only word of caution: "Do not let it affect your work."

Their next meeting was in Connecticut during the summer of 1956. LeG invited Dalton to take her acting classes at the White Barn and to play the role of Oswald to her Mrs. Alving in *Ghosts* at the end of the season. They would then take the production to Milwaukee in November.

During rehearsals, LeG told Dalton that though the final scene, when Oswald goes mad, was usually staged with his back to the audience, this time he was going to face front. Dalton hesitated, then she showed him what she wanted. She got into a chair and played the entire last scene. The hairs stood up on the back of his neck. It was so real and so frightening. At the end of the performances, there was never any applause. The audience was riveted.

Reviewers of *Ghosts* applauded LeG's eloquence and calm and intelligent tone. Lucille Lortel remarked thirty-five years later that it was one of the highlights at the White Barn. Everybody loved it.[30] LeG had failed miserably with this play only eight years earlier. Perhaps the lapse of time had given her perspective. She could now incorporate her own challenges into her performance in order to reveal a struggling and rebellious Mrs. Alving.

It is also possible that LeG had discovered a new freedom in acting with Dalton at her side: "I feel I have reached a point in my work *beyond* technique—I have never felt so completely *free* as I did in my performances of *Ghosts*. . . . I suddenly felt completely liberated and set free from *myself*."[31] It was almost as though she had allowed a mystical force to take over, and she had achieved a state of grace.

A few months later they were together again. LeG asked Dalton to revive their production of *The Corn Is Green* for a short engagement at the Palm Beach Playhouse in Florida. Before starting the long drive south together, he went to Westport and stayed overnight. Gun served a dinner of Danish delicacies, and the next morning, after a breakfast of poached eggs and a look at the *New York Times*, they set out on their journey.

Three days later they arrived in Palm Beach. LeG was to stay with her old friend Alice De Lamar, an eccentric, very shy woman, who had died black hair and chalky white skin, and who often dressed in black.

She reminded Dalton of Mrs. Danvers in *Rebecca*. Although she was a millionaire, her Spanish hacienda had tiny rooms. LeG stayed in what had been a monk's cell. It had slits for windows, cement walls, and the barest of furniture. In the rear of the house was an Olympic-sized pool and a line of royal palms stretching down to the Atlantic Ocean. Dalton stayed in a nearby guest house.

Once rehearsals began, LeG's attitude toward Dalton seemed to change. On the first day she began calling him "Mr. Dearborn." She was very cold, aloof, and distant, and she complained, "Your performance is becoming predictable. It is not springing from anything real. You better work on it. Peculiar things have crept into your performance, my boy." She then climbed into her car, slammed the door, and drove off, leaving Dalton to walk back to his room. The next day, much to his disappointment, she announced that since they only had one week to rehearse the whole play, she was not going to work much on their scenes together.

By opening night, Dalton was ready for blood. He could not understand why she refused to rehearse with him if his scenes needed work. When he got to the scene where Morgan tells off Miss Moffat, Dalton really lit into her in no uncertain terms. It just poured out of him. There was tumultuous applause. When he came off the stage, LeG was standing in her dressing room door blocking his way, with her arms crossed and head cocked. "You caught a fish by the tail tonight," she said with a grin.

After the play closed they stayed for three more days to rest and relax. Dalton moved into a room adjoining LeG's. As they were standing under the palm trees drinking champagne and eating caviar during a going-away party their last night, she admitted the dirty trick she had played on him. They had their arms around each other's waists when the red moon suddenly rose out of the ocean. It turned golden and then yellow. She said very softly that she was proud of him and that he had given a wonderful performance. "I played a dirty trick on you," she said, I'm sorry, but I had to do it to get a performance out of you."

LeG had purposely made Dalton angry so he could resurrect the emotion for the stage. She had created the exact same situation as in the play. Dalton was her protégé just as Morgan in the play is Miss Moffat's, and he got fed up with being treated like a mechanical robot. What LeG needed was to have the boy really tell Miss Moffat off. But Dalton was so in awe of LeG that he had been unable to do it. In fact, he was in love with her.

By her birthday on January 11, LeG was back home in Westport and entertaining May Sarton. She wrote to her house guest a few days later: "I can't tell you what a joy it was to have you here—I only wish it had been *longer*. Some time you must come and stay for a real visit. There are so very few people one can talk to anymore—at least I find it so. . . . You are one of the *very* dearest friends I have—I feel that more and more. . . . Much love to you ever."[32]

On March 9 LeG wrote to May again and described a surprising request that she had made:

It was very sweet of you indeed to think of taking a note to Jo for me. At first I couldn't make up my mind whether to send her a tiny word or not. I think I told you she finds it easier and better *not* to write to me or have me write to her—and it may be she won't want to take the little note I enclose. If not—just tear it up—and tell her I shall completely understand. The main thing is she should know from you that I am very well— that I have ceased beating at the bars of things, and they have therefore miraculously ceased to exist. But—oh!—what a time it's taken me to find that out! I'm so glad you are going to see her—God bless her—she is always and forever in my heart.[33]

The note was delivered to Josie, who was living in California. No one knows what it contained or even if Josie read it. Was it a plea to resume their lost love of twenty-five years ago? Was LeG begging forgiveness for her selfishness? Did she discuss her broken relationships with Gun and Peggy? Did she tell Josie that she had only days earlier rejected Dalton's marriage proposal?

LeG ends her letter to May with these words: "I shall think of you a great deal—and miss you. Not that I see you much—but you will be so *very* far away! . . . Dear love to *you*—it's good to know you are in this world—I've been starting some seeds of delphiniums and pansies in the little green house—and potting up my gloxinia bulbs. What a miracle it all is!"

After the many years of struggle, of suffering and repentance, LeG had finally achieved a sense of serenity. She was finally at peace and ready for the miracle about to take place in her life.

9

The Queen Is Back

LeG had generally resisted acting in revivals in New York, but suddenly an offer came along that was just too good to ignore. Producers Norris Houghton and T. Edward Hambleton asked her to play the role of Queen Elizabeth in Schiller's *Mary Stuart* for the opening of the fifth season at their off-Broadway Phoenix Theatre. The director was the renowned Tyrone Guthrie, and Irene Worth was costarring as Mary.

Nevertheless, this miracle almost eluded LeG. Judith Anderson was the producers' first choice to play the Virgin Queen, but she rejected the salary. LeG's name was then proposed. She was the right age, had vast experience with classical material, and had an imperious, larger-than-life quality to her acting that would fit well with Guthrie's operatic concept for the production. But both Houghton and Hambleton had serious doubts about her:

> There was a good deal of concern about LeG. She had, after the heyday of the Civic, toured with a lot of Ibsen, and somehow the glamour of a star was lost in the process. We thought of her as living in Westport and not having any relationship with the outside world. Her name was pretty dreary at this time. You just didn't associate a star with Le Gallienne. She was certainly nowhere as far as theatre work was concerned.[1]

Since the collapse of the ART ten years earlier, LeG had acted in a mere six plays—four revivals and two new scripts—and had played a total of only fifty-two performances in New York. It seemed as though she had chosen to retire from the New York theatre. Also, her excessive drinking had become more than a rumor; it was a known fact. And with the single exception of her work with Peggy, she had always directed herself in classic revivals. At this point in her life would she be able to submit to the will of another director? Ultimately, Guthrie was sent to Westport to visit with LeG, and soon after he returned to New York with his report, a contract was signed.[2]

LeG spent endless hours dissecting her character, knowing full well that the outcome could determine the rest of her career. For weeks her Blue Room was littered with books about the English Renaissance and about Elizabeth. Using photographs of famous portraits sent to her from England, LeG studied ways to transform herself physically into the very image of her character. Even after the production opened, she labored more than two hours every night applying her makeup, her false nose and eyebrows, and her red wig. She even analyzed the queen's handwriting, so that when she signed Mary Stuart's death warrant in the play's climax she could inscribe an authentic replica of the regal "Elizabeth R."

A young Ellis Rabb played a small role and eagerly observed how Guthrie conducted rehearsals:

What Guthrie did was a surprise. Irene and LeG did not meet until the first rehearsal. There was a brief, very polite, ladylike handshake, and then they sat at opposite ends of the table for the reading. He treated them so differently. He was mean as a snake to Irene. There were these awful scenes. He would say, "No, Irene, you are not going to do that. I want you down here by this word. I am the director. You are the wronged queen. Now go up there and start over again!" With LeG he would walk up close to her and whisper very gently and privately. He treated her almost like the co-director of the production.

One day Irene suddenly turned to LeG and snapped, "Are you going to be over there, Queen?" LeG replied very meekly, "I don't know. Whatever Dr. Guthrie wants." "Just stay where you are, Irene," Tony commanded. There was always an element of tension between them. Just a few years ago, Irene confided to me that in the beginning she didn't think LeG was a very good actress.

Guthrie's technique was amazing. He viewed the play as a duel between these two queens and treated his leading ladies in a way that accentuated their differences. Because the play breaks into the Mary scenes and the Elizabeth scenes, he announced that he would rehearse with two separate casts and that for several weeks he would not rehearse the climactic scene when the two queens meet. When the day finally came, he gathered everybody around and walked the whole thing through for all to see. Then they played the scene. Rabb noticed that "Irene and LeG didn't even say hello that day. They only acted on the stage. The scene was absolutely hair-raising, it was so exciting, it was so vibrant, it was so alive, and they held that through all the performances!"[3]

With all her celebrity, LeG did not misuse her relationship with Guthrie. Actor Paul Ballantyne observed that she behaved "as any star of her era would have behaved. She . . . kept close watch on all developments. . . . This does not mean, however, that she would ever—EVER—have thrown a play out the window or distorted it in any way to satisfy her vanity or any personal desires or whims or ambitions. The play was the thing with her; not just a vehicle for her."[4]

LeG's performance was glorious, one with thrilling bravura. Tom F. Driver of *Christian Century* applauded her electric performance: "It is long since we have seen such command of the stage. . . . [She is] willing to use the body and the voice as instruments which rise on command to the heights demanded by the script." It was acting in the grand style. LeG's queen portrayed a wide range of human emotions: guile, fear, caution, loneliness, jealousy, uncertainty, passion, and ruthlessness. As Walter Kerr reported, "She is giving us her most vigorous, caustic, and shrewdly detailed performance in some years." She made audiences believe that she was indeed the Great Queen Elizabeth. Longtime drama critic Richard Watts, Jr., reported, "This is by all odds the finest portrayal I have ever seen Miss Le Gallienne offer."[5]

Over thirty years later, audience members still shudder when they describe a moment LeG created with chilling intensity. Mortimer had come to the queen as a possible candidate to carry out her plans and knelt before her. Then began a long pause as she decided if she could trust him. LeG did absolutely nothing but gaze at this man. She looked him up and down. Then she studied him from another angle. It went on and on and on and on. Houghton remembers the moment vividly:

> I've never been present at such a long, long, long pause. She knew exactly when to stop it, or she would lose her audience. She took it as long as she dared. It was a most arresting moment as everyone realized what was passing through Elizabeth's mind, as she weighed and judged every facet of Mortimer's character.[6]

The techniques that had brought LeG fame earlier in her career still worked. She was simply incredible as Elizabeth. Thrilled theatregoers claimed that they would never again be able to separate Elizabeth and Eva Le Gallienne. Michael Dewell, a young entrepreneur who would soon serve as her producer for the next ten years, called it "a transfiguring performance. Here this rather petite lady looked tall and commanding. She became Elizabeth!"[7]

The performance was a definite turn in LeG's waning career. Her kind of play and her style of acting had been unpopular for nearly two decades, and she was nearly unknown by the current Broadway crowd. By the late 1950s, however, audiences' tastes had begun to change. The psychological realism of Tennessee Williams, Arthur Miller, William Inge, and Lillian Hellman had lost its fascination. The period of their greatest contributions had come to an end.

The Actors' Studio emphasis on emotional memory and method acting soon began to seem too limiting. Audiences were returning to an appreciation for the artistic use of body and voice and for the studied development of characterization. A critic for *Theatre Arts* explained as he praised *Mary Stuart*: "If nowadays the play suggests escapism, it is just the thing for those seeking to get away from it all—'it,' in this case, being our contemporary realistic acting and stagecraft." LeG certainly recognized the difference: "It's been fun playing Elizabeth. . . . People seem to be so grateful to see 'real theatre' for a change."[8]

"It was striking good luck for us and for her. It was a dream production from the beginning," Hambleton stressed. "It brought her back to center stage and catapulted her into her old position. It was remarkable."[9] Adding to everyone's joy were long lines at the box office and announcements of an extended run.

Because of her regained popularity, LeG was asked to serve on a committee planning a repertory theatre for the new Lincoln Center for the Performing Arts. Even though she knew she would not be asked to be in charge of the company, she was delighted to be included. The honor soon turned sour. She disagreed violently with the committee's focus on architecture and insisted they should be concentrating on actors and plays and on how to build an audience. After a number of frustrating meetings, she resigned in a huff.

Her comeback brought her more work. She appeared in three dramatic specials on television in 1958—*The Bridge of San Luis Rey*, *The Shadow of a Genius*, and *Bitter Heritage*—and she had the opportunity to play opposite such stars as Judith Anderson, Hume Cronyn, Boris Karloff, and Franchot Tone. According to one reviewer, millions of viewers witnessed "acting at its supreme best."[10]

Next, LeG departed for London to appear as Mrs. Dudgeon in a film version of Shaw's *Devil's Disciple*. Regardless of the distinguished cast, which included Burt Lancaster, Kirk Douglas, and Laurence Olivier, LeG did not anticipate the project: "Mrs. Dudgeon is indeed most 'disagreeable'—poor thing! I can't say I look forward to her very much." When the film was released the following year, LeG's part had been edited down to only a few lines. Accustomed to concentrating on the clear development of her characters, she found film acting disturbing. For a stage actor the work is "so bitty," she complained. "There's no opportunity to play a whole scene. It's done in scraps and bits. It's nothing but technical."[11]

Soon after she returned to Westport, LeG received a call from Hambleton. Would she be interested in touring with *Mary Stuart*? Once again, the project had not initially included LeG. About a year earlier, Houghton and Hambleton had hired Michael Dewell and Frances Ann Dougherty to organize a touring wing for their theatre; it was to be called the National Phoenix. The idea was to start with something modest, so they began plans to tour with a staged reading of Sean O'Casey's new play *The Drums of Father Ned* starring Peggy Wood.

Sometime after they began to negotiate bookings, however, their leading lady was injured in a serious accident. As she was turning on the holiday lights for the Christmas tree at Times Square, the tree fell over on her. Her doctor reported that she would be unable to tour. The producers were frantic until Hambleton remembered that LeG had hinted she might be willing to tour *Mary Stuart*.

Though this idea was quite a switch from traveling with "four chairs and dinner jackets," they jumped on the idea. They knew it would be extremely difficult to book a Schiller classic, especially with a star whose name recognition they questioned, but at least they would be assisted by the exceptional acclaim the production had already received in such magazines as *Time*, *Life*, and *Newsweek*. Another coup was Lawrence Langner's decision to make the tour a Theatre Guild attraction. Since his organization controlled a national chain of theatregoers, it provided the struggling company with massive subscription lists at every stop.

Dewell and Dougherty, who were appointed as producers, actually had very few professional credits at that time. Dewell, a graduate of Yale University and London's Royal Academy of Dramatic Arts, had performed in touring companies and on television and had served as stage manager at the off-Broadway Cherry Lane Theatre. Dougherty's theatre background was even less. She had worked with children's theatre in Westport, had served as a play reader for David Selznick, and had been assisting Norris Houghton at the Phoenix. "I don't know what Miss Le Gallienne thought of these kids that were going to be producers," Dewell chuckled. "She probably thought she was going to be producing it anyway."[12]

Although LeG had been involved for several weeks in endless talk about the production and had made a verbal agreement to tour, specific details still had to be worked out with her fearsome agent, Jane Broder. Dewell told her he would send a contract, but Broder said, "No, that is not really the way we're going to do it. I will come to your office and bring you what she will find acceptable." When Broder arrived, Dewell offered her a cup of coffee. "No, we'll see how the conversation goes, and if it goes well, then I'll have a cup." Broder then laid out the conditions. LeG insisted on final approval of the lighting and gels, booking contracts, houses, a follow spot operator who would travel with the company, and all publicity photos. Footlights and an apron stage had to be available at every theatre. She would not participate in publicity schemes, and she would not play in a "miked" house. "There are no dead spots in a theatre," LeG had always proclaimed, "only dead audiences."[13]

One clause Dewell flatly rejected was LeG's refusal to play in Chicago: "Must we play Chicago? You know, Noel tells me that he has it in his contract that he won't play there. I understand Rex Harrison has it in his contract. Why can't I have it?" Apparently many touring companies had suffered from the vicious reviews of *Chicago Tribune's* Claudia Cassidy, and LeG hoped to bypass such problems.[14]

Dewell came to realize that the contract was "the goddamnest thing" he had ever signed. "Even so, she was, thank God, not one of these star ladies. She was interested in every aspect of the production."[15] She wanted the original sets, costumes, and as many of the original cast as possible; she insisted on giving the road the best standards of New York. Since Guthrie was not available to remount the show, LeG agreed to direct and made it clear that she would not go off on her own but would re-create the original staging.

At first, LeG was enormously concerned because Hambleton had rented the sets and costumes to the Vancouver Festival. To guarantee they would be properly cared for, LeG reluctantly consented to perform the play there for a few weeks, with Viveca Lindfors as Mary Stuart and John Reich directing. Since Dewell needed to discuss numerous details with LeG, he flew to Canada and took in the show while he was there. The performances had no spark, and Lindfors was intense to the point of being nearly grotesque. The two strong-willed women undoubtedly had words, for Lindfors has adamantly refused to talk about LeG or the production ever since. When Dewell went backstage afterward, LeG ran up to him crying, "Michael, don't worry! It's not going to be like this! Ours will be better!"[16]

But as LeG started to remount the production for the National Phoenix tour, problems surfaced immediately. Since Irene Worth was unavailable to re-create her role, Dewell hired Signe Hasso, a Swedish actress with an impressive background. Hasso had trained at the Stockholm Royal Academy and, by the age of nineteen, was a major star in her homeland. At twenty she had starred in the title role of *Mary Stuart* at the Royal Dramatic Theatre. In 1940 she had begun her American motion picture career, which included starring roles in *The House on 92nd Street* and the Academy Award-winning *A Double Life*. In 1950 she had journeyed to London to star in Ibsen's *Rosmersholm*. Most recently she had starred on Broadway in *Uncle Vanya* with Franchot Tone and in *The Applecart* with Maurice Evans.

The problem was not Hasso's background, nor was it that she and LeG clashed. In fact, they quickly became good friends. Since rehearsal time was limited, Dewell had mailed a script to Hasso, who was performing in a play in Stockholm. During the long journey to New York by ship, she studied the script and memorized her part. It was very hard to learn, since it was all in blank verse and not in her native tongue. When she started to say her opening line at the first rehearsal in New York, LeG stopped her abruptly, "No, darling, that's not quite right." They soon discovered that Hasso had been sent the wrong translation. They had ten days to rehearse. "Oh, my God, I can't do it!" Hasso cried. "Not in ten days." LeG was beside herself. What Hasso had memorized was similar, yet totally different. "Ask my secretary if she thinks she can get it into my head," Hasso said, "If she says yes, I'll do it. But I don't take any responsibility." The decision was to continue.[17]

They opened on October 2, 1959, in a high school auditorium in Sacramento, California—an odd site for a premiere, but a grand old friend of LeG's, Eleanor McClatchy, persuaded the city to roll out the carpet for the visiting royalty. When reminiscing about the splendid arrangements and all of LeG's female attachments, Dewell quipped, "You know, the title of LeG's biography could really be 'Le Gallienne and Her Ladies!'"[18] As it turned out, the reviewers concurred that it was a tremendously exciting show, a magnificent performance. Their judgment may have been influenced by the fact that McClatchy owned both the *Modesta Bee* and the *Sacramento Bee* newspapers.

Still lacking the support of major reviews, the company headed nervously for San Francisco, where advance sales were sparse. They had been warned of disaster, and Dewell and Dougherty were discouraged as they watched the first part of the performance. The audience seemed so terribly quiet. The play did not seem to be working. To drown their sorrows, they walked across the street to a bar, where they decided to stay until it was over.

Suddenly Dougherty blurted out, "Oh, my God, the flowers!" They had instructed two ushers to run down the aisles with huge bouquets of roses to present to the leading ladies during the curtain call. LeG and Hasso had been told in advance, but they knew they were to act surprised. "It'll be a disaster," Dougherty cried. "The audience will be rushing to get out, and the ushers will be fighting to get to the stage. We've got to stop them." They ran across the street, and as they were about to grab the ushers, a staff member whispered, "Stop! Stop! What are you doing? Listen, they love it." The entire audience was on its feet yelling, "Bravo!" The next morning, there was a line of people around the block trying to buy tickets. Almost overnight the entire engagement was sold out. "Miss Le Gallienne was gratified," Dewell remembers, "but not overwhelmed."[19]

LeG had expected all along to repeat her New York triumph and had been very depressed by the Vancouver Festival. It had been a difficult experience, so she was now quite relieved. From coast to coast, reporters proclaimed that LeG had reached new heights of dramatic power. Tickets were so much in demand during their run in the nation's capital that the company returned there at the end of the tour for another limited engagement. Staats Cotsworth had acted with LeG in many productions, but in his role of Lord Burleigh, he witnessed more than ever how "she was an actress who really looks at you! You could really play with her onstage. She was not a 'star' who was out for her own part."[20] The production received the Circle Award for that year's best road tour in the country and was televised for NBC.

The long tour was not without its moments. The company had traveled by bus and truck from Canada to their next stop in Detroit. All the sets came by rail. Following the regulations of the U.S. Customs office, the doors to the boxcars had remained sealed until an officer checked them. When the company reported to the train for the official inspection, they opened the doors of the boxcar that contained the props and out stumbled an elephant! It seems that their boxcar had been switched with one from a Ringling Brothers circus. LeG was a wreck. "I cannot play without my throne!" she demanded. They wound up flying the throne in, and the curtain went up fifteen minutes late.[21]

As the company ended the tour, plans for a permanent organization began to develop. They wanted the freedom to work with each other and with classical material. They wanted to tour across the country and present full-scale productions in repertory, echoing LeG's earlier attempts in the twenties and forties. With LeG as the inspiration and honorary president, Dewell and Dougherty began to plan. A representative of the company would have to arrive in each city several weeks in advance in order to promote ticket sales, disseminate teaching materials to the schools, prepare publicity campaigns, and appear before civic groups. Members of the cast and crew would meet with students, sometimes after performances and sometimes in their class-rooms. It was LeG's suggestion to call the new group the National Repertory Theatre (NRT).

During the long months of intense activity, Dewell and LeG developed a unique alliance. He was never quite sure of his role, however, and early on concluded that LeG was not about to clarify it. As he confessed years later, "Miss Le Gallienne being Miss Le Galli-enne, she more or less told me what to do." For example, while the company rehearsed in New York, Dewell would spend the mornings working diligently on paperwork in the office. Late in the afternoon, he would rush home, change into dungarees, and return to the theatre to help the stage manager. After several days of this routine, LeG took him aside. "You know, Michael, you're the producer on this. The cast needs a producer that they can look up to. He's their daddy, and actors are children. You should wear a suit and a tie when you are around them. You should act like the producer, and you should not be emptying the wastebasket."[22]

Dewell observed many things. Each time they reached a new theatre on the tour, LeG would immediately test the house. Carrying Miss Midge, her tiny Yorkshire terrier, in one hand, she would walk out to center stage, slowly look around, then cross down and walk back and forth along the curtain line, snapping her fingers. She could tell everything about the acoustics of the theatre and how she would have to pitch her voice. Then she would walk center stage just to the curtain line and reach out her arms. The first time he saw this, Dewell asked her what she was doing. "Oh, I learned that from Sarah Bernhardt. Sarah always said that if you stood at center stage at the curtain line and reached out your arms as if you were going to give a welcoming embrace to someone and if the walls of the theatre lined up with the lines of your arms, then it was a good theatre."

Other observations were not so inspiring. Although LeG was exceptionally disciplined when she was working—never late, always early, never touching a drink even during lunch, and exercising every day—Dewell saw another side when he visited her on Christmas Eve.

He could not ignore the petty fighting, the little unpleasant spats, between LeG and Gun. At issue was LeG's demand that Gun come to cook for her during their engagement in Boston. Though he had been invited for a holiday dinner, there was virtually no food in the house. Trying to make conversation over the sparse table, Dewell blurted out very innocently, "I don't understand. Why is Katharine Cornell called the First Lady of American Theatre. Was she wonderful at one time?" LeG replied bluntly, "No! Kit never could act." End of discussion. They proceeded to drink so heavily that by evening Dewell had to carry LeG up to her bed.

Dewell also noticed that LeG seemed terribly out of touch with the world around her. In one instance, she telephoned him a few months after the *Mary Stuart* tour: "I've just discovered the most wonderful person. I saw this girl give the most extraordinary performance. You must get her. You must hire her. Just wait until you see her. I went to see a movie called *Judgment at Nuremberg*. There is a girl in it that's wonderful; she ought to be famous. Her name is Judy Garland." In another instance, they were driving to Los Angeles for their next engagement, when Dewell casually mentioned to LeG that advance sales were slim because they were competing with the World Series. "The World Series," she muttered. "Couldn't you have arranged for them to have changed it?" It took him a few minutes to realize she did not mean the booking, but rather the date of the World Series!

Although LeG had an offer from the Dallas Theatre Center to direct and star in *John Gabriel Borkman* and *The Seagull*, she chose instead to continue with the NRT. By the time the new tour started in the fall of 1961, LeG was elated: "This tour has a personal meaning. The climate for repertory has improved. . . . It is accepted and wanted. It is a growing movement."[23]

Capitalizing on their success with LeG as Elizabeth I, Dewell and Dougherty starred her again in *Mary Stuart* and added Maxwell Anderson's *Elizabeth the Queen*. The notices equaled those of a year earlier. Richard Coe of the *Washington Post* called her "a sterling star." Philadelphia's Ernest Schier sang her praises: " . . . a spellbinding performance by one of the world's great actresses." Headlines from coast to coast announced, "The Queen is Back."[24]

The royal entourage rarely traveled first class, and more by bus and truck. They would pull into a city in the middle of the night not knowing if it was Omaha, Kalamazoo, or maybe Buffalo. They played in renovated barns and churches, new theatres and old, dragging along with them their ironing boards, hair dryers, bird cages, plants, dogs and cats, and hundreds of bags. When LeG checked into her hotel room, she would immediately set about converting the room more to her liking, moving the furniture, unpacking her own drapes and hanging them over the windows, and installing lower wattage bulbs in all the light fixtures.

As they were making their long trek from Minnesota to Lincoln, Nebraska, they were stranded in a severe blizzard in the middle of the prairie. The snow drifted so high, in fact, that the bus was almost entirely buried. After they huddled in the cold for over twelve hours, running the engine, worrying if they would run out of fuel, fearing carbon monoxide, and trying to keep warm, they were suddenly discovered by a local farmer who was an amateur dogsledder. Faye Emerson, who was touring as Mary Stuart, pulled her fur coat over another mink, climbed out of the bus, and shouted, "Just the thing. My good man, I'm hiring you to . . . "

"Take you to a hotel?" he asked.

"No," she replied, "take me to the nearest liquor store for supplies." She went whooshing off on the dogsled and returned later with a case of scotch. They were finally rescued and taken to a small-town American Legion Hall, where they spent the next few days.[25]

The townspeople were a delight. They brought blankets and food, including homemade pies. Because of her age and star status, LeG was given special treatment and was invited to spend the time in the mayor's home. Gina Shield was assistant to the producers and reported that LeG was a "remarkably good sport about the whole thing and behaved very, very well. We laughed a lot about the idea of Miss LeG being stranded in a small town. Somehow her having to deal with the locals didn't fit in with our picture of her. I'm sure she was utterly charming and delightful."[26]

But LeG wasn't always charming and delightful. After the company finished their evening performance in Texarkana, they flew by chartered plane to New Orleans, arriving in the dim hours of the morning. Even though they had a matinee that day, many of the actors went out on the town. Everybody was really hung over when they arrived at the theatre. LeG was incensed! She was already dressed in her Elizabeth I costume, and she called the entire company onto the stage. She stood up on her throne and reamed them. She was furious! "I've never been so disgusted in my life. Get out of my sight, all of you! Don't you ever dare do this again. Go and find a bakery shop, eat a loaf of bread, and then come back and do the performance. Now get out of my sight!"[27] Everybody ran like hell! Though LeG enjoyed imbibing now and then just as much as the next person, maybe more, she never allowed it to interfere with her work.

LeG's former protégé Dalton Dearborn has unpleasant memories of the tour.[28] As Essex is taken away to be executed at the end of *Elizabeth the Queen*, LeG always sank down at the foot of her throne. The lights would narrow down to her face and get smaller and smaller as the drumroll swelled. Then blackout. The company would walk on for their curtain call. Since LeG was blinded by the light, the actors would guide her as the lights came up. They would walk as a company to the footlights, bow, and then back up as the curtain lowered. One night the actor who usually held her hand missed the curtain call, and Dalton stepped in to fill the gap. As the curtain came down, LeG turned her head and suddenly realized who was standing next to her. She snatched her hand away, and in full view of the audience, snarled under her breath, "It's the snake."

A few days later, Dalton asked the company manager if he could sit in the "star seat," the right front of the bus. The protocol was never dictated, but everyone understood it nevertheless. The seat, of course, first belonged to LeG, but since she preferred to sit further back with her dog, it went to Faye Emerson. For this journey Faye was traveling by car, leaving the seat vacant. Because of the heirarchy, Dalton knew that it was appropriate to ask in advance. When LeG realized what had occurred, she insisted he relinquish the seat to her. "You don't like that, do you?" she said coldly. Later, when Dalton asked Emerson if she could explain what it was that he had done wrong—why LeG had become so distant and aloof—she answered simply, "She's in love with you."

More than likely, LeG resented what she perceived was Dalton's presumptuous and rude behavior. She now felt she could not trust him. As a supporting player, he should not be standing next to her during curtain calls, and he should not be sitting in choice seats on the bus. But whatever the reason for her antagonism, that was the last time she spoke to him for ten years. Though he had nightmares for months and almost suffered a breakdown over their ruptured relationship, LeG never explained or apologized. Many times during the next decade, mutual friends pleaded with her to see him again, but she refused. Again May Sarton's observation applied: "Once LeG finished with someone, she finished!"[29]

Even at the age of sixty-two, LeG could be bewitching. One young member of the company, a twenty-year-old from Australia, had most of the women running after him. Still, he was intent on making love to

LeG; he found her so incredibly sensual. She had that ability to attract. She never used her sexuality, but it was there. It was like she was a mother, grandmother, and lover, all at the same time. One minute, she could be so gentle, feminine, and seductive. The next minute she could be an actual tigress and could turn around and snap your head off.

In twenty-six weeks the company had traveled 40,000 miles and had played in fifty-eight cities to over 250,000 people. The tour had cost nearly $1,000,000. Although business had been brisk, the impossible expense of touring repertory had left them with a deficit of over $150,000.[30] The producers decided, therefore, that in order to make the NRT a permanent company, they would spend the next year campaigning for funds and planning the future.

During that time, LeG cemented her friendship with Ellis Rabb and his new bride, Rosemary Harris.[31] Rabb had first seen "this fabled lady of the theatre" some twenty years earlier, when he was a young apprentice at the Wellesley Summer Theatre, where she had toured with *The Corn Is Green*:

> I was intrigued by the little snippets people would say about her—her starting a repertory company and her career. She was sort of like a legend, but she was living. I thought she must be hundreds of years old, which of course she wasn't. I was told about the time in the twenties when she returned to New York from Paris. As she stepped off the oceanliner she was holding a brace of greyhounds, was wearing a huge Russian hat, and was smoking from a long, elegant cigarette holder. I had heard about her lesbianism, and I think what I really wanted to see was what a dyke looked like.

Rabb had watched from across the street as LeG had whisked into the hotel the day she arrived. Because of the scars from the fire, she had refused to be seen in public without proper makeup. "The mysterious and strange lady left an indelible impression" on the seventeen-year-old actor.

When Rabb and LeG had performed together in the original *Mary Stuart* production in 1957, he had become her "mascot" and had visited her daily backstage. She had joined the NRT about the same time that he had founded the Association of Producing Artists (APA), another company specializing in touring noncommercial plays.

During one of his first seasons, Rabb had hired her with a grant from the Rockefeller Foundation, to coach him during the last four or five days of rehearsals for *Richard II*. He knew she had always liked his voice, so he thought she would be especially impressed with that part of his acting. He distinctly remembers her comments about his big speech in the deposition scene. "I don't understand," she said, "What do you have in mind? Why are you so vocal? You are so terribly vocal." As he tried to justify his serious intensity, she interrupted, "Why don't you just say it? You're using your technique and your voice too much."

Rabb went away cursing and absolutely devastated, wishing LeG would go back to New York. But when he gave the speech at the next rehearsal, he immediately discovered that he was hearing it for the first time: "I realized her note had been brilliant. It was not something a director would normally give an actor. It sounds so negative, but she was so straightforward. She had forced me to become aware of what I was saying."

At the reception prior to the opening night performance, a terrible scene erupted over the future of the company. LeG was present and heard Rabb and some of the university officials squaring off. He lashed out at them and stormed from the room, screaming that he would not perform. LeG went to his apartment and urged him to go on. He eventually gave what he thought was the best performance of his life. All the anger galvanized him: "I didn't give a shit about what anybody else did or said. I didn't worry about the production or the company. I just concentrated on my objective, and I really acted." After the performance, there was a light tapping on his dressing room door. When he looked up in the mirror, he saw LeG standing behind him. She walked in, knelt down beside him, and took his hands in hers. She did not say a word, yet there was such communication: "Tout sera bien" (All shall be well).

To inaugurate the company's residency on the campus of the University of Michigan at Ann Arbor in 1962, Rabb telephoned LeG to see if she would direct and star in *Ghosts*. "Let me call you after I've had time to think about it," she said. Literally no more than five minutes later, she called back and had it entirely cast, including Rosemary Harris as Regina.[32]

When the cast arrived for their first rehearsal at the White Barn Theatre, they discovered that LeG had single-handedly taped out the floor plan and placed all the furniture. After three days in which she totally blocked the play, she said, "OK, I'll see you in two weeks. Spend that time thinking about your character, the blocking, the set, and what you want to accomplish."[33]

That evening LeG invited Ellis and Rosemary to dinner. They drank a lot of wine and looked at LeG's scrapbooks. In one clipping, Isadora Duncan had written about "the young and beautiful actress

Eva Le Gallienne, whom I call my spiritual daughter." She signed another: "My little angel." By two in the morning they were all tiddly and went to bed.

Since Gun was out of town, LeG prepared breakfast the next morning, scrambling eggs with one hand and drinking salty dogs with the other. "She was like a child; she was so happy that we were there." She began to describe how she had made her flying entrance as Peter Pan. She first flopped to the floor; then she began leaping from table to countertop and nearly crashed into Rosemary's arms. Every time she would get midway into some story she was performing, the whole kitchen would cloud with smoke from the burned eggs and toast, and all of them would collapse in fits of laughter. She tried three times, until they finally settled for corn flakes.

As Ellis and Rosemary drove through LeG's gates later in the day and began their journey back to New York, Rosemary became very pensive. "We must be careful, darling," she said. "LeG could devour us!" At first Ellis thought his wife was being overly dramatic and was perhaps even jealous of LeG, but he soon concluded that she was right: "If we had fanned the flames going on at that time and had been like her children, she probably would have given us everything. If we had wanted to do just that, we would soon have been living there and commuting to New York. On the one hand she pushes everyone away, but when she gets somebody she wants, she wants them totally."

LeG asked Rabb to be "her eyes" once they began to rehearse in Michigan:

> I felt very self-conscious about it. I mean she knows everything about Ibsen. She's translated and acted and directed. I mean this *is* Eva Le Gallienne. Very timidly I gave a very technical note, something about the position of one of the plants on the set. A day or two later she came up to me and said very softly, "Ellis, dear, don't you have any notes for me?" I watched again and got an idea. I went backstage, and trembling I tried to give her a note, a conceptual note. I suggested that rather than be so affectionate toward Oswald at the end that she have more anger within herself. It was a complete change in playing the beat.

> Instead of disregarding the note she asked, "What do you mean? Go on, tell me more." That night I could see her mind trying to make it work. I started to go up to her afterwards to tell her to forget it, that it was a stupid idea, and she stopped me. "Don't say anything! I know now exactly what you mean. I didn't do it; I didn't do it. But I'm going to do it. Let's just be quiet." And the next time, there it was.

LeG directed the first act like it was high comedy. It was unbelievably vital, with a brilliant tempo and bright sunlight. Nothing hinted of the typically Ibsenesque gloom. With the sound of the champagne bottle being uncorked at the end of the act, LeG abruptly changed the mood. She sat down in her famous Duse pose, clasping her hands and leaning forward on her knees. Her head came up ever so slowly. Rabb has never forgotten "those eyes. One of them half open, so blue, piercing like diamonds. And then she muttered a hushed 'Ghosts.' She colored the word so richly. It had about seventeen syllables." The audience jumped in fright. They were drawn into the play; they were hooked. Reviewers called her work "magnificently tragic," "intensely real," "a unique theatre experience that may never be duplicated in our generation."[34]

For the next three years LeG returned to the road with the NRT. She was actively involved in all three of the productions in the first season. She played the small part of Mme. Desmermortes in Anouilh's *Ring Round the Moon*. A satirical charade filled with confusion and mistaken identities, the production achieved modest success. LeG, however, had trouble with the flamboyant style and felt intimidated by her character's elegant femininity.

LeG's main contribution of the year was to direct and star as the middle-aged, fading actress in *The Seagull*. It was important to cast everyone a little older than ideal, since LeG was considerably older than her character. She personally selected Anne Meacham to play Nina. Dewell wanted film actor Farley Granger to play Konstantin, since he would have definite box-office appeal, so he took him to Westport to meet LeG. After a leisurely lunch, she asked if Granger could return in a week or so for a private meeting. She thought he might work for the role, but she worried: "He has such a straight back. That's not good. We'll have to see if we can break him down."[35]

When the day finally came, they met at the White Barn, and she proceeded to lead him through a series of exercises. When he looks back on it, Granger can see her "pulling me aside, putting her arm around my shoulder, and talking very quietly. Sometimes she would kneel or sit at my feet as she gave me notes."[36] Persuaded that she could work with him, she handed him a stack of authentic Russian clothes she had ransacked from her trunks and instructed him to wear them when he returned to New York. They would help him build his character.

LeG's insistence on authenticity could have brought a criminal conviction. Among her demands was a real Russian seagull for the set, not American, not fake, but a real Russian seagull. The producers and props department looked everywhere. They knew that the Audubon Society must not get wind of their search. Since the Russian seagull was an endangered species, it was against the law to have one, let alone kill it. Dewell worked through legal channels in Washington, DC, and even flew to Missouri to find one; no luck. He found a dead one, but his hotel refused to store it in the restaurant's freezer. Finally, he had one secretly delivered live to his apartment in Manhattan. Dewell personally strangled it halfway across the George Washington Bridge, as he took it to a New Jersey taxidermist to be stuffed.[37] LeG also required Russian cigarettes, not an easy item to find in the middle of the Cold War.

This was the first production on which designer Tharon Musser worked with LeG, and she was excited to learn that "she was very positive and knew what she wanted, but she was not dictatorial":

> She put people in awe to the point where we didn't really want to displease her. She was not one of those ladies that did summer stock and was specific about the color of gels and position of the lights. LeG was not like that. She was after the right atmosphere and wanted to show off the play, not the star.

Musser had designed a special cue that would slowly bring up the lights by a door just prior to LeG's first entrance. LeG saw it at a technical run and stopped the rehearsal. "No, no, no, darling. That's not right at all." When Musser explained that she was trying to prepare the audience for LeG's entrance by focusing attention in that area, LeG replied, "No, no, no, no, darling. Don't do that; don't worry. They will know when I enter."[38]

There were no real conflicts between them. Musser was much younger then, had no axe to grind, and believed it was her role to work for the director. She came to realize, however, that LeG "could not reconcile herself to the fact that things were not like they had been at the Civic Rep." She wanted lighting designed especially for each play, which would have required hiring union technicians to rehang and focus every night as they changed to the next play. She objected to Musser's general repertory plot, even though it included a few specials for each production. "She understood why, but wouldn't accept it. I guess she never really admitted that theatre existed after the Civic, certainly not in new ways of doing things."[39]

The production became so popular during the tour that Dewell and Dougherty booked it for a five-week run on Broadway at the end of

the season—the first time LeG had returned since 1957. She seemed to
be playing with a renewed confidence. Walter Kerr noticed that when
she tilted her head back to send cigarette smoke into the sky, there was a
regal skip to her foot, "as she decides that she is still 'fresh as a girl.'" At
one point, she took out a puff and powdered her nose with what one
critic called "the neat, calm poise of the performer who has made a
scene count."[40]

Besides the kudos, it was a time for awards. On the evening of April
5, 1964, New York's Belasco Theatre was filled with such notables as
John Gielgud, Katharine Cornell, Lillian Gish, June Havoc, Lillian
Hellman, and Margaret Leighton, as Adlai Stevenson, the U.S. dele-
gate to the United Nations, presented LeG with an engraved silver
bowl from the American National Theatre and Academy, for her fifty
years of service to the theatre.

But it was the special Tony Award that caused a stir. The NRT was
slated for an award for their excellence, with the understanding that
LeG be the person to accept. She had always avoided such huge public
gatherings and at first refused. Dewell promised that he would buy a
large table at the affair and have all of her friends around her. She finally
consented but under one condition—Richard Burton must be the
person presenting.

When the evening arrived, Dewell was aghast:[41] "She was grotesque. She'd had her hair done. I'd known her for nearly ten years, and
I'd never known her to have her hair done. Some old lady out in the
boonies had frizzed it all up. She bought a frilly dress with lots of
ruffles! Oh, God! She looked a fright!" Dewell bit his tongue and
proceeded to tell her that she looked wonderful. When the appropriate
time came, she got up and magestically sailed to the stage.

Burton was drunk out of his mind and made off-color remarks
through his entire speech. "In England we have a thing where we
honor people and make them dames. We should have that here. Miss Le
Gallienne should be a dame. Some people say she's not a dame. Now
there are dames, and there are *dames*." He rambled on and on—was she
or was she not. The whole acceptance was a disaster.

"It was awful," Dewell recalled. "Thank God, they cut to a
commercial for the television broadcast." He still resents the fact that
LeG kept the Tony statuette for herself, since it was meant not for her
but for the company. LeG drove back to Westport ashamed and never
discussed the evening again. When she was nominated for another
Tony nearly twenty years later, she did not want to attend. Not even her
closest friends knew why.

The next year LeG chose not to tour with the NRT, so she could finish writing a book about Eleonora Duse. However, she did direct two plays for the company. Her revival of *Liliom* was met with resistance. In the thirty years since she had presented the play at the Civic, times had changed. Audiences had certainly been thrilled with the musical version, *Carousel*, but that seemed more like a fantasy than did the original play. Even though this revival was some twenty years before consciousness was raised about battered women and domestic violence, audiences objected to the play's basic premise that it was "possible for someone to hit you . . . and not hurt you at all."[42]

Problems also came from LeG's directing. Her casting of Dolores Sutton as Julie was a mistake. Nobody but LeG wanted to hire her. She lacked charm and beauty and showed absolutely no sign that she could convey the pentup emotions of the character. "She was boring!" Dewell charged. The producers bowed to LeG's choice but later wished they had not always been so agreeable. Dewell has commented on her casting ability at length:

> Her casting tended to be conservative, not really exciting. She would go for the mundane, the acceptable. It was so ordinary and lady-like. She could be outrageous in her own performances, but she'd cast less-skilled actors. There was always the question of why she wanted to cast certain women. When I couldn't see it in their talent or in their type or in their looks, I wondered what LeG saw that I didn't see. I felt very often it was some sort of lesbian attraction. I don't mean she was going to put the make on them, but it was an attraction. It was a definite failure. If there was something wrong with an actor's audition, the worst thing she would say was "they have no demon." She meant they had no inner genius, no fire, no special spirit. She knew it was an essential part of genius, but she often settled for less in her casting.

> There is no doubt that her lesbianism affected her casting. She was put off by macho guys; she had trouble dealing with them and worked better with men who were not overly masculine. It was a limitation. She always wanted to hire her old friends, actors like Dickie Waring who was not a good actor. That was the kind of actor she went for, someone she rated as useful and not necessarily good. I remember when we were casting the *Mary Stuart* tour that Frances Ann and I objected to her wanting to cast an actor for the role Leicester who was going to tower over her. When we complained that he was too tall, she said, "He won't be." She wanted someone she knew she could out-act; someone who would not be competition. I suspect that her limitation with casting was at least part of the problem with her old American Repertory Theatre as well.[43]

Farley Granger, who played the title role, saw another problem with *Liliom*. He concluded that LeG simply held on too strongly to her 1920s production concept. Though she did not really try to make the cast imitate her in any way, still her overall approach and intent was rooted in her former renditions. A Chicago reviewer labeled the play "a fragile relic."[44]

Fortunately, LeG's second directing assignment of the season, when she was reunited with Signe Hasso in a revival of *Hedda Gabler*, was a much greater success. LeG had come to feel through the years that Hedda needed to be absolutely charming. That was Hasso's approach as well:

> I played her with much more femininity than LeG did. I thought that was the strength of the whole play, that she was very feminine. I had the most feminine clothes. When they play *Hedda* they usually play it very austere and with no sense of humor. She was a frigid woman, and she teased all the time. She would tease and tease and tease. We played it with lots of fun in the beginning. I wanted her to be pretty and full of charm. That was Hedda. So when the last act comes there is someplace for the actress to go. You cannot start out heavy.[45]

Though the role was known as LeG's signature piece, she allowed Hasso freedom to pursue a new interpretation. "She was wonderful," Hasso stressed. "She embroidered on my ideas. That's why she's a wonderful director. I would do things the way I saw them in rehearsal, and they would give her ideas. She would sort of add and subtract from what I was doing. She sort of edits. She's a very good editor!"

Hasso even urged two script changes that LeG accepted. In her translation of the play, LeG writes that Eilert Lovborg shoots himself in the bowels, but Hasso argued that a better translation of Ibsen's line was that he shoots himself in the groin: "That's the whole play, Lovborg representing fertility and Hedda being rational. It produces a totally different reaction from saying 'bowels,' for then you get to the heart of the play. Groin is now okay to say, but when I said it twenty-five years ago people gasped."

Hasso's other change, one that even Ibsen enthusiasts applauded, came at the end of the play. Ibsen's original ends with one gunshot, and everybody rushes up to the inner room and realizes Hedda had committed suicide. Hasso felt the end was too abrupt and that Ibsen "wouldn't mind a change, because he himself relied on the ideas of a director." She had Hedda fire her pistols twice after she went into the inner room and closed the curtains behind her. The first time was as if she were just practicing, and her husband responded with "Please, dear, not today, not today. Please don't play with your pistols today." She then opened the curtains with a little smile and a laugh. Everybody relaxed. Then came another shot. Her husband stood up and repeated more firmly, "Please, not today! I told you, not today," as he crossed up and threw back the curtains to reveal her body. Both Hasso and LeG agreed that it made the ending much stronger.

Although LeG apparently developed a close working relationship with her leading lady, she certainly had some tense moments with the production staff. Once again her demand for authenticity was incessant. When Hedda burns Eilert's manuscript at the end of act 3, LeG wanted a real burning flame in the porcelain stove. To appease her, the props department created an extremely realistic, fake fire, using an intricate system of colored gels, lights, and fans. Tharon Musser designed the lights and was proud of the effect:

> It was marvelous, but LeG would not have it. She had done it at the Civic Rep, damn it, and she would do it again. When I told her there was no way we could have an open flame, that it was now against all regulations to have a real fire on stage and that we just could not do it in Boston of all places since they had experienced many theatre fires in the past, she said, "Just on opening night when the critics are there, and then after that we'll stop."[46]

Luckily, nobody in the audience that opening night realized they were witnessing a real fire!

For a few days LeG was also at odds with Farley Granger, who was playing Eilert Lovborg. While they were in Boston, he left for a brief weekend to do some Christmas shopping in New York. Since a heavy snowstorm was slowing his return by train, he called ahead at every stop to inform the stage manager of his location. The company was pacing backstage at the theatre, wondering if he would ever make it. As the train pulled into the Boston depot, the stage manager was standing on the platform with Granger's costume. He changed in the car as they rushed wildly to the theatre, and he walked on stage just in time for his cue. LeG was absolutely furious with him. When he invited the entire cast to his hotel room a few days later to decorate a Christmas tree, LeG came, placed one or two ornaments on the tree, and walked out.[47]

The next summer LeG received a surprise telephone call from Terence Scammell, who was rehearsing for the role of Romeo at the

American Shakespeare Theatre in Stratford, Connecticut.[48] He had driven frantically back to New York one evening, had gone to the bars, and had gotten absolutely soused to the gills. He called LeG about three in the morning and told her he was quitting the production. His Juliet, Maria Tucci, was being very proper and would not allow him to kiss her or touch her. The next day LeG offered to coach them both if Allen Fletcher, the director, would approve.

It was incredible what LeG did. The first thing she said after observing a rehearsal was "You know, dear, you cannot play Juliet and hate your Romeo. That's what's coming out. Every time he moves toward you, you move away. When he takes you in his arms, you start to move your buttocks away from him. It's completely contrary to what the play is all about." LeG then suggested that Maria play Juliet to LeG's Romeo. They got up on the stage and started. When Maria began to move away, LeG grabbed her and squeezed her buttocks. "Stay close to me. This is what it's like. This is what it's all about, closeness, love, not this moving away." They would go to her house and rehearse on the balcony at the back of the house. Sometimes LeG would play Romeo and sometimes Juliet. She had so much energy. She was sixty-six, yet she seemed sixteen.

At the opening matinee performance, LeG brought Scammell an enormous bunch of flowers from her garden, arranged in a pewter jug that had belonged to her mother, and a small box containing a ring that LeG had worn when she had played Hamlet. The accompanying card said, "Beware the demon vanity. Don't be nervous, play well, be happy. Much love, LeG."

Scammell asked what she meant by the note "Beware the demon vanity." LeG replied,

> It means how are you going to feel when you get into the wings and when you stand there knowing that the press is going to be there?
>
> Beware the demon vanity. If you are worried about Terence Scammell there is no room for Romeo. You have learned your lines; you know what you've got to do. If you, Terence Scammell, stand in the way, go home. You cannot be an artist. You cannot be what you have to be if you cannot get rid of self. Beware the demon vanity!

Scammell remembered LeG's advice when he walked onto the stage, and he played as never before. The reviews were excellent, and the production became the big hit of the summer season—all because of

LeG. She made everything come alive. Even Lillian Gish, who was playing the Nurse, admitted it, and Helen Hayes called Scammell the Romeo of the century.

The following season, LeG returned to the stage. Dewell and Dougherty announced what was supposed to be LeG's farewell tour of the United States. Peggy Webster was hired to direct her in both *The Madwoman of Chaillot* and *The Trojan Women*. The two former partners had not worked together on stage for many years, not since 1950, when LeG had directed a production of *The Three Sisters* for the Brattle Theatre in Boston. "We were all sort of on edge," Musser recalled.[49] The couple's relationship and split were well known in theatre circles, and nobody knew if there would be fireworks or fawning. As it turned out, everything went smoothly.

Dewell said that "you could tell there was something under the surface. They scrapped occasionally, but it was as if they hadn't worked together for a long time, and they weren't going to let anything screw it up this time. They were very, very careful." Whenever he talked to Peggy about LeG, "she always talked very, very lovingly and with enormous respect for her talent. There was never anything personal said. They were very happy to be working together. That was clear."[50]

It was unfortunate, therefore, that the productions were not more popular. Peggy's directing of *Madwoman* was calm, orderly, and ponderous. Even Dewell, who produced it, described it as "old-fashioned and clutzy." Sloane Shelton played a supporting role and thought she understood the problem: "The Madwoman is a warm, expansive, and eccentric part. Those aspects are helped by a personality star. LeG lacked the bizarre side. She's too delicate and intellectual and has such a sense of solitude. The critics probably would have preferred a personality actress like Angela Lansbury."[51] Critics complained that LeG could barely be heard, but still she would not allow any "miking."

Shelton's reaction to LeG's performance as Queen Hecuba in *The Trojan Women* was quite the opposite. "She played ferociously. She gave you energy through her eyes. It had to do with her own concentration. She was so generous. In my main scene she put herself down-right with her back to the audience and gave me her complete attention. She focused entirely on me."[52] Made up as an old, stooped, white-haired woman wrapped in a rough, blood-red cloak, LeG suggested not a royal queen but a dispossessed refugee who had been living in utter hardship and discomfort for weeks. Coming as it did in 1965, the classic play became, under Peggy's direction, a subtle yet poignant statement about America's involvement in Vietnam.

By the end of the season, Dewell and Dougherty tried to shift the emphasis of the NRT. Although they had achieved national recognition and had brought first-rate productions of the classics to cities around the country, by the spring of 1966 they showed a debt of nearly a half million dollars.[53] They decided to abandon their touring and to become the resident company at the newly restored Ford's Theatre in Washington, DC. After a year, the company totally disbanded.

LeG's six years with the NRT had been personally fulfilling. Of the eleven productions, she had directed three and performed in six. For the most part her work had received great critical acclaim, and obviously the group's dedication to the classics and to repertory had excited her. But when the decision came to move to Ford's Theatre, LeG chose to leave the company. She had no interest in a permanent position so far from her Connecticut retreat.

Dewell had come to appreciate what a unique artist LeG was:

> She is able to transcend her own self so totally. As an actress, I don't think she had any weaknesses. None at all, and you can't say that about very many people. Her nature was so diverse and so crazy and her genius was so all over the place. It wasn't in any bourgeois sense polite or nice or acceptable. She was outrageous, absolutely outrageous. She had a keen intellect so she was able to apply that outrageousness. But she was so self-destructive. It was why things didn't often work out for her because of that war within her of always protecting herself.[54]

Regardless of his admiration, Dewell was not disappointed to see her leave the company. LeG had assumed the role of head of the company and had played it to the hilt. She insisted on the best treatment—all the way. Whenever they flew—which in those days had to be with TWA to accommodate her dog—she sat alone in the first-class section. Not even the producers merited that luxury. The best rooms at the hotels were assigned to her. Rehearsals were built around her schedule. The entire company cooperated with the media for publicity, but not LeG. She claimed weariness and would not accept radio or television interviews. Only on rare occasions would she grant a "class" interview with an important journalist.

Sometimes her behavior rankled the others. Once, in a railroad station in Texas, luggage had been misplaced, and everyone was expressing concern for poor Miss LeG. Faye Emerson exploded: "And where is Miss Le Gallienne? Where is the mighty Miss Le Gallienne? She's off somewhere, no doubt, resting her royal head on a velvet silk pillow! Courtesy of the management!!" Sometimes, there were incredible fights with lots of yelling and screaming, and Dewell often found himself the mediator.

Dewell and his partner were struggling to mold a team of artists who would work together to achieve a unity of style. But LeG was not a collaborator. Dewell learned through the years of working with her that she was "a dictator":

> She was deeply distasteful and would never acknowledge the production team or even the name of the NRT. She would talk about her personal attitudes, about the parts she was playing. She would talk about the Civic Rep or the ART as if she were trying to rewrite history. She never did anything to advance the NRT, only to advance the image and the history and the living legend of Eva Le Gallienne. I'm still mad about it. It was a dreadful way to behave, and it eventually completely alienated my partner from her. She is totally selfish.

Though LeG had no theatre work for several months, she managed to keep extremely busy with writing projects. In 1959 she had published her translations of seven Hans Christian Andersen tales, and now she put the finishing touches on her adaptation of *The Nightingale*. (In 1985 she also translated Andersen's *Snow Queen*.) She drew much praise for her biography of Eleonora Duse, which appeared in 1966. With the assistance of her secretary Eloise Armen, she even began to research a new biography. Because she had always respected the lengthy and descriptive reviews of Boston's H. T. Parker, she wanted to elevate him as the ultimate critic. Publishers were not interested.

May Sarton phoned LeG one morning to warn her about a new book Sarton was completing, *Mrs. Stevens Hears the Mermaids Singing*. The theme focuses on a woman who feels the need to disclose that she is lesbian. The main character is an aging writer who consents to being interviewed because she hopes she will be forced "to confront certain things in her own life and in her work that seem unresolved." She says to the young interviewers that "it isn't worth it any longer to wear a mask" and that "we have to be ourselves, however frightening or strange that self may prove to be."[55] May knew that since the story would be considered autobiographical, she would be revealing her own sexuality.

It was not easy for May to be so transparent; in fact, it was terribly difficult:

> The word "lesbian" I still find hard to use. There's almost always somebody else involved. I couldn't write the book until my parents were

dead; their generation just wouldn't understand. I finally considered it a great responsibility to "come out" because I had no family. Nobody could be hurt. I knew that plenty of people who love my work would be very shocked.[56]

LeG was one of them. When she interviewed Eloise Armen to be her secretary, LeG felt compelled to discuss her own sexuality. She warned Armen that if she accepted the position, some people might whisper that she, too, was a lesbian. In the course of the conversation LeG acknowledged shame and disapproval of May's confessional.[57]

A few years later, when Carolyn Heilbrun was working on a biography of May Sarton, she interviewed LeG in her home and drove away in utter dismay. She told May later that "she could not have been treated with greater distance and coldness." LeG would not discuss May Sarton's personal life, claiming that to do so would be a betrayal. "Obviously, it wouldn't have been," May stressed later. "Poor Carol; she couldn't get anywhere with LeG. It's sad, but it was always used against her probably more than if she had actually come out." Unlike May and the character in her novel, LeG could not remove the mask.

In years past LeG and May had seriously discussed the possibility of a relationship. "I loved her," May claimed, "but we were too alike to be lovers." They had much in common—dedication to careers, love of gardening, passion for solitude, artistic sensibilities—and they were both women who liked to take the initiative.

But as they grew older, their differences became more apparent. One night LeG came to her bedroom when May was visiting. "I was in therapy at the time trying to find out about myself. To her it was terrible! She came in the middle of the night in her nightgown and knelt at my bedside and implored me not to go to a psychiatrist. 'If you can't get through it yourself, then don't lean on some doctor.'"

May, like the character in her novel, had decided that "one of the privileges of old age was that no holds were barred. You were permitted to be absolutely honest." By contrast, as LeG grew older, she became more guarded with her identity and languished in shame.

LeG's relationship with Gun never improved. LeG never talked about any good times they shared. Even after their extended trip to Europe, visiting friends in London and driving through Scotland and Wales, all LeG would ever say was that Gun was an avid sightseer. Then she would sigh, "Oh, Marion was so gloomy. She wasn't Norwegian for nothing."[58]

Shortly after LeG had returned to Connecticut after her last tour with the NRT, she and Gun climbed into the car one evening, after having a few too many drinks. They misjudged a turn and ran over Miss Midge, LeG's favorite Yorkshire terrier. They were both hysterical with tears and sobbing. LeG had always said that she suffered more from the death of animals than of humans, since animals were so helpless. She made a vow then and there to stop drinking. Not long after that, she was having dinner at Ellis Rabb's apartment and was offered one of her favorite drinks, a salty dog. "No, thank you. I've stopped. I've decided I've had my quota," she said.[59]

A wonderful addition to their lives occurred when two very special friends moved nearby. Doris Johanson and Jessalyn Jones were both women who had worked in advertising in New York City and had lived in nearby Redding, Connecticut, for a number of years. They had met Gun in the mid-thirties when they had all stood at the back of the packed Civic Repertory Theatre one night, watching LeG perform in *Camille*. They quickly became close friends. When the caretaker's tiny cottage on LeG's property became available, the two partners moved in, and they remain there to this day.

Doris and Jessalyn were really more loyal and protecting of Gun than intimate with LeG. When LeG was off on her various tours, they would take Gun shopping and invite her to dinner. Sometimes they would even stay in the big house with her. Although they had always idolized LeG, they disliked her treatment of their devoted friend. On the rare occasions when they tried to talk to LeG about it, she would close up and retreat.[60]

Halfway through the 1967–68 season, LeG joined the APA-Phoenix, a merger of the Ellis Rabb and T. Edward Hambleton theatre companies. Her first assignment was to play Queen Marguerite in the American premiere of Ionesco's *Exit the King*, a modern morality play that dramatizes the reality of death. The play opens with the king being told he is going to die in ninety minutes. As the action progresses, he loses his health, his authority, and all his possessions. His first wife, Queen Marguerite, continually reminds him that he is going to die. Dressed totally in black and with her face sharply framed by a wimple, LeG appeared regal and austere.

Actually, LeG thought *Exit the King* was "extremely old-fashioned." What really attracted her to join the company was their promise that she could direct *The Cherry Orchard* toward the end of the season. At first, she wanted to cast Rosemary Harris in the lead, but since she and Rabb had recently divorced, the producers felt it would be risky to have her in the company. LeG's second choice was her old friend Uta Hagen. She was not completely wrong for the part, Rabb insisted.

229 / The Queen Is Back

"She is a great actress, but you felt that any moment she could chop down the cherry trees herself, saw up the lumber, and build condominiums."[61]

Hagen certainly had impressive credits. Her very first role had been as Ophelia in LeG's *Hamlet* three decades earlier. She had toured with Alfred Lunt and Lynn Fontanne. She had played Desdemona in America's first integrated production of *Othello*, starring Paul Robeson and directed by Peggy Webster. Five years later she took over Jessica Tandy's role of Blanche DuBois in *A Streetcar Named Desire*, and in 1951 she played the role of Shaw's Saint Joan for the Theatre Guild. Then came a Tony for her memorable performance of Martha in Albee's *Who's Afraid of Virginia Woolf*. Her friendship with LeG had remained so strong through the years that as part of her costume for Saint Joan, she had worn a special tunic that LeG had personally woven years earlier for their *Hamlet* production.

Tension began from the very first rehearsal. LeG was adamant about using her 1944 translation. More modern versions were suggested, but she would not budge, boasting that hers was best because she was an actress and knew what played—the sounds and rhythms. She scrapped constantly with Hagen during the rehearsals to make her character more frivolous, but Hagen would always argue, "But LeG, then I won't be true to myself." Then LeG would shoot back, "I don't know what all this stuff is, this Method acting and Actors' Studio stuff," and the battle would continue. Hagen begged for the freedom to develop the character as she saw the woman, but LeG would only defend her personal process of acting: "Acting is like planting a garden. If you plant carrots and you plant them very carefully in a row, then the carrots will all grow up in the right way. It is the gardener's job to put them down very carefully in the earth so they can grow."[62]

"The cast never pulled together," Hambleton noted. "I don't think Uta and LeG hit it off." This was truly an understatement. Clive Barnes called the acting "provincial," and other critics complained of the lack of ensemble acting and the absence of character relationships. Hagen became so disillusioned about her own ability that she stopped acting for twelve years. She credits LeG for discovering her and acknowledges her importance to the American theatre, but declined all invitations to visit her and refuses to be interviewed about her mentor: "Although I would like to help, I have a heavy work schedule of my own which doesn't allow me to give even superficial attention to such matters."[63]

The ordeal was just as draining on LeG. She had begun the play with an inexhaustible amount of energy. She would bound up the steps of the theatre every morning and have no patience with younger actors who waited for elevators. "I love APA," she beamed. "I've known Ellis Rabb many years, and I admire him very much. He has the closest thing to real repertory. . . . I haven't been as happy since the Civic Repertory days."[64]

By the time the reviews came out, however, LeG had suffered a heart attack. After a brief stay in the hospital, she went home to recuperate. Her doctors advised that she should never act again. Rather than tell her the truth, everyone agreed to say that she needed to rest for two more weeks. Whenever the time was up, the doctors would say, "I'm sorry, you need another two weeks." They actually played this game for quite a few months. During it all, Rabb would chat with her on the telephone and occasionally visit her in Connecticut.

One morning in late spring, she opened the newspaper and saw the announcement for the next season at the APA-Phoenix. She raced to the phone and called Rabb: "There is absolutely nothing for me. I can't play anything in those.

You know, dear, I don't have much time." Some of the stories he had heard about her suddenly flashed before him. He had often been warned: "If you rile her, if you get her back up, watch out." LeG had even bragged to him one time that in her earlier days, "I was a terror." He now experienced her outrage firsthand:

She was mad! She can just scratch her nails down that board when she wants to. I replied that we had to announce something or other. She was very distant, and I reminded her that the doctors said she should be careful not to exert herself. I got one more telephone call from her. It was very brief, and very icey: "I'm not wanted." And she hung up. I could not tell her the truth, that the doctors said she should not act again.

Then summer came. We were going to do *Exit the King* in repertory for a few performances in a couple of places, and the doctors said it might be good for her to do it. When I called and asked her, she said, "Oh, I didn't think you wanted me." There was nothing I could say; I got this wall. When she arrived in Palo Alto for the first engagement, I had flowers sent to her hotel and to her dressing room for the first rehearsal. I came in to the dressing room because I knew she would be there early; she always is. She was putting on her makeup and would not look at me except through the mirror. I knelt down beside her.

"Thank you very much for the flowers, dear. They're very, very beautiful, but I don't really understand what the note means. It says, 'Welcome

Home.' What does that mean?" Then she turned from the mirror straight to me: "I don't really have a home, do I? You had better go now; I must finish getting ready."[65]

Not too much later, LeG confided to May Sarton that she was in desperate need of a great boost to her morale, "which has taken a bit of a beating in this Year of Grace."[66] It appeared as if the APA-Phoenix did not want her. At the age of sixty-nine, LeG knew she was beyond starting another theatre, and she feared that she was being put out to pasture like some nagging old work horse.

10

Exit the Queen

Anyone who spent fifty years in the theatre was bound to experience reversals. LeG had more than her share. The decade of the twenties saw her on top, but by the mid-thirties she was something of a pariah. Though in the mid-forties she still managed to create national headlines with the ART, her career remained in a stalemate until the late fifties, when she played *Mary Stuart*. For the next ten years, she relished the attention she received as a star with classical repertory companies. Then, the overwhelming problems with *The Cherry Orchard* brought her decade of activity to a screeching halt. It seemed her career was always stopping and starting.

When things had begun to unravel in the past, LeG had fled to Connecticut or sometimes to Europe, where she would agonize over her failure and plot her next move. Her home had always been a place where she could enjoy peace and freedom from public scrutiny before she once again took to the boards. It had been a retreat where she could mount her next attack on the Broadway system. But now it appeared that her options were dwindling.

Her home was no longer a retreat, a place to recoup and dress her battle wounds, but a refuge, a sanctuary, and she developed walls to keep people away. She entertained few friends and even fewer strangers. She might invite Haila Stoddard and June Havoc or maybe Bambi Linn for tea, but she would never venture out to their nearby homes. The extreme isolation fed the rumor that she had become a rude and cranky recluse, but in reality she only wanted to be around people she could trust.

LeG tried to make the best of her forced retirement. She took up hammer and nails and helped a builder add another room to the main house. A bridge was made to connect the upper level of the structure to the barn, and she christened it the "May Sarton Memorial." She personally constructed a new set of bookcases for her Blue Room, and another set as a Christmas gift for Doris and Jess, who were living in the little caretaker's cottage at the bottom of the lane.

LeG's hectic schedule during the past ten years had taken her away from her animals, so now she devoted hours on end to feeding and caring for them. She began a training program for her new Yorkshire terrier, Nana, and even accompanied it to obedience classes. Doris and Jess noticed the uncanny affinity LeG had with animals. In fact, there was no animal that did not come to her. She could be standing nonchalantly in a room, and they would sidle up to her. One day she discovered two baby robins that had fallen from their nest and had injured their wings. She cared for them as lovingly as she would have cared for her own baby, forcing milk into their beaks every two hours with a little eye dropper and later feeding them small pieces of ground hamburger with a pair of tweezers. For a number of years after that, the two robins returned each summer to her garden. The animals brought her such joy that her friends used to say she should have been a veterinarian.[1]

A couple of years earlier, LeG had met a young twelve-year-old boy as he cut through her property on his way to school. At first she simply asked Ted Lockwood if he would like to earn some spending money by helping her in the garden after school and on weekends. Their relationship blossomed as they worked side by side nearly every day. The intensity at which she pursued something that was not her occupation but a mere hobby gave him inspiration. She knew all the botanical names and so many details about pruning and plant diseases. She sparked his interest in ornamental plants. Though she was missing more than half of her left little finger, it did not interfere with her gardening. She would stuff her glove with dirt and carry on. Her hands might have been crippled, but they were exceptionally strong.

Some might have thought that LeG was leading a sad and depressing life. Ted Lockwood would surely disagree. At least in the part of life they shared together, she was very happy—with the garden, the creatures of the forest, the trails in the woods, and her dogs. She was a loner much of the time, but she was not depressed and unhappy. She seldom talked theatre. They had a good time together. She accepted him for what he was, a quiet, shy, reticent, eleventh-generation Yankee. She thought of him as a son or grandson. Years later he opened his own business as a landscaper and gardener and moved into her original old house.

During this time, LeG's professional work was very limited. She taped a series of recordings of Hans Christian Andersen's tales and published a translation of *The Little Mermaid*, a lengthy review of two biographies of Ibsen, and an article about Sarah Bernhardt. She pulled every string imaginable to land the lead female role in the film *Harold and Maude* but ultimately lost to Ruth Gordon.

In June 1970 LeG played the featured role of the Countess of Rousillon in the American Shakespeare Festival's production of *All's Well That Ends Well*. The management had considered her for many roles in the past, but either she was busy or the directors were afraid of working with her.[2] Though it was a real coup for the theatre, Michael Kahn was quite nervous at first about directing her. He had heard all the stories about her temperament and was more than aware of her formidable background, but he found her unbelievably easy to work with:

> She was amenable to direction and terribly professional. I feared she might be a horror, but she wasn't at all. She helped younger members of the company in moving and speaking. She told the girls how to walk in the long gowns and how to hold them. She helped others with the verse. She had a very natural, real, conversational way of speaking verse. It was not old-fashioned or oratorical at all. It was very helpful having her as an example for the others in the company.

Producer Berenice Weiler remembers most vividly how LeG's voice rang through the theatre. There were times when it was a little difficult to hear her, but audiences loved seeing her on stage again.[3] So did the critics.

Despite the positive response, LeG found the engagement disillusioning. In her previous experience in repertory, the scenery was always saved and used again. But Stratford was like Broadway; the scenery was destroyed after each production. "How can you have a theatre like that?" she asked. "No wonder they spend millions. It's ridiculous. The waste is unbelievable. It makes me so angry!"[4] She knew that such waste led to higher ticket prices and therefore sluggish box office.

Soon after the play closed, LeG was haunted by a trail of personal tragedies. Hep died suddenly of a heart attack on July 4 at the age of seventy-six. She had suffered for some time with hardening of the arteries. The only source of irritation that had persisted between the sisters was their father. "*She* knew him as the artist. *I* knew him as the man," Hep explained:

> With Eva it was different. She only met Father from time to time in his studio, and their meetings were accompanied by the romance of a brilliant daughter making contact with a brilliant father. There were no breakfasts, luncheons and dinners en famille, no requests for pocket

money never handed over! None of the shoulder rubbing annoyances of family life—difficult at best.[5]

Hep definitely had her reasons for not idolizing her absent father.

Hep's death meant that LeG's only surviving blood relative was a cousin in Denmark. LeG had been close to Hep's husband through the years, but suddenly there was a sore spot—LeG was not mentioned in her half sister's will.[6] The estate was small, and since LeG owned her home and was still earning some money through her theatre work, Hep apparently saw no need to provide for her.

Fourteen months later, Gun died. In recent years she had been crippled with severe arthritis in her hands and had had heart trouble. A housekeeper-nurse had been hired to help with the daily chores. The morning Gun died, LeG called her friend Terence Scammell, who was living in California, and begged him to come. He arrived the next day and was stunned to see that Gun's bedroom had already been reno-vated—empty closets, fresh paint, new furniture, different paintings on the walls.

At first and for no apparent reason, LeG was irritable and sharp with Scammell, but the next morning she dismissed the previous day with a laugh and acted as if nothing serious had happened. It was only then that he realized the truth of the various tales he had heard about her. Her emotional tirade the day before had been the result of drinking. He had known her for nearly ten years and had never seen her touch a drop, but Gun's death had brought her back to the bottle.

LeG's grief was prompted not from losing a lover of nearly forty years but from a feeling of anger. She resented the years she had been burdened by Gun. When she died, Gun was a very handsome, tall, respectable-looking woman with snow white hair, the kind of woman most people would enjoy introducing to their mother. For most of her time with LeG, she had virtually no money of her own, no allowance, and had to beg LeG for all that she spent. Eloise Armen had urged her a few years earlier to sign up for Social Security. When she finally began to receive her monthly check, she confessed to Eloise that it was so wonderful to have her own spending money and not to have to ask LeG for money to buy stockings.[7]

Gun was virtually ignored in LeG's home and slinked in the shadows whenever there were visitors. LeG had always hidden her from public view as if she were ashamed of her. When asked a few years after Gun's death if she had known the woman, LeG's friend and neighbor Haila Stoddard registered a total blank. She did not recognize the name, and she did not know of any woman ever living in the house with LeG besides Peggy Webster. When Gun died, LeG did not want it reported that a woman lived with her and therefore provided no obituary for the local newspaper. To this day, there is no death certificate recorded in the Weston Town Hall. Gun left no will. Even though LeG was the administrator of Gun's estate, which was valued at less than $10,000, the sole beneficiary was a brother living in Houston, Texas.[8] By not including LeG, perhaps Gun was silently registering her many years of neglect.

A year later LeG was faced with a third death. Peggy Webster had been diagnosed with cancer and had undergone complicated surgery in New York. When it became apparent that the end was fast approaching, Peggy chose to leave her home on Martha's Vineyard and to return to England to die peacefully in London's St. Christopher's Hospice. She did not want prolonged pain and agony or the expense of more surgery. LeG accompanied her. Because England had strict regulations that prevented LeG from entering the country with her dog, she stayed for six weeks at Alice De Lamar's Paris apartment and flew daily to visit Peggy in London. She was at Peggy's bedside when she died on the evening of November 13, 1972.

Peggy's death distressed her more than the others. A former lover, comrade, and confidante was gone. She telephoned Eloise Armen that night to share the news, but Eloise was not home. When Eloise finally returned the call the next day, LeG was furious and screamed at her for not having returned the call sooner. Once again LeG was lashing out at a friend after a drinking binge.[9] When she returned to Connecticut in early January following a trip to Copenhagen, she wrote to her friend Eugenia Rawls:

> I was so exhausted when I got back home I had to stay in bed for ten days and was forbidden to do *anything*. So *silly*. But the last months of 1972 were pretty hard to take. Peggy was wonderful right up to the end. For her sake one can only say thank God it's over. She suffered so horribly for the last year. But oh! How one will miss her![10]

The three deaths, coming as they did in a span of two years, were devastating for LeG. Her good friend Jessalyn Jones took care of her for the next three years and saw her turning to the Bible for comfort. She read it daily as she had her breakfast in the Blue Room. People close to her, such as Ted Lockwood and Doris Johanson, noticed that parts of her seemed to be removed as her friends and loved ones died. During a lengthy interview she gave during this time, she sat silently in the shadows of the late afternoon sun, holding Nana to her chest. She leaned back in her chaise in the Blue Room. "I miss them so," she sighed. "They're all gone now."[11]

Perhaps LeG's grief prompted her to mend the schism she had suffered with one of her closest friends for ten years. Patrick Waddington, an actor who had toured with her in *Mary Stuart*, told Dalton Dearborn that she had expressed an interest in seeing him again. Dalton immediately wrote a note to her in response, and a day or two later she called him quite late at night with a simple message: "I've been mad too long."[12]

As he rode the train to visit her in Westport the following weekend, Dalton felt like a teenager going on his first date. LeG was waiting for him at the station. They climbed into her new car and proceeded to talk as if nothing had ever happened between them. She told him about the deaths in her extended family and about her frustration that she was not working. After dinner, she showed him a book that she had put together, a charming children's story filled with pictures of her dog, Miss Midge. Dalton offered to take it to publishers when he returned to New York. Although he never managed to engage a publisher, LeG seemed grateful for his efforts, and Dalton thought their intimate relationship might be restored.

LeG's feeling of loss and despair was complicated by her mounting awareness that she lacked proper recognition. Some years earlier she had assisted Paul Cooper as he prepared his Ph.D. dissertation about the Civic. She granted several interviews, wrote letters, and talked to him often on the telephone. She detested what he wrote: "I told him so. I felt his attitude towards the Civic was intolerably patronizing. . . . He completely missed the *Spirit*, purpose and not inconsiderable accomplishment of the Civic Rep." When she was asked in 1973 if she would help with another study about her career, she reluctantly consented and snapped, "Couldn't you decide to write about Helen Hayes? I'm sure she'd be much more co-operative!"[13]

In the summer of 1974, LeG was hired to repeat her acting classes at the White Barn. One morning before she drove to the theatre for a planning session, she reached for the *New York Times* and saw the headline on the front page: "Katharine Cornell Is Dead at 81." Cornell was described as "one of the great actresses of the American Theatre." So far, so good. Then she read that Alexander Woollcott referred to her as "The First Lady of the Theatre . . . a reigning Broadway star of the second quarter of the century, an actress without peer in emotional, romantic roles, and one, moreover, who took her plays to the byways and crossroads of America." Then came the ultimate assault: "With Helen Hayes and Lynn Fontanne, her contemporaries and rivals, Miss Cornell epitomized the artistry of acting." There was not a hint of LeG's name! In another article, Brooks Atkinson wrote that if Cornell "had a great reputation . . . it was because she had the integrity and taste of a lady."[14]

LeG flew into a rage. How could she be so forgotten and ignored. She had done as much, if not more, than Kit. Her Juliet was better, and so was her *Three Sisters*. Helen Hayes might have been good as Queen Victoria, but she could never perform classics, and she had sold out to Hollywood. Why did Helen deserve such praise? Just because she worked at promoting her image? And Lynn! Why, she had even begged LeG to help her save her production of *The Sea Gull* in the late 1930s. LeG knew that she was just as good—no, better—than them. How dare Atkinson discuss integrity and taste! Was it a sign of integrity and taste for lesbians such as Kit and Lynn to disguise their sexuality in preposterous marriages? Why should they be praised for their charade?

It was entirely understandable that LeG was forgotten. After all, except for the one-week engagement in *All's Well That Ends Well*, the theatre community had not heard from her for six years. Many people thought that after her heart attack and split with the APA-Phoenix in 1968, LeG had chosen to retire from the stage. The simple truth was that she was out of work. Retirement was hardly on her mind. The phone never rang, so it was up to her to create the project. Actually, she had been working for a number of years on a very intriguing idea that she hoped would restore her name.

Sometime in mid-1970, Peggy had suggested to LeG that she read a novel called *The Dream Watcher*, a charming, comic story about an eccentric eighty-year-old Mrs. Woodfin who helps a young boy find himself. Two years later, in the early fall of 1972, LeG had telephoned the author, Barbara Wersba, and said she would like to play the part of the old woman.

Wersba was forty years old at the time. The call was a miracle, since she had idolized LeG for over twenty years:

She became a role model for me when I was around 19, acting in summer stock on Cape Cod. She was playing *The Starcross Story* in Falmouth, and a group of us young actors drove over to see her. I was terribly impressed by her, her bearing, her voice, and fell in love with her. I was young and idealistic.

I had known for years that LeG was a lesbian. She was a "notorious" lesbian, which is rather sad, since I have never known anyone so reticent about her sexuality. She did, however, at the same time flaunt her preferences—which gave her the reputation.

I remember a snowy day in New York, when a friend and I stood across the street from LeG's apartment on West 12th Street. We stood there for hours, staring at her windows, hoping that she might appear. We were both in love with her, but in a very young and innocent way.[15]

Soon after the telephone call, Wersba had gone to Weston and had tea in the Blue Room with LeG and Peggy. LeG lay on the chaise, in the shadows. "She seemed terribly shy," Wersba recalled, "and that great voice, issuing from the shadows, moved me. Since she had been the heroine of my adolescence, I was stunned by the experience of meeting her."

Eventually they stood in front of the fireplace together, and LeG said very softly, "Why don't you write me a play?"

Wersba, who had published a dozen widely acclaimed children's books and was a book reviewer for the *New York Times*, replied, "I don't know how to write a play."

"Then learn!" LeG advised.

Wersba drove home and, "seduced by [LeG's] personality," began immediately to write a stage adaptation of *The Dream Watcher*. She would write a few scenes, drive to Weston from her home in Rockland County, New York, and work with LeG. Wersba would read Albert, the young boy, and LeG would read Mrs. Woodfin. "To act with her, this way," said Wersba, "was like a dream come true for the actress I still was in my heart."

They had worked all winter and spring, taking time out only when LeG took Peggy to the hospice in London.

I worked like a demon, and she did too. LeG kept complaining that what I was doing was *literary*, and what she needed was something to *act*. What was hard for me to deal with were her shifting moods. Happy one day, suicidal the next, I never knew what to expect from her. LeG is two people—Jekyll and Hyde—and for someone as green as I was in those days, it was baffling. She would be intensely cruel to me about the play— then phone to apologize. She would appear cold and indifferent—only to go out and buy me a wonderful present.

In late 1973 Roger L. Stevens had optioned the play for a production at the Kennedy Center. Since he did not want to spend much money on it, he kept looking for inexpensive tryouts. Ellis Rabb agreed to direct, but he kept asking Wersba for rewrites. One day he would want the play to be a surrealist dream, and the next day he would want it to move like a film. At one point, he suggested turning the young boy into an adult. Finally, Rabb disappeared, and weeks later he sent a letter to LeG saying that he no longer wanted to direct the play.

In June 1974 about the time of Katharine Cornell's death, LeG, Wersba, and their agent Audrey Wood met with Stevens in Weston to finalize plans. Burgess Meredith would direct. The play would first open at the University of Tennessee, then it would move on to the Kennedy Center in December. LeG was a charming hostess. At one point, when LeG had left the room, Audrey Wood whispered to Wersba that "in any other country in the world, Le Gallienne would have her own theatre. In *this* country, she grows roses."

After the meeting, Wersba drove to New York with Stevens and paused in the lobby of his hotel to phone LeG about something. "Only an hour had passed, but she was dead drunk—and in a flash this explained many of her mood swings to me."

The play created a final falling out between LeG and Dalton Dearborn.[16] It was the last time he ever saw her in her home. Because she was so excited about her upcoming role in *The Dream Watcher*, he promised during a weekend visit that he would read the script before he went to bed. He did not like it but was afraid to tell her. Five minutes before he left for the train the next morning, LeG turned around and asked him pointedly, "What did you think? You didn't like it, did you?"

He tried to explain that the writing was not memorable, that the characters did not seem to ring true, and that there seemed to be no credible relationship between the old woman and the young boy. This was not what LeG wanted to hear, and she got incredibly angry. "He does exist," she cried. "He lives right down the lane from me, and he's sixteen." She insisted that the boy was just like her neighbor boy and helper, Ted Lockwood. LeG drove Dalton to the train station, and they did not speak again for seven years.

By late July all plans for the production were canceled. LeG had suddenly learned that the director would not be Burgess but a faculty member at the university and that many of the roles would be played by college students. She could not accept the changes and accused Stevens of sabotaging the production: "That bastard. He's a devious operator!"[17]

LeG knew she was slipping fast into a period of depression and alcohol and that her only salvation would be the challenge of a new project, any new project. Four years had gone by since her last role, and no one seemed to notice. All she could see before her now were more of those "deep, black holes."[18]

11

The Comeback Kid

It was a total surprise to Wersba when LeG called a year later to tell her that Lucille Lortel wanted to present *The Dream Watcher* at the White Barn in late August.[1] Overnight a production evolved. Warren Enters was chosen as director, a cast was assembled, and rehearsals began. LeG and Wersba brought treasured objects from their homes to decorate the set. LeG, who claimed to hate The Method, put into the bookcase on stage only those books she felt Mrs. Woodfin might read. She did everything but climb the ladders and hang the lights. "It was hard on the director," Wersba observed. "It was clear that she was the boss, that this was her play." It had been so long, five years since LeG had been on the stage. She was so eager to act again and to prove not only to her critics but to herself that at seventy-five she was still able.

LeG was nervous and insecure, and once during the rehearsal period, she said to Wersba, "I'm afraid I'll go to pieces opening night."

"You will not go to pieces."

"Well, maybe I'll be like an old circus horse, hearing the music again."

"LeG, dear—you will hear the music."

She was a powerhouse, but sometimes she looked a hundred years old. For the open dress rehearsal, LeG's performance was so subdued, so quiet, that everyone was terrified. "My God," they all thought, "is *this* all she is going to do?" But on opening night, she was electrifying. During her last scene, which takes place on her deathbed in a hospital room, the audience was overwhelmed with tears. With the triumphant curtain call, Wersba dashed down to the lobby, grabbed a glass of champagne, and ran up to hand it to LeG as she came offstage. "Thank you, dear LeG," she said. But there was absolutely no response. "Always perverse," Wersba wrote years later. "She went cold if you showed love to her—was loving when you did not."

The *Variety* review was a marvel: " . . . a moving piece of stage-craft . . . rich in homespun philosophy. . . . In the hands of Eva LeGal-

lienne, it becomes a classic. Her performance is flawless."[2] By the third
performance, the cream of New York theatre was there—agents, producers, stars. And after the performance, Wersba and LeG were
mobbed in the Green Room.

June Havoc was in the audience and wrote a letter of thanks to
Lucille Lortel:

> [I am] hopeful of seeing LeG where she belongs once again: center stage,
> out front, and under proper aegis. . . . What a lovely jewel for your
> crown of achievements! What a rare and soul-satisfying experience for all
> of us, to hear the words and luxuriate in the presence of the very, very
> special.

The militant Audrey Wood was elated. "Wersba," she said, "I don't
know where this play is going, but it's going somewhere. You've done
it. You've pulled it off."[3]

During the weekend of the production, Wersba first met Eloise
Armen, who had come down from her summer home in New Hamp-
shire to take care of LeG. She was surprised when she first heard LeG
call Eloise "Mommy" but realized "it was apt. Gun had been a mommy
too. LeG very much needed one."[4]

For the entire week after the production, LeG was drunk. Wersba
would telephone, and LeG would be unable to speak. Her neighbors
and loyal friends Doris and Jess covered for her. But there were no
contracts, no offers, no nibbles. Everybody waited. Still nothing
happened. It appeared that the play's future was zero and that LeG's
dream of a comeback was pure fantasy. Her fear and dismay became
overwhelming, and she sank into silence.

Then, on October 1, LeG called Wersba with a little chuckle in her
voice to announce the good news—she had been offered a lead role in
The Royal Family, which would be directed by Ellis Rabb at the
Kennedy Center. The raves over LeG's performance at the White Barn
had landed her this job, but Wersba had come out of it empty-handed,
with no offers for her or for her play. Naturally, Wersba was beside
herself with frustration and was astonished that LeG did not show "one
ounce of concern" for her feelings of disappointment. Reluctantly, she
agreed to put *The Dream Watcher* on a back burner for LeG to use at
some future date.[5]

LeG was haughty about the whole thing. She pretended she did
not wish to waste her time on a play as frothy as *The Royal Family*.
Actually, she was elated. Loosely based on the exploits of the Bar-

rymore acting clan, the Kaufman-Ferber spoof reveals witty actors who never stop performing. They make entrances, strike poses, quip one-liners, and recite showstopping monologues. "It's such trivia," LeG scoffed. Then Rabb told her she would get the same star billing and salary as Rosemary Harris and Sam Levene. "Oh, why not. With Rosemary and you, and all of us together we might have some fun, and God knows, we can all use the money. We'll do our best."[6]

LeG's being cast as Fanny Cavendish, the aging matriarch of an acting family, was hardly spontaneous. Rabb's promise to her caused a huge scene with producer Roger Stevens. Stevens had grown to dislike LeG during their negotiations two years earlier and had no intention of casting her this time around. She lacked humor and could not play the frivolous comedy. She was not a big enough star. He wanted someone with more of a personality or at least with greater name recognition, someone like Rosalind Russell or Judith Anderson. But Rabb was adamant—LeG or no production. Ten days before rehearsals were to begin, Stevens finally agreed to cast her, but only after he was guaranteed that she would be reliable and refrain from drinking. There was still a battle over her salary and billing. Not until the very day of the first rehearsal was it settled, and then only because Rabb announced that unless she be granted a star contract, he would not show up.[7]

The one-week tryout at the McCarter Theatre in Princeton was tense. Rabb had intended on recapturing a 1920s atmosphere complete with a grandiose New York apartment decorated with tapestries and flowers, airy costumes, and tinkly, jaunty music. Nothing jelled, and the company was jittery about moving on to the Kennedy Center.

The opening in Washington, however, was one of those unexplainable miracles, and plans began almost immediately to continue the hit. The original idea allowed for a two-week engagement in December at the Brooklyn Academy of Music. But critical reactions to the Brooklyn performance rivaled those in Washington and paved the way for a long Broadway run: "a sparkling revival," "a play and production to love," "absolutely smashing comedy." Emory Lewis called LeG "a national treasure" and acclaimed LeG and Rosemary Harris as "two of the finest actresses in the land."[8] He predicted the play would run forever. How ironic that on December 30, 1975, LeG returned to Broadway in the same theatre where she had first reached stardom as Julie in *Liliom* over fifty years earlier. LeG would refer to the building only by its earlier name, the Fulton Theatre. To her annoyance, it was now called the Helen Hayes.

As the play was actually marching toward Broadway, LeG assured Barbara Wersba that future plans were for a road tour only and that she saw no Broadway run ahead that would delay resuming their plans for *The Dream Watcher*:

> She kept in touch with me—just often enough to be sure that I was not offering *Dream Watcher* to anyone else. And by now, of course, I had become aware that LeG was ruthless. She did not find it odd that I should hold the play for her while she triumphed in another play. And why did I do it? Because I felt we were married.[9]

LeG's performance was clearly part of the miracle of the production. Costar Rosemary Harris remembers that at the very first rehearsal, when the company listened to the incidental music Claibe Richardson had composed, "LeG seemed to hang back a bit as we all started dashing about, but she soon got the hang of things. She chose to play Fanny as an actress ahead of her time rather than one dwelling in the past."[10]

On her first entrance, LeG floated down the sweeping staircase with the youth and vitality of a teenager. "Oh, to move always as gracefully as she does," remarked actress Carole Shelley. "It was one perfect motion from beginning to end."[11] LeG dispensed with the cane called for in the script, for she wanted the audience to believe that this aging trouper might indeed embark on another tour.

The character's advanced age and declining health surfaced later in the performance.[12] At one point, while Fanny is overcome with excitement as she encourages her granddaughter to continue her acting career, she collapses. LeG struggled to her feet, spoke in a whisper, and began to climb up the long staircase as she pulled from something deep within her own feelings. She paused near the top and sighed, "No use. . . . No use fooling myself. . . . I'm through. . . . I'm finished." Though Fanny's son called her "the comeback kid," she knew her career was over. When LeG reentered a few minutes later, she again descended the stairs, not overplaying a decrepit old lady, but carefully and haltingly. The contrast with her first entrance was shocking.

Early in act 2, Fanny's son works his way down the long spiral staircase during a fencing lesson with his instructor. As they finish, the script instructs Fanny to exhibit her own fencing expertise by using a newspaper as a sword. LeG had studied fencing for over fifty years and disregarded the stage directions. She grabbed the sword from her son's hand and demonstrated with grand panache, "Ah, the immortal passado! the punto reverso! the hai!" Then she tossed the sword back to him: "You should have seen your father hold off eight of them." As she said this last line, LeG settled down on a low footstool and held a long pause. Her face, so vibrant moments before, sagged and paled. The brief instant brought a tender sensitivity to the character, as her thoughts wandered back to her deceased husband.

The highlight of LeG's performance came in the last few minutes of the play. The family had toasted the acting debut of the youngest Cavendish, Fanny's great-grandchild, and had moved into the adjoining library. The original script directed Fanny to remain in her chair. She reaches to set down her wine glass on a nearby table, drops her glass to the floor, and dies.

Rabb's suggestion for LeG was quite different. After the rest of the family left the room, she turned to salute with outstretched hand the huge portrait of her husband. Then, she slowly turned to the piano, where she picked up a script and walked part way up the stairs. As she turned around, Fanny started rehearsing the role she planned to tour. She was in absolute joy. She descended the stairs. Suddenly she gasped and collapsed into a chair turned upstage, dropping her script to her side. Like her husband before her, she died while performing. At one point during rehearsals, Rabb had considered turning her chair downstage so the audience could see her. But as Eloise Armen commented, "She holds that death pose for so long. And it is so believable! I watch from the wings every night because it scares me so. She plays it with such honesty."[13]

At first LeG had rejected Rabb's idea:[14] "Ellis, No! We can't do that. I know what you want. Some sort of great bravura for the end. But this play is simply too silly, too trivial, too unimportant to have anything like that. In a great play it would be all right, but not in something as silly as this. You must get the curtain down quickly." Because she objected, Rabb refrained from rehearsing the final scene for days.

Finally, with only a couple of days left before opening, LeG approached him. "Ellis, dear, we're just going to have to rehearse the end. It's very, very late. Now what is it you had in mind? Just explain it to me again." At the run-through the next day, as Rabb began to stop the rehearsal just before the death scene, LeG shot him a look and played on. LeG did everything he had suggested. She remembered all the seventeen pieces of business and the transitions. The rest of the cast had not yet received their blocking, but they improvised, and they all began to cry.

When Rabb signaled, "Curtain," they all rushed to her side. "Oh, LeG you were brilliant. You were so moving."

She rose very sprightly and said, "Oh, What nonsense. We can't do that. I simply won't." But she did. And whenever anyone complimented her work in that scene, she quite uncharacteristically replied, "It was Ellis, all Ellis!" At the end of the season, Rabb received a Tony for Best Director.

Sometimes the work was not easy. During a Kennedy Center performance, for example, Rosemary threw off her coat and accidentally hit LeG in the face. The intermission was extended while a doctor treated her eye, but the show continued uninterrupted. Shortly after the Broadway opening, LeG became ill with bronchitis. For nearly a month she remained in bed all day, arising only in time to travel to the theatre. When the producers hinted that she should be relieved from playing the matinees and that Mildred Dunnock might be available to take over the role, she rallied quickly. Like her character of Fanny Cavendish, LeG never missed a performance.[15]

Because the production was such a bonanza, producers Burry Fredrik and Sally Sears booked a twenty-three week national tour during the 1976–77 season. Rabb continued as director, but Carole Shelley substituted for Harris. Only LeG and Sam Levene represented the original stars of the company. LeG looked forward to the tour. As she stated most simply, "My public wants to see me." She joked about any future plans for *The Dream Watcher*: "I suppose by the time I get out of *Royal Family*, producers will say I'm too old for the part of Mrs. Woodfin!"[16]

Before the tour began, however, LeG telephoned Wersba to say that she was prepared to do *Dream Watcher* in a year, after *The Royal Family* completed its national tour. "Something in me broke then," Wersba recalled. "I said that I could not wait another year. She became abusive, yelled and screamed and called me a 'nobody.' I felt heartsick." They did not speak again for over three months.[17]

LeG retained her enthusiasm for the award-winning production, relished the praise, and carried on like a benevolent queen of the theatre. When Carole Shelley prepared to take over Rosemary Harris's role for the national tour, LeG volunteered to attend all the rehearsals. "She was generosity itself," Shelley commented. "She hardly suggested anything to begin with . . . allowing Ellis to direct me."[18]

LeG helped during the run of the tour as well. After about six weeks on the road, Rabb viewed the production for the first time, noticed that Shelley's performance had become "positively Chekhovian," and advised her to adjust. From then on, whenever she started to become a little too serious, LeG took her aside and said with a smile,

"Getting a little Russian, darling." She would always listen offstage or, if possible, watch from the wings to see if all was going well. "She has an extraordinary sense of timing," Shelley said, "and would be very aware if a scene was starting to slow down and would be able to be quite explicit as to where it was happening."

LeG remained keenly interested in her own performance, too, and she struggled to keep it fresh. Shelley observed that "her performance varied very little to my ear and eye":

> She had a distinct and clear line as to Fanny, and would always pursue that line. Seldom, if ever, do I recall that she added or altered her performance, and yet it always seemed to be fresh and secure. If she added anything, it was absolutely spontaneous and perfect. She was an object lesson in how to retain a role without allowing it to become stale.

LeG was honored highly for her efforts. The American National Theatre and Academy chose her as the fifth recipient of their National Artist Award. Alfred Lunt and Lynn Fontanne, ANTA's first winners, sent a message declaring "it is about time" that LeG joined the circle of honorees. "It makes us very happy to be in her company at last." President Gerald Ford hailed her "excellence of achievement."[19]

Theatre World also presented her with an award. When she and Anne Kaufman Schneider attended the ceremony at the end of the season, LeG was taken aback by one of the women that congratulated her. The energetic, goofy, effusive woman was in her mid-fifties, talked with a heavy nasal tone, and had bright blue eyes, blonde hair, and a smile that went on forever. Jewelry was everywhere. She had been a celebrity since 1949, when she had stopped the show with her rendition of "Diamonds Are a Girl's Best Friend." By the mid-sixties hers was a household name from coast to coast. And yet LeG had never heard of Carol Channing. She became so intrigued by this stranger that she went to a performance of *Hello, Dolly!* that Channing was presenting on Broadway that fall and was absolutely thrilled. She stood applauding through the entire curtain call, almost as if she had personally discovered some new talent.[20]

In spite of the awards, LeG was distressed to learn as she toured that her name no longer had the box-office draw it used to. *Variety* kept yapping about how Katharine Hepburn sold out houses as she toured with *The Matter of Gravity* and how Julie Harris packed them in for *The Belle of Amherst*. Only the one week in San Diego was big for *The Royal Family*; the rest of the bookings lost money.

The problem was not the production but that LeG was difficult to promote. She did only what she absolutely had to do. Publicist Shirley Herz would have to go to her on bended knee with even the simplest request. The internationally known photographer Alfred Eisenstaedt wanted to include LeG's photo in a new book he was preparing devoted to one hundred of the most famous American women. Most people would have jumped for the chance to pose for him. For nearly thirty years his work had been seen in *Life* magazine every week. He had photographed such world-famous celebrities as Mary Martin, Katharine Hepburn, Gloria Swanson, Edith Evans, and Marlene Dietrich.

One evening during the Broadway run of *The Royal Family*, Herz arranged for a backstage meeting between Eisenstaedt and LeG. Eisenstaedt first said he wanted her to pose in her Connecticut garden wearing one of her Fanny Cavendish costumes. When she objected, he suggested a photograph of her wearing a large brimmed hat in her garden. She responded, "I guess I'll have to wear a flower print dress next!" and turned him down. She would not make herself look like something she was not. Her friends begged her: "Do you want him to do Helen Hayes instead?" No discussion. She wanted no part of anything that was not pure Le Gallienne. She was a private person who would not promote herself, but as Herz later remarked, LeG's attitude did not always serve her well. The producers were even approached about taking the play to London. This, too, would have boosted LeG's popularity, but she dismissed the possibility because she would not have been allowed to take her dog.[21]

Anne Kaufman Schneider tried to change LeG's mind about publicity.[22] Since she was the daughter of George S. Kaufman and owned the rights to *The Royal Family*, she became very involved with the revival and its progress. Obviously, she had much to gain from a successful revival. She had never seen LeG perform before this production and really knew little about her. One afternoon during the Princeton tryout, she happened to be seated across the room at a restaurant where LeG and her secretary Eloise Armen were having their lunch. There was total silence, no conversation between them. Anne became further intrigued when Burry Fredrik told her about LeG's lesbianism and the divorce scandal.

A very intimate relationship began to develop between Anne and LeG, a relationship that some gossip-mongers called a latent love affair. During the New York run, LeG lived at the Lowell Hotel on East 63rd Street, directly next door to the building where Anne and her husband lived. Anne visited her daily. They often had tea and sometimes strolled together to the bookstores on Madison Avenue. Anne took on the awkward task of informing LeG that she had not been nominated for a Tony for her performance in *The Royal Family*.

Anne had a firsthand glimpse of LeG's unsocial behavior. For the opening night in New York, the producers hosted a huge party at Sardi's, but LeG did not attend. Burry Fredrik organized a company picnic at her home in Weston to celebrate the Fourth of July. LeG attended this time but looked extremely uncomfortable until she started to examine the garden with Burry's husband. When the tour opened in Washington, DC, Anne and her husband hosted the entire company at a lavish potluck supper in their hotel suite. Everyone entered into the fun of mixing the tossed salad in the bathtub. LeG stayed for five to ten minutes and disappeared. LeG was different when she was in a crowd. She could talk one-on-one about her life in the theatre, but she could not tell a joke and was out of place at a party.

Anne and LeG stayed at the lovely St. Francis Hotel during their two-week engagement in San Francisco. The first three days, LeG refused to leave the hotel except to drive to the theatre. Only after considerable prodding did she agree to join Anne for late lunches at a chic restaurant. The Gleeson Library at the University of San Francisco invited LeG to examine their extensive collection of her father's works—first editions, letters, papers, etc. Guaranteed that there would be no public reception, she finally agreed to go—and actually enjoyed it.

LeG seemed rejuvenated by her new friendship with Anne. LeG was living very much alone at the time. Many acquaintances, such as Burry Fredrik, whose home was just yards away, Haila Stoddard, June Havoc, and even her neighbors Doris and Jess, hesitated visiting her. They knew she liked her privacy and were unsure if they would be welcome. But Anne, who soaked up all of LeG's stories about Duse, Bernhardt, and the Civic, visited her often. Anne filled an enormous need, a void that LeG had felt since the deaths of Hep, Gun, and Peggy. She told her friends that she was LeG's last good friend, her inspirational muse. Indeed, May Sarton suspected that Anne did not fully realize when she initiated the friendship how dependent on her LeG would become.[23]

During *The Royal Family* tour, the Public Broadcasting System contracted with the original cast to televise the production the following summer in Hartford, Connecticut. LeG was grumpy much of the time: "The camera doesn't like me, and I don't like the camera!" She would not play in profile, and she became upset when she noticed the camera with the red light was not always on her. Fanny has a line to her son in the play where she puts down the film industry—"Stay on the stage where you belong, then you won't get mixed up with all this riff-raff!" "You see," LeG said, "I should have taken my own advice. Forty percent of my performance is off-camera!"[24] She went on to win an Emmy that year for Best Supporting Actress in a television special.

LeG had commented two years earlier that she did not really mind that she was not nominated for a Tony; she already had plenty of awards and did not need another cluttering up her shelves. Rosemary Harris was selected to tell her that this Emmy nomination was not for Best Actress but for Best Supporting Actress.[25] Oddly enough, LeG rather forgot about the specific category; she never talked about it.

LeG and Anne watched the awards ceremony on television.[26] Anne knew that LeG would not watch the entire program, so she had learned the approximate time the winner would be announced. At the scheduled hour, the two of them sat in their night clothes on the edge of LeG's bed looking at the tiny television sitting on her dresser. LeG was appalled at the quality of the program. Suddenly, it was interrupted. On came President Carter and the prime ministers of Egypt and Israel for a special report about their Camp David negotiations. "Surely they're not going to go back to that rubbish they were showing before," LeG remarked.

Eventually the program returned, and Hal Linden announced LeG as the winner. Anne shrieked with joy. She looked at the screen and then back at LeG. There was a lot of applause, and Linden explained that LeG was unable to be present to accept the award. With absolutely no visible reaction, LeG then asked Anne to turn off the television. "How ridiculous," she said. "Anne, why are you carrying on so? How can you be so foolish?" There was no expression of pleasure or joy. Not until the next day, when she was reading the announcement in the *New York Times* and receiving congratulatory telephone calls, did it sink in that the award meant something. Then LeG became rather pleased: "Hmm, a lot of people seemed to have watched the program last night."

In the fall of 1976, shortly before *The Royal Family* tour began, LeG had telephoned Wersba again and had told her quite casually that Burry Fredrik was about to option *The Dream Watcher*. It was not a request for an option, or a question of whether Wersba wanted it, but an accomplished fact—LeG's way of holding on to the play while she toured. "And here I made a fatal mistake," Wersba confessed. "I met Fredrik for lunch, did not like her, felt that she was both an amateur and a phony—but allowed her to option the play. And from there on, it was downhill all the way."[27]

Some outsiders argued that LeG, in spite of such selfish behavior, had a generous side to her nature. They cited examples of how she offered to help her friends. When Jess was taken to the hospital for extensive throat surgery, for example, LeG was right there ready to pay the bills. Jess had always been an Anglophile and feared that after her surgery she would never be able to visit England. LeG donated money to make it possible. Though both Doris and Jess appreciated her gifts, they viewed her actions not as an outgrowth of sincere generosity but as a manifestation of LeG's intense need to love and her need to be loved.[28]

Plans and auditions began for *The Dream Watcher* during the summer of 1977. They would open in Seattle and move on to Boston before premiering on Broadway. There was trouble from the beginning. The playwright, the producer, the director, and the star were at odds with one another. There were meetings and arguments, violent scenes and reconciliations. "Each person involved wanted the play to be his," remarked Wersba. "So it wound up being no one's. Throughout the summer, LeG was paranoid about the proceedings—and often drunk."[29]

The rehearsals in Seattle were a terror. Director Brian Murray threw emotional tantrums. Burry Fredrik devoted most of her time to the two plays she was producing in New York. And Wersba, with no experience in playwrighting, kept rewriting. LeG was kind one day, demonic the next. She would be silent and sullen with Wersba and then embrace her warmly. During one rehearsal, Wersba complimented LeG, saying that some business she did was very funny. "Shut up!" LeG screamed. "Or it will never be funny again." In her naïveté, Wersba had felt married to LeG, and yet during the time in Seattle, she lived alone in a shabby apartment, while LeG and Eloise Armen stayed in a comfortable hotel six miles away.

At the first technical rehearsal, everyone knew it was hopeless. The set designed by Ed Wittstein was mountainous and grotesque. Built on a turntable that would not turn properly, it was backed by a cyclorama painted in cartoon style. "The whole thing was like a bad joke," Wersba moaned. "I sank into a seat and tried not to cry. LeG, however, *dealt* with it all—and for this I admired her. In two minutes she was up on stage, coping with the monstrous set, trying to make it work—and the pro in her was never more apparent."

All Seattle was elated over the premiere about to take place. Two years earlier LeG had thrilled theatregoers at the Seattle Repertory Theatre with her exciting direction of Jeannie Carson in *A Doll's House*.

It was considered one of the best productions the theatre had enjoyed in years, so the locals naturally thought another triumph was in the offing.

What a disappointment! On the night of the first preview, props (including a television set) flew off the turntable and into the audience. The turntable would not work properly, and when it did, it creaked. The actor playing the young boy forgot his lines, and LeG was inaudible. On opening night, the audience was silent and barely applauded at the curtain calls. The reviews were scathing. Critics attacked the unbelievable dialogue, stick-figure characters, and hollow sentiment. Only the work of LeG was praised. Rex Reed hailed her for giving her role "a gentle beauty and haunting verisimilitude." "Such is the magic of Miss Le Gallienne," explained a local critic, "that she makes the cliche disappear before your very eyes. Such style! Such class!"[30]

After the reviews, Wersba decided to close the play and LeG agreed. Fredrik's option on the script had just lapsed, and Wersba would not renew it. Telling all this to a weeping cast in the green room one night, LeG said, "My friends, we are not going on with this play. Our butterfly has been cloaked in iron."[31]

The night before Wersba flew back to New York, she went to LeG's dressing room to say goodbye. "Go on, get out of here," LeG said harshly. "Go back to your life."

That was the end of their seven-year relationship. The marriage that Wersba had fantasized with LeG ended with bitterness:

> I walked away from the theatre, in the rain, and looked back once to see my name in lights on the marquee. And then it was over. What LeG liked was to charm, to seduce, to beguile, and that she did brilliantly. Where her character faltered was in the area of being a *star*. There, she was vain and foolish and could be easily taken in by flattery. And like all great actors, there was a huge emptiness in her. She only lived fully when acting someone else.

LeG had used Wersba, had perhaps misused her. And now that her usefulness was over and she could not further LeG's dreams for a comeback, she was told to leave.

LeG's frustration was profound. At seventy-eight she wanted another hit and knew her time to make a lasting impression with contemporary audiences was diminishing. Also, she needed money. She had managed to tuck away some savings from *The Royal Family*, but without more cash, she would never be able to afford spending her last years in her own home. Once she retired she would have only Social Security. She had lived in her home for half a century. The prospect of an apartment, a condominium, or—God forbid—a retirement home was frightening beyond belief.

An unexpected inheritance gave her some hope. Frank Soyer of Glendale, California, died in 1978 and left his entire estate to LeG. She had never met him, had never received a letter from him, and had never even known of his existence. All she knew about his life was set forth in his will:

> I hereby give, devise and bequeath all of my estate and property of whatsoever nature and wherever situated to the woman I love, Miss Eva Le Gallienne, actress of last known address in Weston, Connecticut, providing she survives me.
>
> I have never been married and I have no children.
>
> I hereby make no provisions for my brothers and sisters, although they are my nearest relatives, since they are persons of sufficient means and are not in need.
>
> I hereby nominate, constitute and appoint the sole beneficiary of this will, Miss Le Gallienne, as the Executrix of this will and further direct she should not be required to post any bond for the faithful performance of her duties.
>
> In witness whereof, I have here unto set my hand and seal, this 23rd day of November, 1964.[32]

The "woman I love" was an odd echo from 1936 and England's Edward VIII.

After LeG's lawyer, Virginia P. Boyd, received a copy of the will from Frank Soyer's brother, she found a Los Angeles attorney to investigate the matter. She did not know if the will was valid or if there were any assets in the estate, when the probate wheels slowly began to turn. In the end, LeG received the entire distributable estate—$55,000. For the moment, she was financially secure.

But LeG still needed to work and soon was involved in her first film role in twenty years. Producers Renee Missel and Howard Rosenman and director Daniel Petrie were considering both LeG and Mildred Dunnock for the role of Grandma Pearl in *Resurrection*, an uplifting story about a reluctant faith healer. They asked their leading lady, Ellen Burstyn, to interview them. From the time of their first breakfast meeting at a hotel in New York, Burstyn adored LeG.[33] She had been aware of LeG for many years, had read her book on Duse, had seen her performance in *The Royal Family*, and knew of her impressive reputation in the theatre.

Though she turned eighty during the filming, LeG's energy level was very high. She never complained of the breathtaking heat as they shot every day in the Texas sun. The only complaint she ever expressed occurred just seconds before they were to begin the master shot of a picnic, and she was holding a crying baby. Once the filming had started, she would be forced to hold the baby the entire day as they completed all the various takes—close-ups, dolly shots, tracking, and so on. She ran up to Burstyn: "I don't think I should be holding the baby, do you?"

Burstyn agreed and turned to the director, who then yelled out: "Let's have the mother of the baby, please; she will hold the baby during the shot. Action." Everybody knew that LeG was right; the baby and LeG would have been miserable all day otherwise.

Burstyn recalls that LeG had very little problem adapting her stage acting for the camera.

> I remember her first shot. She was a little bit broad; it was stage technique. At the lunch break I said to the director that she was too broad and asked him to tell her that she didn't need to do anything. All she needed was just to think and to let the camera do the rest; the camera would read her thoughts. He gasped and said, "You are telling me to tell one of the the the Great Ladies of the American Theatre how to act?" He did, though, and immediately after lunch she was splendid, with perfect technique. I told her later during the filming how impressed I was with how quickly she had adjusted to film technique. She said, "I was watching you, dear." She was just wonderful.

The close rapport between the two actresses was immediate and very deep. They never talked about it, but Burstyn believed "there was a direct link between Eleonora Duse to Le Gallienne to me. I had read a lot about Duse and felt there was some kind of lineage." The scene where granddaughter and grandmother say goodby to each other for the last time was emotionally moving for Burstyn:

> I could hardly look at her; I would break down so. For every take she was so consistent, and the tears would well-up in her eyes. When she would

say, "If we could just love each other . . . I suspect there wouldn't be the bother in the world there is," it was like the word "love" just dropped into her heart; the sound came from deep within, deep within her being.

She used her voice in a very conscious way and played her voice like an instrument. It seemed to me that Miss LeG, having really studied with that full intelligence of hers, combined the technique of Bernhardt with the soul of Duse. LeG's soul always showed through, at the same time she had really well-thought-out phrasing. I don't know that anybody works that way any more.

Every scene I played with her was special because of the quality of her being. She had a way of really looking and really listening, which is the essence of fine acting, particularly film acting. I always felt her radiant love.

For the first time, LeG adored working on a film, perhaps because they filmed all the scenes in sequence. Before flying to Texas for the filming, she rehearsed in California for a couple of weeks and even hired a voice coach to help her with the backwoods, Georgia dialect. Anne Kaufman Schneider was paid to accompany her for the three weeks of shooting and reported that LeG was always prepared and never once stumbled over her lines. They worked on one particular scene for two entire days in blistering heat and wind, but LeG carried on with no problems.

Burstyn and the director of photography, Mario Tosi, were so moved by the dailies of the final goodbye scene that they went to see LeG in her apartment late at night. Schneider remarked that it was as if LeG was holding court in her small, two bedroom apartment. Burstyn hugged her and wept. Italian-speaking Tosi threw his arms around her shoulders and said, "Missa LeG, you makea me cry."[34]

The role of a weathered farm woman was quite unlike anything LeG had ever played in her career, and Stanley Kauffmann of *New Republic* remarked that it was "completely realized, completely beautiful." *Saturday Review*'s Judith Crist called LeG's performance "glowing."[35] A few months later LeG was nominated for an Academy Award for Best Supporting Actress, the oldest woman ever to be nominated. *Resurrection* epitomizes the poignancy of her style. Since most of her career was limited to the stage, video cassettes of the film will enable future generations to appreciate the high quality of her acting.

LeG had only begun to delight in the glorious reviews when she was approached by Burry Fredrik about starring in a new play by

Joanna Glass, *To Grandmother's House We Go*. The time of the play is Thanksgiving evening, and all the relatives who have gathered have designs on grandmother's big house. In no time at all, Alan Schneider was signed to direct, with Kim Hunter and Shepperd Strudwick costarring. Problems began, however, when Schneider became ill and was forced to withdraw from the production. Since the premiere had already been announced to open the fall season at the Alley Theatre in Houston, the scramble began for another director. Eventually, Clifford Williams, an associate director for the Royal Shakespeare Theatre in England, was hired.

LeG's daily routine was to sleep late, eat a tiny breakfast, report to the theatre in slacks and a hat, rehearse five hours, and return home for her only major meal. If she had a break in rehearsal, she would go to her dressing room to play with her dog or to put up her feet. Williams marveled at LeG's exceptionally incandescent face and her tiny but strong body: "When I hug my mother who is the same age it feels as if there is no body there. But with LeG, if she isn't holding her dog, you feel a body with a bosom. She is very sensual, tactile, touching."[36]

LeG opposed rewrites once rehearsals began. She would usually come around, but only after great resistance. Williams felt that "she knew she was slipping in her ability to retain things and feared line changes could throw her." She would sit in her dressing room and listen to the rehearsal over the public address system, complaining when she heard line changes taking place. If the changes were not in her scenes, she said nothing. As a matter of fact, she did have frequent memory lapses, so the producers hid a prompter for her in the fireplace of the set.[37]

In England Williams had directed such stars as Alec Guinness, Glenda Jackson, and Claire Bloom, but he was duly impressed with LeG's ability:

It seems like she doesn't do anything. It looks so simple. She has blazing ability and is the greatest of naturalistic actresses. She has extraordinary technical ability that is totally disguised. With the nod of a head, a gesture, or a pause she can get a laugh. With her comic timing she can get polar bears to laugh.

She plays as things are in real life. She doesn't move much on stage; all is extremely economical and controlled. Every little thing is planned—a touch, a smile—yet nothing ever looks planned. She knows what she does and why; nothing is an accident.

One feature of her acting is that she has difficulty understanding why other actresses have problems with a role. She sees and knows clearly what is needed. She loves interaction. If I asked for a change in an actor's performance, LeG enjoyed the exploration and adaptation. She'd become very annoyed with actors who had lazy voices and frozen lips.

It's hard to believe she has been so under-used. In England she'd be busy all the time—look at Cathleen Nesbitt who was busy into her nineties.[38]

They had one physical problem with the staging. LeG had a chair in which she often sat, just left of stage center. It could have been angled full front to let her play directly to the house. It could have been angled in a definite profile toward stage center, but then she would be facing a wall on the other side of the set. Williams wanted it angled a bit toward the audience so they could see and hear her more easily, but LeG disagreed. During the entire six-week run in Houston, she would walk on stage in advance of the opening curtain, see the chair positioned the way Williams wanted it, and proceed to move it so it faced slightly upstage. It was her insistence on being natural and playing within an ensemble. As Williams observed, "She refused to appear like a star. I think Stanislavsky wrote that stars liked to show their ankles. Well, LeG *never* showed her ankles."

New York's Roundabout Theatre wanted to book *Grandmother's House* for their off-Broadway theatre. They sent LeG truckloads of flowers and flew down to Texas to talk to her. The cast, however, was reluctant to accept the offer. They felt that what might be LeG's last play should be on Broadway or not at all. She was clearly moved by their unanimous decision.

Overwhelming tributes greeted LeG when the play opened on Broadway on January 14, 1981. Frank Rich of the *New York Times* wrote, "It is easy to fall in love all over again with Eva Le Gallienne . . . her face, her voice, her poise and her beauty. She is as lyrical as any Juliet. She has no equal on Broadway." ABC's Joe Siegel said, "She is a consummate actress, a queen of the theatre." CBS's Dennis Cunningham added, "Eva Le Gallienne is a glory." And Rex Reed declared, "Eva Le Gallienne and Kim Hunter are the epitome of what craftsmanship is all about."[39]

The same year she had been nominated for an Oscar in *Resurrection*, LeG was nominated for a Tony for Best Dramatic Actress of the year. Though she put up a fuss, she agreed to attend the huge, public ceremony. Anne picked her up at her home and drove her to the theatre.

LeG refused to attend any dinners or parties and would not allow Anne to park the car until fifteen minutes before the event was scheduled to begin. When it was announced that Jane Lapotaire won for her performance in *Piaf*, LeG grabbed Anne's hand and ran up the aisle of the Hellinger Theatre. By the time everyone else arrived at their parties, Anne and LeG were safely back in Connecticut.[40]

After the play closed on Broadway at the end of the season, the producers booked a short tour. They had been approached by two young entrepreneurs to book the production throughout the midwest, but because Fredrik had lost so much money touring *The Royal Family*, she rejected the offer. Instead, they played two summer theatres in New England, traveled to Baltimore, and went on to Palm Beach by the end of the year.

For the opening night at the Cape Playhouse the performance went on in candlelight. A raging thunderstorm knocked out the electricity, but not a line was missed. At first, the actors struggled on in total darkness, not knowing what the management was going to do and not knowing if the lights would ever come back on. They inched their way around the stage for their entrances and exits, sometimes bumping into each other or into furniture. But the show must go on with or without electricity. After the intermission, they played in the golden glow of candlelight. The audience loved it.

LeG experienced another first in Palm Beach, but it was a first that was concealed from her. She had abhorred the modern practice of miking actors and always forbade their use in her productions. But she was now eighty-two and lacked the vocal energy of her youth. Audiences often complained that they simply could not hear her. The management in Palm Beach insisted, therefore, that she be miked. When she threatened to walk out, they pretended to comply with her wishes but in reality placed mikes overhead where she would not notice them.

The younger members of the touring company particularly idolized LeG. Caroline Lagerfelt said, "LeG reminded me of why I went into the theatre in the first place. She loved the theatre and saw it as a way of communicating and expressing."[41] Harriet Harris admired LeG's stamina; she was touring in her eighties! Although they were just beginning their careers and had not even been in the Broadway production of *Grandmother*, LeG was exceptionally open and helpful. She did not want them to copy earlier interpretations and instead urged them to create their own characters.

Both actresses were especially impressed with LeG's curtain call. After the entire company took their bow, they would back up and quickly clear the stage as the curtain descended. LeG would pretend to be surprised when the curtain then rose and caught her alone at center stage. It looked to the audience as if she had "no intention of taking a solo bow. She was so cagey, so amazingly clever. It was so beautiful to watch her body feeling the applause. Her bow was graceful, completely self-effacing, and like a little performance. She did it every night."[42]

Harris often sat with LeG backstage as they waited for their entrances. LeG talked about her gardening and her animals. She described the fire and how she had learned to use her crippled hands. They talked about books and writers. Regularly, she poked fun at Kim Hunter, who often stood in the wings doing Method-acting exercises. One night she showed Harris pictures of herself as a young woman and pointed to her unusually strong legs. "Would you like to see them?" she teased.[43]

In spite of her advanced years, she was now in her eighties, LeG was still embarrassed about her lesbianism. When Anne Schneider suggested they attend a performance of Molly Picon's one-woman show at the White Barn Theatre in 1978, LeG had resisted. She feared being seen in public with another woman; people might gossip about their relationship. She could still remember the awkward evening she had spent years earlier when she, Gun, Doris, and Jess dined at The Elms restaurant in nearby Ridgefield. A woman across the room kept staring at their party through the entire meal, and it made LeG self-conscious and uncomfortable. The woman was Jackie Kennedy Onassis.[44]

The truth of the matter was that people had long ago stopped gossiping about LeG. No one really seemed to care anymore. As friendly as Ellen Burstyn and LeG became during their work together, at the time Burstyn never knew anything about LeG's sexuality. Nobody on the set talked about it; no one made any remarks. The reality did not reach Burstyn until a few years later, when she was filming a documentary for the Actors' Studio at LeG's home and suddenly saw LeG strike a pose. "It shocked me; it looked so masculine and made me chuckle," she said.[45]

To Anne's credit, she did not let LeG's phobia totally control their social life, though she felt sometimes that she was literally shoving LeG out the door. Anne convinced LeG to see her first film in nearly a decade. LeG was intrigued by Julie Andrews in the role of the transvestite cabaret singer in *Victor/Victoria*, especially since it took place in the 1920s in her favorite city, Paris. They took in Christopher Plummer's Iago at the American Shakespeare Theatre, and they drove to New York to see the highly acclaimed Royal Shakespeare production of *Nicholas Nickleby*.

One evening they invited LeG's old friend Ina Claire as well as Shepperd Strudwick and his wife to LeG's home for dinner. Her housekeeper did the cooking, so it should not have been much of an effort. But LeG fretted over the menu and whether she had the proper linens. Although Anne thought the evening was delightful, she realized that for LeG it was difficult and exhausting. She simply could not relax and engage in idle chitchat for an evening, even with people she knew and liked.

In September 1981, Jane Alexander invited LeG to a dress rehearsal of *Hedda Gabler* at the Huntington Theatre in Boston. They had met a couple of times before—once at a dinner party at Michael Kahn's house. Another time Alexander went to LeG's home to get advice on how to play Hilde in Ibsen's *The Master Builder* for a production she was rehearsing for Washington's Arena Stage. "I grew up wanting to be an Eva Le Gallienne," Alexander confessed. "I wanted to be a part of a repertory company and do the kinds of plays she did. She was always an idol of mine. People call Helen Hayes 'The Grande Dame of the Theatre,' but really it should be LeG. There is nobody else like her; she did it all."[46]

Alexander hoped her lifelong idol would give her some words of approval on her new interpretation, but she doubted it would be forthcoming. Alexander wanted an up-to-date production and made her Hedda quick and impulsive, whereas LeG's had always been reflective and manipulative. Besides that major difference between their approaches, Alexander did not particularly like the character and did not enjoy playing it. She realized that with LeG it was different: "She finds something that she identifies with, relates to, understands about Hedda that leaves the rest of us in the dust. She was, after all, the Hedda of the century." LeG was gracious with the company after the rehearsal, but she made only polite comments. Anne had accompanied her and wanted to explore Boston for a few days, but LeG demanded they drive home without even spending the night. She had no interest in staying over; no spirit of adventure.

All the recent recognition for her acting could not suggest that the next project LeG took on would be her theatrical farewell, as well as one of the most embarrassing failures of her long career. LeG proposed to producers Sabra Jones and Anthony D. Marshall that they revive *Alice in Wonderland*. If they opened in 1982, it would commemorate the fiftieth anniversary of the original production. The plan was that

LeG would re-create her role of the White Queen and that Tommy Tune would direct. Though he was deeply involved with *La Cage aux Folles* at the time, he was excited about the script and agreed to do it.

LeG suddenly demanded, however, that she should be the director. The producers should have known better than to give in to her whim. Since 1964 she had directed only twice: *The Cherry Orchard* fiasco in 1968 and *A Doll's House* at a regional theatre in 1975. Her recent track record was not impressive, and she was, after all, eighty-two years old. Nevertheless, since she owned the rights to the play, they reluctantly consented.

It appeared to most people involved that LeG had such a desire to succeed that she was determined to control everything. The producers objected to casting Kate Burton as Alice, but LeG was insistent, arguing that since she was the daughter of Richard Burton, it would be good box office. With the exception of Mary Louise Wilson, who had worked with LeG on *The Royal Family*, most of the cast were proficient but not particularly flamboyant. Nothing suggested that they would be able to play the wacky and eccentric quality the script demanded.

Problems began at the first rehearsal. Following her traditional approach, LeG proceeded to read the entire script to the cast, hardly a normal practice in the contemporary, Broadway theatre. The actors were all eager for an exciting experience, but they received a deadly start that set a Victorian mood for the entire production. As the rehearsals progressed, the actors seemed strangled, unable to explore and create. There was no sense of fun.

Eventually, the producers approached LeG about the problem and suggested bringing in Tommy Tune to look at the show. There was quite a scene, with screaming and yelling. As it turned out, Tune did come to the theatre one night after LeG had gone and rechoreographed all the dance numbers. She would not accept any of his changes and threatened to sue if the producers continued in challenging her authority. Needless to say, the cast was frazzled.

The costumes were another problem. Although Patricia Zipprodt's designs were intended to re-create the original Tenniel drawings, LeG was constantly making changes. They used Naugahyde, a man-made leather imitation, for many costumes. At one point during the construction, designer John Lee Beatty proclaimed that if the ideas continued to change they would have to "go out and shoot another nauga."[47]

The only element that seemed to succeed was the advance publicity. Shirley Herz convinced LeG to stage a casting call where she auditioned twenty live pigs for a featured role in the production. The media went wild with their cameras. LeG walked around the room, picked them all up, and talked to them. Photos of LeG cuddling the piglets appeared on television and in *Time* magazine. Newspapers around the country and as far away as London, England, carried the story with the headline "But Will She Hog the Limelight?" The winner was a fifteen-pound piglet named Michelle. Another gimmick was to sell all tickets for the first night preview at the 1932 price of $1.50 top instead of the normal $40.00. The day tickets went on sale, people were lined up for blocks.

Perhaps the critics expected too much. In any case, they were disappointed and called it "a flat revival," "a rather staid 'Alice,'" and "a wonderland of colorful confusion."[48] Kate Burton was earnest but boring, the actors rarely moved, and when they spoke they seemed remote and disembodied. Virtually the only showstopper was LeG's airborne entrance in the second act. She was the one thing in the performance that was completely magical. Looking like a figure dipped in white spun sugar, the octogenarian flew in from the wings on wires, wrestling with her shawl as if it were a boa constrictor, and hooting madly.

LeG should not take the total blame for the production's failure. According to Anne Schneider, producer Sabra Jones was disappointed when she was not cast as Alice. Her dream was to be an actress-manager like LeG, and she thought this would be her entry. She certainly accomplished a herculean task, raising the money and contracting such top designers as Zipprodt, John Lee Beatty, and Jennifer Tipton; but when rehearsals began to die she panicked and apparently treated LeG badly. Mary Louise Wilson, whom LeG handpicked to play the Red Queen, thought the producers were "crude and insensitive" to LeG: "The producers were idiots, as they usually are." They were rude and dismissive. LeG was the director, but she was always the last person to know what secret changes were being debated and negotiated.[49]

Anne Jackson, Eli Wallach, and Ellen Burstyn were having dinner with Burgess Meredith in California when they saw the reviews. They phoned LeG at once and told her not to worry: "After all, you did it! Who cares what the critics say." May Sarton also phoned and later wrote in her journal that "the ring in her voice makes it very clear that she will not be downed."[50] Unfortunately, Sarton was wrong; LeG was definitely downed. She would never again be seen on the Broadway stage.

In less than three weeks, the $2 million production, backed by Rockefeller and Astor fortunes, was closed. To recoup some of their losses, the producers sold their rights to television's "Great Performances." The small screen adaptation bears little semblance to the Broadway version. When Kirk Browning was selected to direct, LeG washed her hands of the project entirely. Maureen Stapleton took the role of the White Queen. Other replacements in the star-studded cast included Richard Burton, Colleen Dewhurst, Eve Arden, James Coco, Donald O'Connor, and Fritz Weaver. LeG wrote to one of her friends that "if the TV 'Alice' should come your way *don't bother with it*. I had nothing to do with it—and I hear it's awful."[51]

In retrospect, people close to LeG should have advised her against directing *Alice*. Eloise Armen and Anne Kaufman Schneider certainly knew the difficulties she had experienced with memorizing her lines and projecting her voice during *Grandmother's House*. She would need all her available energy just to perform eight times a week. The summer of 1982, LeG was supposed to be revising the script for *Alice*. Whenever Eloise was given something to type, she noticed there were no changes being made and anticipated trouble, yet she told no one. When Burry Fredrik heard about the plans for the revival, her response echoed that of the Broadway crowd: You can't go home again.[52] They knew that to re-create so precisely the *Alice* of 1932 would never work fifty years later, not after a world war, a cold war, Korea, the sexual revolution, women's liberation, race riots, Vietnam, and Watergate.

But another, more troubling factor surfaced that should have alerted them. Five years earlier, when Anne and LeG had flown first class back to Connecticut at the end of *The Royal Family* tour, LeG had accepted a free glass of wine. As far as Anne can remember, that was the first time she had ever seen LeG drink alcohol. Gradually, her drinking accelerated, usually with scotch and water. Anne, who is a very light drinker, remembers that one summer LeG drank entirely too much white wine and soda. Perhaps prompted by the frustration of her memory lapses during *Grandmother*, she revived her "tussles with the bottle," even before preparations had begun for *Alice*.

Anne believed, especially after consulting with her own doctor, that LeG suffered some sort of breakdown during *Alice*. Physically, she remained in fine fettle through the entire debacle, running up the winding stairs backstage and never missing a performance. But the humiliation and hurt she experienced seemed to trigger even more memory loss. When Anne referred to *Alice* no more than six months after it closed, LeG's mind was a blank; she had no memory of it whatsoever. All she could recall was her 1947 revival and Bambi Linn's portrayal of Alice.[53]

LeG's financial security was unexpectedly guaranteed for the rest of her life. Her longtime admirer Alice De Lamar died on August 31, 1983, and included LeG in her will. She was an immensely wealthy recluse, whose father had made his millions in Texas oil. She lived not far from LeG, on a sprawling estate that included her huge home, gardens, a swimming pool, servants, and several cottages that she lent out to female friends. She was known to host lavish parties attended mostly by other women, but she seldom ventured off her estate except to go to her home in Palm Beach or to her apartment in Paris.

Alice had provided LeG's financial structure often over the years. She had bailed her out when *Jehanne d'Arc* failed in Paris in the early twenties, and she had been a major patron of both the Civic and the ART. She had helped LeG purchase her Connecticut home and occasionally had given her money to make improvements. LeG was breathless when the will was read. She assumed she might inherit something, but the magnitude of the gift was overwhelming. In essence, the will bequeathed to LeG all dogs, cats, birds, and other small pets that Alice owned at the time of her death; two acres of land on Hillside Road, which adjoined LeG's property; and one-fourth of Alice's entire estate. LeG's share totaled over $1 million![54]

Although she hardly needed the income, within a few months LeG and Eloise were flying to California where she taped a segment with Blythe Danner and Brenda Vaccaro for the popular *St. Elsewhere* television series. It was her last role.

After *Alice*, LeG had begun drinking excessively and had gone on several extended binges. She had become violent and abusive to her friends and had often been seen at the local bars. Eloise and Anne persuaded her to accept the television offer, hoping the return to work and discipline would be the answer. She did stop for awhile, but when she and Eloise were flying to California, she once again accepted a free drink, this time a glass of champagne.

That was it. She was drunk practically the entire week of the taping. She battled over her costume and insisted on wearing the same wig she had worn a half-century earlier when she had played Juliet. It looked ludicrous on her. Eloise worked and worked with her on her lines, but it was hopeless. At the time, Eloise thought the problem was because of her drinking, but later she came to realize that the alcohol was more the result than the cause. LeG realized she was no longer able to memorize her lines, so she turned to the bottle. In the end, LeG was forced to read all her lines from hidden cue cards.[55]

Still not accepting her condition, LeG nearly begged for the lead role in A. R. Gurney's new play, *The Golden Age*. She lost out to her old friend Irene Worth. Without her work to feed her ego and to create purpose in her life, LeG felt more frantic than ever. She had never truly recovered from her split with Josephine Hutchinson nearly fifty years earlier, so she thought she had found the solution to her prayers when she asked Josie to move in with her. Josie, like Gun, had been like a mother to her, had cared for her and looked after her. Maybe she would do it again.

Since Josie's second husband, Staats Cotsworth, had died in 1979, LeG was hopeful. Josie was also alone and surely would want to return. This was something that May Sarton had always dreamed of, to have LeG and Josie back together again for their final years. Eloise thought the idea was unlikely. LeG talked often of Josie and of all the good times they had shared in their relationship—triumphs at the Civic, trips to Paris, planting their first garden, romantic dinners together. She seemed to forget all the bad times—her own infidelities, the scandal, the fire. She always wanted to see Josie, but whenever they were together they really had very little to discuss. They spent most of the time in silence. Sadly for LeG, Josie was still bitter and declined the offer.[56] LeG's dream for a happy ending with the woman she had always loved was not to be.

With the exception of the daily visits of her cook and housekeeper, LeG was alone. One very late night, after everyone had gone for the day and she had downed a number of drinks, she wandered outside with a glass of wine. She strolled a few yards into the woods and rested at the bench where she had always sat to study her scripts. She walked back into the house to refill her glass, and then she made her way to the barn where she had built so many of the models for her sets. Many of them were still there, but they were now dusty and in cobwebs. In tears she staggered out of the barn and down the lane. She passed by some houses and realized she knew so few of the people that lived around her.

At about two in the morning, LeG knocked on a neighbor's door. "I must talk to you," she cried. "If you have any thoughts of being a lesbian, don't do it. Your life will be nothing but tragedy," and she turned to retrace her steps in the dim of a cold Westport night. How very alone and sad she was.

In the last ten years, LeG had achieved a remarkable comeback. She had earned glowing reviews for *The Royal Family*, *Resurrection*, and

Grandmother's House, had won major acting awards and had been nominated for others. No period of her seventy-year career had been as rewarding since the twenties. Even though no one wanted to admit that she was aging, LeG, and her close friends knew in their hearts that her day had passed. From her poignant speech in *The Royal Family*, LeG knew there was "no use. . . . No use fooling myself. . . . I'm through. . . . I'll never go back again. . . . I'm finished."

12

Winter Bound

In spite of LeG's dismal showing with *Alice* and the catastrophe of *St. Elsewhere*, for the next three years her name was still bandied about for several new projects. Would she be interested in playing the role of the Dowager Empress in a musical version of *Anastasia*? The production never made it off the drawing boards, but if it had, she would have been playing, ironically, the same role Helen Hayes had performed for the 1956 film that earned an Oscar for Ingrid Bergman. There was also talk of LeG costarring in a new English play with film star Gloria Swanson, but it was canceled when Swanson became ill.

LeG rejected some of the offers herself. Tammy Grimes approached her about re-creating the Gladys Cooper role of the eccentric Mrs. St. Maugham in her planned revival of *The Chalk Garden*. They went so far as to meet in Connecticut about production plans and even discussed how Edith Evans had played the part in the film adaptation. Finally, LeG decided that at her advanced age she did not wish to play women who were ill, dying, or on the edge of death. Instead, as she told Burry Fredrik, she wanted to play women who were still alive, still full and vibrant and wonderful.

Lucille Lortel and her assistant Vincent Curcio considered starring LeG at the White Barn with Anne Meacham in a revival of *The Aspern Papers*, a play based on a Henry James novel that Wendy Hiller and Maurice Evans had played off-Broadway in 1962, and they asked LeG if she would teach her acting classes again. Eloise Armen blocked both proposals.

Eloise screened all of LeG's mail, answered most of her correspondence, and took care of her day-to-day finances. She was tremendously faithful and devoted to LeG, literally mothered her, and always thought she knew what was best. She decided it would be good for LeG, for example, to celebrate holidays with a family, so one Thanksgiving she invited LeG and Josie to join the Armens for a typical turkey dinner. What a colossal mistake. LeG hated being away from her home and having to talk to strangers, and she fussed the entire time. Josie got upset when she saw LeG getting upset. The invitation was never repeated.

A protective, perhaps overly protective, Eloise told Lucille Lortel that though LeG had the desire to return to the stage and work, she would not be able to come through in the end.[1] Eloise certainly had LeG's best interests at heart, and yet maybe if she had left the door slightly ajar for the right project, the right role, the work would have been therapy for LeG and would have enriched her fading years.

Physically, LeG seemed thirty years younger. In good weather she spent hours tending her garden and looking after the animals. One day Ted Lockwood came over to repair the roofs on her sheds and barn and brought with him two nail aprons. LeG grabbed one and strapped it around her waist, and together they reroofed the buildings, even replacing some new sections of siding. She was still able to climb down the ladders in her typical fashion, facing front.

LeG's routine was interrupted by occasional visitors, such as Tammy Grimes, the playwright Joanna Glass, and Shirley Herz, who brought a hundred-pound bag of peanuts for LeG's animals. Eloise Armen visited her every afternoon for a couple of hours. One spring day, Rosemary Harris, her daughter Jennifer, and Ellis Rabb drove to Connecticut so that Rosemary could talk to LeG about a project she was contemplating on Isadora Duncan. LeG showed them notes and letters that the revolutionary dancer had sent to her back in the twenties. "It was a wonderful early spring day," Rosemary wrote, "and all the snowdrops and aconites were out in her garden." LeG gave Rosemary some clumps to transplant into her own garden when she returned home to North Carolina. At last report they were thriving.[2]

Anne Kaufman Schneider, who continued her regular visits, began to notice that LeG was becoming unusually forgetful.[3] One day the cook served them an English cream tea, complete with homemade scones and cakes. LeG loved it and ate everything in front of her, but no more than an hour later, she asked Anne if she was ready to have tea served. LeG would always insist on a vow of silence during breakfast but would talk nonstop as Anne tried to read the newspaper.

LeG also started repeating her favorite stories, so that Anne soon had them memorized word for word. One occurred in 1917 when LeG was waiting backstage to make her entrance with Maxine Elliott in *Lord and Lady Algy*. When LeG commented to the older star about the bad performance someone was giving, Elliott peaked through the curtain, saw the packed theatre, and whispered, "Never mind, dear, we have their money."

Another favorite concerned Ethel Barrymore, who was once asked in an interview what the three most dreadful words were in the English language. Barrymore, who was acutely jealous of all her contemporary rivals, replied in a deep and resonating voice, "Cornelia Otis Skinner." No doubt LeG would have said, "Helen Brown Hayes." Every time she ended one of the stories, LeG would break into peals of laughter. As LeG entered her nineties, Anne noticed that even her memory of these stories was fading, and Anne would typically need to prompt or finish the story for her.

It seemed that sometimes LeG's mind was not tracking; an increasing part of the past was disappearing. An old acquaintance would phone or come to visit, and LeG would carry on as if she were comprehending everything. No one ever suspected that as they walked out the door, LeG might turn to Eloise and ask, "Who was that?" She often had no recollection of who the visitor was and literally performed through the entire conversation. For awhile her memory only included things up through the time of *The Royal Family*, a time when she was feeling fulfilled and appreciated. But soon even those memories began to fade. Since the effort to remember and to play her part well in conversation was so exhausting, Eloise tried to shield her from visitors. Sometimes people slipped through her protective screen.

As the months wore on, Anne realized more and more that her dear friend was often very selfish. She was enormously hurt when LeG showed absolutely no interest in her life. Once, Anne flew to England for a West End revival of one of her father's plays and phoned LeG regularly. Each time, however, the conversation reverted quickly to LeG's activities and needs. LeG never once asked how the production was progressing, making Anne wonder why she was bothering to keep in daily contact. Anne drove to see LeG soon after her return to New York, and even then LeG showed no interest.

On another occasion, Anne and her husband went on a two-week holiday to Greece with Alec Guinness and his wife. LeG became quite distraught when she learned of the plans and accused Anne of deserting her. All she could talk about was the loneliness she would feel while Anne was gone. She was unable to share anything resembling joy or excitement. It turned out to be a wonderful holiday, and Anne had a marvelous time as they sailed on their boat around the Greek islands. Yet LeG would not discuss it when Anne returned. The trip did not concern her, so she was not interested.

In 1985 May Sarton had a mastectomy and suffered a stroke that nearly took her life. Anne begged LeG to phone or to send a note to this faithful confidante who had been so important in LeG's life, but all LeG did was instruct Eloise to send a plant. Whenever Anne repeated the request, the answer was always, "Oh, maybe sometime." But she never did call her. Anne eventually came to feel very fortunate that she had other support, such as her husband and friends, to turn to and did not have to rely on LeG for her emotional needs.

Meanwhile, LeG received notice that she was to be awarded the National Medal of the Arts, the highest award any artist could receive from the United States government. She was invited to a luncheon at the White House, where President Reagan himself would make the presentation. Although LeG was perfectly capable of attending, she sent Anne in her place. After passing through the FBI security check, she was ushered to her seat of honor next to Mrs. Reagan. When she accepted the award after lunch, Anne recited the one thing that LeG had instructed her to say: "Tell him how much I admire him."

Anne was so thrilled by the attention and ceremony that she rushed to tell LeG all about it the next day. She took everything she could with her—the menu, a place card, the program, a book of matches, the award, and a flower from the centerpiece—and she even wore the same dress she had selected for the occasion. She proceeded to reenact the entire afternoon. Kitty Carlisle was a guest also, but because she was not one of the honorees, she was not given the same courtesies as Anne and had to enter through a back door. Mrs. Reagan was interesting, charming, and very gracious, though Anne felt that if they had met the very next day, the First Lady would have been oblivious. LeG was barely interested in the story and within a week had forgotten it altogether.

The periodic visits were becoming increasingly frustrating for Anne. LeG's memory lapses were more frequent, and she continued to accuse Anne of neglecting her. Anne would spend an entire afternoon with her and then phone the next day, only to be reproached for having stayed away so long. Soon Anne began to find excuses for not calling.

In the meantime, LeG began to drink heavily again. May Sarton believed that "it had to do partly with the relationship she had entered into with Anne. She is an extremely nice woman, but she got into something with LeG, not quite aware of what was involved. When Anne began to cut back on her visits, LeG turned more to drinking again."[4]

Eloise consulted an alcohol clinic and begged LeG to go, but LeG refused and became abusive. On the morning of the Fourth of July, 1987, Eloise drove over to visit her, but LeG locked all the doors and would not let her in. When Eloise returned home, LeG was on the phone, screaming that she was not through with her. She drove back to LeG's but still could not get past the locked doors. The next morning, the cook who lived nearby discovered that LeG had gotten drunk, fallen down a flight of stairs, and was unconscious and bleeding. LeG was hospitalized for nearly three weeks.

LeG was never left alone after that. Eloise decided to pay a staff of people to be in the house at all times—a cook and housekeeper during the day and a nurse at night. Luckily the inheritance from Alice De Lamar covered the expenses, which came to more than a thousand dollars a week. All liquor was removed, and the keys to LeG's car were hidden so she could not steal out by herself to search for some scotch.

LeG spent her days forever reassessing herself and reflecting on her past, her arrogance and insecurity, her enemies and her admirers. She wished to be left alone and said very little when friends visited. She would sit in the Blue Room and occasionally shuffle around her furniture, admiring all the pieces. There were stacks of books by her chair, the Bible and volumes dealing with religious mystics. She was incredibly hard on herself and muttered that she would have been a better actress if she had been a better person. She lay back in her chaise; her eyes shut. Every now and then she asked Eloise about her relatives, how old her children and grandchildren were, and what she had been doing with her family. "I don't have anyone," LeG often said. "I've never had anyone. I'm just selfish." She repeated often how selfish she had been. More and more of her time was spent in bed with her eyes closed. She was sad and so full of remorse.

When the backward glances became too painful, LeG turned to her scrapbooks. Though most of them were donated to the Beinecke Library at Yale University, she had kept a few of her favorite, more personal volumes. The weight of her failures seemed lighter as she gazed at clippings of her prime. What a stunning beauty she was during *The Swan*—before the fire destroyed her hands and burned her face. The theatre world was at her feet when she played *The Master Builder* and *John Gabriel Borkman* in repertory. Such joy she had during the first years at the Civic, when money was not a concern and the critics were lauding her. She could almost hear the children laughing and squealing as she flew out over them as Peter Pan.

As she turned the pages, she leaned down to retrieve a clipping that had slipped to the floor, not having been pasted alongside the others. Her smile dimmed as she recalled a less pleasant memory. Folded over was the review of a production that had opened in mid-November

1929, the same year LeG was delighting her Civic audiences with Chekhov's *Seagull* and Tolstoy's *Living Corpse*. The play reviewed was notable because it presented Broadway with a most vivid look at a lesbian relationship. It ran little more than a month but managed in that time to raise the ire of many patrons and of such homophobic critics as George Jean Nathan and John Mason Brown. Response ran from confusion to cries of sexual abnormality.

Thomas H. Dickinson's *Winter Bound* concerns two women from urban backgrounds who set out to live alone in a country farmhouse in Connecticut, away from a male-dominated society. Tony is described as a virile-looking woman in a blouse and short trousers, with bobbed hair, an athletic body, and great magnetism. She is cynical, selfish, a wayward spirit with a harsh directness in her manner. She smokes, wears pants, has a love of animals, and is an artist who earns her living creating characters in clay. Her partner, Emily, wears dresses and enjoys housework. She is feminine and easily charmed.

Early in the play, Tony tries to persuade Emily to reject her former boyfriend. In the second scene they argue because Emily resents being left alone all day while Tony is out enjoying life. When Emily threatens to return to her lover, Tony is emphatic: "If you want a man, I guess you'll have to have one. None for me." Later Tony discovers Emily and a neighbor man laughing, teasing, and embracing. When she confronts her about this budding relationship, Emily says she resents depending on Tony for everything and does not like living in her shadow. She calls Tony a "female bully" who has an "air of masculine superiority." Emily marries her young man, and as the curtain falls, Tony is left to pursue a lonely life, winter bound in her rustic Connecticut home.[5]

Only two years prior to this production, LeG and Josie had bought their country retreat in Connecticut, and in six months their relationship had been exposed in headlines across the country. Was this mere coincidence? Or did the playwright develop his theme with LeG and Josie in mind? The possibility is certainly there, since LeG's exploits were already whispered in many circles. Though she had often created gossip, she was still horrified when she first heard of the production. The similarity was entirely too close. Surely this could not be their story, she thought, for she and Josie were very much together—and always would be. That LeG, sixty years later, would be alone and winter bound in her Connecticut home was eerie.

LeG had a very strange fascination with death, an obsession she exhibited her entire life. When Duse died, LeG knelt by the corpse for almost an entire day. When Peggy was on her death bed, LeG insisted on being at her side, regardless of Peggy's objection. The day before Alice De Lamar died, LeG felt compelled to visit, even though the woman was not conscious. When Lisl M. Goodman canvassed hundreds of famous women about their willingness to talk about death for a book she was preparing in 1981, LeG was the very first woman to respond. Eloise and Anne tried to persuade LeG against the interview, but it was something she had to do.[6]

Although she may have colored her responses with an eye for a future book, LeG made some revealing comments.[7] When the author asked what she would do to achieve perfection in her performances, LeG answered, "Anything! My profession has been the passion of my life. I would sacrifice everything for it. As a matter of fact, I have."

"Are you afraid of death?"

"I don't think so," LeG replied. "Of course this is something one cannot know for sure, but I don't feel any fear. It's part of life, part of the rhythm of the universe. And I am not a believer, so I don't fear anything that may come afterwards. I don't think that there is anything. Going to sleep is certainly not frightening. The very best thing is just going to sleep—eternal sleep. Remember, "tis a consummation / Devoutly to be wish'd.'"

"How often do you think about your own death?"

"Very seldom. Every now and then. For instance, when someone says something like, 'In five years you should be . . .' I think, 'who knows where I am going to be in five years.'"

If the truth were known, she was a very religious person, though not in any traditional sense. After the deaths of Gun, Hep, and Peggy in the early seventies, she contacted a local priest in Westport and began taking instruction in the Roman Catholic faith. She eventually stopped when she became disillusioned about the priest's lack of knowledge, and she later cautioned Eloise against allowing the church to bury her when she died. She often repeated the credo "What must be, shall be," which she had adopted years earlier from the writings of St. Julian of Norwich, and she was very realistic about her future. Three or four times in an afternoon, she would ask how old she was and observe, "Hmm! Imagine that. Well, it won't be long now."[8]

LeG died at the age of ninety-two on June 3, 1991, the night of the annual Tony Awards in New York City. As her colleagues applauded the current Broadway stars, LeG made her final exit. It was not a dramatic scene, not a Juliet falling on her dagger or a Marguerite coughing with tuberculosis.

LeG's nurse routinely helped her to bed and then chatted with her a few minutes before leaving the room. This particular evening seemed to be going like all the others in recent months. They chatted, the nurse put LeG's Yorkshire terrier on her patient's lap, and she began to leave. As she was about to close the door, she suddenly felt the room become unusually silent. She turned back for one last look, to see if her patient was alright. LeG was sitting up in her bed, holding Dimpy at her side. She had simply stopped breathing.

For some time LeG and Anne Schneider had been engaged in a friendly wager whether or not LeG's name would make the front page of the *New York Times* when she died. LeG must have been pleased that she lost the bet. Indeed, news of her death did make the front page, and the half-page obituary that followed in another section included two photographs and called her the "Grand Lady of the American Stage." Newspapers across the country reported the death of this "giant of the theater."9

Though often appearing selfish and uncaring about others, LeG's last will and testament was an act of great generosity. Cash bequests to Ted Lockwood, Anne Kaufman Schneider, Eloise Armen, Jessalyn Jones, and Doris Johanson totaled more than a half million dollars. Doris and Jess inherited the cottage they had lived in for over thirty years; Eloise received the home LeG had been living in and LeG's private papers and royalty rights; Anne was given LeG's tangible personal property; and Ted received the eighteenth-century original house along with all of its contents. LeG donated thirteen additional acres of her property to the Aspetuck Land Trust to provide a "small sanctuary dedicated to quiet in an increasingly noisy world." She willed the remainder of her estate to the Actors' Fund of America.10

LeG had often fantasized about living to be one hundred, because then she would have lived in three centuries. In her one century, however, she achieved enough for three. She either acted in and/or directed nearly one hundred fifty live theatre productions, sixteen film and television performances, dozens of radio broadcasts, and a score of records and tapes. She authored four books, published translations of Ibsen and Hans Christian Andersen, provided prefaces and introductions to several volumes, and wrote numerous articles for periodicals, playbills, and newspapers.

LeG's many awards included honorary degrees from a dozen universities, a Tony, an Emmy, an Oscar nomination, a National Artist Award from ANTA, a Citation for Distinguished Service from the American Theatre Association, and the National Medal of the Arts from the United States government. In recognition for her Ibsen translations, the King of Norway presented her with the Cross of the Royal Order of St. Olav, the highest award given to a foreigner. The only major honor that eluded her was the Kennedy Center Honors, which is broadcast on television each year. Irene Worth and Jane Alexander lobbied seriously for LeG's selection in the late eighties, but they were informed by the officials in charge that all honorees must be present at the ceremony. LeG was no longer able to make the journey.[11]

LeG's range of acting was incredible. She went from the classic *Trojan Women* to the contemporary *Exit the King*, from sentimental *Liliom* to the bare simplicity of *Ghosts*, from the romanticism of *Camille* to the realism of *Hedda Gabler*, from the fantasy of *Peter Pan* to the operatic bravado of *Mary Stuart*. No other actress in her time, certainly not Katharine Cornell or Helen Hayes, could possibly boast such a colorful palette.

With her European vision and uncompromising determination, LeG spent over forty years struggling to establish a classical repertory theatre in this country. In 1986, when *American Theatre* magazine celebrated the silver anniversary of the nonprofit theatre movement in America, they featured LeG and proclaimed that her efforts in the twenties, thirties, and forties "presaged a changing role for the theatre a generation in advance." Along with Tyrone Guthrie, John Houseman, and Zelda Fichandler, LeG is credited for being one of the theatre artists who "played a part in shaping America's nonprofit theatre."[12]

All this and still LeG is unknown and underrated. Most Americans, even those in theatre, do not appreciate or even recognize her name. Perhaps memories are short, and celebrities are toasted today and forgotten tomorrow, but the reasons for her neglect are more complex.

With her narrow focus, LeG unconsciously orchestrated her own obscurity. For too long she blindly devoted herself to the classics, insisting they were the pure, and only, art form. Her noble goal to reach the masses sounded hollow when she selected plays that lacked audience appeal. And with strong support from only the chosen few who appreciated the classics, LeG limited her following.

LeG's European sensitivity may have inspired her and given her a vision of what was needed in American theatre, but her elitism and intellectualism became barriers to universal name recognition. She rarely demeaned herself or her art with advertising schemes, for she looked on publicity as a wedge into her private life that could result in catastrophe. She was openly bitter about the success of Helen Hayes, but what did she expect? Hayes was about the same age as LeG and stopped acting in 1971, but she never stopped promoting herself. Perhaps a Greta Garbo could insist on privacy and still be famous. She was a film star and therefore known more to the masses from the outset. Also, reruns of her films and the popularity of video cassettes brought her name and mystique before younger generations. LeG did not enjoy that advantage.

LeG's solitude certainly worked against her. She avoided being in the public eye and wanted nothing to do with the superficialities of life. She never traveled with celebrities or associated with them, and she never capitalized on her successes. She admitted to Anne Kaufman Schneider that for many years she had great difficulty opening her arms wide on stage as she did in *The Royal Family*, because it made her feel so exposed.[13] Perhaps she felt that she shared so much of herself when she performed that after the curtain went down she needed to keep to herself.

But LeG's consummate retreat and seclusion meant that she lost out on human contacts and the sheer joy of living that could have nourished her. May Sarton said, "She seemed to understand everything about human relations at their deepest and most subtle level, and yet it was not true of her as a person, only as an actress." When May visited her for the last time in the early eighties, she still felt an odd wall between them. "I have known her for over fifty years, and I still always have to break the barrier. It is so hard to connect with her. Usually I get her to talk about things at the Civic."[14] Since LeG did not enjoy being around people, she could not allow them to help her grow as a person or as an artist. Instead, she grew out of touch in her Connecticut tower.

Undoubtedly, LeG's private life affected her in a way difficult for Americans to appreciate a half-century later. For her generation, one's sexual orientation never became public except through hostile exposure that inevitably meant disgrace and ruin. Though obstinately reticent and embarrassed by her sexuality, LeG would not cover it up or deny it. She was true to herself even if she did not like what she was. If she had exploited it as some of her friends advised, perhaps she could have developed an exoticism like Alla Nazimova's or a personality cult like Tallulah Bankhead's. But that was not her choice. Acting was a natural outlet for her. It was a way of expressing in public the feelings she regarded as personal. And though LeG could not unbuckle the Victorian belt of propriety, she was able to reveal her soul when she performed. Some have said that her struggle was a drain on her creative energy; others have said it was the very source of it. Regardless, this confinement profoundly directed her art.

Should LeG have been more open, more public? "It behooves all of us to respect and support any woman's choice to stay where she is," advises lesbian psychologist B. Dunker. An older lesbian "has had to develop skills to protect her privacy. She has had to deal with feelings of inadequacy and a lot of anger and guilt. She can bear witness to the difficulty of living as one is not." Dunker adds,

> Old lesbians, out or closeted, have had to develop skills and character traits in order to survive. . . . We've had to support ourselves. . . . We've had to develop a degree of solid, stubborn, self-confidence and courage. . . . We have had to be autonomous and in charge of our own lives. . . . Not all of us have developed all of these traits in equal measure, but our survival is proof that we have some of them.[15]

It is understandable that contemporary lesbians searching for heroes to serve as role models might well complain that LeG should have been more in the public eye. It might be difficult for them to read about a woman who was so diminished by her sexuality. But in spite of her limitations, LeG should be credited for being as honest as she was. When one considers her unique upbringing, her father's rejection, her mother's disapproval, her insecurities, her living in a repressed and alien society, her keen intellect, her propensity to depression and alcoholism, and her choosing a very public career in the early twentieth century, it becomes easier to understand the choices she made.

In *The Dream Watcher*, Mrs. Woodfin, the character inspired by LeG, dares a young boy to be unique. You have a quality, she says, "which puts you in the company of saints and geniuses. Shakespeare was different. Beethoven was different." Then she quotes the famous lines of Thoreau: "If a man does not keep pace with his companions, perhaps it is because he hears a different drummer. Let him step to the music which he hears, however measured or far away."[16]

If only LeG could have followed her own advice. She certainly was contrary to what was allowed in her society and to what was expected of a star, but she could not really meet the challenge head on. Her music was strained. What prominence LeG might have realized if circumstances had not forced her to waste so much precious energy on her shame and seclusion.

In the last scene of the *The Dream Watcher*, the playwright ponders over the leading character—or perhaps it was really Eva Le Gallienne: "Mrs. Woodfin's life had been sad, and yet she had made poetry out of it."[17]

Appendixes
Notes
Index

Appendix A

Works by Eva Le Gallienne

All works are listed chronologically

Books and Translations

Eva Le Gallienne's Civic Repertory Plays. New York: W. W. Norton, 1928.

Foreword to *Plays, Players, Playhouses*, by Irma Kraft. New York: George Dobsevage, 1928.

Preface to *The Plays of Anton Tchekhov*, translated by Constance Garnett. New York: Carlton House, 1929.

Coauthor with Florida Friebus. *Alice in Wonderland*. New York: Samuel French, 1932.

At 33. London: John Lane, The Bodley Head; New York: Longmans, Green, 1934.

Introduction to *The Cry of the Little Peoples*, by Richard Le Gallienne. Camden, NJ: Haddon Craftsman, 1941.

Flossie and Bossie. New York: Harper, 1949.

Introduction to and translation of *Six Plays by Henrik Ibsen*. New York: Modern Library, 1950.

Preface to and translation of *Hedda Gabler*, by Henrik Ibsen. London: Faber and Faber, 1953.

With a Quiet Heart. New York: Viking, 1953.

Foreword to *The Story of Young Edwin Booth*, by Alma Power-Waters. New York: E. P. Dutton, 1955.

Preface to and translation of *The Master Builder*, by Henrik Ibsen. London: Faber and Faber; New York: New York University Press, 1955.

Foreword to and translation of *Seven Tales*, by Hans Christian Andersen. New York: Harper, 1959.

Introduction to and translation of *The Wild Duck and Other Plays*, by Henrik Ibsen. New York: Modern Library, 1961.

Translation of *The Nightingale*, by Hans Christian Andersen. New York: Harper and Row, 1965.

The Mystic in the Theatre: Eleonora Duse. London: John Lane, The Bodley Head; New York: Farrar, Straus and Giroux, 1966. Reprint. Carbondale: Southern Illinois University Press, 1973.

Translation of *The Little Mermaid*, by Hans Christian Andersen. New York: Harper and Row, 1971.

282 / Appendix A

Translation of *The Spider and Other Stories*, by Carl Ewald. New York: Thomas Crowell Company, 1980.

Introduction to and translation of *Eight Plays by Henrik Ibsen*. New York: Modern Library, 1982.

Translation of *The Snow Queen*, by Hans Christian Andersen. New York: Harper and Row, 1985.

Periodicals and Playbills

"My Adventures in Repertory." *Theatre Magazine* 45 (April 1927): 12, 52B.

"What Is Wrong with the Theatre." *Woman Citizen* 11 (April 1927): 22–23, 45.

"Grim Ibsen Triumphs at His Centenary." *New York Times Magazine* (March 18, 1928): section 5, p. 3.

"Sir James Barrie, Peter Pan, and I." *Theatre Magazine* 49 (January 1929): 15.

"What Is Repertory." *Outlook and Independent* 155 (June 18, 1930): 263, 280.

"Plays of the Month." *Civic Repertory Theatre Magazine* (December 1930).

"Isadora Remembered." *Civic Repertory Theatre Magazine* 1 (February 1931): 4.

"Woman's Role in the Theatre." *Smith College Alumnae Quarterly* 22 (February 1931): 135–37.

"The Renaissance of the Theatre." *Civic Repertory Theatre: 1926–1932*. Souvenir program.

"Footlights." *Pictorial Review* 35 (November 1933): 7–9, 66–71.

"Sarah Bernhardt and Eleonora Duse." *Stage* 14 (January 1937): 96–99.

"We Believe . . ." *Theatre Arts* 30 (March 1946): 176–78.

"Repertory . . . When?" *Theatre Arts* 42 (September 1958) 14–16, 76–77.

"Ibsen's *Hedda Gabler*." *Hedda Gabler*. Program of the National Repertory Theatre, 1964–65.

"Director's Note." *The Cherry Orchard*. Program of the APA-Phoenix, 1968.

"Ibsen: The Shy Giant." *Saturday Review*. 54 (August 14, 1971): 23–26, 35–36.

"S. B. Quand-Meme." *Forum* 11 (Summer–Fall 1973): 32–42.

"Hedda Gabler." *Classic Theatre: The Humanities in Drama*. Boston: WGBH-TV, 1975.

"The Joy of 'Alice.'" *Playbill* 1 (November 1982): 20, 22, and 24.

"On Repertory and Audiences." *American Theatre* 3 (November 1986): 20–21.

Newspapers

"My Beauty Recipe." *Austin Statesman*, November 17, 1924.

"Reasons for Repertory." *New York Times*, October 24, 1926.

"Broadway vs. Fourteenth Street." *New York Sun*, October 22, 1927.

"Eva Le Gallienne Makes an Appeal for a Stage Dedicated to Public Service." *New York American*, February 12, 1928.

"'L'Invitation au Voyage.'" *Brooklyn Daily Eagle*, March 17, 1929.

"A Voice From 14th Street." *New York Herald-Tribune*, January 26, 1930.
"Discoveries in Ibsen's Notebooks." *New York Times*, May 29, 1932.
"Eva Le Gallienne Explains Her 'Romeo and Juliet.'" *Baltimore Morning Sun*, October 1, 1933.
"The Summary of a National Tour." *New York Times*, May 6, 1934.
"The Government and Art." *New York Times*, December 8, 1935.
"Hobbies for Everybody." *Philadelphia Evening Bulletin*, April 20, 1940.
"Back to the Road." *Christian Science Monitor*, November 30, 1940.
"The Critic." *New York Times*, February 15, 1942.
"Acting in Repertory." *New York Times*, July 21, 1946.

Miscellaneous

"The Open Door to the Child's Imagination." Manuscript, Summer 1928. Billy Rose Theatre Collection, New York Public Library for the Performing Arts.
"Bringing the Theatre to the People." Speech delivered before Boston's Old South Church, November 18, 1928. Theatre Collection, Museum of the City of New York.
"American Woman and the American Theatre." Manuscript, 1928. Billy Rose Theatre Collection, New York Public Library for the Performing Arts.

Appendix B

Production Record of
Eva Le Gallienne

Title	Date	Function*	Location
Stage			
Monna Vanna	1914	A	London
Le Baiser	1915	A	London
The Bridegroom	1915	A	London
Miss Elizabeth's Prisoner	1915	A	London
Soeur Beatrice	1915	A	London
Laughter of Fools	1915	A	London
Peter Ibbetson	1915	A	London
Mrs. Boltay's Daughters	1915	A	New York
Bunny	1916	A	New York
The Melody of Youth	1916	A	New York
Mr. Lazarus	1916	A	New York; tour
Mile-a-Minute Kendall	1916	A	Stamford, CT
The Cinderella Man	1917	A	San Francisco, CA
The Rio Grande	1917	A	San Francisco, CA
Pierre of the Plains	1917	A	San Francisco, CA
Saturday to Monday	1917	A	New York
Lord and Lady Algy	1917	A	New York
The Off Chance	1918	A	New York; tour
Belinda	1918	A	New York; tour
Lusmore	1919	A	New York
Elsie Janis and Her Gang	1919	A	New York
Tilly of Bloomsbury	1920	A	Washington, DC
Not So Long Ago	1920	A	New York; tour
Liliom	1921	A	New York; tour
Aglavaine and Selysette	1922	A	New York
Sandro Botticelli	1923	A	New York
The Rivals	1923	A	New York
The Swan	1923	A	New York; tour

*A-actress; D-director: P-producer; T-translator

Title	Date	Function*	Location
The Assumption of Hannele	1924	A	New York
La Vierge Folle	1924	A	New York
The Master Builder	1924	A	Rose Valley, PA
Jehanne d'Arc	1925	A	Paris
The Call of Life	1925	A	New York
The Master Builder	1925	DAP	New York; tour
John Gabriel Borkman	1925	DAP	New York; tour
Saturday Night	1926	DAP	New York
The Three Sisters	1926	DAP	New York
The Master Builder	1926	DAP	New York
La Locandiera	1926	DAP	New York
Twelfth Night	1926	DAP	New York
The Cradle Song	1927	DAP	New York; tour
Inheritors	1927	DAP	New York
The Good Hope	1927	DAP	New York
2 × 2 = 5	1927	P	New York
The First Stone	1928	DAP	New York
Improvisations in June	1928	DAP	New York
Hedda Gabler	1928	DAP	New York
The Open Door	1928	DA	New York
The Would-Be Gentleman	1928	DP	New York
L'Invitation au Voyage	1928	DAP	New York
The Cherry Orchard	1928	DAP	New York
Peter Pan	1928	DAP	New York
The Lady From Alfaqueque	1929	DP	New York
On the High Road	1929	DP	New York
Katerina	1929	DP	New York
A Sunny Morning	1929	DAP	New York
The Seagull	1929	DAP	New York
Mademoiselle Bourrat	1929	DP	New York
The Living Corpse	1929	DAP	New York
The Open Door	1930	DAP	New York
The Women Have Their Way	1930	DAP	New York
Romeo and Juliet	1930	DAP	New York; tour
The Green Cockatoo	1930	DP	New York
Siegfried	1930	DAP	New York
Alison's House	1930	DAP	New York
Camille	1931	AP	New York
Liliom	1932	DAP	New York
Dear Jane	1932	DAP	New York
Alice in Wonderland	1932	DAP	New York; tour

*A-actress; D-director; P-producer; T-translator

Title	Date	Function*	Location
The Cherry Orchard	1933	DAP	New York
Hedda Gabler	1933	DAP	New York; tour
The Master Builder	1934	DAP	Tour
A Doll's House	1934	DAPT	Tour
L'Aiglon	1934	DAP	New York; tour
The Cradle Song	1934	DA	New York
Rosmersholm	1935	DAPT	New York
Camille	1935	DAP	New York; tour
The Women Have Their Way	1935	DAP	New York
A Sunny Morning	1935	DAP	New York
Love For Love	1936	A	Westport, CT
Camille	1936	DA	Tour
Prelude to Exile	1936	A	New York
The Mistress of the Inn	1936	DA	Tour
Hamlet	1937	DA	Dennis, MA
Madame Capet	1938	A	New York
Frank Fay's Vaudeville	1939	A	New York
Private Lives	1939	A	Tour
The Master Builder	1939	DAT	Tour
Hedda Gabler	1939	DAT	Tour
Mary, Mary, Quite Contrary	1940	A	Dennis, MA
Hedda Gabler	1941	DAT	Stockbridge, MA
Ah, Wilderness	1941	D	New York; tour
The Rivals	1942	D	New York; tour
Uncle Harry	1942	A	New York; tour
The Cherry Orchard	1944	DA	New York; tour
The Tempest	1945	Designer	New York
Therese	1945	A	New York
Henry VIII	1946	AP	New York
What Every Woman Knows	1946	AP	New York
John Gabriel Borkman	1946	DAPT	New York
Alice in Wonderland	1947	DAP	New York
Ghosts	1948	AT	New York; tour
Hedda Gabler	1948	DAT	New York; tour
Recital Tour	1948	DAP	Tour
The Corn Is Green	1949	A	Tour
Recital Tour	1950	DAP	Tour
The Three Sisters	1950	DAT	Cambridge, MA
Evening with Shakespeare	1950	A	Tour
The Starcross Story	1954	A	New York; tour
The Strong Are Lonely	1953	T	New York .

*A-actress; D-director; P-producer; T-translator

Title	Date	Function*	Location
The Southwest Corner	1955	A	New York
The Corn Is Green	1955	DA	Milwaukee, WI
			Palm Beach, FL
Ghosts	1956	DAT	Westport, CT
			Milwaukee, WI
Mary Stuart	1957	A	New York
Listen to the Mocking Bird	1958	A	Tour
Mary Stuart	1959	A	Tour
Elizabeth the Queen	1961	A	Tour
Mary Stuart	1961	A	Tour
Ghosts	1962	DAT	Ann Arbor, MI
The Seagull	1963	DAT	New York; tour
Ring Round the Moon	1963	A	Tour
Liliom	1964	D	Tour
Hedda Gabler	1964	DT	Tour
The Madwoman of Chaillot	1965	A	Tour
The Trojan Women	1965	A	Tour
Exit the King	1968	A	New York
The Cherry Orchard	1968	DT	New York
All's Well That Ends Well	1970	A	Stratford, CT
A Doll's House	1975	DT	Seattle, WA
The Dream Watcher	1975	A	Westport, CT
The Royal Family	1975	A	New York; tour
The Dream Watcher	1977	A	Seattle, WA
To Grandmother's House We Go	1981	A	New York, tour
Alice in Wonderland	1982	DA	New York

Film and Television

Title	Date	Function*	Location
Alice in Wonderland	1955	A	TV
Prince of Players	1955	A	Film
Southwest Corner	1955	A	TV
The Corn Is Green	1956	A	TV
Mary Stuart	1957	A	TV
The Bridge of San Luis Rey	1958	A	TV
The Shadow of a Genius	1958	A	TV
Bitter Heritage	1958	A	TV
The Devil's Disciple	1959	A	Film
Mary Stuart	1960	A	TV
Therese Raquin	1961	A	TV

*A-actress; D-director; P-producer; T-translator

Title	Date	Function*	Location
Hedda Gabler	1975	Interview	TV
The Royal Family	1977	A	TV
The Dick Cavett Show	1977	Interview	TV
Resurrection	1980	A	Film
St. Elsewhere—The Women	1984	A	TV

Radio

A Doll's House	1930	AD	NBC
Romeo and Juliet	1931	AD	NBC
The Twelve Pound Look	1931	AD	NBC
The Bluebird	1933	Reading	NBC
Peter Pan	1933	Reading	NBC
The Snow Maiden	1933	Reading	NBC
Alice in Wonderland	1933	Reading	NBC
Sleeping Beauty	1933	Reading	NBC
A Midsummer Night's Dream	1933	Reading	NBC
The Swan	1935	Reading	NBC
Evangeline	1937	Reading	NBC
Peter Pan	1937	Reading	NBC

Discography

The Rivals	1943	D	Harvard
Alice in Wonderland	1948	AD	RCA
Album of Stars, vol. 1	1950	A	Decca
Romeo and Juliet	1951	A	Atlantic
Hedda Gabler	1952	ADT	Theatre Masterworks (TM)
Evening with Shakespeare	1953	A	TM
Eva LeG Reads English . . .	1953	A	TM
Les Fleurs du Mal	1954	A	Caedmon
Camille	1963	A	Caedmon
Styles in Shakespeare	1963	A	Creative
The Twelve Pound Look	1971	A	Center for Cassette Studies (CCS)
The Swan	1971	A	CCS
Eva LeG Reads . . . Andersen	1973	A	Miller-Brody (M-B)
The Happy Family and It's Absolutely True	1973	A	M-B

*A-actress; D-director; P-producer; T-translator

Title	Date	Function*	Location
The Steadfast Tin Soldier	1973	A	M-B
Thumbelisa	1973	A	M-B
The Tinder Box	1973	A	M-B
The Ugly Duckling	1973	A	M-B
The Snow Queen	1974	A	M-B
The Velveteen Rabbit	1975	A	M-B
Dick Cavett Talks with LeG	1979	Interview	CCS

*A-actress; D-director; P-producer; T-translator

Notes

Preface

1. *New York Record*, December 19, 1975; *Los Angeles Times*, December 23, 1976; *Cleveland Press*, December 8, 1976.
2. Barry Paris, *Louise Brooks* (New York: Anchor Books, 1989), p. 431; Thomas Wright, *Hind Head* (London, 1898), p. 38.
3. *New York Times*, December 2 and 3, 1990.
4. Interview with May Sarton, April 27, 1989.

1. Water Baby

1. Richard Le Gallienne, *The Romantic '90s* (New York: Doubleday, Page, 1925), p. 223.
2. Richard Whittington-Egan and Geoffrey Smerdon, *Richard Le Gallienne: The Quest of the Golden Boy* (London: Unicorn, 1960), pp. 45–46.
3. Richard Le Gallienne, *The Romantic '90s*, pp. 270–71.
4. Richard Ellmann, *Oscar Wilde* (New York: Alfred A. Knopf, 1988), p. 283; Rupert Hart-Davis, ed., *The Letters of Oscar Wilde* (New York: Harcourt, Brace and World, 1962), pp. 230, 242.
5. Rupert Croft-Cooke, *The Unrecorded Life of Oscar Wilde* (New York: David McKay, 1972), pp. 157–58.
6. Richard Le Gallienne, *The Romantic '90s*, pp. 75–76.
7. Whittington-Egan and Smerdon, *Richard Le Gallienne: The Quest of the Golden Boy*, p. 197.
8. Ibid., p. 270.
9. Ibid., pp. 255–56, 262.
10. Ibid., pp. 265–67.
11. Eva Le Gallienne, *With a Quiet Heart* (New York: Viking, 1953), pp. 282, 42.
12. Whittington-Egan and Smerdon, *Richard Le Gallienne: The Quest of the Golden Boy*, pp. 273, 275.
13. Richard Le Gallienne, *The Quest of the Golden Girl* (London: John Lane, The Bodley Head, 1896), pp. 35–36.
14. Ibid., p. 274.
15. Ibid., p. 332.
16. *New York Telegraph*, March 31, 1898.
17. Julia Cooley Altrocchi, "Uncle Richard," *Poet Lore* 61 (Winter 1966): 343.
18. Whittington-Egan and Smerdon, *Richard Le Gallienne: The Quest of the Golden Boy*, p. 340.
19. *Cincinnati Post*, February 21, 1932.

20. Eva Le Gallienne, "S. B. Quand-Meme," *Forum* 11 (Summer–Fall 1973): 34.
21. Ibid.
22. Whittington-Egan and Smerdon, *Richard Le Gallienne: The Quest of the Golden Boy*, pp. 355–56.
23. Ibid., pp. 358–59.
24. Ibid., pp. 363–64, 368.
25. Ibid., pp. 379–80.
26. Ibid., p. 403.
27. Ibid., pp. 387, 389.
28. Richard Le Gallienne, *An Old Country House* (New York: Harper and Brothers, 1902), pp. 27, 29.
29. Ibid., pp. 46, 48.
30. Richard Le Gallienne, *Little Dinners With the Sphinx* (New York: Moffat, Yard, 1905), pp. 231–33.
31. Ibid., pp. 234–40.
32. *New York Times*, March 5, 1916.
33. Whittington-Egan and Smerdon, *Richard Le Gallienne: The Quest of the Golden Boy*, pp. 395–96.
34. Ibid., pp. 405–6.
35. Ibid., p. 407.
36. Altrocchi, "Uncle Richard," p. 355.
37. Interview with Doris Johanson and Jessalyn Jones, July 28, 1989; Eva Le Gallienne, *With a Quiet Heart*, p. 282.

2. Mad about Her

1. Shari Benstock, *Women of the Left Bank* (Austin: University of Texas Press, 1986), p.47.
2. Richard Whittington-Egan and Geoffrey Smerdon, *Richard Le Gallienne: The Quest of the Golden Boy* (London: Unicorn, 1960), p. 14.
3. Ibid., p. 420.
4. Eva Le Gallienne, *At 33* (New York: Longmans, Green, 1934), p. 20.
5. Whittington-Egan and Smerdon, *Richard Le Gallienne: The Quest of the Golden Boy*, pp. 423–24.
6. Eva Le Gallienne, "S. B. Quand-Meme," *Forum* 11 (Summer–Fall 1973): 33.
7. *Philadelphia Record*, April 18, 1930.
8. *New York Post*, October 11, 1930.
9. Eva Le Gallienne, trans., *Seven Tales by H. C. Andersen* (New York: Harper and Row, 1959), pp. 5–6.
10. Interview with Anne Kaufman Schneider, April 26, 1989.
11. Constance Collier, *Harlequinade: The Story of My Life* (London: John Lane, The Bodley Head, 1929), pp. 220–21.

12. Eva Le Gallienne, "S. B. Quand-Meme," p. 35.
13. Ibid., p. 36.
14. Ibid., p. 38.
15. Ibid., pp. 38–39.
16. Genevieve Parkhurst, "Pictorial Review's $5000 Achievement Award," *Pictorial Review* 29 (January 1928): 2.
17. *New York Times*, September 23, 1916.
18. Eva Le Gallienne, "S. B. Quand-Meme," p. 42.
19. Eva Le Gallienne, *At 33*, pp. 79–80.
20. "The Laughter of Fools," *Times*, (London) May 31, 1915.
21. Elsie Janis, "Don't Weaken," *Liberty* (December 29, 1928), n. pag.
22. Unmarked clipping, Billy Rose Theatre Collection, New York Public Library for the Performing Arts.

3. *Tout Sera Bien* (All Shall Be Well)

1. Joseph Wood Krutch, *The American Drama Since 1918* (New York, 1957), pp. 7–8.
2. Richard Whittington-Egan and Geoffrey Smerdon, *Richard Le Gallienne: The Quest of the Golden Boy* (London: Unicorn, 1960), p. 460.
3. *New York Times*, January 5, 1916.
4. Unmarked clipping, Billy Rose Theatre Collection, New York Public Library for the Performing Arts.
5. Interview with Dalton Dearborn, August 2, 1989.
6. "Russian Artiste Becomes an American Star," *Theatre Magazine* 7 (January 1907): vii; unmarked clipping, Billy Rose Theatre Collection, New York Public Library for the Performing Arts; Ada Patterson, "An Interview with a Multiple Woman," *Theatre Magazine* 7 (August 1907): 221.
7. Eva Le Gallienne, ed., *Eva Le Gallienne's Civic Repertory Plays* (New York, 1928), p. ix; interview with Eva Le Gallienne, July 26, 1974, as quoted in Robert A. Schanke, "Eva Le Gallienne: First Lady of Repertory" (Ph.D. diss., University of Nebraska, 1975), p. 45.
8. Interview with Anne Kaufman Schneider, April 26 and May 18, 1989.
9. Kaier Curtin, *We Can Always Call Them Bulgarians* (Boston: Alyson, 1987), p. 57.
10. *New York Globe*, May 8, 1920; interview with Eva Le Gallienne, July 26, 1974, as quoted in Schanke, "Eva Le Gallienne: First Lady of Repertory," p. 47.
11. Interview with Anne Kaufman Schneider, May 18, 1989.
12. Joseph Schildkraut, *My Father and I* (New York: Viking, 1959), p. 159.
13. Interview with Eva Le Gallienne, July 26, 1974, as quoted in Schanke, "Eva Le Gallienne: First Lady of Repertory," p. 48.
14. Eva Le Gallienne, *At 33* (New York: Longmans, Green, 1934), p. 150; Theresa Helburn, *The Wayward Quest* (Boston: Little, Brown, 1960), pp. 172-73; interview with Michael Dewell, February 5, 1991.

15. Schildkraut, *My Father and I*, p. 161.
16. *New York Times*, April 21, 1921; Lawrence Langner, *The Magic Curtain* (New York: Dutton, 1951), p. 162; *New York Times*, May 1, 1921; *Cleveland Plain Dealer*, October 17, 1922.
17. *Boston Herald*, February 12, 1922.
18. Interview with Eva Le Gallienne, July 26, 1974, as quoted in Schanke, "Eva Le Gallienne: First Lady of Repertory," p. 53.
19. Unmarked clipping, Theatre Collection, Free Library of Philadelphia.
20. *Cincinnati Billboard*, July 16, 1921; Pearl Malvern, "Mediums of Art," *Shadowland*," (n.d.).
21. *New York Times*, November 15, 1925.
22. *Austin Statesman*, November 17, 1924.
23. Interview with Michael Dewell, February 5, 1991. For over sixteen years Michael Dewell was married to actress Nina Foch, daughter of Dirk Fock. The spelling of the family name was slightly altered to improve the pronunciation.
24. Mercedes de Acosta, *Here Lies the Heart* (New York: Reynal, 1975), p. 113.
25. *New York Times*, January 4, 1922.
26. Interview with Eva Le Gallienne, July 30, 1974, as quoted in Schanke, "Eva Le Gallienne: First Lady of Repertory," p. 56.
27. de Acosta, *Here Lies the Heart*, p. 148.
28. Eva Le Gallienne, *The Mystic in the Theatre: Eleonora Duse*, reprint ed. (Carbondale: Southern Illinois University Press, 1973), p. 5; Eva Le Gallienne, *At 33*, pp. 162–64.
29. Eva Le Gallienne, *At 33*, p. 165; Eva Le Gallienne, *The Mystic in the Theatre: Eleonora Duse*, p. 106.
30. Eva Le Gallienne, *At 33*, pp. 167–68; Eva Le Gallienne, *The Mystic in the Theatre: Eleonora Duse*, pp. 108–10.
31. *New York Times*, October 24, 1923; *New York Telegram*, October 24, 1923.
32. Eva Le Gallienne, *The Mystic in the Theatre: Eleonora Duse*, p. 148.
33. Ibid., pp. 152–53.
34. Ibid., pp. 111, 116; Eva Le Gallienne, *At 33*, p. 168.
35. Arthur Hornblow, "Mr. Hornblow Goes to the Play," *Theatre Magazine* 38 (December 1923): 15.
36. Interview with Haila Stoddard, May 19, 1989.
37. Interview with May Sarton, April 27, 1989; interview with Dalton Dearborn, August 2, 1989.
38. Letter from Eva Le Gallienne to an unknown recipient, January 26, 1925, Otto Kahn Collection, Princeton University Library.
39. Interview with Eva Le Gallienne, July 30, 1974, as quoted in Schanke, "Eva Le Gallienne: First Lady of Repertory," p. 65.
40. Letter from Eva Le Gallienne to Irina Skariatina, March 27, 1925, Otto Kahn Collection, Princeton University Library.

41. Letter from Eva Le Gallienne to Helen Lohmann, May 3, 1925, Theatre Collection of the Museum of the City of New York.
42. *l'Action Francaise* (Paris), June 18, 1925.
43. *New York Times*, July 12, 1925.
44. *New York Review*, July 11, 1925; letter from Eva Le Gallienne to George E. Bogusch, December 30, 1967, quoted in George E. Bogusch, "An American in Paris," *Theater Design and Technology* (October 1969): 8.
45. Noel Coward, *Present Indicative* (New York: Doubleday, 1937), p. 216.
46. Interview with May Sarton, April 27, 1989.
47. *New York Times*, October 10, 1925; *New York Herald-Tribune*, October 10, 1925.
48. Interview with Eva Le Gallienne, July 26, 1974 as quoted in Schanke, "Eva Le Gallienne: First Lady of Repertory," p. 55.

4. Abbess of Fourteenth Street

1. *New York World*, November 11, 1925; *New York Times*, November 15, 1925.
2. Eva Le Gallienne, trans., *The Master Builder*, by Henrik Ibsen (New York: New York University Press, 1955), p. 11.
3. *Brooklyn Daily Times*, January 1926; Eva Le Gallienne, *The Master Builder*, p. 29.
4. Promptscript for *The Master Builder*, Civic Repertory Theatre Collection, Beinecke Library, Yale University; Eva Le Gallienne, *The Master Builder*, p. 162.
5. *New York Sun*, October 22, 1927.
6. Interview with Eva Le Gallienne, July 26, 1974, as quoted in Schanke, "Eva Le Gallienne: First Lady of Repertory" (Ph.D. diss., University of Nebraska, 1975), p. 76.
7. *New York Herald-Tribune*, January 30, 1926; *New York Times*, January 30, 1926; *New York Sun*, January 30, 1926.
8. *New York Times*, December 14, 1925.
9. *Chicago Daily News*, May 3, 1926; *Philadelphia Public Ledger*, n.d., Theatre Collection, Free Library of Philadelphia; Eva Le Gallienne, "Bringing Theatre to the People," a typed transcription of an address delivered before Boston's Old South Church Forum, November 18, 1928, Theatre Collection of the Museum of the City of New York.
10. Letter from Eva Le Gallienne to Otto Kahn, May 25, 1926, Otto Kahn Collection, Princeton University; interview with Eva Le Gallienne, July 26, 1974, as quoted in Schanke, "Eva Le Gallienne: First Lady of Repertory," p. 90.
11. Letter from Eva Le Gallienne to Otto Kahn, May 3, 1926, Otto Kahn Collection, Princeton University Library.
12. George Jean Nathan, "The Theatre," *American Mercury* 14 (May 1928): 122.

13. Eva Le Gallienne, *At 33* (New York: Longmans, Green, 1934), p. 199; Cole Lesley, *The Life of Noel Coward* (London: Jonathan Cape, 1976), p. 90.

14. Edouard Bourdet, *The Captive* (New York: Bretano's, 1926), pp. 148, 178.

15. *New York Times*, September 30, 1926; *New York Morning Telegraph*, October 10, 1926; Arthur Hornblow, "Mr. Hornblow Goes to the Play," *Theatre Magazine* 44 (December 1926): 16; George Jean Nathan, "Theatre," *American Mercury* 12 (March 1927): 373.

16. Kaier Curtin, *We Can Always Call Them Bulgarians* (Boston: Alyson, 1987), p. 53.

17. Lesley, *The Life of Noel Coward*, p. 101.

18. *New York World*, October 27, 1926.

19. *New York World*, January 25, 1927.

20. *Boston Transcript*, n.d., Billy Rose Theatre Collection, New York Library for the Performing Arts.

21. Grace Cooper, "Eva Le Gallienne," *The Independent Woman* 6 (December 1927): 10–11.

22. All references to specific finances of the Civic Repertory Theatre are from auditor's statements, ledgers, and financial statements in the Civic Repertory Theatre Collection, Beinecke Library, Yale University, as quoted in Schanke, "Eva Le Gallienne: First Lady of Repertory."

23. *New York American*, February 12, 1928.

24. Eva Le Gallienne, "My Adventures in Repertory," *Theatre Magazine* 45 (April 1927): 52B.

25. *New York Sun*, October 19, 1927; John Mason Brown, "Broadway in Review," *Theatre Arts Monthly* 11 (December 1927): 895; Herman Heijermans, *The Good Hope* (New York: Samuel French, 1955), p. ix.

26. *New York World*, January 14, 1928.

27. George Jean Nathan, "The Theatre: Blah in Another Direction," *American Mercury* 13 (March 1928): 377–78.

28. Interview with Eva Le Gallienne, July 26, 1974, as quoted in Schanke, "Eva Le Gallienne: First Lady of Repertory," p. 114.

29. Eva Le Gallienne, ed., *Eva Le Gallienne's Civic Repertory Plays* (New York: W. W. Norton, 1928), p. 91.

30. Promptscript for *Hedda Gabler*, Civic Repertory Theatre Collection, Beinecke Library, Yale University; May Sarton, "The Genius of Eva Le Gallienne," *Forum* 11 (Summer–Fall 1973): 48; Eva Le Gallienne, trans., *Eight Plays by Henrik Ibsen* (New York: Modern Library, 1951), p. 574.

31. Interview with Glenda Jackson, May 13, 1982, as quoted in Robert A. Schanke, *Ibsen in America* (Metuchen, New Jersey: Scarecrow Press, 1988), p. 268; *New York Journal*, March 27, 1928.

32. Interview with Tonio Selwart, April 29, 1989.

33. Interview with Richard Waring, August 1, 1989.

34. Interview with Tedd Fetter, July 15, 1973, as quoted in Schanke, "Eva Le Gallienne: First Lady of Repertory," p. 120; *New York Times*, June 16, 1974;

Cindy Adams, *Lee Strasberg: The Imperfect Genius of the Actors Studio* (Garden City, NJ: Doubleday, 1980), p. 2.

35. Interview with Paul Vincent, July 31, 1989.
36. Lesley, *The Life of Noel Coward*, p. 90.
37. Promptscript for *The Cherry Orchard*, Civic Repertory Theatre Collection, Beinecke Library, Yale University.
38. Videotaped interview with Eva Le Gallienne, September 22, 1975, Billy Rose Theatre Collection, New York Public Library for the Performing Arts.
39. Eva Le Gallienne, "Sir James Barrie, Peter Pan, and I," *Theatre Magazine* 49 (January 1929): 68.
40. *Chicago Examiner*, December 22, 1933.
41. Interview with Eva Le Gallienne, July 26, 1974, as quoted in Schanke, "Eva Le Gallienne: First Lady of Repertory," p. 131.
42. Interview with Eva Le Gallienne, July 26, 1974, as quoted in Schanke, "Eva Le Gallienne: First Lady of Repertory," p. 131; *Baltimore Morning Sun*, October 1, 1933.
43. *Hartford Times*, October 16, 1933.
44. Sarton, "The Genius of Eva Le Gallienne," p. 48.
45. *New York American*, April 22, 1930; Joseph Wood Krutch, "Drama," *The Nation* 130 (May 14, 1930): 579; *New York Herald-Tribune*, April 22, 1930; *New York Times*, April 22, 1930; interview with Richard Waring, August 1, 1989.
46. Radclyffe Hall, *The Well of Loneliness* (New York: Avon, 1981), p. 437.
47. Interview with May Sarton, April 27, 1989; interview with Tonio Selwart, April 29, 1989.
48. The cartoon is located in the "Lesbian Scrapbook," p. 4, Manuscript Collection, Kinsey Institute, Bloomington, Indiana.
49. Eva Le Gallienne, *With a Quiet Heart* (New York: Viking, 1953), p. 93.

5. My Life in Two

1. *New York American*, July 8, 1930; *New York Evening Journal*, July 8, 1930; *New York Daily News*, July 9, 1930; *New York Herald-Tribune*, July 9, 1930; *New York Sun*, July 9, 1930.
2. *New York Daily News*, July 8, 1930; *New York Daily Mirror*, July 9, 1930.
3. The Complaint, Answer, Findings of Fact, Judgment, and Decree, file 32315, July 7, 1930, Second Judicial District Court, Reno, Nevada.
4. Clement Wood, *Amy Lowell* (New York: Harold Vinal, 1926), pp. 13, 173; Martha Dickinson Bianchi, *Emily Dickinson Face to Face: Unpublished Letters with Notes and Reminiscences* (Boston: Houghton Mifflin, 1932).
5. Promptscript for *Alison's House*, act 3, Civic Repertory Theatre Collection, Beinecke Library, Yale University.
6. Unmarked clipping, Theatre Collection, Free Library of Philadelphia.

7. Interview with Eva Le Gallienne, July 26, 1974, as quoted in Schanke, "Eva Le Gallienne: First Lady of Repertory" (Ph.D. diss., University of Nebraska, 1975), p. 139.
8. Eva Le Gallienne Collection, Billy Rose Theatre Collection, New York Public Library for the Performing Arts.
9. *New York Evening Telegram*, February 9, 1931.
10. *New York Sun*, February 7, 1931.
11. *New York Herald-Tribune*, May 3, 1931.
12. Herbert L. Gravitz and Julie D. Bowden, *Recovery: A Guide for Adult Children of Alcoholics* (New York: Simon and Schuster, 1985).
13. Most of the information about the fire is taken from Eva Le Gallienne's second autobiography, *With a Quiet Heart* (New York: Viking, 1953), pp. 3–14.
14. Ibid., pp. 5–6.
15. Ibid., p. 11.
16. *New York Evening Telegram*, December 19, 1930; *Philadelphia Public Ledger*, May 7, 1933.
17. Interview with Eloise Armen, May 19, 1989.
18. Eva Le Gallienne, *At 33* (New York: Longmans, Green, 1934), p. 236.

6. The Greater Depression

1. Souvenir Program of the Civic Repertory Theatre, Beinecke Library, Yale University.
2. Auditor's statements of the Civic Repertory Theatre, May 23, 1931, and August 31, 1932, Beinecke Library, Yale University.
3. Herschel Williams, "*Liliom*," *Theatre Arts Monthly* 17 (January 1933): 14.
4. Letter from Paul Ballantyne, September 15, 1974.
5. *New York World-Telegram*, October 27, 1932.
6. *Women's Wear Daily*, December 6, 1935; *The Stage*, December 1932.
7. *New York Post*, December 12, 1932.
8. Pressbooks of the Civic Repertory Theatre and auditor's statement of May 6, 1933, Beinecke Library, Yale University.
9. Letter from Richard Le Gallienne to Otto Kahn, February 3, 1930, Otto Kahn Collection, Princeton University; letter from Otto Kahn to Richard Le Gallienne, March 4, 1930, Otto Kahn Collection, Princeton University Library.
10. Jack Poggi, *Theater in America: The Impact of Economic Forces* (Ithaca, NY: Cornell University Press, 1968), pp. 49–50.
11. *New York Sun*, February 6, 1933.
12. Auditor's statement of the Civic Repertory Theatre, May 6, 1933, Beinecke Library, Yale University.
13. Auditor's statements of Eva Le Gallienne Productions, Inc., December 2 and December 30, 1933, Beinecke Library, Yale University.

14. Letter from Eva Le Gallienne to May Sarton, August 4, 1933, Berg Collection, New York Public Library.
15. Unmarked clipping, Theatre Collection, Free Library of Philadelphia; *Philadelphia Evening Bulletin*, November 23, 1933.
16. *Baltimore Evening Sun*, November 10, 1943.
17. All references to the telegrams are from FERA "Old General Subject" Series, Miscellaneous Correspondence, Record Group 69 of WPA, National Archives.
18. Letter from Eva Le Gallienne to May Sarton, August 27, 1933, Berg Collection, New York Public Library.
19. *Christian Science Monitor*, December 4, 1933; untitled Pittsburgh newspaper, December 4, 1933, Theatre Collection, Free Library of Philadelphia.
20. Auditor's statements of Eva Le Gallienne Productions, Inc., March 24, April 28, and August 31, 1934, Beinecke Library, Yale University.
21. Untitled Minneapolis newspaper, February 7, 1934, Billy Rose Theatre Collection, New York Library for the Performing Arts.
22. *St. Paul Press*, March 6, 1934.
23. Interview with May Sarton, April 27, 1989.
24. Ibid.
25. Ibid.
26. Letter from Eva Le Gallienne to May Sarton, January 29, 1934, Berg Collection, New York Public Library.
27. *New York Post*, November 10, 1934.
28. Kaier Curtin, *We Can Always Call Them Bulgarians* (Boston: Alyson, 1987), p. 205.
29. *Boston Herald*, November 19, 1935.
30. *New York Sun*, December 7, 1935.
31. Pressbooks of the Civic Repertory Theatre, Beinecke Library, Yale University.
32. Mollie B. Steinberg, "History of the Fourteenth Street Theatre," *Civic Repertory Theatre Magazine* (April 1931): 9.
33. *New York Times*, February 15, 1931; Robert Benchley, "Early Christmas Flopping," *New Yorker* 6 (December 15, 1930): 36.
34. *New York Herald-Tribune*, February 17, 1929.
35. Letter from Paul Ballantyne, September 15, 1974.
36. Genevieve Parkhurst, "Pictorial Review's $5000 Achievement Award," *Pictorial Review* 29 (January 1928): 66.
37. Interview with Howard da Silva, October 1964, as quoted in Paul Reuben Cooper, "Eva Le Gallienne's Civic Repertory Theatre," (Ph.D. diss., University of Illinois, 1967), p. 123.
38. Letter from Paul Ballantyne, September 15, 1974.
39. Alfred L. Bernheim, *The Business of the Theatre: An Economic History of the American Theatre, 1750-1932* (New York: Actor's Equity Association, 1932), p. 75.

40. Interview with May Sarton, April 27, 1989.
41. Auditor's statements of the Civic Repertory Theatre, August 31, 1929, and August 31, 1935, Beinecke Library, Yale University.
42. Letter from Eva Le Gallienne to William Lyon Phelps, December 9, 1935, Beinecke Library, Yale University.
43. Unmarked clipping, Theatre Collection, Free Library of Philadelphia.

7. Beyond Joy

1. Eva Le Gallienne, *The Mystic in the Theatre: Eleonora Duse*, reprint ed., (Carbondale: Southern Illinois University Press, 1973), p. 58.
2. Ibid., p. 121.
3. *New York World Telegraph*, July 3, 1936.
4. Eva Le Gallienne, *With a Quiet Heart* (New York: Viking, 1953), pp. 97–98.
5. Letter from Eva Le Gallienne to Butler Davenport, January 3, 1937, Amherst College Library.
6. Eva Le Gallienne, *With a Quiet Heart*, p. 107.
7. Ibid., p. 105.
8. *Boston Transcript*, August 24, 1937; *New York Telegram*, August 24, 1937; *New York Times*, August 24, 1937.
9. Eva Le Gallienne, *With a Quiet Heart*, p. 114.
10. Ibid., p. 163.
11. Letter from Eva Le Gallienne to Chamberlain Brown, May 24, 1939, Theatre Collection, New York Public Library.
12. *New York Times*, March 6, 1942.
13. Interview with Haila Stoddard, May 19, 1989; Rosamond Gilder, "Broadway in Review," *Theatre Arts Monthly* 26 (March 1942): 154.
14. Interview with Haila Stoddard, May 19, 1989.
15. Interview with May Sarton, April 27, 1989.
16. Joseph Schildkraut, *My Father and I* (New York: Viking, 1959), p. 223.
17. *New York Morning Telegram*, May 22, 1942; *New York Herald-Tribune*, May 21, 1942; *New York Post*, May 21, 1942.
18. Letter from Eva Le Gallienne to May Sarton, October 22, 1942, Berg Collection, New York Public Library.
19. Eva Le Gallienne, *With a Quiet Heart*, pp. 230–31.
20. Margaret Webster, *Don't Put Your Daughter on the Stage* (New York: Alfred A. Knopf, 1972), p. 124.
21. Letter from Eva Le Gallienne to May Sarton, February 22, 1945, Berg Collection, New York Public Library.
22. Letter from Eva Le Gallienne to May Sarton, April 9, 1945, Berg Collection, New York Public Library.
23. Letter from Eva Le Gallienne to May Sarton, January 26, 1946, Berg Collection, New York Public Library.

24. Letter from Tennessee Williams to Margo Jones, August 1944, Harry Ransom Humanities Research Center, University of Texas at Austin.
25. Letter from Eva Le Gallienne to May Sarton, January 26, 1946, Berg Collection, New York Public Library.
26. *New York Times*, November 3, 1946.
27. Webster, *Don't Put Your Daughter on the Stage*, p. 156.
28. Interview with Eli Wallach, March 16, 1991.
29. *New York Times*, November 3, 1946.
30. Eva Le Gallienne, *With a Quiet Heart*, p. 263.
31. Ibid., p. 267.
32. Ibid., p. 260.
33. Eva Le Gallienne, *At 33* (New York: Longmans, Green, 1934), pp. 251–52.
34. *New York World-Telegram*, January 30, 1947.
35. Cheryl Crawford, *One Naked Individual* (New York: Bobbs-Merrill, 1977), p. 154.
36. *New York Journal-American*, February 28, 1947.
37. George Jean Nathan, *Encyclopaedia of the Theatre* (New York: Alfred A. Knopf, 1940), p. 231; letter from George Jean Nathan to Sean O'Casey, December 30, 1949; *New York Journal-American*, n.d., Theatre Collection, Billy Rose Theatre Collection, New York Public Library for the Performing Arts.
38. Interview with Anne Jackson, March 16, 1991.
39. Webster, *Don't Put Your Daughter on the Stage*, pp. 248–49; interview with Anne Jackson, March 16, 1991.
40. Webster, *Don't Put Your Daughter on the Stage*, p. 273.
41. Jonathan Ned Katz, *Gay/Lesbian Almanac* (New York: Harper and Row, 1983), pp. 613–16; Jonathan Ned Katz, *Gay American History* (New York: Thomas Y. Crowell, 1976), p. 92; interview with Anne Jackson, March 16, 1991.
42. *Boston Post*, September 17, 1947.
43. Eva Le Gallienne, *With a Quiet Heart*, pp. 284–85.
44. John Joseph Evoy, *The Rejected: Psychological Consequences of Parental Rejection* (University Park: Pennsylvania State University Press, 1981), p. 72.
45. Ibid., p. 124.
46. Letter from Eva Le Gallienne to Robert Carver of Actors' Equity Association, March 14, 1948, Margaret Webster Collection, Library of Congress.
47. *New York World-Telegram*, February 25, 1948.
48. George Jean Nathan, *The Theatre Book of the Year: 1947–1948* (New York: Alfred A. Knopf, 1948), p. 277; *New York Journal-American*, March 8, 1948.
49. Letter from Lawrence Langner to Eva Le Gallienne, March 18, 1948, Beinecke Library, Yale University; letter from Margaret Webster to Brooks

Atkinson, March 3, 1947, Margaret Webster Collection, Library of Congress.

50. Letter from Paul Ballantyne, October 1, 1974.
51. Letter from May Sarton to Eva Le Gallienne, March 10, 1948, Berg Collection, New York Public Library.
52. *Variety*, May 12, 1948.
53. Letter from Eva Le Gallienne to May Sarton, March 21, 1948, Berg Collection, New York Public Library.

8. Buying Some Freedom

1. Eva Le Gallienne, *Flossie and Bossie* (New York: Harper and Row, 1949).
2. Interview with Eva Le Gallienne, July 30, 1974, as quoted in Schanke, "Eva Le Gallienne: First Lady of Repertory" (Ph.D. diss., University of Nebraska, 1975), p. 196; Debbi Wasserman, "Developing an American Acting Style," *New York Theatre Review* 2 (February 1978): 6.
3. Letter from Eva Le Gallienne to May Sarton, June 7, 1949, Berg Collection, New York Public Library.
4. Ibid.
5. Interview with Richard Waring, August 1, 1989.
6. Letter from Eva Le Gallienne to May Sarton, December 27, 1949, Berg Collection, New York Public Library.
7. Letter from Eva Le Gallienne to May Sarton, March 2, 1951, Berg Collection, New York Public Library.
8. Margaret Webster, *Don't Put Your Daughter on the Stage* (New York: Alfred A. Knopf, 1972), p. 273.
9. Eva Le Gallienne, Introduction to *Six Plays by Henrik Ibsen* (New York: Modern Library, 1957), pp. vii–viii.
10. Ibid., p. xii.
11. Ibid., p. xii, xv.
12. Program insert for *Hedda Gabler* recording.
13. Eva Le Gallienne, *With a Quiet Heart* (New York: Viking, 1953), pp. 302–3.
14. *New York World-Telegram*, January 9, 1954.
15. *Detroit Free Press*, September 20, 1953.
16. Letter from Eva Le Gallienne to May Sarton, March 1, 1954, Berg Collection, New York Public Library.
17. *New York Post*, August 16, 1963; John Cottrell and Fergus Cashin, *Richard Burton: An Intimate Biography* (London: Arthur Baker, 1971), p. 154.
18. Interview with George Morfogen, June 3, 1990.
19. Mariette Hartley, *Breaking the Silence* (New York: G. P. Putnam's, 1990), pp. 75–82.
20. Interview with George Morfogen, June 3, 1990.
21. Interview with Paul Vincent, July 31, 1989.

22. Ibid.
23. Ibid.
24. Unless otherwise cited all references to Peter Falk's acting classes with Le Gallienne are from an interview with Peter Falk, February 7, 1991.
25. Letter from Peter Falk to Eva Le Gallienne, March 18, 1987.
26. Ibid.
27. Interview with Lucille Lortel, July 29, 1989; interview with George Morfogen, June 3, 1990.
28. *Cleveland Press*, January 25, 1955.
29. All references to the relationship between Eva Le Gallienne and Dalton Dearborn are from interviews with Dalton Dearborn, August 2, 1989, and June 2, 1990.
30. Interview with Lucille Lortel, July 29, 1989.
31. Letter from Eva Le Gallienne to May Sarton, March 21, 1948, Berg Collection, New York Public Library.
32. Letter from Eva Le Gallienne to May Sarton, January 16, 1957, Berg Collection, New York Public Library.
33. Letter from Eva Le Gallienne to May Sarton, March 9, 1957, Berg Collection, New York Public Library.

9. The Queen Is Back

1. Interview with Norris Houghton, May 31, 1990; interview with T. Edward Hambleton, October 18, 1990.
2. Ibid.
3. Interview with Ellis Rabb, September 16, 1989.
4. Letter from Paul Ballantyne, October 1, 1974.
5. Tom F. Driver, "Drama," *Christian Century* 74 (November 6, 1957): 1324; *New York Herald-Tribune*, October 9, 1957; *New York Post*, October 20, 1957.
6. Interview with Norris Houghton, May 31, 1990.
7. Interview with Michael Dewell, February 5, 1991.
8. "Mary Stuart," *Theatre Arts* 41 (December 1957): 83; letter from Eva Le Gallienne to Arthur William Row, n.d., Billy Rose Theatre Collection, New York Public Library for the Performing Arts.
9. Interview with T. Edward Hambleton, October 18, 1990.
10. *New York Times*, January 26, 1958.
11. Letter from Eva Le Gallienne to Mr. Cordell, July 9, 1958, Lilly Library, Indiana University; *Milwaukee Sentinel*, November 15, 1955.
12. Interview with Michael Dewell, February 5, 1991.
13. Ibid.
14. Ibid.
15. Ibid.
16. Ibid.

17. Interview with Signe Hasso, February 6, 1991.

18. Interview with Michael Dewell, February 5, 1991.

19. Ibid.

20. Interview with Staats Cotsworth, June 2, 1975, as quoted in Schanke, "Eva Le Gallienne: First Lady of Repertory" (Ph.D. diss., University of Nebraska, 1975), p. 273.

21. Interview with Signe Hasso, February 6, 1991.

22. This and the immediately following references to observations made by Michael Dewell are from an interview with Michael Dewell, February 5, 1991.

23. *New York Times*, July 18, 1961; *New York Times*, November 24, 1963.

24. *Washington Post*, October 24, 1961; *Philadelphia Evening Bulletin*, November 29, 1961; *Detroit Free Press*, April 4, 1962.

25. Interview with Michael Dewell, February 5, 1991; interview with Dalton Dearborn, August 2, 1989.

26. Interview with Gina Shield, December 18, 1989.

27. Interviews with Michael Dewell, February 5, 1991; Tharon Musser, December 19, 1989; Gina Shield, December 18, 1989; Dalton Dearborn, August 2, 1989.

28. The immediately following is from an interview with Dalton Dearborn, August 2, 1989.

29. Interview with May Sarton, April 27, 1989.

30. *New York Times*, May 11, 1962 and November 24, 1963; NRT Cumulative Fiscal Fact Sheet, Billy Rose Theatre Collection, New York Public Library for the Performing Arts.

31. Except where otherwise indicated, the immediately following discussion of Rabb's relationship with Le Gallienne is from an interview with Ellis Rabb, September 16, 1989.

32. Interview with Rod Bladel, May 29, 1975, as quoted in Schanke, "Eva Le Gallienne: First Lady of Repertory," p. 277; interview with Rosemary Harris, March 31, 1982.

33. Ibid.

34. Ibid.; *Detroit Free Press*, October 26, 1962; *Ann Arbor News*, October 25, 1962; *Michigan Daily*, October 25, 1962.

35. Interview with Michael Dewell, February 5, 1991.

36. Interview with Farley Granger, December 18, 1989.

37. Interview with Tharon Musser, December 19, 1989; interview with Michael Dewell, February 5, 1991.

38. Interview with Tharon Musser, December 19, 1989.

39. Ibid.

40. *New York Herald-Tribune*, April 6, 1964; *New York Times*, April 6, 1964.

41. The following discussion of the Tony Awards ceremony is from an interview with Michael Dewell, February 5, 1991.

42. Ferenc Molnar, *Liliom* (New York: Samuel French, 1945), p. 137.

43. Interview with Michael Dewell, February 5, 1991.
44. Interview with Farley Granger, December 18, 1989; *Chicago American*, March 5, 1965.
45. Interview with Signe Hasso, February 6, 1991.
46. Interview with Tharon Musser, December 19, 1989.
47. Interview with Farley Granger, December 18, 1989.
48. Interview with Tharon Musser, December 19, 1989; interview with Berenice Weiler, August 2, 1989; interview with Gina Shield, December 18, 1989.
49. Interview with Tharon Musser, December 19, 1989.
50. Interview with Michael Dewell, February 5, 1991.
51. Interview with Michael Dewell, February 5, 1991; interview with Sloane Shelton, June 11, 1975, as quoted in Schanke, "Eva Le Gallienne: First Lady of Repertory," p. 289–90; *Louisville Times*, January 18, 1966.
52. Interview with Sloane Shelton, June 11, 1975, as quoted in Schanke, *Eva Le Gallienne: First Lady of Repertory*, p. 288.
53. NRT Cumulative Fiscal Fact Sheet, Billy Rose Theatre Collection, New York Public Library for the Performing Arts.
54. Interview with Michael Dewell, February 5, 1991.
55. May Sarton, *Mrs. Stevens Hears the Mermaids Singing* (New York: W. W. Norton, 1965), pp. 16, 78.
56. This and the following comments by Sarton are from an interview with May Sarton, April 27, 1989.
57. Interview with Eloise Armen, May 19, 1989.
58. Interview with Anne Kaufman Schneider, May 18, 1989.
59. Interview with Ellis Rabb, September 16, 1989.
60. Interview with Doris Johanson and Jessalyn Jones, July 28, 1989.
61. Interview with Ellis Rabb, September 16, 1989.
62. Interview with Ellis Rabb, September 16, 1989.
63. Interview with T. Edward Hambleton, October 18, 1990; *New York Times*, March 20, 1968; interview with Anne Kaufman Schneider, April 26, 1989; letter from Uta Hagen, June 3, 1974.
64. *New York Times*, March 17, 1968.
65. Interview with Ellis Rabb, September 16, 1989.
66. Letter from Eva Le Gallienne to May Sarton, September 16, 1968, Berg Collection, New York Public Library.

10. Exit the Queen

1. Interviews with Doris Johanson and Jessalyn Jones, July 28, 1989; Eloise Armen, May 19, 1989; Anne Kaufman Schneider, April 26, 1989.
2. Interview with Berenice Weiler, August 2, 1989.
3. Interview with Michael Kahn, May 31, 1975, as quoted in Schanke, "Eva Le Gallienne: First Lady of Repertory" (Ph.D. diss., University of Nebraska,

1975), p. 307–8; interview with Berenice Weiler, August 2, 1989.

4. Interview with Eva Le Gallienne, July 26, 1974, as quoted in Schanke, "Eva Le Gallienne: First Lady of Repertory," p. 308.

5. Richard Whittington-Egan and Geoffrey Smerdon, *Richard Le Gallienne: The Quest of the Golden Boy* (London: Unicorn, 1960), p. 464.

6. Telephone conversation with the probate office, Redding, Connecticut, March 20, 1991.

7. Interview with Eloise Armen, May 19, 1989.

8. Interview with Haila Stoddard, May 19, 1989; interview with Anne Kaufman Schneider, April 26, 1989; telephone conversations with Weston Town Hall and Westport Probate Office, March 12, 1991.

9. Interview with Eloise Armen, May 19, 1989.

10. Letter from Eva Le Gallienne to Eugenia Rawls, January 8, 1973 (see also letter from Margaret Webster to Eugenia Rawls, October 2, 1972), Southern Historical Collection, University of North Carolina Library, Chapel Hill, North Carolina.

11. Interview with Doris Johanson and Jessalyn Jones, July 28, 1989; interview with Eva Le Gallienne, July 26, 1974, as quoted in Schanke, "Eva Le Gallienne: First Lady of Repertory," p. 313.

12. Interview with Dalton Dearborn, August 2, 1989.

13. Letters from Eva Le Gallienne to Robert A. Schanke, n.d. and July 30, 1973.

14. *New York Times*, June 10, 1974.

15. This and the following comments by Wersba are from a letter from Barbara Wersba, August 4, 1989.

16. Interview with Dalton Dearborn, August 2, 1989.

17. Telephone conversation with Eva Le Gallienne, July 22, 1974.

18. Letter from Eva Le Gallienne to May Sarton, March 2, 1951, Berg Collection, New York Public Library.

11. The Comeback Kid

1. The following account of rehearsals and opening night are from a letter from Barbara Wersba, August 4, 1989.

2. *Variety*, September 10, 1975.

3. Letter from June Havoc to Lucille Lortel, September 3, 1975, Lortel Collection, Westport Public Library; letter from Barbara Wersba, August 4, 1989.

4. Letter from Barbara Wersba, August 4, 1989.

5. Ibid.

6. Interview with Ellis Rabb, September 16, 1989.

7. Ibid.; interview with Burry Fredrik, July 28, 1989.

8. *New York Record*, December 19, 1975; AP Release, n.d., Billy Rose Theatre Collection, New York Public Library for the Performing Arts; NBC Radio Review, December 18, 1975.

9. Letter from Barbara Wersba, August 4, 1989.

10. Interview with Rosemary Harris, March 31, 1982.

11. Letter from Carole Shelley, September 16, 1977.

12. The passages discussed and quoted are from George S. Kaufman and Edna Ferber, *The Royal Family* (Garden City, New York: Nelson Doubleday, 1956), pp. 122–25.

13. Discussion with Eloise Armen, November 21, 1975, as quoted in Robert A. Schanke, "Eva Le Gallienne: The Comeback of a Star," *Southern Theatre* 13 (Fall 1978): 8.

14. The following discussion of the final scene is from an interview with Ellis Rabb, September 16, 1989.

15. Discussion with Eloise Armen, January 12, 1976, as quoted in Schanke, "Eva Le Gallienne: The Comeback of a Star," p. 9; interview with Rosemary Harris, March 31, 1982.

16. Discussion with Eva Le Gallienne, July 2, 1976, as quoted in Schanke, "Eva Le Gallienne: The Comeback of a Star," p. 10.

17. Letter from Barbara Wersba, August 4, 1989.

18. This and the following comments by Shelley on her performance and Le Gallienne's are from a letter from Carole Shelley, September 16, 1977.

19. *Variety*, January 12, 1977.

20. Interview with Anne Kaufman Schneider, May 18, 1989.

21. Interview with Shirley Herz, July 27, 1989.

22. Interview with Anne Kaufman Schneider, April 26, 1989.

23. Ibid.; interview with May Sarton, April 27, 1989.

24. Interview with Ellis Rabb, September 16, 1989; interview with Rosemary Harris, March 31, 1982.

25. Interview with Rosemary Harris, March 31, 1982.

26. The following details of that night are from an interview with Anne Kaufman Schneider, April 26, 1989.

27. Letter from Barbara Wersba, August 4, 1989.

28. Interview with Doris Johanson and Jessalyn Jones, July 28, 1989.

29. This and the following discussion of the rehearsals are from a letter from Barbara Wersba, August 4, 1989.

30. *Variety*, December 14, 1977; *Seattle Times*, December 1, 1977.

31. This and the following comments on the close of the play are from a letter from Barbara Wersba, August 4, 1989.

32. This excerpt from Soyer's will and the discussion of the inheritance are from a letter from Virginia P. Boyd, November 15, 1989.

33. Burstyn's comments and the discussion of the filming are from an interview with Ellen Burstyn, July 31, 1989.

34. Interview with Anne Kaufman Schneider, May 18, 1989.

35. Stanley Kauffmann, "Books and the Arts," *New Republic* 183 (November 15, 1980): 22–23; Judith Crist, "Three Provocative Gambles," *Saturday Review* 7 (November 1980): 82–83.

36. Interview with Clifford Williams, April 22, 1982.

37. Ibid.; interview with Eloise Armen, May 19, 1989.

38. Interview with Clifford Williams, April 22, 1982.

39. *New York Times*, January 16, 1981; *New York Times*, January 21, 1981.

40. Interview with Anne Kaufman Schneider, April 26, 1989.

41. Interview with Caroline Lagerfelt and Harriet Harris, December 19, 1989.

42. Ibid.

43. Interview with Harriet Harris, December 19, 1989.

44. Interview with Anne Kaufman Schneider, April 26, 1989; interview with Doris Johanson and Jessalyn Jones, July 28, 1989.

45. Interview with Ellen Burstyn, July 31, 1989.

46. This and the following comment by Alexander are from an interview with Jane Alexander, June 1, 1990.

47. Peter Hay, *Theatrical Anecdotes* (New York: Oxford University Press, 1987), p. 223.

48. *New York Times*, December 24, 1982; *Des Moines Sunday Register*, January 2, 1982.

49. Interview with Anne Kaufman Schneider, May 18, 1989; interview with Mary Louise Wilson, December 16, 1989.

50. Interview with Anne Jackson and Eli Wallach, March 16, 1991; May Sarton, *At Seventy: A Journal*. (New York: W. W. Norton, 1984), pp. 227–28.

51. Letter from Eva Le Gallienne, October 25, 1983.

52. Interview with Anne Kaufman Schneider, May 18, 1989; interview with Eloise Armen, May 19, 1989; interview with Burry Fredrik, July 28, 1989.

53. Interview with Anne Kaufman Schneider, May 18, 1989.

54. Alice De Lamar, Last Will and Testament, Westport Probate Office, Westport, Connecticut; Eva Le Gallienne, Last Will and Testament, Westport Probate Office, Westport, Connecticut.

55. Interview with Eloise Armen, May 19, 1989.

56. Interview with May Sarton, April 27, 1989; interview with Eloise Armen, May 19, 1989.

12. Winter Bound

1. Interview with Clifford Williams, April 22, 1982; interview with Burry Fredrik, July 28, 1989; interview with Lucille Lortel, July 29, 1989; interview with Eloise Armen, May 19, 1989.

2. Letter from Rosemary Harris, February 17, 1990.

3. The following recollections of Anne Kaufman Schneider are from interviews with Anne Kaufman Schneider, April 26 and May 18, 1989.

4. Interview with May Sarton, April 27, 1989.

5. Thomas H. Dickinson, *Winter Bound*, act 1, scenes 2 and 4, typewritten copy, Billy Rose Theatre Collection, New York Public Library for the Performing Arts.

6. Interview with Eloise Armen, May 19, 1989; interviews with Anne Kaufman Schneider, April 26 and May 18, 1989.

7. Lisl M. Goodman, *Death and the Creative Life* (New York: Springer Publishing, 1981), pp. 57–60.

8. Interview with Eloise Armen, May 19, 1989; interviews with Anne Kaufman Schneider, April 26 and May 18, 1989.

9. *New York Times*, June 5, 1991; *Los Angeles Times*, June 5, 1991.

10. Eva Le Gallienne, Last Will and Testament, Westport Probate Office, Westport, Connecticut; interview with Eva Le Gallienne, July 26, 1974, as quoted in Schanke, "Eva Le Gallienne: First Lady of Repertory" (Ph.D. diss., University of Nebraska, 1975), p. 313.

11. Interview with Jane Alexander, June 1, 1990.

12. Peter Zeisler, "Toward Brave New Worlds," and Eva Le Gallienne, "On Repertory and Audiences," *American Theatre* 3 (November 1986): 5, 20.

13. Interviews with Anne Kaufman Schneider, April 26 and May 18, 1989.

14. Interview with May Sarton, April 27, 1989.

15. Buffy Dunker, "Aging Lesbians: Observations and Speculations," in *Lesbian Psychologies*, ed., Boston Lesbian Psychologies Collective (Urbana: University of Illinois Press, 1987), pp. 76–77.

16. Barbara Wersba, *The Dream Watcher* (New York: Atheneum, 1968), pp. 31, 72–73.

17. Ibid., p. 171.

Index

National Phoenix Theatre. *See* Phoenix Theatre
National Repertory Theatre (NRT), 210–14, 217–26
National Woman's Party, 75
Nazimova, Alla, 48–50, 54, 80, 81, 82, 103, 116, 161, 277; in *The Cherry Orchard*, 81; and Eva, xvii, 47, 80; lesbianism of, xviii; reputation of, 46–47
Norregaard, Julie. *See* Le Gallienne, Julie
Not So Long Ago, 31, 49–50

Oberfelder, Arthur M., 165
Odéon Theatre, 62
Off Chance, The, 46
Old Manor, The. *See* Chiddingfold
Olivier, Laurence, 172, 205
Open Door, The, 111

Palm Beach Playhouse, 199
Pater, Walter, 5
Peggy. *See* Webster, Margaret
Pepi. *See* Schildkraut, Joseph
Peter Ibbetson, 39–40
Peter Pan, 42, 43, 81–82, 115–16, 175, 216
Petrie, Daniel, 254–55
Philipson, Ralph H., 38, 56
Phoenix Theatre, 202, 206, 208
Picon, Molly, 260
Pierre of the Plains, 45
Pons, Helene, 162
Prelude to a Kiss, 161
Prince of Players, 192 93
Private Lives, 164
Pulitzer Prize, 91

Rabb, Ellis, 228, 269; and the APA-Phoenix, 228–29; and *The Dream Watcher*, 240; and *Ghosts*, 215–17; on *Mary Stuart*, 203; relationship with Eva, 214–17, 230–31; in *Richard II*, 214–15; and *The Royal Family*, 243–47
Rathbone, Basil, 60, 72, 190
Reagan, Ronald, xv, 271

Reed, Ethel, 11, 16, 17
Reed, Joseph Verner, 173
Reich, John, 207
Reicher, Frank, 50
Resurrection, 254–56
Rice, Elmer, 113
Richardson, Claibe, 245
Riise, Frederick, 11
Ring Round the Moon, 217
Rio Grande, 45
Rivals, The, 165–66
Roberts, Leona, 70, 110, 114
Robins, Elizabeth, 12
Rockefeller, John D., Jr., 175–76
Romeo and Juliet, 31, 32, 33, 39, 43, 83–84, 103–4, 107, 111, 159, 164, 190, 222–24
Roosevelt, Franklin D., 105, 107, 189
Roosevelt, Mrs. Franklin D., 105
Rose Valley Theatre, 60
Rosmersholm, 111–12
Ross, Robert, 90
Rostand, Edmond, 36
Roundabout Theatre, 258
Row, Arthur, 54
Royal Family, The, xix, 243–51
Royal Theatre (Copenhagen), 31

St. Elsewhere, 265–66, 268
Saint Joan, 61
Sandro Botticelli, 55–56, 59
Sarton, May, 80, 90, 101, 108, 109, 116, 191, 232; on *Alice in Wonderland*, 263; on the Civic Repertory Theatre, xii; correspondence with Eva, 104 5, 106, 109, 171, 182–83, 186–88, 192, 201, 231; on Eva's acting, xi–xiii, 84; on Eva's career, xiii; on Eva's lesbianism, 85, 108, 226–27; on Eva's personality, xx, 109, 213; on Eva's relationship with Anne Kaufman Schneider, 250; on Eva's relationship with Marion Evensen ("Gun"), 167; relationship with Eva, 227, 270–71, 277
Saturday Night, 70, 73
Scammell, Terence, 222–24, 235

Robert A. Schanke is professor and chairman of the Department of Communication and Theatre and director of theatre at Central College, Pella, Iowa. He has published numerous articles on American theatre history and has contributed to *Women in American Theatre*, *Cambridge Guide to World Theatre*, *Cambridge Guide to American Theatre*, *Oxford Companion to the Theatre*, *American Theatre Companies*, and *Shakespeare Around the Globe*. While living in Great Britain, he was guest lecturer at Manchester, Swansea, and Loughborough universities, as well as before the British Society for Theatre Research. He served on the Board of Directors of the American Theatre Association and as president of the Mid-America Theatre Conference. He is the author of *Ibsen in America: A Century of Change* and *Eva Le Gallienne: A Bio-Bibliography* and serves as editor of the international theatre journal *Theatre History Studies*.